TEACHING CHILDREN WITH LEARNING DISABILITIES

PERSONAL PERSPECTIVES

**THE MERRILL PERSONAL PERSPECTIVES
IN SPECIAL EDUCATION SERIES**

edited by James M. Kauffman

TEACHING CHILDREN WITH LEARNING DISABILITIES

PERSONAL PERSPECTIVES

edited by

James M. Kauffman

The University of Virginia

Daniel P. Hallahan

The University of Virginia

CHARLES E. MERRILL PUBLISHING COMPANY
A Bell & Howell Company
Columbus, Ohio

This book was set in Schoolbook.
The production editor was Francie Margolin.
The cover was designed by Will Chenoweth.

Published by
CHARLES E. MERRILL PUBLISHING COMPANY
A Bell & Howell Company
Columbus, Ohio 43216

Photographs of children courtesy of Susan Locke and Edgar Bernstein.

Library of Congress Catalog Card Number: 75-18205
International Standard Book Number: 0-675-08664-7

1 2 3 4 5 6 7 8—80 79 78 77 76

Printed in the United States of America

SERIES EDITOR'S FOREWORD

As members and future members of the special-education profession, we are in many ways at an adolescent stage of development. We are being pulled in opposite directions, not really knowing whether we should separate ourselves from the educational mainstream and assert our independence or embrace and merge with the disciplines from which we spring. It is an awkward and painful stage that is full of conflicting urges and perplexing characteristics. We realize that our self-assurance is accompanied by self-doubt, that our growth is rapid and uneven, and that our desire to perform exceeds our knowledge and skill. We keenly sense our own tendency to be argumentative and we are constantly aware that our economic needs outstrip our ability to acquire financial support.

In order to survive this difficult period in our history, we may need to engage in serious introspection—not in a spirit of inducing biting self-criticism or remorse, but in order to clarify our origins, our current perspectives, and our future directions. We must realize that only by trying to determine where we have been and where we are going can we be certain that the process of getting there will continue to be rewarding.

The Merrill Personal Perspectives in Special Education Series is a project designed to facilitate this introspection and to communicate major points of view regarding issues and problems in the field. The series features original contributions from persons whose work has left an indelible mark on the profession. These individuals have contributed summaries of their professional development and current perspectives which are free of the vagaries and distortions which inevitably accompany interpretation by another writer. The mosaic created by their contrasting and complementary origins, experiences, ideas, and personalities provides a picture of the profession which should help us to see ourselves, our work, and our goals as special educators with greater clarity.

James M. Kauffman

The University of Virginia

FOREWORD

Having prepared for a number of years to be a historian and historical researcher, I can give my total support to books of this type. If this
volume had been published earlier, perhaps the late Dr. Newell C. Kephart could have written a chapter from his personal vantage point. Of
course, autobiographical writing, with its obvious orientation to the past,
contains subjective elements, but so does history written by even the most
objective historian. Historical research emphasizes the use of primary
sources over secondary ones, and what is more primary than the people
who have lived and are living history. Metternich once said that "the men
who make history have not time to write it." This volume proves Metternich wrong (as he was about other events too) in that the women and men
who contributed to this book not only make history, but do write about
it. Probably they would not have undertaken an introspective examination
without a stimulus from the editors, but the fact remains that they did.
For that, we can and should be grateful.

When the editors asked me to write this foreword, I readily accepted
the invitation, for two central reasons. First, I firmly believe that the
Personal Perspectives Series is important because it disseminates the
humanism as well as scholarship of those individuals who have made
many positive contributions to the profession. Second, the contributors to
this volume, as well as those in the others in the series, express a profound
respect for the past. They do not dwell in the past, but they do discern that
without understanding events which have already occurred, future
changes have little chance of realization.

There were other reasons for my eager acceptance. I have known and
respected Jim Kauffman as friend and colleague for many years. While
I haven't known Dan Hallahan as many years, he, like Jim Kauffman, is
dedicated to standards of quality in any task he undertakes.

The first question that came to my mind, as it will to many others,
is "What does someone who has devoted many years to learning from
seriously emotionally disturbed children know about the category of
learning disabilities?" In answer to that question, I believe that the cognitive, perceptual, motor, and other behaviors of emotionally disturbed

children are as variable as are their affective and social behaviors. In fact, I have yet to meet a disturbed youngster who does not exhibit learning disabilities. All too often, the problems of academic learning are antecedents of social and affective behavioral manifestations. Even the emotionally disturbed child who is "making it in school" with average grades could achieve much closer to his capacity if relevant, remedial intervention were provided.

I myself have had some formal ties to the field of learning disabilities. In the early 1960s, I presented a paper at one of the first U.S. Office of Education sponsored workshops on learning disabilities. Also, I was fortunate in participating with Norris G. Haring in applying for research on the feasibility of early identification of children with learning disabilities. I even gave a paper at one of the national conventions of the Association for Children with Learning Disabilities.

Every educator, special or otherwise, must attempt to know and practice his profession in ways which enhance children's learning. In that sense, all of us "area-identified" folk are in the same business—arranging environments which promote behavioral change, hopefully for the better, in children and in ourselves. If the area of learning disabilities has done no more than bring to the profession a recognition of the fact that the principles of learning are fundamental to all humans, then its contribution is of historic magnitude. In reality, the field, through its advocates, has contributed much more than this. This volume describes some of those additional contributions through brief autobiographies which reflect the very personal and human insight, understanding, and knowledge of people who have literally devoted their lives to handicapped children.

Even though it is obvious, it must be written; This volume cannot begin to include all of the individuals who have made, and are continuing to make, contributions to the learning disabilities area. The contributors to this volume are unique in that they bring full and exciting histories, events occurring over a period of time, to each page. Each and every one of them has roots in areas other than learning disabilities. This is easily understood; when they began their careers, the idea of learning disabilities did not exist. Yet, when their individual and collective pasts are analyzed and synthesized, all are persistent in learning about learning. There are others, not included in this volume, who have quite similiar pasts. Their stories should be told, and perhaps they can be in subsequent volumes the Personal Perspectives Series. I hope so. As for those advocates who are recent graduates of learning disabilities programs with specific theoretical orientations, they are now establishing their own unique pasts and will be heard from as time passes. They, along with the contributors to this volume, are the hope for the future. They will not dwell in the past. Rather, they will take from it what is beneficial and use it to construct even more relevant programs for the handicapped. Old or new, young or old, the contributors to this volume, and those whose unique personal perspectives are not yet written, share this volume of the relationship between the past and the future.

The editors requested that I read this entire volume before I wrote the foreword. I agreed, since having taken a speed reading course many years ago, I read rapidly. I thought I would just go through the chapters very quickly and then write a brief, and probably innocuous, foreword. That was foolish, and deep down, I recognized it as such. As I began to read, I was immediately overwhelmed with the power of the words of the contributors, even though all were far too modest. This is a powerful book. Those who pick it up should be prepared for an adventure in development, defeat, victory, humor (particularly the willingness to laugh at oneself), and just plain human goodness, as reflected in the lives of very generous and loving human beings.

In talking with contributors to other volumes of the Personal Perspectives Series, the most frequent comment was that writing an account of one's life is similar to writing your own funeral service. Upon first hearing that, I agreed, but at the same time, I thought that it was also morbid and sad. Something happened to change my mind, though. The day before I began to write this foreword, I attended the funeral of my 92-year-old uncle. He had been a farmer and rancher all his life. I couldn't begin to fathom the number of sixteen- to eighteen-hour days he worked to nurture both crops and animals. Even though he never accumulated money, he achieved something worth much more. As the minister said, my uncle was more wealthy than most of us in what really mattered. He had spent a lifetime working with the most fundamental of God's creations, the soil and the animals. My uncle worked with God's creations, not man's creations. With this insight, I began to understand that my uncle's funeral was neither sad (not that he will not be deeply missed) nor morbid, but was indeed the moment for celebration of accomplishment. Then how could an examination of one's past efforts, hopes, and achievements be saddening? As special educators, we, like my uncle, work with the most important of God's creations, the children who come to us for help, support, and understanding. Is there a higher calling? I think not. Therefore, the opportunity to share with others those deeply personal inner thoughts and goals should be a signal for rejoicing. To be honest in writing, or even thinking, about oneself requires diligence, high tolerance for pain, recognition of weakness as well as strength, and dedication. After such a writing task has been completed, one can then reflect upon it with satisfaction, joy, and probably awe. I feel and believe that the ten very humanistic people who wrote chapters for this volume went through that sometimes wrenching but ultimately satisfying and happy process of creating knowledge which can be shared and used by others.

I have read representative professional publications of each and every one of the contributors. In fact, I use their articles and books in my teaching. I have also known most of them personally for many years or have had the priviledge of listening to them, even if briefly, tell of their important endeavors for the handicapped. To some of them I owe a very personal debt in that they exerted both an indirect and direct influence upon my life.

In a way, Bill Cruickshank is a symbolic grandfather to me since I learned of his work through one of his students, Norris Haring, who, in turn, profoundly influenced and still influences my efforts in education. Over the years I have had the opportunity to learn from Professor Cruickshank. His vitality, understanding of people, and knowledge never cease to amaze me.

Tom Lovitt is a long-time personal friend and colleague. We were doctoral students together, suffering, developing, and most importantly, sharing what we learned. That relationship still exists. I eagerly read his latest articles and other publications. Tom's description of his transfer from learning disabilities to "interrelated," for program-funding purposes, contains both humor and insight into the problem of categorizing and labeling children. Programs can be interrelated (generic), but I have yet to see an interrelated child in the sense that the term is typically used in special education. The profession is finally beginning to make this very subtle discrimination. It should help us get over an irrelevant hurdle so that we can settle down to investigate those relevant problems of learning which constantly confront us.

Another individual who has made significant contributions to the profession for many years is Jim Gallagher. His work in the areas of the gifted, brain-injured, and learning disabled is constantly cited. He also brought excellence to those federal programs which still continue to be vital in providing leadership and advocacy for a largely unrecognized minority group, the handicapped. His leadership in the development of early childhood programs and technical assistance procedures will have a profound and enduring impact. As is true with the other contributors, Jim's humanism makes possible an extensive range of conceptual and "can do" compentencies.

What can I write about Sam Kirk? Like Bill Cruickshank, he is truly a pioneer, one individual whose work has influenced every other individual in the field. His design, and implementation of a research institute is still a model for replication. About thirteen years ago, Sam made a very brief visit to the Children's Rehabilitation Unit of the University of Kansas Medical Center. He had also visited the staff of the Menninger Foundation in Topeka and had stopped at the Unit to see Norris Haring. I vividly recall Sam, cigar in mouth, giving information at a very high rate. In the span of a few minutes, he conveyed the real issues in the field, those related to learning processes. Then he was on his way again. He still is a "high-rate individual." Our profession could ask for no finer representative.

I am pleased that this volume includes chapters by Ray Barsch, Marianne Frostig, and Gerald Getman. I first met Ray when he was at the University of Wisconsin, in the process of refining the Movigenic concept.

His writings are as refreshing as he is in person. Marianne Frostig is a clinician in the finest sense of that label. She has "been there," and, in fact, still *is* there as conveyed in her chapter and the descriptions of her clinical work with children. I know Gerald Getman through his writings and also indirectly because of a quirk in timing. During the 1964 summer session at Texas Woman's University, I taught a three-week course in the emotionally disturbed. Dr. Getman was a visiting professor that summer too, but he was scheduled for the first three weeks and had left the campus before I arrived. However, I did get to know him through his former students who had enrolled in my class. Their excitement with what they had learned from Dr. Getman was contagious. I caught it and have tried to follow his work over the years since that summer. The chapters written by these three individuals are a *must* reading assignment. Their theories, concepts, and programs have generated many adherents and opponents. Their chapters convey what all of us should know but which is rarely practiced in daily affairs. In essence, what is conveyed is that innovators provide a much broader perspective on the problems and potential solutions than their interpreters. While these three educators have chosen to concentrate upon what appear to be circumscribed aspects of the field, they, as their chapters make clear, are Gestalt-oriented in their thinking and action. They never lose sight of the total child; and, after all, that is what all educators should consistently stress.

Edward Frierson's chapter gets right to the issue of talking versus doing. He is, like his colleagues in this book are, a doer. They are known by their actions and the literature which describes those actions. Dr. Frierson's chapter is informative from a technical or pedagogical view, but in every line a fine sense of humor, perspective, and balance comes through. Like the other contributors, Ed must work a twenty-hour day which includes teaching, writing, research, and direct service to children. Even his written words exude energy.

As a former student of Sam Kirk, Jeanne McRae McCarthy has continued to model the excellence which was ever present in her doctoral studies. Of course, she brought a history of excellence to that program, so its continuation has been no surprise. She has been a clinician, teacher, and program administrator. I wish that I had known Jeanne when she was at the Wichita Guidance Center. I have great empathy for her problem of trying to explain to a group of "pure clinical" psychologists why it is important to know about children's acquisition of reading and other academic skills. I went through a similar process too, and I surely could have used her help.

Sheldon R. Rappaport's chapter is especially poignant. Not only has he been active in those endeavors common to most professionals in the field, but he has also experienced the perspective of one who has had problems which are subsequently resolved. One can feel his pain, confusion, and anguish at being told that he would not be promoted to the second grade from the first. He overcame, though, and thus provides hope that solutions, rather than just problems, can be identified.

I could write on ad infinitum about those who have contributed to this volume. However, that would take another volume. Besides, the contributors have done a far better job than any synthesizer of their work could do. I could not do justice to them by interpreting. They need no one for that. Rather, the commonalities among these individuals should be stressed.

All the contributors have a deep and abiding respect for their historical roots. They acknowledge their debt to history by describing significant others who influenced their lives. Those others may have been parents, but there were also teachers along the way who exerted positive influences. As one reads the chapters, the characteristics of honesty and candor come through. The contributors write as they saw it then, see it now, and hope to see it in the future. There is no vagueness about where they stand on the issues. Yet each is open for the processing of new information, concepts, and practices. They are not happy with the status quo, and want to foster change based upon rational thought and action. All of them possess and exhibit a difficult-to-define trait which is important in making the difference between adequacy and excellence. Even though some are associated with specific intervention programs, all stress individualization of programs for children, the unique totality of a child, and clinical child-based experiences in the preparation of professionals. All the contributors are practiced observers of behavior. They use all of the senses to take in information, process it, and put it to good use. They are great analyzers and synthesizers. As such, each has the ability to discern the relationship, particularly the commonality, between general and special education. From knowing some of the contributors personally, and all of them through their writing and speeches, it is evident that they are not afraid of taking risks if by doing so, the lives of handicapped children can be improved. They constantly seek new ways to serve. Individually and collectively, they are models with which we can identify in going about meeting our daily and long-range responsibilities.

There are also two chapters in this book which will enable the serious student to assimilate the magnitude and depth of the information which the personal perspectives chapters convey—the overview chapter by Sara Tarver and Daniel P. Hallahan, which summarizes the past and current developments in the field of learning disabilities, and the last chapter by Hallahan and Elizabeth D. Heins, which is a review of the current issues and problems confronting professionals in special education. These chapters build a conceptually understandable framework in which the chapters by the contributors will provide a comprehensive past, present, and future perspective on the field.

I hope that this book will be read and reread by the "old timers," "new timers," and perpetual students (which should include every special educator). I intend to do so, and it will be required reading for the students in my classes. The book contains significant conceptual and technical information, plus the personal perspectives which put it all together. The contributors have given of themselves in writing their chapters. That is the best tradition of special education. One can not ask for more from another human being.

Richard J. Whelan

The University of Kansas
  and
The University of Kansas Medical Center

PREFACE

Two decades ago learning disabilities did not exist as a field of study, although there is no question that learning disabled children have always existed. The phenomenal growth of this newest area of special education has led to confusion regarding every aspect of the field: definition, etiology, treatment, and evaluation. Confusion among professionals working in the field has led, quite predictably, to consternation among students who must attempt to sort out the essentials and avoid being blown about by every wind of doctrine. The problem of the student is compounded by the fact that most publications present only one perspective on the field, contain only scattered selections of the writings of major figures, or represent a third party's attempts to abstract and interpret the viewpoints developed by others. As a result, even the perseverant and fortunate student often remains ill-equipped to formulate his own coherent approach to the field or to develop and evaluate educational methods on any rational basis.

This book is designed to give students in special education a personalized synopsis of the development of educational practice for children with learning disabilities. The contributors to this book are, without exception, individuals who, in our judgment, have made major contributions to the development of the field. We have attempted to go beyond the typical textbook format by providing a tête-à-tête between reader and author. Persons representing widely differing approaches to the field have contributed material for the book. No attempt has been made to categorize or classify the writers as belonging to particular schools of thought, a task which is probably as fruitless as attempting to fit children into diagnostic categories. As a result, we hope our own biases and distortions have been minimized and the reader is left to form his own evaluation of the authors' contributions. The authors' vitae provide guidance for additional study of the work of individuals in whom the student may have further interest.

It must be recognized that to summarize your work in the field in a few manuscript pages is an extraordinarily demanding task, particularly when your involvement has been long and arduous. Inevitably, under such circumstances many things must be left unsaid. Those who have contributed to this volume must be admired for their courage and willingness to share their professional development under such constraints. In this case, brevity is not the soul of wit but of modesty. The reader must recognize also that vitae, as well as ideas, are constantly evolving. The material presented in this book captures facets of the development of the field at a particular moment in its history. The chapters themselves are but vignettes of professional lives which are still evolving.

In Chapter 1, Tarver and Hallahan provide an overview of the development and status of the field, including essential information related to the controversies surrounding definition, characteristics, etiology, and evaluation. This introduction provides a framework for approaching the chapters which follow. Chapters 2 through 11, titled only by the authors' names, contain personal accounts of the authors' professional lives. In Chapter 12, Hallahan and Heins summarize major concepts and current issues in the field.

The success of an endeavor like this book depends on the assistance and competence of many people other than the contributors and editors. We are especially grateful to Tom Hutchinson for his help as special education editor for C.E.M., to Francie Margolin for her expertise as our production editor, and to Anne Benassi for preparing the index.

James M. Kauffman
Daniel P. Hallahan

The University of Virginia

CONTENTS

TEACHING
CHILDREN WITH
LEARNING DISABILITIES

PERSONAL PERSPECTIVES

1
Children with Learning Disabilities:
An Overview

TERMINOLOGY

The term *learning disabilities* was introduced by Samuel Kirk in 1963 to designate a segment of the school-age population which did not seem to fit into any of the existing categories of exceptional children, but which nevertheless was in obvious need of special education services. In an attempt to provide parents and professionals with some common basis of understanding regarding the children to whom the term was meant to refer, Kirk (1963) made the following comments:

> As I understand it, this meeting is not concerned with children who have sensory handicaps, such as the deaf or the blind, or with children who are mentally retarded, or with delinquent or emotionally disturbed children caused by environmental factors. It is concerned primarily with children who can see and hear and who do not have marked general intellectual deficits, but who show deviations in behavior and in psychological development to such an extent that they are unable to adjust in the home or to learn by ordinary methods of instruction in school.

Despite a relatively brief history, the term has very quickly come to be used by parents, the lay public, and a diversity of professionals to refer to a heterogeneous group of children. Depending upon where one travels in the United States, one can find different interpretations of the LD category. Too often the learning disability label has been applied by those who have only a superficial grasp of the identity of this new category of children, their characteristics, and their needs. Probably because the commonly accepted definitions of learning disabilities specify that the children in question are of normal or near normal intelligence and because many of these children have traditionally been in the charge of the regular classroom teacher, the unproven assumption that almost any teacher with just a few special education courses can become a qualified LD teacher has arisen. This assumption is most unfortunate because all the available evidence indicates that learning disability children present as many (and, in fact, the very same) challenges as those faced by teachers of the retarded and behaviorally disordered (Hallahan & Kauffman, 1976).

The terminological and semantic confusion surrounding the birth of this term was an inevitable result of the multifaceted history of its evolution. During the half-century preceding the learning disabilities era, the child who failed to learn in school in spite of average intellectual potential and adequate emotional stability had attracted the interest of a wide variety of specialists within many disciplines, including medicine, psychology, language, and education (Lerner, 1971). Each profession had attempted to label, define, diagnose, and remediate the child within its own limited frame of reference. Cases were reported in which the same child was labeled in different settings by a variety of terms such as *brain injured, dyslexic, slow learner, educationally handicapped,* and *aphasic.* Equally inconsistent reports of characteristics and recommendations for treatment and/or remediation added to the mass confusion confronting parents seeking help for their children.

As parents and professionals began to recognize commonalities in this group of children who had been viewed from so many different angles, the need for increased interdisciplinary communication and a consolidated effort became apparent. Some professionals felt that the logical first step was the derivation of terminology, both an identifying term and a definition, that would be acceptable to all concerned professions and to parents as well. As history has revealed, this preliminary task proved to be a formidable one. Although the questions of the efficacy of labels in general, the desirability of particular labels as opposed to others, and the nature of appropriate definitions for the various labels had been debated at length prior to the 1960s, they had primarily existed at the intradisciplinary level. Now the magnitude of these issues was multiplied by the need for resolution at a multidisciplinary level.

The major points of the controversy have revolved around the questions of whether labels and definitions are necessary, and, if so, whether they should be etiologically or behaviorally oriented. The following objections to the establishment of a new category of special children via a common label were summarized by Hammill and Bartel (1971): (a) Labels, no matter how neutral they are intended to be, acquire a stigma. (b) Negative labels reduce teacher expectations, which may further reduce the child's chances for academic progress. (c) Labels are often interpreted causally, e.g., the child is said to be not learning to read because he is dyslexic. Such an interpretation can lead to a false sense of resolution of the child's problems. (d) A common label for children exhibiting such a hetergeneous assortment of behavioral traits is meaningless.

Proponents of identifying terminology point to the necessity to think in terms of categories for purposes of legislation and funding, administration of special education programs, and research. Regarding the conceptual and empirical importance of a definition, McCarthy (1971) stated:

... the most important decision you will make is that of definition—
because your definition will dictate for you the terminology to be used in
your program, the prevalence figures, your selection criterion, the characteristics of your population, and the appropriate remedial procedures
[p. 14].

Substantial support for identifying terminology is indicated by the
vast amount of professional time and energy which has been devoted to
the selection of an appropriate term and formulation of a viable definition. A major effort to study the problems of terminology was made by a
task force appointed by the National Society for Crippled Children and
Adults, Inc., and the National Institute of Neurological Diseases and
Blindness of the National Institutes of Health in 1964 (Clements, 1966).
The task force directed by Sam D. Clements grouped thirty-eight frequently used terms into two categories—those which related the organic
etiology of the condition and those descriptive of the consequence or
behavioral manifestation of the disorder. Included in the first category
were terms such as *organic brain disease, organic brain dysfunction, minimal brain damage, minimal brain injury,* and *minimal cerebral damage.*
The behavioral category included terms such as *hyperkinetic syndrome,
dyslexia, perceptually handicapped, specific reading disability, aphasoid
syndrome,* and *learning disabilities.* After much deliberation the term
minimal brain dysfunction syndrome was selected by the task force to
refer to children of near average, average, or above average general intelligence with learning or behavioral disabilities associated with deviations
of function of the central nervous system. The word "dysfunction" was
considered to be preferable to the word "damage" because it conveys the
concept that not all children exhibiting the group of symptoms associated
with the syndrome necessarily have demonstrable brain damage. The
substitution of the term "dysfunction" for "damage" reflects a softening
of the neurological position. Whereas at one time it was quite popular to
posit that learning disability children suffer from subtle neurological
lesions, educators and even some neurologists have more recently questioned this assumption. In particular, some educators have pointed out
that the issue of neurological etiology is, in many respects, irrelevant for
the classroom teacher. The teacher must deal with the behavior of the
child, regardless of its etiology. The word "dysfunction" is thus preferred
because it connotes less finality than "damage."

Terminological issues were also discussed extensively at two major
conferences in the early 1960s. The first, a conference on problems of the
perceptually handicapped held by parents in 1963, was the occasion at
which Kirk introduced the term *learning disabilities.* This term was
accepted, though not without debate, by the convention's vote to organize
the Association for Children with Learning Disabilities.

Terminological issues arising at the second significant conference, a
Seminar on Brain-Injured Children held in 1965, have been described in

detail by Hallahan and Cruickshank (1973). Cruickshank was instrumental in assembling twenty-seven leading professionals, representative of a wide variety of disciplines, to discuss topics relevant to the study of the brain-injured child. The most controversial topic discussed was terminology. Gallagher voiced objections to the term *brain injury,* pointing out that it connotes irreversibility, creates negative reactions, and is often applied without conclusive evidence that the brain is damaged. His major objection to the label of *brain injury* was its lack of educational relevance. Gallagher proposed, instead, that the term *developmental imbalance* be accepted. Both Freidus and Cruickshank further elaborated the need for terminology emphasizing behavioral manifestations rather than etiology. Advocating continued usage of the term *brain injury,* Rappaport pointed out that lack of concern for a possible organic etiology could result in overlooking conditions which might jeopardize the child's life. Realizing that no one definition could serve the purposes of all concerned disciplines, Reitan suggested that several definitions be formulated for purposes of (a) etiology, (b) classification and administration, and (c) education. No consensus regarding a term and a definition was reached at this meeting, but a trend toward the rejection of etiologically oriented terms in favor of educationally relevant, behaviorally oriented terms was evident.

Although these terminological issues have by no means been resolved to the satisfaction of all concerned parties, sufficient agreement has been reached to facilitate progress in legislation and funding at the national, state, and local levels. Congressional acceptance of the term *learning disabilities* was marked by passage of the Children with Specific Learning Disabilities Act in 1969. Incorporated into this legislation was a definition formulated by the National Advisory Committee on Handicapped Children (1968):

> Children with special learning disabilities exhibit a disorder in one or more of the basic psychological processes involved in understanding or using spoken or written languages. These may be manifested in disorders of listening, thinking, talking, reading, writing, spelling, or arithmetic. They include conditions which have been referred to as perceptual handicaps, brain injury, minimal brain dysfunction, dyslexia, developmental aphasia, etc. They do not include learning problems which are due primarily to visual, hearing, or motor handicaps, to mental retardation, emotional disturbance, or to environmental disadvantage.

Seven other definitions of a learning disability which have been frequently cited in the literature are reported by Chalfant and Scheffelin (1969). Although these definitions differ in phraseology and emphasis, two common elements are discernible, either by explicit statement or by implication: children who fall into other categories of exceptionality are excluded, and a discrepancy between intellectual potential and actual achievement is necessary.

In attempting to classify individual children as learning disabled in adherence with commonly accepted definitions, several practical problems have frequently been encountered: (a) In most cases of learning disorders, there is no evidence of actual brain damage. Therefore, a definition using evidence of demonstrable brain damage as a criterion rules out large numbers of children who may exhibit the same debilitating symptoms as those children for whom an organic etiology has been established. (b) The distinction between primary causative factors and secondary symptoms is exceedingly difficult to determine in children presenting both learning problems and other symptoms more commonly associated with emotional disturbance, cultural deprivation, and mental retardation. (c) The nonspecific nature of the discrepancy clause in most definitions has resulted in wide variations of judgments regarding the magnitude of discrepancy characteristic of a learning disability. While a more specific discrepancy clause would be preferable for purposes of research, such a specific criterion would present a problem in early identification and prevention. The goal in these endeavors is to identify the LD child as early as possible and institute preventive measures before enough time has elapsed for the child to develop a significant academic discrepancy.

Failure to resolve these problems has led some to view the term *learning disabilities* as a generic term which refers to all children who have learning problems, regardless of etiology, classification, or severity of the problem. In particular, Hallahan and Kauffman (1975; 1976) have suggested that children identified as learning disabled, emotionally disturbed, and educable mentally retarded have more in common than they do not. Their viewpoint is that the same behavioral characteristics are found in each of these populations with differentiation only with regard to the relative frequency of some behaviors. For example, social maladjustment is a problem in all three categories, although it occurs somewhat more often in the emotionally disturbed. *How much more often* is of great importance. Hallahan and Kauffman believe that the available evidence indicates that there is considerable overlap among categories on relevant behaviors, and they thus posit that it is not logical to have classes established on the basis of the labels the children may carry. This position should not be confused with the idea of doing away with special classes —a position which is currently in vogue. Instead, Hallahan and Kauffman are recommending that special class teachers be more aware of the particular deficits and strengths of individual children, regardless of the diagnostic label attached to individual pupils. In contrast to this view is one which, though not intended as a denial of the presence of learning disorders in other types of exceptional children, contends that the term *learning disability* describes a specific type of exceptional child, that differential diagnosis can be made, and that such a distinction is of utmost importance because the educational needs of the different types of exceptional children may not be identical (Myers & Hammill, 1969).

The wide range of prevalence estimates of learning disabilities, from 1 to 30 percent (Lerner, 1971), reflects the uncertain state of affairs regarding identifying criteria. However, even the conservative estimate of 1 to 3 percent recommended by the National Advisory Committee on Handicapped Children (1968) recognizes that this elusive group of children constitutes a substantial segment of the school-age population.

ETIOLOGY

Learning disabilities have most often been considered to be a result of neurological dysfunction caused by organic factors such as brain damage, genetic variations, and biochemical imbalances. However, a number of emotional and environmental factors have also been postulated to play an etiological role in learning disabilities, either as sole causative agents or as contributing factors.

Organic Factors

It has long been known that brain damage or dysfunction may arise from pathologies such as unfavorable intrauterine environment, premature birth, anoxia, physical trauma, RH factor, and congenital malformations (Lerner, 1971). The medical histories of many children with learning disabilities indicate one or more of these potential sources of dysfunction.

Theories of neurological etiologies have primarily been formulated by medical professionals. Alfred Strauss (Strauss & Lehtinen, 1947), a physician working with mentally retarded children during the first half of this century, and Heinz Werner, a developmental psychologist, noted that the medical histories of many of these children revealed sources of possible brain injury. In addition, the behavioral characteristics of some of the children were found to be similar to those of brain-injured adults. Strauss and Werner therefore theorized that brain injury was the etiological factor involved in some cases of mental retardation. According to them, the brain injury was exogenous, that is, caused by an injury outside the genetic structure rather than by impairment of the inherited pattern or structure of the brain. The major criticism of their theory concerns the circularity of diagnosing brain injury on the basis of behavioral traits and then attributing these same behaviors to brain injury (Sarason, 1949).

Samuel Orton (1937), a neuropathologist who related the language disorders of children of average intelligence to brain functioning, hypothesized that language disorders are the result of failure to establish cerebral dominance in the left hemisphere of the brain, that hemisphere which specializes in language functions. Orton's theory also postulated that motor integrading, i.e., right handedness and left eyedness or vice versa, reflects this lack of cerebral dominance. Although current research strongly supports the contention that the left hemisphere plays the primary role in language functioning, the mixed dominance aspect of Orton's theory has fallen into disrepute. Current research indicates that mixed dominance is not a *significant* factor in reading retardation (Belmont & Birch, 1965; Tinker, 1965).

The theories of both Lauretta Bender, a psychiatrist, and Katrina de Hirsch, a language pathologist, reflect Orton's influence. Bender (1963) views failure to establish cerebral dominance as one symptom of a basic maturational lag in certain aspects of neurological development. De Hirsch (1963), expanding upon Bender's maturational lag theory, described a maturational or developmental lag as immaturity of Gestalt functioning which, in many cases, may be restricted to a single sensory modality. The theories of Orton, Bender, and de Hirsch are discussed more fully in the language characteristics section of this overview. However, one important difference in the etiological views of these three language theorists and the etiological views of Strauss should be mentioned at this point. Orton, Bender, and de Hirsch all considered the neurological dysfunctions underlying learning disorders to be genetically determined, at least in most cases. Strauss, as previously mentioned, considered exogenous brain injury to be the cause of the learning problems of his mentally retarded subjects.

Ophthalmologists have also been interested in the interrelationship of brain dysfunction, vision, and learning problems. Hinshelwood (1917), an English ophthalmologist, referred to severe reading disability in children of normal intelligence as "congenital word blindness" and hypothesized the etiology to be a congenital defect of that area of the brain in which visual memories of words are registered. More recently, a number of peripheral visual defects such as visual acuity, refractive errors (strabismus, inadequate fusion, aneseikonia), and binocular difficulties (myopia, hyperopia, and astigmatism) have been postulated to be associated with reading disabilities (Lerner, 1971). Reviews of research studies regarding the relationship between these ocular defects and reading ability do not support the view that such defects cause reading problems (Goldberg & Schiffman, 1972; Lawson, 1968; Park, 1968). It is generally agreed, however, that centrally processed visual functions such as visual perception and visual discrimination play a more significant role in reading than do the peripheral visual defects which have been mentioned (Lerner, 1971).

Other medical disorders more recently hypothesized to cause learning difficulties are biochemical irregularities involving glandular disorders (Eames, 1962; Smith & Carrigan, 1959), hypoglycemia and narcolepsy complex (Roberts, 1969), vitamin deficiencies (Cott, 1972), and allergies (Wunderlich, 1970). Because both the study of the biochemistry of neurology and the theories postulating biochemical etiologies are relatively recent, these hypotheses have not been sufficiently tested to justify conclusions at this time.

Emotional Factors

Symptoms of emotional maladjustment or disturbance frequently coexist with learning disabilities (Rubin, 1971; Connolly, 1971; Goldberg & Schiffman, 1972). The classic study of Morse, Cutler, and Fink (1964) indicated that underachievement is a frequent characteristic of children educated in public school classes for the emotionally disturbed. The nature of the relationship between the various symptoms of emotional disturbance and learning disabilities is far from clear.

At one time emotional disturbance due to child-rearing practices was probably the most commonly cited cause of learning disabilities (Clements & Peters 1962; Connolly, 1971). Some other causative emotional factors reported in the literature are anxiety (Natchez, 1968; Spielberger, 1966), negative attitudes toward parents (Blanchard, 1935), and disturbances of exploratory functions (Sylvester & Kunst, 1943). A review by Gates (1941) of eight investigations of the relationship between emotional disturbance and reading difficulty was influential in shifting the focus from emotional factors to other possible etiological factors. Some of Gates' (1941) major conclusions were:

1. There is no single personality pattern among reading disabled children of adequate intelligence. Reading disability occurs in all sorts of personality types, home backgrounds, parental relationships, and emotional patterns.

2. Good readers are consistently superior to poor readers in almost no single personality or emotional trait.

3. Emotional, motivational, or dynamic patterns revealed by clinical analysis may, in some cases, comprise at least a partial cause of reading difficulty; situations which appear to lead to emotional tension, anxiety, fear, or resistance may interfere with learning to read.

4. Personality maladjustment is a relatively rare cause of serious reading defect. Personality maladjustment, when occurring along with reading disability, is the cause of the defect in only approximately one or two cases out of ten.

5. Symptoms such as nervousness, withdrawal, aggression, defeatism, and chronic worry appear among cases in which the maladjustment is the cause, the result, or the concomitant of reading disability. It is therefore impossible to tell whether these symptoms are causes, effects, or concomitants.

6. About 75 percent of children with reading difficulty show personality maladjustment. The maladjustment is estimated to be the cause of the reading difficulty in one-quarter of these cases.

Most recent psychiatric views of learning disabilities reflect a concern for the effects of a learning disability on emotional stability as well as concern for emotional instability as a causative factor (Giffin, 1968; Rubin, 1971). Rappaport (1966) contends that the child with a brain dysfunction fails to develop basic ego functions such as frustration tolerance and concern for others, partially because of his own lack of intactness and partially because of the feedback he gets from others. The child's inadequacies and failures lead to feelings of ineptness and to rejection by others.

Rubin (1971) formulated a model to depict the relationship between environmental stress and vulnerability due to an inadequately developing cognitive-perceptual-motor system. According to this model, interactions between vulnerability and stress result in four possible outcomes (Rubin, 1971):

1. High vulnerability, low stress—may not show maladjustment.
2. High vulnerability, high stress—most serious disability.
3. Low vulnerability, low stress—freedom from disability.
4. Low vulnerability, high stress—show maladjustment when stress is high.

Environmental Factors

Research indicating that environmental factors such as poor nutrition, a lack of environmental stimulation, and a number of related sociological variables may contribute causally to learning disabilities is rapidly accumulating. A comprehensive review of the research in this area is included in Cravioto and DeLicardie (1975) and Hallahan and Cruickshank (1973). They focus on the interrelationship of neurological dysfunction, perception, and learning disorders, suggesting that environment contributes to neurological dysfunctioning which, in turn, contributes to perceptual disorders and resulting learning disabilities.

Dyspedagogia is another type of environmental condition which has been hypothesized to be the cause of learning disabilities (Bruner, 1971; Cohen, 1971). Cohen (1971) states that "Research indicates that most reading retardation stems from the dreaded psychoeducational disease we have labeled dyspedagogia—poor teaching [p. 271]." He goes on to say that the cure for dyspedagogia is intensive, effective teaching. While this view does not seem to provide a tenable explanation of neurological and perceptual dysfunction, it does make the important point that children can learn in spite of basic neurological deficits if appropriate teaching is provided. This concept of dyspedagogia is also in accord with the general educational philosophy of radical behaviorism (Throne, 1973). Throne states that extraordinary environmental conditions devised by the teacher can have profound positive effects on the damaged organism's learning. In other words, the radical behaviorist places the onus of responsibility for the child's progress on the teacher.

Subgroups Based on Differential Etiologies

Rabinovitch and Ingram (1962) and Bannatyne (1971) have attempted to delineate subgroups of children with learning disabilities on the basis of clinical data. These investigators have hypothesized differential etiologies for subgroups exhibiting different, though overlapping, behavioral syndromes. Rabinovitch and Ingram (1962) defined three major groupings in reading retardation:

1. A *primary reading retardation* group in which capacity to learn to read is impaired in the absence of indications of brain damage by medical history or neurological examination. The basic cause is biological and reflects disturbed neurological organization.

2. A *brain injury with resultant reading retardation* group in which capacity to learn to read is impaired by brain damage as indicated by the medical history.

3. A *secondary reading retardation* group in which capacity to learn to read is intact but is utilized insufficiently because of negativism, anxiety, depression, emotional blocking, psychosis, limited schooling opportunity, or other external factors.

Bannatyne (1971) assigns different original causes to four types of dyslexia:

1. *Primary emotional communicative dyslexia* caused by a poor communicative relationship between mother and child during the critical period of language development.

2. *Minimal neurological dysfunction dyslexia* caused by brain damage or brain malformation.

3. *Genetic dyslexia* caused by the absence of inherited potential to acquire language functions easily.

4. *Social, cultural, or educational deprivation dyslexia* caused by deprivation in the home, school, or neighborhood environment.

CHARACTERISTICS

Perusing the professional literature quickly reveals that a vast number and variety of characteristics have been attributed to children with learning disabilities. A task force appointed to study the terminology and identification of children with minimal brain dysfunction, called Task Force I (Clements, 1966), reviewed over 100 publications concerned with symptomatology. A total of ninety-nine characteristics, grouped into fifteen categories, were reported. The ten most frequently cited characteristics, listed in order of their frequency (the rank ordering may be more a reflection of the interests of professionals than of the actual incidence of these characteristics) were:

1. Hyperactivity
2. Perceptual-motor impairments
3. Emotional lability
4. General coordination deficits
5. Disorders of attention (short attention span, distractibility, perseveration)
6. Impulsivity
7. Disorders of memory and thinking
8. Specific learning disabilities (reading, arithmetic, writing, spelling)
9. Disorders of speech and hearing
10. Equivocal neurological signs and electroencephalographic irregularities.

Other characteristics revealed by the Task Force I review will be listed in appropriate sections of this overview. While many of the characteristics reported are based on a substantial body of clinical data and classroom observations, there is relatively little experimental research to show that the majority of these characteristics occur more frequently in the LD population than in the non-learning-disabled population. The primary focus of this overview will be on research findings and on theories which have been formulated to explain the relationship between the various characteristics and learning difficulties.

The division of characteristics into three types—perceptual-motor, intellectual and cognitive, and language—represents an arbitrary classification scheme, as many characteristics are applicable to more than one category.

Perceptual-Motor Characteristics

A review of articles in six major professional journals between the years 1936 and 1970 led Hallahan and Cruickshank (1973) to conclude that

Both the articles concerned with brain injured children and those dealing with learning disabled children have reflected a continuous predominance of interest in perceptual-motor behaviors as compared to cognitive-language behaviors and especially to socioemotional aspects of behavior. The field of learning disabilities, in particular, has been primarily attentive to perceptual-motor development and maldevelopment [p. 157].

This disproportionate interest in the perceptual-motor characteristics of children with learning disabilities has been attributed to the influence of the pioneering efforts of Goldstein with brain-injured adults, Werner and Strauss with brain-injured mentally retarded children, and Cruickshank with brain-injured children of average intelligence (Hallahan & Cruickshank, 1973).

Goldstein (1939) observed soldiers who had received head injuries in World War I and reported bizarre behavioral and psychological characteristics. Patients exhibited disorganized behaviors, disorientation, and extreme emotional lability when confronted with tasks which they could not easily perform. This cluster of behaviors was referred to as a "catastrophic reaction." Excessive orderliness, meticulosity, and perseveration were also observed and postulated by Goldstein to represent the patients' attempts to avoid a catastrophic reaction. Other psychological characteristics reported by Goldstein included figure–background confusion, forced responsiveness to stimuli, and concrete behavior, i.e., poor abstracting and categorizing abilities.

Goldstein's observations had a strong influence upon the direction of the later experimentation of Werner and Strauss with brain-injured, mentally retarded children. Under the direction of these two men, a series of studies was carried out to compare the performance of exogeneous (brain-injured) mentally retarded children with that of endogenous (familial) mentally retarded children. Their findings revealed that the exogenous group exhibited visual-motor disorganization (Werner & Strauss, 1939), deficiencies in vocal reproductions of melodic patterns (Werner & Bowers, 1941), figure-background confusion (Werner & Strauss, 1941), and deficiencies in concept formation, i.e., categorizing on the basis of inessential elements (Strauss & Werner, 1942). In addition, Strauss and Kephart (1940) found the exogenous subjects to be more uncoordinated, erratic, impulsive, disinhibited, socially unaccepted, and uncontrolled. In summary, the same types of behaviors observed by Goldstein in brain-injured adults were found to be characteristics of the exogenous mentally retarded children studied by Werner and Strauss.

Cruickshank, probably more than any other one individual, was instrumental in extending the concepts and findings of Werner and Strauss to the population presently described as learning disabled. Influenced by his association with Werner and Strauss, Cruickshank first directed a series of experimental studies in which the performance of cerebral-palsied children of average, near average, and above average IQ was compared to that of their normal counterparts on tasks similar to those employed by Werner & Strauss. Essentially the same characteristics exhibited by Werner and Strauss's exogenous subjects were revealed in the cerebral-palsied children, i.e., poor figure-ground discrimination (Dolphin & Cruickshank, 1951a), concept formation deficiencies (Dolphin & Cruickshank, 1951b) poor visual-motor performance (Dolphin & Cruickshank, 1951c), and poor tactual-motor performance (Dolphin & Cruickshank,

1952). Cruickshank also pointed to the accumulation of clinical evidence that many of these same behaviors are characteristic of some children with no known brain damage, those children who were frequently being referred to as "minimally brain injured."

While Cruickshank and his colleagues experimented to describe the characteristics of the cerebral-palsied population, no experimental studies were being done at that time to verify these same characteristics in the minimally brain-injured population. Cruickshank and his colleagues, however, accepted clinical data as sufficient evidence for the existence of these characteristics and proceeded with the task of designing programs to meet the needs of children exhibiting such characteristics (Cruickshank, Bentzen, Ratzeberg, & Tannhauser, 1961). More recently, experimental studies comparing learning disabled children to their normal peers on measures of some of these characteristics have been conducted, sometimes yielding inconsistent findings. These studies will be discussed in the cognitive characteristics section of this overview, as the present trend is to include studies of hyperactivity, distractibility, and impulsivity under the rubric of cognitive functioning.

Impairments of perception and concept-formation reported by Task Force I (Clements, 1966) were:

1. Impaired discrimination of size.
2. Impaired discrimination of right–left and up–down.
3. Impaired tactile discriminations.
4. Poor spatial orientation.
5. Impaired orientation in time.
6. Distorted concept of body image.
7. Impaired judgment of distance.
8. Impaired discrimination of figure–ground.
9. Impaired discrimination of part–whole.
10. Frequent perceptual reversals in reading and in writing letters and numbers.
11. Poor perceptual integration (child cannot fuse sensory impressions into meaningful entities).

Under disorders of motor function were listed:

1. Frequent athetoid, choreiform, tremulous, or rigid movements of hands.
2. Frequent delayed motor milestones.
3. General clumsiness or awkwardness.
4. Frequent tics and grimaces.
5. Poor fine or gross visual-motor coordination.

6. Hyperactivity.

7. Hypoactivity.

Perceptual-Motor Theories

Many of the characteristics investigated by Goldstein, Werner and Strauss, and Cruickshank appear to pertain to emotional and cognitive functioning as well as to perceptual-motor functioning. However, several theories more purely perceptual-motor in nature have grown from the influence of these historical precursors. Newell C. Kephart (1960, 1971), Ray H. Barsch (1967, 1968), and Gerald Getman (1965) were each associated, either directly or indirectly, with Werner and with Strauss in the course of their careers (Hallahan & Cruickshank, 1973), and each developed a perceptual-motor theory reflecting that influence. The theories developed by Kephart, Barsch, and Getman differ in the extent to which they emphasize the perceptual as opposed to the motor aspects of development, with Kephart and Barsch emphasizing the role of movement and motor development in learning and Getman emphasizing the role of vision. Nevertheless, all three postulate that adequate conceptual development and language-communicative abilities are dependent to some extent upon motor development.

Kephart's perceptual–motor theory: Kephart (Kephart, 1971; Roach & Kephart, 1966) viewed the process of development as one in which the child progresses from motor patterns to percepts, matches the percepts to motor patterns, proceeds through higher levels of perceptual integration, and finally forms concepts. Inadequate development at any level of the hierarchy affects development at all higher levels.

In Kephart's theory, the beginning stages of development involve two concurrent processes. One is the patterned differentiation of specific elements from a mass; the other is the patterned integration of specific elements into a structured whole. After both patterned differentiation and patterned integration have developed, movement patterns can emerge. At this stage, Kephart's theory emphasizes the distinction between motor patterns and motor skills. Motor skills are specific activities which contribute little to later stages of development, whereas motor patterns encompass the purpose and outcome of the movement and provide the basis for more complex learnings. Only the development of motor patterns can lead to generalization of motor behaviors. The development of laterality, i.e., the awareness within the body of the differences between left and right, is dependent upon generalization of motor patterns and the development of spatial concepts is dependent upon the establishment of laterality.

During the next stage of development, the perceptual-motor match stage, previously acquired motor information and perceptual information come to mean the same thing. To achieve this match, the child must observe objects perceptually while manually or motorically manipulating them. From this matching process, visual-auditory and tactual-kinesthetic integration develop, which, in turn, promote the learning of form perception. The development of both the perceptual-motor match and laterality enables the child to develop directionality, i.e., the projection of the inner awareness of left and right to objects outside the body.

The final stage of development elaborated in Kephart's theory is that of concept formation. This involves the manipulation of relationships between percepts in such a way that unique elements emerge.

Barsch's theory of movigenics: This is a theory of the origins and development of movement and its relationship to learning efficiency. The extraordinary emphasis which Barsch (1968) places upon the role of movement in learning is illustrated by the statement that "perception is movement and movement is perception" [p. 299]. Ten postulates form the basis of Barsch's theory (Barsch, 1967).

1. Man is designed for movement.
2. The objective of movement is survival.
3. Movement occurs in an energy surround.
4. Man acquires information through his percepto-cognitive system, i.e., the six senses of taste, touch, muscle feeling, smell, sight, and hearing.
5. The terrain of movement is space.
6. Developmental momentum thrusts the learner toward maturity.
7. Movement occurs in a climate of stress.
8. Feedback is essential for efficiency.
9. Development occurs in segments of sequential expansion.
10. Communication of efficiency is derived from the visual spatial phenomenon called language.

Getman's visuomotor theory: Getman, an optometrist, contends that 80 percent of all learning is acquired visually (Getman & Kane, 1964). He uses the terms *vision* and *visual perception* synonymously, defining vision as the ability to interpret and understand the world of things that cannot be touched, tasted, smelled, or heard (Getman, 1965). He points out however, that vision and sight, i.e., visual acuity, cannot be equated.

The major concepts underlying Getman's theory are:

1. Vision is a psychological function which is learned.
2. Experiences can be provided which will enhance perceptual development.
3. Vision is based upon a developmental sequence of physiological actions.

4. Visual development and motor development are inextricably interwoven and should not be considered as separate developmental phenomena.

Getman's (1965) visuomotor theory is based on Skeffington's (1926–1965) model of perceptual performance. In Skeffington's model, four components merge to produce vision: (a) the Anti-Gravity Process, (b) the Centering Process, (c) the Identification Process, and (d) the Speech-Audition Process. Getman (1965) expanded Skeffington's model to describe these components of vision in a developmental schema. The resulting visuomotor complex portrays the sequence of processes as a pyramid of learning composed of six levels or systems which develop prior to and result in vision:

1. *The innate response system* refers to the innate reflexes of the infant.
2. *The general motor system* represents locomotor skills such as creeping, walking, running, jumping, skipping, and hopping.
3. *The special motor system* encompasses elaborate combinations of motor skills involved in the two systems developed earlier, e.g., eye–hand relationships, bimanual relationships, hand–foot relationships, voice, and gesture relationships.
4. *The ocular motor system* is composed of the ocular skills of fixation, saccadics, pursuits, and rotation.
5. *The speech motor system* includes babbling, imitative speech, and original speech.
6. *The visualization system* represents both immediate and past–future visualization. Visualization refers to imagery, i.e., the ability to recall or remember not only what has previously been seen, but also what has been heard, touched, or felt.

Getman (1962, 1965) repeatedly emphasizes the importance of the child's active participation and involvement in experiences at each level of development. As such experiences result in the formation of many perceptions, the perceptions are integrated to form concepts.

The neurological organization theory of Doman and Delacato: The neuropsychological theory formulated by Glenn Doman and Carl Delacato at the Institutes for the Achievement of Human Potential contends that language disorders are symptoms of a central cause—a lack of neurological organization. The continuum of language disorders, from most severe to least severe, encompasses aphasia, delayed speech, stuttering, retarded reading, poor spelling and handwriting, and reading below performance in mathematics.

The concept of neurological organization was fully elaborated by Delacato (1959) in *Treatment and Prevention of Reading Problems.* Later,

Delacato (1966) capsuled the theory as it relates to the diagnosis and treatment of reading problems in ten basic premises:

1. Reading is a perceptual act and is a function of the human nervous system.

2. The human nervous system is the result of a phylogenetic process.

3. The ontogenetic development of each individual's nervous system, in general, recapitulates that phylogenetic process. Man has superimposed one unique aspect . . .

4. The basic difference between the nervous system of man and that of slightly lower forms of mammals lies not in the number of cells, but in the differentiation and organization of those cells. Thus, we have for man the concept of Neurological Organization in addition to neurological development.

5. Neurological Organization is a "whole." . . . Segmentation into parts results in misdiagnosis, and poor treatment follows.

6. Deprivation, trauma, or enrichment all affect the development and organization of the human nervous system.

7. Children who have problems with reading have either been traumatized or have been deprived environmentally, resulting in a lack of complete Neurological Organization, which in turn, creates the reading problem.

8. The diagnosis of a reading problem, therefore, becomes an evaluation of the state of Neurological Organization.

9. Where development or organization of the nervous system is found lacking, increased opportunity for its development must be given if the reading problem is to be eliminated.

10. Reading problems can be avoided by the prevention of trauma to the nervous system and by providing maximal environmental opportunity for the development and organization of the nervous system [pp. 5–6].

The Doman–Delacato theory of neurological organization and its associated treatment program have been widely publicized and controversial. A review of the controversy surrounding this theory sponsored by numerous professional educational and medical organizations resulted in the adoption of an official statement. Two of the statement's most crucial criticisms of the theory were based on a review by Robbins and Glass (1969), in which evidence was cited to discredit the tenets (a) that ontogeny recapitulates phylogeny, and (b) that uniform dominance or sidedness is a significant factor in the etiology and therapy of language problems. The statement also points out that present information does not support the view that all language problems can be represented on a single continuum of neurological disorganization. In addition, attempts by those at the Institutes for the Achievement of Human Potential to explain anthropological and cultural differences in terms of restrictions on creeping and crawling were referred to as an exceedingly narrow and questionable view. In brief, this official statement reflects agreement with the conclusion drawn by Robbins and Glass (1969) that "As a scientific hypothesis the theory of neurological organization seems to be without merit" [p. 346].

General Criticisms of Perceptual-Motor Theories

Perceptual-motor theories of learning disabilities have been the target of two general types of criticisms: (a) perceptual-motor theorists have been accused of overemphasizing the roles of movement and visual perception, while underemphasizing or neglecting the roles of cognition, auditory perception, and language, and (b) some basic assumptions on which the perceptual-motor approach to learning disabilities is based have been called into question. These assumptions are that adequate perceptual-motor development is prerequisite to adequate conceptual, language, and academic functioning and that inadequate perceptual-motor development will result in learning problems.

The validity of the first criticism regarding the neglect of cognitive functioning depends to some extent upon the criteria employed in making the distinction between perceptual and cognitive characteristics, a distinction which is by no means crystal clear. As already mentioned, several of the characteristics investigated by Werner and Strauss which have typically been considered to be perceptual-motor characteristics are also frequently viewed as cognitive characteristics.

The extent to which the study of auditory perception and language have been neglected has been discussed by Wepman (1972). Citing Gibson's (1969) classic review of research on normal perceptual development, Wepman pointed out that only 10 percent of over one thousand studies reviewed by Gibson (1969) referred to auditory perception and/or language acquisition. Visual perception was investigated in the vast majority of the studies. Wepman (1972) offered the following reasons. (a) In the past, visual learning has been thought to be directly related to cognitive development, while auditory perception has been viewed as related to speech but not to the higher mental processes. (b) Visual representation in the central nervous system is greater than the auditory, and the visual decoding system is more complex than the auditory; therefore, it has been assumed that impairments were more likely to occur in the visual modality than in the auditory.

The second general criticism of the perceptual-motor approach pertains to the underlying assumption that perceptual-motor functioning and academic functioning are related. Correlational evidence lends support to the assumption that perceptual deficits are related to reading, at least at some age levels (Keogh & Smith, 1967; Skubic & Anderson, 1970; Snyder & Freud, 1967). However, the relationship may not be one of cause and effect. For a comprehensive review of the research pertaining to the interrelationship of perceptual-motor development, cognition, and academic achievement, the reader is referred to Hallahan and Cruickshank (1973).

Hammill and his colleagues have also questioned the positing of a relationship between visual perception and learning problems. They, in fact, have raised concerns about the underlying assumptions of a "disability" position, whether it be visual, auditory, or psycholinguistic (see Hammill & Larsen, 1974a, 1974b for statements of their argument).

Intellectual and Cognitive Characteristics

Clinicians and school psychologists have traditionally used individually administered standardized intelligence tests, such as the *Wechsler Intelligence Scale for Children (WISC)* and the *Stanford-Binet,* to assess the intellectual functioning of children for purposes of classification and placement. Current concern with functional analysis and the processes, as opposed to the products, of learning has resulted in attempts to use these same instruments for diagnosis by analyzing subtest patterns. A substantial number of studies have been conducted to investigate the usefulness of *WISC* subtest patterns in the identification and diagnosis of learning disabilities, particularly reading disabilities.

Three *WISC* subtest patterns were reported to be characteristic of children with minimal brain dysfunction by Task Force I (Clements, 1966): (a) "scatter" within both Verbal and Performance scales, (b) high Verbal–low Performance, and (c) low Verbal–high Performance. Similar subtest patterns were reported by Owen, Adams, Forrest, Stolz, and Fisher (1971) and Huelsman (1970). Owen and colleagues (1971) delineated one subgroup of educationally handicapped children with relatively high Performance IQs in relation to their Verbal IQs and another subgroup with the reverse subtest pattern. They also reported that the total group of educationally handicapped children demonstrated significantly greater variability of Verbal scale subtest scores than did a control group of academically successful peers. However, no significant difference in variability of Performance scale scores was found for the two groups. Huelsman (1970) found that high Performance IQs were characteristic of about 20 percent of a group of disabled readers.

Attempts have also been made to analyze *WISC* subtest scores by grouping the subtests into categories other than Verbal and Performance. For example, Bannatyne (1971) suggests that pertinent information regarding a child's strengths and weaknesses can be obtained by reanalyzing *WISC* subtests as follows:

1. Spatial ability: Picture completion, Block design, Object assembly.
2. Conceptualizing ability: Comprehension, Similarities, Vocabulary.

3. Sequencing ability: Digit span, Picture arrangement, Coding.

4. Acquired knowledge: Information, Arithmetic, Vocabulary.

Witkin (Witkin, Dyk, Faterson, Goodenough, & Karp, 1962) proposes a slightly different three-factor process analysis of the *WISC* in which the subtests are grouped in three major categories purported to measure relatively independent functions:

1. A Verbal-comprehension factor tapped by the Vocabulary, Information, and Comprehension subtests.

2. An Attention-concentration factor tapped by the Arithmetic, Digit span, and Coding subtests.

3. An Analytic-field-approach factor tapped by the Object assembly, Block design, and Picture completion subtests.

Keogh and Hall (1973) analyzed the *WISC* subtest scores of educationally handicapped children by using Witkin's three-factor process analysis and reported the following results: (a) Educationally handicapped boys had significantly higher Verbal-comprehension and Analytic-field-approach factor scores than educationally handicapped girls. (b) For educationally handicapped boys, Verbal-comprehension and Analytic-field-approach factor scores were significantly higher than Attention-concentration factor scores. (c) For educationally handicapped girls, no significant differences between factor scores were found. These results are consistent with those reported by Owen's group (1971) who found educationally handicapped children to have significantly lower scores than normal controls on the Arithmetic, Digit span, Coding, and Information subtests. Huelsman (1970) also reported essentially the same low subtest pattern for retarded readers. In brief, results of the studies of *WISC* subtest analyses by Keogh and Hall (1973) and Owen et al. (1971) and a review by Huelsman (1970) all indicate that children with learning disabilities or subgroups of the LD population exhibit deficiencies on those *WISC* subtests purported to measure Attention-concentration abilities.

Further evidence of attention disorders in LD children is provided by both clinical data and experimental research. Task Force I (Clements, 1966) reported that short attention span for age, over-distractibility for age, impaired concentration ability, motor or verbal perseveration, and impaired ability to make decisions are characteristic of children with minimal brain dysfunction. Tarver and Hallahan (1974) reviewed twenty-one experimental studies of attention deficits in children with learning disabilities, including studies of distractibility, hyperactivity, impulsivity, vigilance (sustained attention), and intersensory shifting of attention, and drew the following conclusions:

1. Children with learning disabilities tend to be more highly distracted than controls by the distractors involved in figure-back-

ground tasks and by some types of incidental stimuli spatially contiguous to the central task. They do not appear to be differentially distracted by environmental stimuli such as flashing lights, white noise, and color cues.

2. Children with learning disabilities tend to be more impulsive, that is, less reflective, than controls.

3. Hyperactivity may be situation specific; that is, children with learning disabilities tend to be more active than controls in social situations where they are required to be motorically inactive but this is not necessarily the case in all situations.

4. Evidence regarding deficiencies in ability to shift attention from the visual to the auditory modality is inconclusive.

5. Children with learning disabilities tend to be deficient in ability to sustain attention over time.

The concept-formation deficiencies reported by Werner and Strauss have also been interpreted within an attentional framework. The inability of exogenous children to categorize and form abstractions efficiently was postulated to be the result of overattraction to and grouping on the basis of inessential characteristics of the stimuli (Strauss & Werner, 1942; Werner & Strauss, 1941). While concept-formation deficiencies in LD children have not been the subject of extensive experimentation since this early work, there has been much theorizing regarding the consequences of poor concept formation. Lerner (1971) points out how poor conceptual abilities can result in the confusion of attributes of an object with the concept of the object, inability to comprehend multiple meanings of words, and deficiencies in reading comprehension. Engelmann (1969) also views deficiencies in reading comprehension as the result of inadequacies in concept formation.

Language Characteristics

As mentioned, the language characteristics and closely related auditory deficits of children with learning disabilities have been studied less extensively than have visual and perceptual-motor characteristics, particularly in basic experimental studies. The neglect of these important learning variables no doubt reflects the status of the fields of psychology and linguistics. While visual perception has been researched extensively since the birth of psychology in the late nineteenth century, the scientific study of language and auditory perception is more recent and has taken place largely within the relatively new field of psycholinguistics. Wepman (1972) points out, however, that recent child development abstracts show a growing interest in language acquisition, language development, and auditory perception.

Although the language problems of children with learning disabilities have been the subject of relatively little basic research, several theories of language disabilities were developed even before the perceptual-motor theories.

Samuel Orton: The earliest observations and investigations of language problems in children with normal intelligence came from within the medical profession. Before the turn of the century, both Kerr (1897), an English physician, and Morgan (1896), an English ophthalmologist, published reports of reading disabilities in children with normal intelligence. Hinshelwood (1917), also an English ophthalmologist, observed similarities in cases of congenital word blindness, i.e., severe reading disability in children of normal intelligence, and acquired word blindness, the inability of adults to read after the destruction of certain areas of the brain.

Samuel Orton (1937), a neuropathologist, also observed similarities in the language disorders of adults suffering from brain damage to the dominant hemisphere of the brain and children with normal intelligence who had suffered no known brain damage. Orton devoted most of his career to the clinical study of these children and formulated a comprehensive theory of language disabilities. The views of Orton (1937) and Hinshelwood (1917) differ in two major respects: Orton viewed reading disability as a functional variant in the establishment of hemispheric dominance which was genetically determined, whereas Hinshelwood viewed the disorders as a congenital brain defect. Hinshelwood restricted his theory to severe reading disability, whereas Orton considered reading disability to range from mild to severe, depending upon the degree of cerebral dominance which the child had developed.

Rejecting Hinshelwood's term *congenital word blindness* as misleading, Orton introduced the term *strephosymbolia,* meaning twisted symbols, to accurately depict the symptomatology of the condition without implying actual brain damage. The major symptoms of reading disability reported by Orton (1937) were:

1. Difficulties in differentiation of letters such as *p* and *q,* and *b* and *d.*

2. Confusion of pallindromic words such as *was* and *saw.*

3. Reading from right to left instead of left to right, evidenced by reversals of paired letters, syllables within words, and whole words within sentences.

4. Capacity to mirror read and produce mirror writing.

Orton attempted to explain these symptoms in terms of motor integrading, i.e., mixed dominance. According to Orton's theory, records, or engrams, stored in the cells of the nondominant hemisphere of the brain form mirrored or antitropic patterns of those records stored in the dominant hemisphere. Thus, the mirrored counterpart of the word *was* as stored in the dominant hemisphere would be stored as *saw* in the nondominant hemisphere. With the establishment of complete hemispheric dominance, the dominant hemisphere comes to control language functions and suppresses the engrams laid down in the nondominant hemisphere. When complete hemispheric dominance is lacking, the mirrored images from the nondominant hemisphere often emerge, and the child reads *b* as *d* and *was* for *saw,* etc.

Although Orton's study of language problems in children began with the study of specific reading disability (developmental alexia), he later extended his work to the study of other syndromes, including specific writing disability (developmental agraphia), developmental word deafness, motor speech delay (developmental motor aphasia), unusual clumsiness (developmental apraxia), stuttering, and combinations of these syndromes. He also found that difficulty sequencing or repicturing the exact order of letters, sounds, or other language units was common to all six syndromes.

Orton's observation of sequencing difficulties is consistent with the more recent clinical observations of Eisenson (1972). In reference to children with developmental aphasia, a disorder considered by many language clinicians to represent a subgroup of LD children, Eisenson (1972) stated that "Sequencing difficulties are pronounced for auditory events and especially for speech, but may also be present for visual events" [p. 63]. Further evidence of sequencing difficulties in children with learning disabilities is provided by Doehring's (1968) correlational study. In this study, 109 measures of language and nonlanguage abilities were obtained for retarded readers. Reading disabilities was more highly correlated with visual and verbal tasks requiring the sequential processing of related material than with any of the other measures.

Lauretta Bender: Lauretta Bender, a clinical psychiatrist working at Bellevue Hospital in New York, was associated with Orton during the early years of his career. She noted that many of the boys referred to Bellevue Hospital for psychiatric treatment were severely retarded readers and hypothesized the reading disability to result from a common cause of emotional maladjustment, behavior disorders, and delinquency. Like Orton, Bender (1963) related language disorders to cerebral dominance, explaining the disorders in terms of a maturational lag in the development of central nervous system functions in the following way:

> ... those parts of the neopallium which serve the specifically human functions of unilateral cortical dominance, unilateral handedness for tool or pen and pencil usage, unilateral eyedness for close focus, auditory and visual recognition of signs and symbols, and the learning processes for the spoken and written language, show a wider range of maturation age than do parts associated with other maturation or habit patterns [p. 27].

Bender (1963) listed the following symptoms of the maturational lag syndrome:

1. Slow maturation of language skills, most often recognizable by difficulties in learning to read at the usual age.
2. Slower maturation in neurological patterning, revealed in the developmental history of motor skills, soft neurological signs, and motor awkwardness.
3. An uneven pattern of intellectual development with variability in I.Q.
4. In preschool years, weaknesses in drawing and form perception, ill-defined handedness, and atypical directionality.
5. Frequent occurrence of left-handedness and mixed dominance.
6. Right-left confusion or lack of orientation.
7. Immature personality development.
8. Higher frequency among boys than among girls.
9. Familial histories of other cases with left-handedness, mixed or incomplete cerebral dominance, language disabilities, stuttering, or left–right disorientation.

Thus Bender (1963) associated poor motor development with language disabilities. She developed the *Bender Visual Motor Gestalt Test* (Bender, 1938), which has frequently been used in the clinical diagnosis of learning disabilities, to assess visual-motor development.

Bender (1963) also studied childhood schizophrenia extensively and similarly considered this disorder to be the result of a maturational lag. In comparing childhood schizophrenia with language disorders, Bender (1963) wrote:

> The language lags are more strongly localized in the areas of language, dominant cerebral control, and mentation, and are therefore not as all-embracing or as severe as childhood schizophrenia. Furthermore, the language lags tend to be self-correcting and are never as malignant as childhood schizophrenia may be. However, the mechanisms and defenses are similar. It may be difficult to differentiate between a severe, uncorrected language lag and a mild schizophrenia . . .
>
> They are also comparable because in both there is evidence for genetic or familial etiological factors; both show lags in maturation with primitive features in organization of this behavior; both show evidence for a basic abstractiveness in function and secondary or reactive concreteness [p. 42].

Katrina de Hirsch: The influence of both Orton and Bender is reflected in the theories of Katrina de Hirsch (1963), a speech pathologist and language theorist. De Hirsch (1963) uses the term *specific dyslexia* to refer to the same types of language disorders which were described by Orton (1937). Like Bender, de Hirsch (1963) views language deficits as manifestations of central nervous system immaturity, i.e., a maturational or developmental lag. Like both Orton and Bender, she theorizes that immature psychoneurological functioning is genetically determined.

De Hirsch (1952) described in detail both the receptive and the expressive language deficits of dyslexic children, including difficulties with processing complex verbalizations, difficulties with syntactical formulations, dysnomia, cluttering, disorganized verbal expression, and difficulties in grasping spatial and temporal categories.

Having studied Gestalt psychology in Germany, de Hirsch was also interested in the perceptual-motor characteristics of dyslexic children. She observed that many of the perceptual-cognitive characteristics investigated by Werner and Strauss were frequently associated with dyslexia, and she attempted to explain language deficits in terms of underlying perceptual-motor deficits such as immature motility patterning, poor fine motor control, undifferentiated perception, and poor spatial and temporal organization. In turn, she explained these perceptual-motor deficits as basic immaturity in Gestalt functioning, that is, that function of the organism which responds to a given constellation of stimuli as a whole.

Like Orton, de Hirsch contends that language disorders—oral, written, and printed—represent a continuum of verbal symbolic disturbances. She noted that many children who exhibit speech problems during the preschool years also have difficulties later learning to read, write, and spell. These observations directed her interest toward the development of a test battery to identify potential academic failures prior to school entrance. Her efforts in this direction are discussed in the early identification section of this overview.

Helmer Myklebust: In his early career, Myklebust worked with deaf (1960) and aphasic (1957) children. During this time, he detected auditory dysfunctions of less severity than those generally associated with aphasia in children with no measurable hearing loss. These findings channeled him into the study of auditory disorders and closely associated language disorders. Myklebust (1968) uses the term *psychoneurological learning disabilities,* which reflects both the behavioral characteristics and the underlying central nervous system dysfunction, to refer to children with language disorders (Myklebust & Boshes, 1960).

Myklebust's (1960) theory of language acquisition entails five levels of verbal language development. The first level, that of inner language, involves the formation of simple concepts. The development of inner language permits transformation of experience into verbal or nonverbal symbols. At the second level, auditory receptive language skills develop. Symbols and experience are associated, enabling the child to comprehend spoken words. Next, the development of auditory expressive language is evidenced in the child's speech. The fourth developmental level, that of visual receptive language, involves the comprehension of printed words, i.e., reading. At the last level of development, visual expressive language is evidenced in the ability to express oneself through writing. Like most language theorists, Myklebust contends that receptive language precedes expressive language development and that expressive language disabilities usually reflect inadequate receptive language development.

Myklebust's concept of semiautonomous brain systems encompasses both interneurosensory and intraneurosensory learning (Johnson & Myklebust, 1967). In intraneurosensory learning, a system functions almost independently of others. For example, the auditory system functions independently, to a large extent, in the acquisition of oral language. Interneurosensory learning refers to integrated learning which involves the simultaneous functioning of two or more systems. In interneurosensory learning, a transducer system within the brain translates information from one system to another. Myklebust contends that some children with learning disorders are able to process information through a single modality, but become overloaded when information received simultaneously through several modalities must be integrated. Dyslexia and apraxia are cited as examples of disorders resulting from deficits in interneurosensory learning. There is some evidence that those children who are brain damaged, or are thought to be brain damaged, are more likely to have intersensory than intrasensory problems (Deutsch & Schumer, 1967). In addition, other theorists and researchers (c.f. Birch & Belmont, 1964, 1965) have stressed the importance of auditory–visual integration in the ability to read.

Johnson and Myklebust (1967) described five types of psychoneurological learning disorders:

1. *Disorders of auditory language.* Three types of auditory language disorders are (a) generalized auditory deficits, in which the child hears but does not interpret environmental sounds or speech, (b) receptive auditory disorders, in which the child interprets nonverbal environmental sounds but does not comprehend the auditory symbols involved in oral language, and (c) auditory expressive disorders, which may involve problems of reauditorization and word selection (anomia), difficulties in production of motor movements necessary for speech (dyspraxia), and defective syntax.

2. *Disorders of reading.* Myklebust differentiates visual and auditory dyslexia. The visual dyslexic may exhibit characteristics such as confusion of similar letters and words, frequent letter reversals and inversions, poor visual sequencing, poor visual memory, poor visual analysis, and visual integration skills. The auditory dyslexic is likely to have difficulty reauditorizing phonemes and words, blending sounds, and learning phonetic word attack skills in general.

3. *Disorders of writing.* Dysgraphia, revisualization deficits, and deficiencies in formulation and syntax are included as disorders of writing. Dysgraphia is a disorder of the visual-motor system which results in the inability to copy letters, words, or numbers. Revisu-

alization problems reflect a basic deficiency in visual memory. Disorders of formulation and syntax usually reflect deficiencies in ideation and may be manifested in behaviors such as word omissions, distorted word order, incorrect word endings, faulty punctuation, and improper verb and pronoun usage.

4. *Disorders of arithmetic.* Myklebust makes a distinction between arithmetic disorders related to language disorders and those related to disturbances in quantitative thinking. The first type of disorder may result from auditory receptive language problems which interfere with the comprehension of oral instructions and explanations or from an inability to write the answers to arithmetic problems. Disturbances in quantitative thinking are manifested in the inability to calculate.

5. *Nonverbal disorders of learning.* Problems in gesturing, motor learning, body image, spatial orientation, right–left orientation, social imperception, distractibility, perseveration, and disinhibition are included in this category.

Myklebust also developed a formula for establishing a child's learning quotient, a quantification of the severity of a learning disability. The formula takes into account the child's mental age, life age, grade age, expectancy age, and achievement level.

EARLY IDENTIFICATION

The need to identify children with potential learning problems before they are exposed to the academic demands of first grade is rapidly gaining recognition. Advocates of the early identification movement point out that preventive measures instituted at early ages are more economical and short-term than remediation at later ages and that preventive treatment may preclude the development of secondary emotional disturbance.

Most attempts to identify high-risk children before the failure syndrome has been firmly established have focused on the kindergarten and first-grade child. Several significant investigations, however, have sought to delineate those characteristics of infants which are predictive of future learning problems. One such study of particular significance is a ten-year longitudinal study reported by Thomas, Chess, and Birch (1968). In this study, 128 infants were rated on a three-point scale for nine temperamental characteristics—activity level, rhythmicity, approach or withdrawal, adaptability, intensity of reaction, threshold of responsiveness, quality of mood, distractibility, and attention span and persistence. The children were subsequently examined periodically over a ten-year period. By the age of ten, 42 of the 128 children had been referred to clinics for learning and behavioral problems. These clinical cases differed from the children who did not develop behavioral disturbances in either high or low activity, irregularity, withdrawal response to novel stimuli, nonadaptability, high intensity, persistence, and distractibility. Although single traits were not found to be indicative of behavioral disorders, clusters of traits were associated with increased risk of behavioral disorders.

Thomas, Chess, and Birch (1968) stress that there is no direct cause-and-effect relationship between patterns of temperament and behavioral disorders. Some children with negative temperamental qualities did not develop behavior disorders, while others with favorable characteristics did. The authors subscribe to an interactionist point of view, contending that both normal and deviant development result from the interaction of the child's temperament with significant features of his environment. They emphasize the importance of achieving a match between the child's temperament and the manner in which the child is handled by parents, teachers, and other significant persons.

Denhoff, Hainsworth, and Hainsworth (1971) also attempted to delineate identifying criteria during the neonatal period and the first year of life by having pediatricians rate over 800 items pertaining to neurological symptoms and defects during pregnancy, delivery, and first-year development. From these ratings, two neurological outcome indices, a neonatal outcome index and a first-year outcome index, were derived. Six years later these two indices were found to correlate significantly with scores on the *Wide Range Achievement Test,* the *Meeting Street School Screening Test,* and the *WISC.*

A major study designed to predict reading failures among kindergarten children was conducted by de Hirsch, Lansky, and Langford (1966). A battery of thirty-seven tests assessing perceptual-motor, body image, and linguistic performance was administered to fifty-three children during their kindergarten year and again at the completion of the second grade. A Predictive Index, composed of ten of the thirty-seven tests, was found to identify ten of the eleven children who were reading failures by the end of the second grade. Tests included in the Predictive Index were Pencil Use, *Wepman Auditory Discrimination Test,* Number of Words Used in a Story, *Bender Visual Motor Gestalt Test,* Categories, *Horst Reversals Test, Gates Word Matching Test,* Word Recognition I, Word Recognition II, and Word Reproduction. Because this Predictive Index was found to require too much administration time to be useful as a screening device with large groups of children, the index was reassessed (Jansky & de Hirsch, 1972) and a simplified Screening Index which requires only about fifteen minutes to administer was devised (Jansky, 1973). This Screening Index is composed of Letter Naming, Picture Naming, *Gates Word Matching Test, Bender Visual Motor Gestalt Test,* and the Binet Sentence Memory.

Evidence that teacher perceptions are a valid means of identification at the kindergarten level is provided by studies conducted by W. D. Kirk (1966), Ferinden and Jacobson (1970), and Haring and Ridgway (1967). In the Kirk study, kindergarten teachers were asked to provide a motor assessment for each child and, in addition, to rate children in nine ability areas: reasoning, speed of learning, verbal comprehension, ability to deal with abstract ideas, perceptual discrimination, psychomotor abilities, verbal expression, number and space relations, and creativity. Results of the study indicated that: (a) Although teachers tended to select younger children as slower, their identification of bright and slow children was accurate, with identification of slow children being more accurate than identification of bright children. (b) Teachers showed high interrater reliability (0.88). (c) A score composed of the nine ability areas was more accurate than the motor assessment.

In the Ferinden and Jacobson (1970) study, teachers' subjective evaluations were found to be 80 percent correct in predicting which children would experience learning difficulties in school. The predictive validity of the teacher evaluation was higher than that of the *Bender Visual Motor Gestalt Test* and the *Metropolitan Reading Readiness Test,* but less than that of the *Wide Range Achievement Test* and the *Evanston Early Identification Scale.*

Haring and Ridgway (1967) provided kindergarten teachers with a screening scale to objectify their observational evaluations in eleven areas: personal appearance, psychological characteristics, gross muscle coordination, verbal fluency, speech development, auditory memory, auditory discrimination, visual memory, visual discrimination, visual motor performance, and directionality-laterality. They found that the teachers were able to identify children by specific areas of developmental retardation.

A number of rating scales, checklists, and other screening tests useful for the identification of high-risk children at the kindergarten and prekindergarten ages have been developed. For a more comprehensive listing and description of such screening devices, the reader is referred to Wallace and Kauffman (1973) and Irwin, Moore, and Rampp (1972).

Lewis has been engaged in some interesting research in the development of attention and perception in infants which has implications for early identification (see Lewis, 1975, for a summary of this research). He has collected some data which suggest that one can use laboratory measures of heart rate deceleration (an indicator of attentional responding) to predict later learning problems. Although the results are extremely tentative at this time, Lewis' works holds promise for a method of identifying infants who are "at risk" of later school failure.

Some Problems of Early Identification

Although much effort has been devoted to the early identification movement and progress has been achieved on many accounts, some pertinent questions have been raised. Keogh and Becker (1973) summarized the problems in early identification with three major questions:

1. How valid are the identifying or predictive measures?
2. What are the implications of diagnostic data for remediation or educational intervention?
3. Do benefits of early identification outweigh possible damaging or negative effects of such recognition? [p. 6].

Regarding the validity of identification techniques, Keogh and Becker (1973) said: (a) Most techniques and/or tests are too limited in validity to allow definitive prediction about individual children. (b) Learning problems are often attributable to the interaction of the child with the learning situation; yet, most identifying procedures are focused entirely upon the child. The accuracy of the prediction is thus reduced. (c) The development of instruments with high predictive validity is limited by ethical considerations. After a child has been identified as high risk, educational intervention is called for. If the intervention is effective, the child becomes a successful achiever, and thus the predictive validity of the instrument is reduced.

Early identification is based upon the assumption that the educational programs of high-risk children will be modified to reduce the likelihood of the development of a learning problem. Keogh and Becker (1973) point out, however, that it is often difficult to match a child with the appropriate preventive or remedial strategy on the basis of the data collected by early identification techniques. They state that "assignment of children to a particular intervention may be in large part a matter of program availability, point of view of the diagnostician, intuition, and a little bit of faith" [p. 7].

Regarding the negative effects of early identification, Keogh and Becker (1973) point to a possible built-in expectancy phenomenon. Lowered teacher expectations may affect the child's performance. Also, overemphasis of certain inabilities may cause anxieties on the part of parents and teachers which may have further debilitating effects upon the child. They suggested the following guidelines for early identification:

1. *Specification of expected outcomes.* This suggestion implies that the most accurate screening measures are those which are tied to criterion or outcome measures in both content and time.

2. *Focus on competence.* Identification should provide information about the child's compensatory abilities so that they can be incorporated into preventive educational strategies.

3. *Inclusion of task and situation.* Identification procedures must be broadened to include task components, situational variables, and expectancies.

4. *Assessment of school behavior.* The child's classroom behavior and problem-solving strategies should be included in the identification process.

5. *Identification and remediation.* Behavioral observation techniques are more useful than standardized tests in pinpointing those aspects of the child's performance which might be used as the basis for instruction.

DIAGNOSIS

Diagnosis is closely related to both identification and remediation. As suggested by Keogh and Becker (1973), identification techniques should provide diagnostic information about the child's strengths and weaknesses so that an appropriate individualized instructional program can be developed. With early identification, the instructional program is aimed at prevention, whereas the broader concept of diagnosis can be applied to evaluation after a learning problem has developed. In either case, the goal is to acquire information about the child that will be useful in planning an effective instructional program.

Diagnostic information can be obtained through case histories or interviews, clinical and teacher observations, informal tests and trial teaching sessions, and formal standardized tests. Comprehensive listings and discussions of such diagnostic tools are included in Lerner (1971), Smith (1969), and Waugh and Bush (1976).

This overview will discuss two diagnostic tests which have been used extensively and are representative of standardized tests used within the field of learning disabilities—the *Illinois Test of Psycholinguistic Abilities* and the *Marianne Frostig Developmental Test of Visual Perception.* Both of these diagnostic tools were designed specifically to assess specific abilities and disabilities so that the resulting information could guide remediation and/or prevention.

Illinois Test of Psycholinguistic Abilities (ITPA)

In his early career, Samuel Kirk, the senior author of the *ITPA,* was primarily concerned with attempting to increase the rate of mental development of disadvantaged and institutionalized mentally retarded children (Paraskevopoulos & Kirk, 1969). Kirk noted that many mentally retarded children displayed wide discrepancies in abilities and recognized the need for tests to isolate their specific abilities and disabilities. The *ITPA* grew out of the early attempts of Kirk and his colleagues to devise such tests. An experimental edition of the *ITPA* (Kirk, McCarthy, & Kirk, 1961) was published first; a revised edition was issued in 1968 (Kirk, McCarthy, & Kirk, 1968).

The *ITPA* is based on the concept of intraindividual differences, that is, differences of ability within a single child. It measures a number of discrete areas of psychoeducational development which can be compared to determine developmental imbalances. Because LD children are noted for wide discrepancies in abilities, the *ITPA* has come to be widely used within the field of learning disabilities.

The *ITPA*, adapted from the communications model of Osgood (1957a, 1957b), is based on a three-dimensional model which contains two channels of communication, three psycholinguistic processes, and two levels of organization:

1. *Channels of communication* are the modalities through which sensory impressions are received and responses expressed. The *ITPA* includes only those two channels which were deemed to be most educationally relevant—the auditory-vocal and the visual-motor.

2. *Psycholinguistic processes* are the receptive, organizing, and expressive processes involved in the acquisition of language. Reception involves the ability to recognize and understand what is seen or heard. Organization refers to the internal manipulation of percepts, concepts, and linguistic symbols. Expression refers to the ability to express ideas either verbally or nonverbally.

3. *Levels of organization* are the degree to which communication habits have been developed by the individual. The automatic level encompasses those communication habits which are less voluntary but highly organized and integrated. The representational level refers to those communication skills involving a mediating process of utilizing symbols which carry meaning.

The *ITPA* is composed of twelve subtests, six at the representational level and six at the automatic level of organization. Psycholinguistic functions tested at the representational level include auditory reception, visual reception, auditory association, visual association, verbal expression, and manual expression. The six functions tested at the automatic level are grammatic closure, auditory closure, sound blending, visual closure, auditory sequential memory, and visual sequential memory.

The validity of the *ITPA* has not been conclusively established. Hallahan and Cruickshank (1973) reviewed validity studies of the *ITPA* and concluded that "While the literature pertaining to the experimental edition is inconclusive or negative with regard to construct and to concurrent and predictive validity, the authors have demonstrated fairly adequate concurrent validity with the new edition" [p. 112]. Despite this possible limitation of the *ITPA*, the work of Kirk and his colleagues in the development of this test has generally been lauded by professionals in the field of learning disabilities on two accounts: (a) it focuses on the relatively neglected psycholinguistic functioning of children with learning disabilities, and (b) it reflects a basic concern for diagnosis leading to remediation. Again, Hammill and his colleagues have argued that the reliance of the *ITPA* on underlying psycholinguistic processes is not warranted (e.g.,

Hammill & Larsen, 1974a). They have also concluded that the efficacy of psycholinguistic training is questionable.

Marianne Frostig Developmental Test of Visual Perception (DTVP)

Marianne Frostig, the senior author of the *DTVP*, believes that most learning is acquired through the visual modality (Frostig & Horne, 1964). She contends that failure to develop visual perceptual skills between the ages of three and one-half and seven and one-half years is likely to result in some degree of emotional disturbance and academic failure. Disturbances in visual perception are by far the most frequent symptoms exhibited by children referred to the Frostig Center of Educational Therapy, and Frostig has related the academic failure of these children to inadequate development in five aspects of visual perception:

1. *Eye–motor coordination* is essential for writing and an important prerequisite to reading.
2. *Figure–ground perception* is required in the analysis and synthesis of written words, phrases, and paragraphs.
3. *Form constancy* is necessary for the recognition of familiar words presented in unfamiliar contexts.
4. *Position in space* is required in the differentiation of letters which have the same form but different spatial positions, e.g., *b* and *d*.
5. *Spatial relations* is involved in the recognition of letters in a word and words in a sentence.

Frostig's experience with the study of visual perception in young children led her to believe that visual perception consists of a number of different, relatively independent, functions. She does not contend that these five visual perceptual abilities are the only ones involved in the total process of visual perception (Frostig, Maslow, Lefever, & Whittlesey, 1964), but chose to study these particular aspects of visual perception because they seem to be particularly relevant to school performance. The *DTVP*, constructed to assess visual perceptual performance in five areas, includes the following subtests (Frostig, Lefever, & Whittlesey, 1966):

1. *Eye–Motor Coordination*—a test of eye–hand coordination involving the drawing of continuous straight, curved, or angled lines between boundaries of various width or from point to point without guidelines.
2. *Figure–Ground*—a test involving shifts in perception of figures against increasingly complex grounds. Intersecting and "hidden" geometric forms are used.
3. *Constancy of Shape*—a test involving the recognition of certain geometric figures presented in a variety of sizes, shadings, textures,

and positions in space, and their discrimination from similar geometric figures. Circles, squares, rectangles, ellipses, and parallelograms are used.

4. *Position in Space*—a test involving the discrimination of reversals and rotations of figures presented in series. Schematic drawings representing common objects are used.

5. *Spatial Relationships*—a test involving the analysis of simple forms and patterns. These consist of lines of various lengths and angles which the child is required to copy; using dots as guide points [p. 5].

The *DTVP* yields scaled scores and age equivalents for each of the five subtests for children between the ages of four and eight years. In addition, an overall measure of the child's visual functioning in relation to that of his age peers, a Perceptual Quotient, is derived.

The *DTVP* has been criticized on three accounts (see Hallahan & Cruickshank, 1973):

1. The standardization sample consisted primarily of white middle-class children; thus the usefulness of the test with children of lower socioeconomic classes has been questioned.

2. The basic assumption that five different and relatively independent components of visual perception are assessed has been called into question.

3. Validity and reliability studies have yielded equivocal results. Reliability coefficients for total scores have generally been high, although reliability coefficients for subtest scores have been much lower. A review of studies investigating the predictive validity of the *DTVP* led Myers and Hammill (1969) to conclude that total scores of the *DTVP* predict reading readiness adequately at the first-grade level, but do not predict first-grade reading achievement, and *DTVP* scores are related to reading in the second and third grades to a small degree.

Despite these criticisms of the *DTVP*, Frostig, like the authors of the *ITPA,* has been credited with making a commendable early effort to provide a diagnostic instrument to detect specific impairments so that remediation could be tailored to the individual child's needs.

Criterion-Referenced Testing

The *ITPA* and the *DTVP* are normative in nature in that they were developed with the idea that the performance of the child being tested would be compared to his peers. A different popular approach to diagnostic testing is criterion-referenced testing. Advocated for use within the classroom situation, criterion tests are usually teacher-made instruments of specific academic materials. For example, a teacher may administer twenty sight-words to a child. He then determines that the pupil should be able to recognize eighteen out of the twenty. He instructs and tests until this criterion is reached. This kind of testing is directly related to the subject matter of the classroom. Criterion-referenced testing need not be considered a substitute for normative testing. In order for the teacher to determine that the child has a problem worth working on in the first place, he may wish to rely upon normative test data. Drew, Freston, and Logan (1972) have developed a model for combining normative and criterion testing in special education.

Those who favor the use of criterion testing hold that it is more directly applicable to the teaching situation. It aids the teacher in setting goals and aids in specifying what each individual child does and does not know. The major drawbacks to criterion testing are that the teacher must develop reliable tests and set the appropriate criterion. Given the usual lack of sophistication of teachers in test construction, these criticisms should not be taken lightly.

Behavioral Assessment

While we discuss behavioral assessment later in this chapter in conjunction with behavior modification, we mention it here as a method of assessment. There is a rapidly expanding school of thought within the learning disabilities field, and the field of special education in general, that deemphasizes the use of standardized tests. These practitioners are more interested in measuring the exact academic responses a child must make rather than relying upon data obtained from assessment of behaviors required to perform on standardized tests. Advocates of this approach, intimately associated with the practice of behavior modification, are interested in specifying those responses necessary for achievement that the child lacks or produces in a deficient manner. To specify the source of the problem, then, the user of behavioral assessment must first break down the academic skill into its component parts. This process is usually referred to as *task analysis*.

While at first glance task analysis and behavioral assessment appear easy, the precision and level of specificity required make them extremely difficult to perform with any degree of rigor. In order to analyze a task in terms of its component parts, the teacher needs to know the sequential steps necessary for the child to complete the task. The measurement of these specific behaviors must then be made. A large portion of the teacher's job becomes the daily measurement of the child's acquisition of discrete responses. Such procedures can only be successful if the teacher is committed to taking these measures accurately. The effort is well worth it, however, because of the educationally useful information that can be gained from behavioral assessment.

MEDICAL TREATMENT

The medical profession has been involved to a greater extent in the etiological and preventive aspects of learning disabilities than in treatment. Nevertheless, several types of medical treatment which have been prescribed for LD children should be mentioned—pharmacological treatment, orthomolecular treatment (megavitamins), and allergy treatment.

Pharmacological treatment has most often been used to control hyperkinetic behavior. Four groups of commonly used drugs are stimulants, antihistamines, anticonvulsants, and tranquilizers (Baldwin & Kenny, 1966). Evidence regarding both the positive and the negative efforts of drug treatment is inconclusive. Among the negative side effects of drugs which have been reported are anorexia, insomnia, headaches, and abdominal pain (Laufer, 1971), loss of appetite, interferences with sleep, crying jags, nervousness, and palpitations (Solomons, 1971), psychological addiction, increased hyperactivity, and loss of independence and control (Ladd, 1971), and growth depression of height and weight (Safer, Allen & Barr, 1972).

In presenting the positive side of drug treatment, Conners (1973) states that:

> ... drugs have uniformly been shown to produce substantial academic and behavioral improvement, and, therefore, when indicated they deserve to be used under proper circumstances. Side effects may be annoying but can be regulated; toxic effects are very rare and seldom encountered. Although available long-term follow-ups are scarce, the information from several studies gives no support to the commonly voiced fears that these drugs produce a susceptibility to addiction or drug abuse in later life. If anything, the evidence suggests that treated children are less likely to suffer the vicissitudes of adolescence, ego-failure, and cumulative failure that are true of untreated children ... [p. 351].

Freeman (1966) reviewed forty-three controlled studies of the effects of a variety of drugs on brain-damaged and behavioral-disordered children, finding twenty-one of the studies to report positive results and twenty-two negative or inconclusive results.

The newer treatment approaches of megavitamin therapy (Cott, 1972), diet control (Roberts, 1969; Cott, 1972), and allergy desensitization (Wunderlich, 1970) have been subjected to less scientific scrutiny than has pharmacological treatment. As pointed out by Cott (1972), positive clinical reports of megavitamin treatment and dietary regulation indicate that "investigation of this type of treatment by controlled studies should be given the highest priority, ... such treatment satisfies the first dictum of good medical practice—that of doing the patient no harm [p. 257]."

Most professionals involved in the medical treatment of children with learning disabilities agree that such treatment in combination with special educational provisions is more effective than either alone (Conners, 1973; Edgington, 1970).

EDUCATIONAL PROVISIONS

Many of the educational methods and techniques currently being recommended for children with learning disabilities can be traced back to the early works of Montessori (1912), Itard (1962), Seguin (1907), and even Quintillian, a Roman teacher of the first century A.D. (Murphy, 1965). They have, of course, undergone modification and refinement to take into account the abilities and disabilities characteristic of LD children.

Necessity demands that the educational approaches mentioned in this overview be described very briefly. To do justice to any single approach would require a complete volume. For a more comprehensive, single-volume summary, critique, and comparison of methods, the reader is referred to Myers and Hammill (1969).

The various methods and procedures described here are, for the most part, not mutually exclusive. In fact, the nature of some requires that they be used in conjunction with others. Behavior modification, for example, is not a program with content of its own, but a set of procedures which may be used effectively in conjunction with a variety of instructional programs. In the case of most of the other methods, they may be, and often are, employed concurrently or at different points in a child's educational program, either in their entirety or in part.

Structured Classrooms

The rationale for the current emphasis upon the structuring and controlling of the educational environments of children with learning disabilities can be found in the writings of Werner, Strauss, Cruickshank, and their co-workers. Strauss and Kephart (1939; Kephart & Strauss, 1940) found that the IQs of endogenous mentally retarded children increased over a four- to five-year period of institutionalization, while the IQs of the exogenous children decreased. To explain these findings, they hypothesized that the exogenous children were unable to benefit from the highly stimulating institution environment, i.e., that they were hyperresponsive to external stimulation. Strauss and Lehtinen (1947) described educational strategies for the exogenous children which involved both control of the overstimulating environment and education of the child to control his environment. They hypothesized that control of the external environment would decrease hyperactivity and distractibility which, in turn, would result in increased learning. The increased learning was hypothesized to produce greater self-control on the part of the child. As self-control developed, control of the external environment was gradually decreased.

Among the numerous classroom structuring procedures recommended by Strauss & Lehtinen (1947) are:

1. Small class size.
2. Covered or painted windows.
3. Plain, unornamented clothing.
4. Use of screens to shut out distracting stimuli.
5. Absence of inessential visual stimuli in the classroom, e.g., colorful pictures on walls, bulletin boards, etc.
6. Uncluttered pages with widely spaced written materials.
7. Covers for reading materials which allow for exposure of small areas of material at one time.
8. Motor involvement in learning activities to increase and maintain attention.

In a pilot demonstration project, the Montgomery County–Syracuse University Study and Teacher demonstration, Cruickshank and his colleagues (Cruickshank, Bentzen, Ratzeburg, & Tannhauser, 1961) refined and extended the teaching procedures of Strauss and Lehtinen (1947) and applied them to the teaching of children with average and near-average intelligence. In this study, forty hyperactive children were divided into four classes of ten children each. Two of the classes were designed as experimental classes and two as control classes. The experimental classes were exposed to a highly structured environment incorporating many of the recommendations of Strauss and Lehtinen. In addition, the experimental classes were provided with individual cubicles designed to eliminate distracting external stimuli and promote attention to the learning task.

At the end of one academic year, the data indicated that the experimental program had resulted in improved perceptual-motor performance on the *Bender Gestalt* and improved attention on the *Syracuse Visual Figure-Background Test*. Higher level cognitive abilities, as assessed by achievement and intelligence tests, were not affected, however. In addition, follow-up of the children revealed that the gains were lost after reentrance into the traditional classroom environment. This, of course, is not surprising. It may simply mean that one year of intervention is not enough. The results obtained after the one year are more disturbing.

In addition, some recent studies and theories have called into question the effectiveness of minimizing external stimulation. A review of research, for example, led Somervill, Warnberg, and Bost (1973) to conclude that "there is no single study which clearly indicates that minimizing external stimulation has a beneficial effect on task performance or is associated with a reduction in hyperactive behavior" [p. 172]. Hallahan and Kauffman (1975), however, have reviewed the stimulus attentuation studies and have concluded that, in general, stimulus reduction has been effective in increasing attentional abilities. They state that the evidence *does not* support the notion that stimulus reduction results *directly* in cognitive gains. Cruickshank (1975) notes, also, that none of the studies of stimulus reduction has been a replication of the total educational program used in the Montgomery project. It seems safest to conclude that stimulus reduction can aid in developing the *inattentive* child's attention, but achievement gains also rely upon channeling the child's attention appropriately.

Another important point is that stimulus reduction should only be effective for those children who are distractible. While group data may indicate that *some* learning disabled children are distractible, it is logical to assume that some are not. In other words, it makes more sense to provide children with educational procedures based upon observed and/ or tested behavioral characteristics than on diagnostic labels. For example, in contrast to the popular view that brain-injured children and/or LD children are hyperresponsive to external stimulation is a hyporesponsiveness hypothesis formulated by Browning (1967), who interprets many of the behaviors of brain-injured children as hyporesponsiveness to external stimulation. He contends that high levels of stimulation often increase attention abilities and result in improved performance. To test these contrasting hypotheses, Somervill, Warnberg, and Bost (1973) conducted an experiment in which boys rated as distractible and nondistractible by their teachers were exposed to one of three treatment conditions: (a) minimal stimulation condition in which cubicles were used, (b) control condition in which no effort was made to increase or decrease stimulation, and (c) high stimulation condition in which subjects were subjected to high levels of auditory and visual stimulation. Results of the study indicated that neither high levels of stimulation nor minimal stimulation had a significant effect on the performance of either the distractible or the nondistractible subjects.

Behavior Modification

The structured educational approaches of Strauss and Lehtinen (1947) and Cruickshank (Cruickshank, Bentzen, Ratzeburg, & Tannhauser, 1961) were significant precursors of behavior modification (Hallahan & Kauffman, 1975, 1976; Kauffman, 1975). Behavior modification has been proposed and used as an effective means of structuring the classroom by Haring, a former student of Cruickshank's. In the Arlington County Experiment (Haring & Phillips, 1962), two experimental (structured) classrooms were compared with a control classroom which was nonstructured. Academic achievement gains were reported to be significantly greater for the experimental group than the control group. Hewett's (1968) "engineered classroom" is another example of the application of behavior modification procedures to structure the classroom. He has designed a token-based classroom environment for children with behavioral and learning problems.

Behavior modification has been defined by Kauffman (1975) as follows:

> Behavior modification is the systematic control of environmental events to produce specific changes in observable behaviors. It is not restricted to the use of consequences or to the removal of maladaptive behaviors. Environmental events preceding the behavior in question (i.e., instructions, cues, models, prompts, etc.) as well as events following the behavior (i.e., positive reinforcers or aversive stimuli) may be arranged to modify an individual's performance. Furthermore, procedures which strengthen appropriate behavior are equally as important as techniques designed to eliminate undesirable behavior [p. 395].

Kauffman (1975) suggests that the most significant contributions of behavior modification to previously developed structured methodology lie in the development of measurement and evaluation techniques. He described a wide variety of such techniques. One measurement method which is rapidly gaining recognition and usage within the field of learning disabilities is precision teaching (Lindsley, 1971). In precision teaching, the beginning, intermediate, and ending points of desired behaviors are precisely described, and behaviors are measured as "movement cycles."

Worell and Nelson (1974) divided general behavior modification procedures into the following sequence of six stages:

1. *Select a target behavior.* The target behavior, i.e., the behavior to be changed, must be defined as an observable, countable, repeatable, specific action of the child, e.g., hitting, talking, out-of-seat.

2. *Measure and record baseline.* The target behavior is recorded before environmental changes are instituted. Behaviors are frequently recorded as rate of behavior, percentage of correct responses, or percentage of intervals during which the behavior occurred. The behavior is also measured and recorded during the intervention and evaluation stages of the behavior modification program.

3. *Develop an ABC analysis.* Antecedents (A) that may contribute to the occurrence of the behavior (B) and the consequences (C) which may be reinforcing and maintaining the behavior are observed. Analysis of this information is used to determine whether intervention strategies should focus on antecedents, consequences, or both.

4. *Initiate an intervention strategy.* The strategy employed depends upon whether the target behavior is to be decreased or increased. Positive reinforcement, i.e., following a behavior with a conse-

quence that increases the behavior in question, is the most effective means of increasing appropriate behavior. Contingency contracting (Homme, 1969) and token economies (Stainback, Payne, Stainback, & Payne, 1973) are two systems which are based largely upon the use of positive reinforcement and which allow for individualization of reinforcers. Extinction and punishment (involving either the presentation of aversive stimuli or the withdrawal of reinforcement after an inappropriate behavior has been emitted) are used to decrease inappropriate behavior. Antecedent events may be manipulated either to increase desired behavior or decrease undesired behavior. These procedures include modeling, class structuring, and curriculum modifications.

5. *Evaluate results.* After the intervention strategy has been in effect long enough for the target behavior to stabilize, the effectiveness of the intervention strategy is evaluated. In one commonly used evaluation procedure, reversal, the intervention strategy is withdrawn and recording of the behavior is continued. If the behavior returns to baseline level, the behavior change was a function of the intervention strategy employed. After the evaluation has been completed, the intervention strategy can be reinstated.

6. *Communicate results.* Positive progress should be reported to the child, his parents, his teachers, and other school personnel.

The ultimate aim of behavior modification, like that of the structured approach of Strauss & Lehtinen (1947), is to educate the child to exercise self-control over his own behavior. Behavior modifiers recognize, however, that imposed external control is often a necessary prerequisite to self-management. Both Haring and Whelan (1968) and Hewett (1967) have outlined the stages which a child goes through in making the transition from dependence upon external motivation to reliance upon self-motivation.

Behavior modification techniques are more fully described in Kauffman (1975), Krasner and Ullmann (1965), and Wallace and Kauffman (1973) and their application demonstrated in numerous case studies reported by Ullmann and Krasner (1965) and Worell and Nelson (1974). Those contemplating the use of behavior modification in school settings will be well advised to heed the cautionary note offered by Gearheart (1973): "Behavior modification procedures should be fully understood, including both potentials and limitations, before launching into a classroom program" [p. 121].

Voluminous studies of the effectiveness of behavior modification in the control of hyperactive, disruptive, aggressive, and inattentive behaviors have been reported (Hallahan & Kauffman, 1975). Although comparatively little research has been conducted on the modification of academic behaviors, an area of study which seems to have particular relevance to the field of learning disabilities, Kauffman's (1975) review of the literature indicates that studies of this type are rapidly accumulating. He cites a substantial number of studies in which behavior modification procedures were found to result in improved reading, handwriting, spelling, composition, oral language, and arithmetic.

In most of the studies cited by Kauffman, the effectiveness of the manipulation of consequences was investigated. Of particular recent interest, however, are a series of studies conducted by Lovitt and his colleagues in which the manipulation of antecedent events was found to improve academic performance. Results of these studies have shown that: vocalizing arithmetic problems before writing the answer improves arithmetic performance (Lovitt & Curtiss, 1968), specific modeling procedures influence the acquisition of computational arithmetic skills (Smith & Lovitt, 1975), explicit verbal instructions improve linguistic performance (Lovitt & Smith, 1972), and teaching aids and instructions affect subtraction performance (Smith, Lovitt, & Kidder, 1972). Lovitt (1973) has also taught LD children to type faster than they were able to write without reinforcement other than that inherent in the activity of typing itself. In addition, Lovitt (1967a, 1967b, 1968a, 1968b) has developed techniques for measuring the auditory and visual modality preferences of learning disabled children.

Perceptual-Motor Training Programs

The perceptual-motor training programs in current use with LD children are more similar than dissimilar. This is particularly true of the training programs developed by Kephart (1960, 1971), Barsch (1965), and Getman (Getman & Kane, 1964; Getman, Kane, & McKee, 1968). Kephart's program includes activities for sensory–motor training, chalkboard training (visual–motor), ocular control training, and form perception training. Getman's training program is divided into six categories—general coordination, balance, eye–hand coordination, eye movement, form perception, and visual memory. Barsch's movigenics curriculum includes activities for each of twelve dimensions of development and learning—muscular strength, dynamic balance, spatial awareness, body awareness, visual dynamics, auditory dynamics, kinesthesia, tactual dynamics, bilaterality, rhythm, flexibility, and motor planning. While Barsch's curriculum makes more specific mention of auditory training, some auditory training is also inherent in the training programs of Kephart and Getman. Nevertheless, all three programs' emphases are on perceptual-motor development.

The Frostig–Horne program of visual perception (Frostig & Horne, 1964) is more highly test-related than are the programs of Kephart, Barsch, and Getman. Although the *Purdue Perceptual-Motor Survey* (Roach & Kephart, 1966) has been used with Kephart's program, the assessment is less formal than that involved with Frostig's *DTVP* (Frostig, Maslow, Lefever, & Whittlesey, 1964). In the Frostig-Horne program, specific activities are directly related to the specific deficits assessed by the *DTVP*. Suggested activities and materials are provided in order of difficulty in the five areas of visual perception assessed by the *DTVP*— eye motor, figure–ground, perceptual constancy, position in space, and spatial relations.

Doman and Delacato also state that their program of neurological organization (Delacato, 1959, 1963; Doman, Delacato, & Doman, 1964) is based upon evaluation procedures. Performance is assessed in six areas —mobility, language, manual competence, visual competence, auditory competence, and tactile competence. This information is used to determine the child's lowest level of neurological organization so that treatment (often called *patterning*) can be instituted at the next level, that level at which neurological organization is incomplete. Treatment procedures recommended at each level (brain stage) of development, from lowest to highest level, include:

1. Medulla and cord level—opportunities for reflex movements and imposed movements of the arms and legs without body movement.
2. Pons level—homolateral patterning, proper sleep patterns, and binocular visual exercises.
3. Midbrain level—bilateral activities, cross-pattern creeping, eye coordination exercises, and music.
4. Early cortical level—cross-pattern walking, spatial relations games, and near–point visual exercises.
5. Cortical hemispheric dominance—sleep patterns consistent with sidedness and activities designed to develop consistent foot, hand, and eye dominance.

Over the past ten years or so, a large number of studies have been conducted to test the effectiveness of perceptual-motor training programs. Hallahan and Cruickshank (1973) reviewed these studies and summarized:

> Although no persuasive empirical evidence has been brought to the fore in support of perceptual-motor training, neither has there been solid negative evidence. Owing to the lack of satisfactory research studies with proper methodological controls, it is injudicious to decide wholeheartedly that perceptual-motor training deserves or does not deserve approval. The ultimate acceptance or rejection of these theorists and their procedures ought to depend upon systematic, empirical investigations yet to be done [p. 216].

Linguistic Approaches

McCarthy and McCarthy (1969) classified techniques of teaching children with learning disabilities in two categories, those reflecting a process orientation and those reflecting a tool-subject orientation. The perceptual-motor approaches and some others reflect a process orientation, i.e., they attempt to identify the learning processes underlying academic performance and apply remediation at that more basic level. The linguistic approaches—the Gillingham–Stillman, Fernald, and McGinnis methods—are tool-oriented, i.e., designed to teach the tool subjects of reading, writing, and spelling.

Gillingham and Stillman: Because the techniques and methods of teaching reading, writing, and spelling to children with specific language disability developed by Gillingham and Stillman (1956) are based on the theories of Samuel Orton, they have often been referred to as the Orton–Gillingham approach. The approach consists of a highly sequential set of techniques for teaching reading, writing, and spelling concurrently. In the initial stages of the remedial program, each new phonogram is taught by a series of procedures, referred to as *linkages,* which involve associations between visual, auditory, and kinesthetic symbols. After these linkages have been firmly established, sounds are blended into whole words and words into sentences and stories.

Although both the Gillingham–Stillman method and another method based on Orton's theory, *The Writing Road to Reading* by the Spaldings (1969), have been referred to as *phonic systems* by Myers and Hammill (1969), they are more frequently referred to by their advocates as *multisensory systems.* An adaptation of the Orton–Gillingham approach for use in the classroom is called *A Multi-Sensory Approach to Language Arts for Specific Language Disability Children* by the author, Beth Slingerland (1971).

Fernald: Like the Gillingham–Stillman method, Fernald's (1943) remedial reading method has been referred to as a *multisensory approach.* However, the Fernald method differs from the Gillingham–Stillman method in several significant respects. First, the Fernald approach emphasizes meaningfulness and motivation. It is purported to increase the child's interest in reading through having him compose his own stories. Secondly, the Fernald method is a whole-word approach in which the child is not allowed to sound out words. The Gillingham–Stillman approach, on the other hand, is a synthetic blending approach which emphasizes the acquisition of basic skills thought to be involved in the process of decoding words.

In stage one of the Fernald remedial reading method, the child tells a story. The teacher then writes each word from the story that is to be learned, the child traces and pronounces aloud each word that the teacher has written, and finally, the child writes each word from memory and checks it for correctness. In stage two, tracing is eliminated. The child looks at the word, says it to himself, and then writes the word from memory. In stage three, the child learns directly from the printed word, without vocalizing or copying. The final stage, stage four, has been reached when the child is able to read new words by generalizing from known words.

McGinnis: McGinnis's association method (1963) is designed for the younger language disabled child or for the older, more severely language delayed or aphasic child. Although the primary emphasis is on the teaching of oral language skills, the method also provides for the teaching of academic language skills.

Like the Gillingham–Stillman method, the association method introduces words by a phonetic approach. Words are produced sound by sound and gradually combined into more complex language units. McGinnis contends that precise articulation production of words precedes recognition of the meanings of words.

At the first stage or level of the association method, attention activities are presented. The second level is comprised of three language units. In the first unit, nouns are taught. In the second, articles, pronouns, prepositions, and present progressive verbs are taught and used in both oral and written sentences. In unit three, more complex verb tenses and language forms are taught.

Eclectic Approaches and Clinical Teaching

The orientation toward eclecticism in teaching children with learning disabilities is perhaps best illustrated in the clinical teaching approaches described by Frierson (1967) and Lerner (1971). Frierson points out that clinical education may or may not be conducted in a clinical setting, and that, regardless of the type of setting in which it is conducted, its effectiveness rests upon three things: (a) a thorough diagnosis which yields educationally relevant information about each child's strengths and weaknesses, (b) selection of sound teaching procedures which fit the diagnostic information for each child, and (c) objective measurement of success and empirical validation of specific procedures.

Regarding the necessity for clinical educators to be knowledgeable of many reading methods, Frierson (1967) states:

> The clinical educator must know the differences that make a difference in reading approaches. It is altogether likely that the clinical approach will selectively incorporate a combination of reading experiences drawn from several approaches. The combination will vary with each individual based upon a complete differential diagnosis. If a clinic approach is "packaged," it ceases to be a clinical approach! [p. 480].

Several eclectic approaches to the remediation of language disabilities are based upon diagnostic results of the *ITPA* (Bush & Giles, 1969; Karnes, 1968; S. A. Kirk, 1966). These approaches do not constitute a method per se, but are more appropriately described as a compilation of activities designed to promote development of each of the psycholinguistic processes assessed by the *ITPA*. Johnson and Myklebust (1967) also suggest numerous activities to remediate a wide variety of specific language deficits; however, their approach is not based upon a single diagnostic instrument.

Clinical teaching is an outgrowth of recognition of the need to match the learning style of the learner with the demands of the task to be learned, an approach advocated many years ago by Werner and Strauss. In order to achieve this match, it is necessary not only to diagnose the child's strengths and weaknesses, but also to analyze the task to be learned. Too frequently in clinical teaching, diagnosis has been thorough, while task analysis has been relatively neglected. Two somewhat different types of task analysis have been described by Johnson and Myklebust (1967) and Engelmann (1969). In Johnson and Myklebust's (1967) approach, the task is analyzed according to manner of presentation and expected mode of response. The analysis involves determination of the perceptual channels required in understanding the task and making the required responses, whether the task is essentially unisensory or cross-modal, the verbal or nonverbal nature of the task, and the levels of perceptual, memory, symbolic, and conceptual skills involved in the task. The task analysis recommended by Engelmann (1969) is an outgrowth of behavioristic psychology and an essential component of behavior modification. This approach demands that educational objectives be operationally stated, that the task be broken down into small sequential components, and that required appropriate responses be specified for each step in the sequential hierarchy. Johnson and Myklebust's (1967) task analysis approach seems to lend itself to process-oriented remediation, while the approach of Engelmann (1969) seems to be more appropriate for tool-oriented remediation.

REFERENCES

Baldwin, R. W., & Kenny, T. J. Medical treatment of behavior disorders. In J. Hellmuth (Ed.), *Learning disorders*. Vol. 2. Seattle: Special Child Publications, 1966.

Bannatyne, A. *Language, reading and learning disabilities*. Springfield, Ill.: Charles C Thomas, 1971.

Barsch, R. H. *A movigenic curriculum*. Madison, Wisc.: Department of Public Instruction, Bureau for the Handicapped, 1965.

Barsch, R. H. *Achieving perceptual-motor efficiency*. Vol. 1. Seattle: Special Child Publications, 1967.

Barsch, R. H. *Enriching perception and cognition*. Vol. 2. Seattle: Special Child Publications, 1968.

Belmont, L., & Birch, H. G. Lateral dominance, lateral awareness and reading disability. *Child Development,* 1965, **34,** 57–71.

Bender, L. A Visual-Motor Gestalt Test and its clinical use. *American Journal of Orthopsychiatry Monograph,* 1938, No. 3.

Bender, L. Specific reading disability as a maturational lag. *Bulletin of the Orton Society,* 1963, **13,** 25–44.

Birch, H. G., & Belmont, L. Auditory-visual integration in normal and retarded readers. *American Journal of Orthopsychiatry,* 1964, **34,** 852–61.

Birch, H. G., & Belmont, L. Auditory-visual integration, intelligence and reading ability in school children. *Perceptual and Motor Skills,* 1965, **20,** 295–305.

Blanchard, P. Psychogenic factors in some cases of reading disability. *American Journal of Orthopsychiatry,* 1935, **5,** 361–74.

Browning, R. M. Hypo-responsiveness as a behavioral correlate of brain-damage in children. *Psychological Reports,* 1967, **20,** 251–59.

Bruner, E. C. Teaching disorders. In B. Bateman (Ed.), *Learning disorders.* Vol. 4. Seattle: Special Child Publications, 1971.

Bush, W. J., & Giles, M. T. *Aids to psycholinguistic teaching.* Columbus, Ohio: Charles E. Merrill, 1969.

Chalfant, J. C., & Scheffelin, M. A. Central processing dysfunctions in children: A review of research. *NINDS Monograph,* 1969, No. 9. Bethesda, Md.: U.S. Department of Health, Education and Welfare.

Clements, S. D. Minimal brain dysfunction in children: Terminology and identification, Phase one of a three-phase project. *NINDB Monograph,* 1966, No. 3. Washington, D.C.: U.S. Department of Health, Education and Welfare.

Clements, S., & Peters, J. Minimal brain dysfunctions in the school-age child. *Archives of General Psychiatry,* 1962, **6,** 185–97.

Cohen, S. A. Dyspedagogia as a cause of reading retardation: Definition and treatment. In B. Bateman (Ed.), *Learning disorders.* Vol. 4. Seattle: Special Child Publications, 1971.

Conners, C. K. What parents need to know about stimulant drugs and special education. *Journal of Learning Disabilities,* 1973, **6,** 349–51.

Connolly, C. Social and emotional factors in learning disabilities. In H. R. Myklebust (Ed.), *Progress in learning disabilities.* Vol. 2. New York: Grune & Stratton, 1971. Pp. 151–78.

Cott, A. Megavitamins: The orthomolecular approach to behavioral disorders and learning disabilities. *Academic Therapy,* 1972, **7,** 245–59.

Cravioto, J., & DeLicardie, E. Environmental and nutritional deprivation in learning disabilities. In W. M. Cruickshank & D. P. Hallahan (Eds.), *Perceptual and learning disabilities in children.* Vol. 2. *Research and theory.* Syracuse: Syracuse University Press, 1975.

Cruickshank, W. M. The psychoeducational match. In W. M. Cruickshank & D. P. Hallahan (Eds.), *Perceptual and learning disabilities in children.* Vol. 1. *Psychoeducational practices.* Syracuse: Syracuse University Press, 1975.

Cruickshank, W. M., Bentzen, F. A., Ratzeburg, F. H., & Tannhauser, M. T. *A teaching method for brain-injured and hyperactive children.* Syracuse: Syracuse University Press, 1961.

de Hirsch, K. Specific dyslexia or strephosymbolia. *Folia Phoniatrica,* 1952, **4,** 231–48.

de Hirsch, K. Psychological correlates of the reading process. *Bulletin of the Orton Society,* 1963, **13,** 59–71.

de Hirsch, K., Jansky, J. J., & Langford, W. S. *Predicting reading failure.* New York: Harper, 1966.

Delacato, C. H. *The treatment and prevention of reading problems: The neurological approach.* Springfield, Ill.: Charles C Thomas, 1959.

Delacato, C. H. *The diagnosis and treatment of speech and reading problems.* Springfield, Ill.: Charles C Thomas, 1963.

Delacato, C. H. *Neurological organization and reading.* Springfield, Ill.: Charles C Thomas, 1966.

Denhoff, E., Hainsworth, P., & Hainsworth, M. Learning disabilities and early childhood education: An information-processing approach. In H. R. Myklebust (Ed.), *Progress in learning disabilities.* Vol. 2. New York: Grune & Stratton, 1971.

Deutsch, C. P., & Schumer, F. *Brain-damaged children: A modality-oriented exploration of performance.* Final Report to Vocational Rehabilitation Administration. U.S. Department of Health, Education and Welfare, 1967.

Doehring, D. G. *Patterns of impairment in specific reading disability.* Bloomington: Indiana University Press, 1968.

Dolphin, J. E., & Cruickshank, W. M. The figure–background relationship in children with cerebral palsy. *Journal of Clinical Psychology,* 1951, **7,** 228–31. (a)

Dolphin, J. E., & Cruickshank, W. M. Pathology of concept formation in children with cerebral palsy. *American Journal of Mental Deficiency,* 1951, **56,** 386–92. (b)

Dolphin, J. E., & Cruickshank, W. M. Visuo-motor perception of children with cerebral palsy. *Quarterly Journal of Child Behavior,* 1951, **3,** 198–209. (c)

Dolphin, J. E., & Cruickshank, W. M. Tactual motor perception of children with cerebral palsy. *Journal of Personality,* 1952, **20,** 466–71.

Doman, G. J., Delacato, C. H., & Doman, R. *The Doman-Delacato Developmental Profile.* Philadelphia: Institutes for the Achievement of Human Potential, 1964.

Drew, C. J., Freston, C. W., & Logan, D. R. Criteria and reference in evaluation. *Focus on Exceptional Children,* 1972, **4,** 1–10.

Eames, T. H. Physical factors in reading. *The Reading Teacher,* 1962, **15,** 427–32.

Edgington, R. Letter on drugs. *Academic Therapy,* 1970, **6,** 47–50.

Eisenson, J. *Aphasia in children.* New York: Harper, 1972.

Engelmann, S. *Preventing failure in the primary grades.* Chicago: Science Research Associates, 1969.

Ferinden, W. E., & Jacobson, S. Early identification of learning disabilities. *Journal of Learning Disabilities,* 1970, **3,** 589–93.

Fernald, G. M. *Remedial techniques in basic school subjects.* New York: McGraw-Hill, 1943.

Freeman, R. Drug effects on learning in children: A selective review of the past thirty years. *Journal of Special Education,* 1966, **1,** 17–64.

Frierson, E. C. Clinical education procedures in the treatment of learning disabilities. In E. C. Frierson & W. B. Barbe (Eds.), *Educating children with learning disabilities: Selected readings.* New York: Appleton-Century-Crofts, 1967.

Frostig, M., & Horne, D. *The Frostig program for the development of visual perception: Teacher's guide.* Chicago: Follett, 1964.

Frostig, M., Lefever, W., & Whittlesey, J. R. B. *Administration and scoring manual for the Marianne Frostig Developmental Test of Visual Perception.* Palo Alto: Consulting Psychologists Press, 1966.

Frostig, M., Maslow, P., Lefever, D. W., & Whittlesey, J. R. B. *The Marianne Frostig Developmental Test of Visual Perception, 1963 standardization.* Palo Alto: Consulting Psychology Press, 1964.

Gates, A. I. The role of personality maladjustment in reading disability. *The Journal of Genetic Psychology,* 1941, **59,** 77–83.

Gearheart, B. R. *Learning disabilities: Educational strategies.* St. Louis: C. V. Mosby, 1973.

Getman, G. N. *How to develop your child's intelligence.* Luverne, Minn.: Author, 1962.

Getman, G. N. The visuomotor complex in the acquisition of learning skills. In J. Hellmuth (Ed.), *Learning disorders.* Vol. 1. Seattle: Special Child Publications, 1965.

Getman, G. N., & Kane, E. R. *The physiology of readiness: An action program for the development of perception for children.* Minneapolis, Minn.: Programs to Accelerate School Success, 1964.

Getman, G. N., Kane, E. R., & McKee, G. W. *Developing learning readiness programs.* Manchester, Mo.: McGraw-Hill, 1968.

Gibson, E. J. *Principles of perceptual learning and development.* New York: Meredith Corp., 1969.

Giffin, M. The role of child psychiatry in learning disabilities. In H. R. Myklebust (Ed.), *Progress in learning disabilities.* Vol. 1. New York: Grune & Stratton, 1968.

Gillingham, A., & Stillman, B. *Remedial training for children with specific disability in reading, spelling, and penmanship.* Cambridge, Mass.: Educators Publishing Service, 1956.

Goldberg, H. K., & Schiffman, G. B. *Dyslexia. Problems of reading disabilities.* New York: Grune & Stratton, 1972.

Goldstein, K. *The organism.* New York: American Book, 1939.

Hallahan, D. P., & Cruickshank, W. M. *Psycho-educational foundations of learning disabilities.* Englewood-Cliffs, N.J.: Prentice-Hall, 1973.

Hallahan, D. P., & Kauffman, J. M. Research relevant to the education of distractible and hyperactive children. In W. M. Cruickshank & D. P. Hallahan (Eds.), *Perceptual and learning disabilities in children.* Vol. 2. *Research and theory.* Syracuse: Syracuse University Press, 1975.

Hallahan, D. P., & Kauffman, J. M. *Introduction to learning disabilities: A psychobehavioral approach.* Englewood Cliffs, N.J.: Prentice-Hall, 1976.

Hammill, D. D., & Bartel, N. R. Background and overview to learning disorders. In D. D. Hammill & N. R. Bartel (Eds.), *Educational perspectives in learning disabilities.* New York: Wiley, 1971.

Hammill, D. D., & Larsen, S. C. The effectiveness of psycholinguistic training. *Exceptional Children,* 1974, **41,** 5–14. (a)

Hammill, D. D., & Larsen, S. C. The relationship of selected auditory perceptual skills and reading ability. *Journal of Learning Disabilities,* 1974, **7,** 429–35. (b)

Haring, N. C., & Phillips, E. L. *Educating emotionally disturbed children.* New York: McGraw-Hill, 1962.

Haring, N. G., & Ridgway, R. W. Early identification of children with learning disabilities. *Exceptional Children,* 1967, **33,** 387–95.

Haring, N. G., & Whelan, R. J. Experimental methods in education and management. In N. J. Long, W. C. Morse, & R. G. Newman (Eds.), *Conflict in the classroom: The education of emotionally disturbed children.* Belmont, Calif.: Wadsworth, 1968.

Hewett, F. M. A hierarchy of educational tasks for children with learning disorders. In E. C. Frierson & W. B. Barbe (Eds.), *Educating children with learning disabilities: Selected readings.* New York: Appleton-Century-Crofts, 1967.

Hewett, F. M. *The emotionally disturbed child in the classroom.* Boston: Allyn & Bacon, 1968.

Hinshelwood, J. *Congenital word blindness.* London: H. K. Lewis & Co., 1917.

Homme, L. E. *How to use contingency contracting in the classroom.* Champaign, Ill.: Research Press, 1969.

Huelsman, C. B. The *WISC* subtest syndrome for disabled readers. *Perceptual and Motor Skills,* 1970, **30,** 535–50.

Irwin, J. V., Moore, J. M., & Rampp, D. L. Nonmedical diagnosis and evaluation. In J. V. Irwin & M. Marge (Eds.), *Principles of childhood language disabilities.* New York: Appleton-Century-Crofts, 1972.

Itard, J. M. *The wild boy of Aveyron.* New York: Appleton-Century-Crofts, 1962.

Jansky, J. J. Early prediction of reading problems. *Bulletin of the Orton Society,* 1973, **23,** 78–89.

Jansky, J., & de Hirsch, K. *Preventing reading failure: Prediction, diagnosis, and intervention.* New York: Harper, 1972.

Johnson, G. O., & Myklebust, H. R. *Learning disabilities: Educational principles and practices.* New York: Grune & Stratton, 1967.

Karnes, M. B. *Helping young children develop language skills: A book of activities.* Arlington, Va.: Council for Exceptional Children, 1968.

Kauffman, J. M. Behavior modification. In W. M. Cruickshank & D. P. Hallahan (Eds.), *Perceptual and learning disabilities in children.* Vol. 2. *Research and theory.* Englewood Cliffs, N.J.: Prentice-Hall, 1975.

Keogh, B. K., & Becker, L. D. Early detection of learning problems: Questions, cautions, and guidelines. *Exceptional Children,* 1973, **40,** 5–11.

Keogh, B. K., & Hall, R. J. Functional analysis of WISC performance of children classified EH and EMR. Technical Report, University of California, Los Angeles, 1973.

Keogh, B. F., & Smith, C. E. Visual-motor ability and school prediction: A seven year study. *Perceptual and Motor Skills,* 1967, **25,** 101–10.

Kephart, N. C. *The slow learner in the classroom.* Columbus, Ohio: Charles E. Merrill, 1960.

Kephart, N. C. *The slow learner in the classroom.* (2nd ed.) Columbus, Ohio: Charles E. Merrill, 1971.

Kephart, N. C., & Strauss, A. A. A clinical factor influencing variations in IQ. *American Journal of Orthopsychiatry,* 1940, **10,** 343–50.

Kerr, J. School hygiene in its mental, moral and physical aspects. *Journal of Statistic Society,* 1897, **60,** 613.

Kirk, S. A. Behavioral diagnosis and remediation of psycholinguistic abilities. In Proceedings of the Conference on Exploration into the Problems of the Perceptually Handicapped Child, First Annual Meeting, Vol. 1, Chicago, April 16, 1963.

Kirk, S. A. *The diagnosis and remediation of psycholinguistic abilities.* Urbana: University of Illinois Press, 1966.

Kirk, S. A., McCarthy, J. J., & Kirk, W. D. *Illinois test of psycholinguistic abilities* (Experimental ed.) Urbana: University of Illinois Press, 1961.

Kirk, S. A., McCarthy, J. J., & Kirk, W. D. *Illinois test of psycholinguistic abilities.* (Rev. ed.) Urbana: University of Illinois Press, 1968.

Kirk, W. D. A tentative screening procedure for selecting bright and slow children in kindergarten. *Exceptional Children,* 1966, **4,** 235–41.

Krasner, L., & Ullmann, L. (Eds.), *Research in behavior modification: New developments and implications.* New York: Holt, Rinehart & Winston, 1965.

Ladd, E. L. Pills for classroom peace? *National Elementary Principal,* 1971, 42–47.

Laufer, M. W. Long-term management and some follow-up findings on the use of drugs with minimal cerebral syndromes. *Journal of Learning Disabilities,* 1971, **4,** 518–22.

Lawson, L. J. Ophthalmological factors in learning disabilities. In H. R. Myklebust (Ed.), *Progress in learning disabilities.* Vol. 1. New York: Grune & Stratton, 1968.

Lerner, J. W. *Children with learning disabilities.* Boston: Houghton Mifflin, 1971.

Lewis, M. Development of attention and perception in the infant and young child. In W. M. Cruickshank & D. P. Hallahan (Eds.), *Perceptual and learning disabilities in children.* Vol. 2. *Research and theory.* Syracuse: Syracuse University Press, 1975.

Lindsley, O. R. Precision teaching in perspective: An interview with Ogden R. Lindsley. *Teaching Exceptional Children,* 1971, **31,** 114–19.

Lovitt, T. C. Free-operant preference for one of two stories: A methodological note. *Journal of Educational Psychology,* 1967, **58,** 84–87. (a)

Lovitt, T. C. Use of conjugate reinforcement to evaluate the relative reinforcing effects of various narrative forms. *Journal of Experimental Child Psychology,* 1967, **5,** 164–71. (b)

Lovitt, T. C. Operant preference of retarded and normal males for rate of narration. *Psychological Record,* 1968, **18,** 205–14. (a)

Lovitt, T. C. Relationship of sequential and simultaneous preference as assessed by conjugate reinforcement. *Behaviour Research and Therapy,* 1968, **6,** 77–81. (b)

Lovitt, T. C. Applied behavior analysis techniques and curriculum research. Report submitted to the National Institute of Education, 1973.

Lovitt, T. C., & Curtiss, K. A. Effects of manipulating an antecedent event on mathematics response rate. *Journal of Applied Behavior Analysis,* 1968, **1,** 329–33.

Lovitt, T. C., & Smith, J. O. Effects of instructions on an individual's verbal behavior. *Exceptional Children,* 1972, **38,** 685–93.

McCarthy, J. J., & McCarthy, J. F. *Learning disabilities.* Boston: Allyn & Bacon, 1969.

McCarthy, J. M. Learning disabilities: Where have we been? Where are we going? In D. D. Hammill & N. R. Bartel (Eds.), *Educational perspectives in learning disabilities.* New York: Wiley, 1971.

McGinnis, M. *Aphasic children: Identification and education by the association method.* Washington, D.C.: Volta Bureau, 1963.

Montessori, M. *The Montessori method.* A. E. George (Trans.) New York: Frederick Stokes, 1912.

Morgan, W. P. A case of congenital word blindness. *British Medical Journal,* 1896, **2,** 1378.

Morse, W. C., Cutler, R. L., & Fink, A. H. *Public school classes for the emotionally handicapped: A research analysis.* Washington, D.C.: Council for Exceptional Children, 1964.

Murphy, J. J. (Ed.) *Quintilian. On the early education of the citizen-orator.* New York: Bobbs-Merrill, 1965.

Myers, P. I., & Hammill, D. D. *Methods for learning disorders.* New York: Wiley, 1969.

Myklebust, H. R. Aphasia in children. In L. Travis (Ed.), *Handbook of speech pathology.* New York: Appleton-Century-Crofts, 1957.

Myklebust, H. R. *The psychology of deafness.* New York: Grune & Stratton, 1960.

Myklebust, H. R. Learning disabilities: Definition and overview. In H. R. Myklebust (Ed.), *Progress in learning disabilities.* Vol. 1. New York: Grune & Stratton, 1968.

Myklebust, H. R., & Boshes, B. Psychoneurological learning disorders in children. *Archives of Pediatrics,* 1960, **77,** 247–56.

Natchez, G. Causation of learning disorders: Editor's introduction. In G. Natchez (Ed.), *Children with reading problems.* New York: Basic Books, 1968.

National Advisory Committee on Handicapped Children. *Special education for handicapped children.* First Annual Report. Washington, D.C.: U.S. Department of Health, Education and Welfare, January 31, 1968.

Orton, S. T. *Reading, writing and speech problems in children.* New York: Norton, 1937.

Osgood, C. E. A behavioristic analysis of perception and language as cognitive phenomena. In J. S. Bruner (Ed.), *Contemporary approaches to cognition.* Cambridge, Mass.: Harvard University Press, 1957. (a)

Osgood, C. E. Motivational dynamics of language. In M. R. Jones (Ed.), *Nebraska symposium on motivation.* Lincoln: University of Nebraska Press, 1957. (b)

Owen, F. W., Adams, P. A., Forrest, T., Stolz, L. M., & Fisher, S. Learning disorders in children: Sibling studies. *Monographs of the Society for Research in Child Development,* 1971, **36,** 1–77.

Paraskevopoulos, J. N., & Kirk, S. A. *The development and psychometric characteristics of the revised Illinois Test of Psycholinguistic Abilities.* Urbana: University of Illinois Press, 1969.

Park, G. E. The etiology of reading disabilities: An historical perspective. *Journal of Learning Disabilities,* 1968, **1,** 318–30.

Rabinovitch, R. D., & Ingram, W. Neuropsychiatric considerations in reading retardation. *Reading Teacher,* 1962, **15,** 433–39.

Rappaport, S. R. Personality factors teachers need for relationship structure. In W. M. Cruickshank (Ed.), *The teacher of brain-injured children.* Syracuse: Syracuse University Press, 1966.

Roach, E. G., & Kephart, N. C. *The Perceptual-Motor Survey.* Columbus, Ohio: Charles E. Merrill, 1966.

Robbins, M., & Glass, G. V. The Doman-Delacato rationale: A critical analysis. In J. Hellmuth (Ed.), *Educational therapy.* Vol. 2. Seattle: Special Child Publications, 1969.

Roberts, H. A clinical and metabolic reevaluation of reading disability. In *Selected papers on learning disabilities, fifth annual convention, Association for Children with Learning Disabilities.* San Rafael, Calif.: Academic Therapy Publications, 1969.

Rubin, E. Z. Cognitive dysfunction and emotional disorders. In H. R. Myklebust (Ed.), *Progress in learning disabilities.* Vol. 2. New York: Grune & Stratton, 1971.

Safer, D., Allen, R., & Barr, E. Depression of growth in hyperactive children on stimulant drugs. *New England Journal of Medicine,* 1972, **24,** 561–63.

Sarason, S. B. *Psychological problems in mental deficiency.* New York: Harper, 1949.

Sequin, E. *Idiocy: And its treatment by the physiological method.* 1864; New York: Columbia University Press, 1907.

Skeffington, A. M. *Papers and lectures.* Duncan, Okla.: Optometric Extension Program, 1926–1965.

Skubic, V., & Anderson, M. The interrelationship of perceptual-motor achievement, academic achievement, and intelligence of fourth-grade children. *Journal of Learning Disabilities,* 1970, **3,** 413–20.

Slingerland, B. H. *A multisensory approach to language arts for specific language disability children. A guide for primary teachers.* Cambridge, Mass.: Educators Publishing Service, 1971.

Smith, D. D., & Lovitt, T. C. The use of modeling techniques to influence the acquisition of computational arithmetic skills in learning disabled children. In E. Ramp & G. Semb (Eds.), *Behavior analysis & education—1973.* Englewood Cliffs, N.J.: Prentice-Hall, 1975.

Smith, D. D., Lovitt, T. C., & Kidder, J. D. Using reinforcement contingencies and teaching aids to alter subtraction performance of children with learning disabilities. In G. Semb (Ed.), *Behavior analysis & education—1972.* Lawrence, Kan.: Kansas University Department of Human Development, 1972.

Smith, D. E. P., & Carrigan, P. *The nature of reading disability.* New York: Harcourt Brace, 1959.

Smith, R. M. *Teacher diagnosis of educational difficulties.* Columbus, Ohio: Charles E. Merrill, 1969.

Snyder, R. T., & Freud, S. L. Reading readiness and its relation to maturational unreadiness as measured by the spiral after-effect and visual-perceptual techniques. *Perceptual and Motor Skills,* 1967, **25,** 841–54.

Solomons, G. Guidelines on the use and medical effects of psychostimulant drugs in therapy. *Journal of Learning Disabilities,* 1971, **4,** 470.

Somervill, J. W., Warnberg, L. S., & Bost, D. E. Effects of cubicles versus increased stimulation on task performance by first-grade males perceived as distractible and nondistractible. *The Journal of Special Education,* 1973, **7,** 169–85.

Spalding, R. B., & Spalding, W. T. *The writing road to reading.* New York: Morrow, 1957.

Spielberger, D. D. *Anxiety and behavior.* New York: Academic Press, 1966.

Stainback, W. C., Payne, J. S., Stainback, S. B., & Payne, R. A. *Establishing a token economy in the classroom.* Columbus, Ohio: Charles E. Merrill, 1973.

Strauss, A. A., & Kephart, N. C. Rate of mental growth in a constant environment among higher grade moron and borderline children. Paper presented at American Association on Mental Deficiency, 1939.

Strauss, A. A., & Kephart, N. C. Behavior differences in mentally retarded children as measured by a new behavior rating scale. *American Journal of Psychiatry,* 1940, **96,** 1117–23.

Strauss, A. A., & Lehtinen, L. E. *Psychopathological education of the brain-injured child.* New York: Grune & Stratton, 1947.

Strauss, A. A., & Werner, H. Disorders of conceptual thinking in the brain-injured child. *Journal of Nervous and Mental Disease,* 1942, **96,** 153–72.

Sylvester, E., & Kunst, M. Psychodynamic aspects of the reading problem. *American Journal of Orthopsychiatry,* 1943, **13,** 69–76.

Tarver, S. G., & Hallahan, D. P. Attention deficits in children with learning disabilities: A review. *Journal of Learning Disabilities,* 1974, **7**, 560–69.

Thomas, A., Chess, S., & Birch, H. G. *Temperament and behavioral disorders in children.* New York: New York University Press, 1968.

Throne, J. M. Learning disabilities: A radical behaviorist point of view. *Journal of Learning Disabilities,* 1973, **6**, 543–46.

Tinker, K. J. The role of laterality in reading disability. In *Reading and inquiry.* Newark, Del.: International Reading Association, 1965.

Ullmann, L. P., & Krasner, L. (Eds.) *Case studies in behavior modification.* New York: Holt, Rinehart & Winston, 1965.

Wallace, G., & Kauffman, J. M. *Teaching children with learning problems.* Columbus, Ohio: Charles E. Merrill, 1973.

Waugh, K. W., & Bush, W. J. *Diagnosing learning disabilities.* 2nd ed. Columbus, Ohio: Charles E. Merrill, 1976.

Wepman, J. Auditory processing disturbances: Current status of research. In D. Rampp (Ed.), Proceedings of the first annual Memphis State University symposium on auditory processing and learning disabilities, 1972.

Werner, H., & Bowers, M. Auditory-motor organization in two clinical types of mentally deficient children. *Journal of Genetic Psychology,* 1941, **59**, 85–89.

Werner, H., & Strauss, A. A. Types of visuo-motor activity in their relation to low and high performance ages. *Proceedings of the American Association on Mental Deficiency,* 1939, **44**, 163–68.

Werner, H., & Strauss, A. A. Pathology of figure-background relation in the child. *Journal of Abnormal and Social Psychology,* 1941, **36**, 236–48.

Witkin, H. A., Dyk, R., Faterson, H. E., Goodenough, D. R., & Karp, S. A. *Psychological differentiation.* New York: Wiley, 1962.

Worell, J., & Nelson, C. M. *Managing instructional problems: A case study workbook.* New York: McGraw-Hill, 1974.

Wunderlich, R. *Kids, brains, & learning.* St. Petersburg, Fla.: Johnny Reads, Inc., 1970.

2
Ray H. Barsch

Ray H. Barsch

Ray Barsch *is founder of the Ray Barsch Center for Learning in Canoga Park, California. Since 1970 he has been a lecturer in the Department of Special and Rehabilitation Education, California State University at Northridge, and in the Division for Continuing Education, the University of Santa Clara. He is also a consultant to eight school systems in the Southern California area. From 1967 to 1970, he was professor of special education and director of the Learning Disabilities Clinic at Southern Connecticut State College. He was director of research and development for the DeWitt Reading Clinic in San Rafael, California, from 1966 to 1967. During the years 1963 to 1966 he was director of teacher preparation programs in the areas of the physically handicapped and neurologically impaired in the Department of Counseling and Behavioral Studies at the University of Wisconsin. From 1950 to 1964 he was director of the Easter Seal Child Development Center and director of professional services for Jewish Vocational Services in Milwaukee, Wisconsin.*

Dr. Barsch was born in Milwaukee, Wisconsin, in 1917. His education included a B.S. degree in special education for the mentally handicapped, received from the University of Wisconsin at Milwaukee in 1950. In 1952, he received a M.Ed. degree in school psychology from the same university. He received his Ph.D. degree in educational psychology from Northwestern University in 1959.

In addition to his other professional activities, Dr. Barsch has served as a lecturer at several other universities and as a consultant and advisor to many institutions and organizations. He is a Fellow of the American Psychological Association and a member of the American Academy of Cerebral Palsy, the American Association on Mental Deficiency, and the Council for Exceptional Children. He served as charter president of the Division for Children with Learning Disabilities of the Council for Exceptional Children. In 1974 he was awarded the International Milestone Award of the International Federation of Learning Disabilities at its World Congress in the Netherlands.

Dr. Barsch has been the director of many research projects and has published widely in professional journals and books. He is an associate editor of Exceptional Children *and the* Journal of Learning Disabilities. *A selected bibliography of works by Dr. Barsch appears on page 93.*

PROLOGUE TO PERSPECTIVE

The invitation to contribute a chapter to this impressive volume gained an immediate, positive response, compelled by the convergence of three factors: First, the opportunity to share these pages with so many respected and prestigious colleagues was perceived as a singular honor. Second, the chance to subject my position, stance, and posture on various issues to contemporary comparisons in this emerging field sparked the embers of my disposition to controversy and divergence. And third, the editors' delightful choice of the term *Perspectives* to characterize the nature of the content warmed the cockles of my space-oriented heart. What a happy, spatializing word ... *perspectives* ... an unsuspecting confirmation in linguistic disguise!

In the first flush of enthusiasm the writing of a personal perspective appeared to be a primer-simple assignment ... a few hours at most ... double-spaced and into the envelope ... but this proved to be an illusion. In short order it became a challenge which turned into a chore and finally into a burden. The limitations of vocabulary constantly defeated the thoughts. Only the compulsion to closure forced a completion.

SEMINAL SOURCES

Any exercise in cognigraphy must begin with a listing of acknowledgements ... those compelling experiences of mind shape perspective ... factors of influence. Omission of biographic antecedents is a deliberate economy in the journey to expression of personal stance.

In the semantic fashion of the moment there are a number of *seminal sources* which must be credited as converging vectors in stimulation and provocation of whatever inspirations, insights, and ideations characterize my present and emerging professional mind. Three main vectors must be noted.

The retrospective process of "auditing my cognitive books" to prepare this manuscript brought to mind Chapter V in the Book of Genesis which follows the course of "Adam begat Seth and Seth begat . . ." covering a span of many generations. In the same style it would be possible to list a series of "begattings" dating back to Itard, Seguin, Rousseau, Plato, Montessori, etc., extending to a lengthy assortment of revered names in educational and psychological thought up to the leading contemporary minds which captivate my attention.

I Have Had Many Teachers

Some were gifted professors who not only provided foundations but offered expansions, unique insights, and stimulations to inquiry. Some have been giant minds encountered at conferences and personal meetings. I have been privileged to enjoy dialogues with many of the cutting-edge contemporary leaders, sharpening my own thoughts in the process. Others were silent teachers, conveying fascinating perspectives on pages of print, influencing and modifying my mind, unaware of their impact.

While the collective body of knowledge contained in the rich minds of those teachers, live and immediate, as well as those who write books and articles, has always been awesome in expanse, I have been most appreciative for their inspirations to independent thought. I was, fortunately, guided to "read between the lines," critically evaluate, extrapolate, extend upon promising threads, and most of all . . . to retain independent perspective. The profundity of such liberation is a cherished cognitive possession.

Without seeking to diminish the significance of the literature and the hundreds of personal dialogues with thoughtful contemporaries, major credit for shaping my present mind must be given to a vast army of unacknowledged educators—thousands of children who have patiently granted me the privilege of learning from them.

Blissfully unaware of profound criteria, charming in their ignorance of normative standards, and desperate in their search for comfort and integrity—one by one, in lengthy procession, they have persistently challenged the platitudes and clichés which were always so conveniently at hand. In countless ways, subtly and unconsciously, they have insisted upon understanding rather than classification. In their innocence they have posed behavioral and functional questions which could not, confidently, be answered by prevailing diagnostic and therapeutic assumptions. As each child, in turn, displayed his idiosyncratic composite of efficiencies and inefficiencies, my book learning was constantly put to the test, my sensitivity challenged, and my collegiate confidence shaken—but I learned . . . slowly and gradually . . . as my guides provided the lessons.

Textbook model behaviors, neat clusters of developmental inadequacies which confirm the postulates of normative psychology, and categorical qualifications which facilitate classification lull the clinical mind into a production- or assembly-line mode of thinking. Enigmatic children, however, have a way of perturbing evaluative confidence. In their engaging naïveté, they beg for special understanding and defy the practices of convenience.

Gradually I came to realize that no child was a routine or standard case—all were enigmatic in some way. So long as I separated the child-world into routine and enigmatic cases, I learned only from the enigmatic; but when I began to regard every child as enigmatic, I learned something new and fascinating from each one.

EMERGING SELF

Like many other conscientious clinicians, I have experienced a number of disenchantments during the past three decades of professional life —those sad and painful moments of insight and conscience which rise up to perturb the clinical soul—when previously comforting platitudes become shallow verbalizations, when traditionalized terminology becomes an obfuscating game of semantics, when carefully rehearsed procedures of analysis fail to analyze, and when faithfully memorized characteristics and constellations of categories become nothing more than rote recitations with little or no substance. Disenchantment is always prelude to growth.

My disenchantments have been too numerous to detail, but a few deserve comment here to support my present convictions and to identify some of the contributing vectors which prompted the composition of Movigenics. Purist minds will take offense, but rebel minds will be kindred to my accounts. The chronology of disenchantment is blurred, but the outcome is clear.

Normative Psychology

In the cloister of my collegiate years I was thoroughly saturated with the doctrines of normative psychology and properly awed by the impressive documentations of the developmentalists. Several years of clinical confrontation passed before the first heretical thoughts entered my mind.

Enigmatic children, unrehearsed in the Tables of Development, persistently defied the canons which I had learned to recite but did not understand. In my college years I had paid little attention to the fact that no developmental finding had ever reached a 100 percent density. Findings of 66 to 80 percent were judged to be sufficient for declaration of norm. More and more I was impressed by the fact that I was seeing so many who probably fell into the small percentage of "does not apply."

In college there seemed to be an amazing abundance of normative schedules; but after several years of real-life contact, the supply seemed to be pitifully scant. The cause was, apparently, abandoned long before a comprehensive listing had been achieved, and the professional world was left with a noble but incomplete concept.

It was disillusioning to discover that so little of human behavior had been subjected to the normative process, leaving so vast an expanse open to local interpretation. Every conscientious clinician, sooner or later, faces the fact that the main part of the journey to human understanding must be traveled in lonesome cognition—or become a hodgepodge of fragments and platitudes.

Normative psychology, so proudly membered for the past forty years, is on the wane—nourished only by the regimented mind of Education, insisting upon the myths of homogeneity and maturation, lulled by the platform melodies of the "average child" and the administrative convenience of the model. I, for one, do not mourn its passing. I welcome wholeheartedly the advent of dynamic individuality—the complex composite, the incomparable self—idiosyncratically resistant to defeating comparisons.

Scientist Identity

At one time I entertained aspirations to become an educational scientist. Seduced by tantalizing promises of scientific fulfillment and the prospect of entry into the sanctuary of the elite, I carried on a brief fling with the .01 level of confidence, faithfully rehearsing the proper ritualistic incantations to the gods of significance. On several occasions I was embarrassed by the .06 level and politely informed by colleagues of the distinctive difference between science and horseshoes. On other occasions I found it difficult to breathe comfortably in the rarified atmosphere of the computer terminal—something about a digital allergy.

By clinical persuasion I became a conscientious objector in the conflict between paradigms and computers. Freed from the compulsion to affiliation, I have continuously enjoyed the liberties of imagination and the unbridled quest for satisfaction of my curiosity while ignoring any urgency to R.S.V.P. to the scientific committee in charge of affairs.

Personal enchantment with the games and rituals of science did not lead to a rejection of the concept of quantified confirmation. Some of my best friends are scientists. Only my passionate fervor for identity has cooled. Being of divergent mind, as a matter of acquired disposition, I have always found intervening variables far more fascinating than control factors. Human variability became a more exciting focus than human similarity. Humanity somehow loses vitality in a computer print-out. I remain content with empiricist status, fully cognizant of such low order classification in the phylum of science.

Psychometry

I joined the ranks of the psychometrically disenchanted some twenty years ago, before it was fashionable to express doubts. The glow faded in gradual stages. For several years after graduation I was faithful to the percentile, quotient, and the raw score. Collegiate indoctrination had filled me with the proper awe of standardization and imbued my psychometric soul with the majestic sense of power which accompanied the administration of tests and the subsequent canonic interpretations. With the customary respect and virtue of the metric novice, I applied myself to the prescribed rituals. Gradually, however, a deep urgency for independent thought nagged at my psychometric being, and religious doubts began to enter my mind. I confess to a period of psychometric agnosticism in which I experimented with highly personalized variations of all existing tests, deliberately violating the Persian laws of standardization and scoring. Happily my heretical urges led me to the discovery of child dynamics.

The dynamics of human variability became my focus in assessment rather than the attainment of some categorical rubric. Each child was, and still is, granted an inalienable right to distinctive self—to project his unique personal organization in utter defiance of preconceived trait constellations, categorical criteria, and normative standards. Once freed from the provincial bonds I began to see children in context, adapting and reacting to environmental stresses of siblings, economics, teaching styles, and parental life models, regardless of their designated diagnosis. Test boxes became vehicles for eliciting behavior in complex displays of efficiencies and inefficiencies instead of mystically endowed shrines, compelling worship. Solo flights of induction and deduction became far more exciting than routine listings of percentiles and quotients.

Descriptive analysis of the complex functioning of a single child in context, drawn from many different subtests, insightful observations, and a clinical appraisal of environmental influences replaced the urgency for peer comparisons. The understanding of human dynamics is not equivalent to the computation of a raw score.

The Interdisciplinary Diagnostic Team

The sacred concept of interdisciplinary diagnostic teams, functioning in holy and respectful alliance, in schools, clinics, and agencies across the land, must be classified as one of the major nobilities of the twentieth century education mind. The prospect of expert practitioners engaged in the exercise of collective wisdom for the benefit of a single individual is exciting!

The possibility that massive provincial walls, which had been erected so carefully to insure disciplinary privacy and guarantee territorial rights on the human domain, might be reduced to casual guideposts here and there, without fear of trespass, is, indeed, a joy to contemplate. Unfortunately, noble purposes must find their way to implementation—and the seeds of disenchantment again begin to sprout.

Boundaries of province have been so deeply etched in the disciplinary mind that comparatively few practitioners have been able to implement plans with unqualified respect, a mutualized sense of responsibility, and a dynamic spirit of interactional equality. Certainly there are examples of idealized implementations, standing as testimonials to the worth of the concept; but most efforts have been thwarted by dynamic interplays which were quite remote from nobility of mind.

Interdisciplinary identity is not guaranteed by invitation to membership. Many so-called "teams" are little more than show-and-tell experiences with each member adhering to provincial protocol, guarding against infringements—token representations of the concept in practice but not in full nobility of mind.

"Interdisciplinariness," instead, is a professional state of mind, open to adoption by practitioners in any field, regardless of degree, impressiveness of vitae, station of prestige, or invitation to become a member of a team. Possession of a library card and an inquiring mind constitute the sesame to interdisciplinary identity. The full array of provincial objectives, principles and practices, issues and controversies in any discipline are accessible on library shelves to inquisitive readers. Beyond the literature, I have found that most practitioners are more than happy to "teach" an interested novice about the glories and the heartaches of their respective discipline.

True, interdisciplinariness requires constant and diligent effort and a firm commitment to acquisition, but the effort can be highly rewarding. The respective insights which have emerged, driven by provincial fervor and compartmentalized thought, constitute a remarkably worthy composite, deserving of integration into a dynamic wholeness. No single discipline can claim a territorial imperative in human affairs. Collective wisdom is the sole hope of any individual beset with problems.

The abiding conviction that the essence of the interdisciplinary concept resides in the individual mind has led me to search in and among many professions for insights that could add bits of understanding to the complexity of human dynamics. The effort has been a source of constant cognitive joy to me, but also a source of repeated embarrassment among colleagues who classified my endeavors as fraternization with the enemy. The true interdisciplinarian must be sufficiently committed to the cause to adopt a multiple identity while seeking to crystallize a larger self. Interdisciplinariness is an invitation to mind. Only when this is fully realized will the concept achieve the nobility it deserves.

MOVIGENICS

The term *Movigenics* dates back about fifteen years. It emerged from a growing conviction in clinical practice that the origin and development of movement patterns across a wide expanse of human behavior promised a mother lode in the understanding of learning. It was, and is, an attempt to give identity to a particular cognitive composite.

At the moment of conception it seemed a thrilling experience to name a cognitive offspring with a fanciful title, but there have been many occasions when I have doubted the wisdom of such baptism. Like the classic Percival, Movigenics became a "fighting" name to be defended on all sides from taunting colleagues. Through the years it has been ridiculed and praised, rejected and embraced, approached and avoided, mispronounced and misspelled—and all too seldom understood.

The invitation to present a personal perspective is a welcomed opportunity to clarify some of the misinterpretations and misconceptions regarding the nature and purpose of Movigenics which seem to be floating around the troubled seas of Education. It is equally an occasion to expand and extend upon the principles and constructs which I have previously presented (Barsch, 1967a, 1969) in the hope that the full potential of the orientation might be considered.

In its initial and constantly evolving state, the composite has been personally regarded as an orientation—a cognitive map to guide practitioners toward a goal of practical synthesis amid a diverse assortment of theories, differing and seemingly conflicting methodologies, and variant experimental data abounding on the contemporary psychological, social, and educational scenes. Movigenics is not a theory, in the customary sense of the term, since it does not contain a distinctive set of hypotheses which lend themselves to neat experimental paradigms on their way to cherished levels of significance.

It is, likewise, not a method, complete with prescribed and defined sequences of instruction, a kit of materials, and a convenient supply of duplicating masters or workbooks. The orientation has, however, given impetus to the formulation and structuring of several patterns of instruction which can be classified unto themselves as methods. These are not the substance of the composite but are, rather, offshoots or spin-offs. For example, I have recently presented a *visualization impress method* for attaining proficiency in spelling (Barsch, 1974a), a *pacing method* for attaining temporal consciousness among learners through the use of metronomically temporized activities (Barsch, 1974b) and a *visualization method* to improve listening efficiency (Barsch, 1975).

These methods, and others yet to come, do involve prescribed sequences of instruction and were designed in conformity to a specific hypothesis which emerged from the Movigenic orientation. As such, they are open to critical comparison with any other existing, direct approach to instruction, and they are subject to statistical confirmation or denial. Being an avowed empiricist, concerned with direct-action forms of demonstration and study in the dynamic interactional context of the classroom, I do not feel any heavy compulsion to proof. I will, happily, transfer the hallowed historical models of control-experimental, test-retest forms of research which constitute a personal Grail for so many to those who are so disposed.

If these practical extensions along the spatial perspective serve only to introduce a novel contrast to the monotony of traditionalized procedures, to generate excitement for learning among students, to provide teachers with an escape clause from the drudgery of writing objectives and defining outcomes, and generally to add a little spice to routine curricular menus, they will have accomplished their main intent. Happy learners, instructed by happy teachers in a context of personal excitement for mutual advancement, is a preferred objective to the elusive .01 probability level.

There is yet another purpose for delineating an assortment of emerging methods. Firing line personnel, enthused by the provocative nature of the Movigenic orientation, often find it difficult to implement the principles and constructs in any other way than through the conduct of a daily motor activity. These methods will, hopefully, serve to demonstrate the range of application inherent in the spatial perspective and exemplify in daily practice the expanded intent of the composite.

The whole of Movigenics is unresearchable. Orientations are only models of thought fashioned along a particular perspective. They are neither right nor wrong—only more or less useful.

From its point of origin to its point of termination in some remote future, Movigenics has been, and will continue to be, a massive exercise in eclecticism—a continuing journey to synthesis. Like most conscientious clinicians and teachers I became weary of hopping from one theoretical formulation to another, from one authoritatively advocated method to another, and from one renowned opinion to another, in accord with whatever fragment of human behavior became my focus of the moment. A single child's emotional conflicts sent me scurrying to the manifold interpretations available in the psychological literature. The same child's language difficulties invited an extended expedition into the literature on language development and all possible expressions of disorder. His perceptual problems, once I could divorce myself from exclusive focus on his drawing of geometric forms, led me to a massive body of literature on perception with all of its variant viewpoints. The child's reading difficulties suggested another search, his computing dilemma another, his social impasse another. ... and on and on. ... collecting bits of wisdom and fragments of insight but never unity or synthesis.

I extended my cherished disposition to "read between the lines" to reading "between the books" and "between the theories" in a compelling quest for common threads, for clarification of precise points of contact and divergence, in a continuous effort to disentangle the vines of semantic idiosyncrasy. Eclecticism, properly advanced to its logical end, must inevitably yield an independent product—a unique synthesis ... embodying a multitude of valued thoughts of others in union with convictions growing out of personal experiences and a liberal sprinkling of imagination ... and some daring. Heated by the fires of personal cognitive style, the fusion occurred and formed a new Gestalt.

Movigenics became such a Gestalt, an attempt to establish order and organization in the face of diversity, variance, contrast, and fragmentation. From the beginning, there has been no effort to deny or reject traditional or contemporary points of view, plausible data, and compelling statements of conviction. Human perception being what it is, variance in focus, emphasis, and priority must be expected. The canons of scientific respectability demand isolations and fragmentations. Intervening variables must be eliminated and pure forms must be studied. Unfortunately, human behavior remains a domain of hopelessly entangled variables which defy isolation. The plethora of opinions and data require a commitment to synthesis, if any order is to be achieved.

In the practice of Movigenics the teacher and therapist simply exercise a right of translation, converting the plethora into a singular perspective. Contemporary and historical thoughts are not rejected, but only translated and reinterpreted in spatial terms. The privilege of idiom is respected; but in the interest of achieving a single mind, a space overlay is made. The emotional organization of an individual is converted into a spatial model of psychological distance, approach-avoidance tendencies, attacks and retreats, etc. The social organization of the individual is viewed in spatial terms of mobility strivings, congestions, isolations, and cultural attitudes. In the academic world, reading, mathematics, writing, and spelling are converted into spatializing experiences. Recreational and sports experiences are studied as spatial events. One model of reference is employed throughout the effort to understand the dynamics of a given individual in the hope of achieving an integrated understanding of the whole instead of disparate fragments.

The ten constructs which serve as the foundation stones of the Movigenics orientation are substantially confirmed by a massive body of literature and thought. Supportive thought as well as data may have been presented in differing dialect; but with a slight amount of reinterpretation, the reinforcement is assured.

There can be no argument that the human organism is designed for mobility, that he or she moves in space, that he or she must process information to achieve independent survival, and that the ability to perceive is crucial to the survival. Similarly, there can be no argument regarding the developmental forward thrust to maturity. In recent years the dynamics of stress in human affairs have been abundantly studied, and the feedback model is no longer in doubt. There is also consensus on the belief in the orderliness of development. The fact that man is a communicating being is another certainty.

None of these constructs or facts is subject to exclusion in the study of human dynamics. Opinions may differ in regard to assigning relative values to each construct. Some voices may insist upon adding to the listing; others may argue against the manner in which these constructs have been translated into considerations for educational practice; but there can be no denial of import.

The fifteen components of Movements Efficiency are, likewise, open to debate regarding interpretation, but cannot be dismissed from consideration if human dynamics are to be understood. Muscular strength and dynamic balance are so vital to human performance that current status must always be questioned. The import of body awareness is no longer debatable. Since space and time are universal dimensions for mobile Man, every person's prevailing state of sophistication in these dimensions must be assessed. The six channels of perceptual function—gustatory, olfactory, tactual, kinesthetic, auditory, and visual—and their respective states of utility in processing multivariant information cannot be disregarded. During the past decade the evidence of Man's bilateral nature has mounted. Denial of rhythm as an essential component in human behavior would be foolhardy. Few would attempt to argue against the need for flexibility in performance if the adaptable character of man is to be studied. Finally, man's capability to plan, revise, remodel, project, invent, and organize must always be taken into account.

The interrelatedness and the interdependence of these fifteen components within each individual becomes an expression of the distinctive self at variance with others. The study of the unique interactional composite constitutes the objective of assessment in the spatial perspective.

Since the conventions of psychometry have been structured in accord with a principle of fragmentation, there is no convenient battery of tests. Instead the clinician and the teacher must rely upon extensive observations, formulations of clustered generalizations, and a conviction of interrelatedness.

It is the Movigenic premise that all fifteen components interact in each individual at varying states of integrity and utility. No component can be studied in isolation. No component can be classified as a highly developed function and dismissed from further attention while concentration is accorded to the weak function. It is the togetherness of the whole which is important. No child can truly be considered totally free of coordination problems as long as he is experiencing academic difficulty. The conventional model of fragmentation has led many educators to dismiss motoric factors from consideration just because a child demonstrates some expertise in sports. But membership on a local Little League team does not constitute motoric absolution, as any astute observer will attest. In twenty years of diligent observation we have yet to encounter a child whom we were prepared to designate as well-coordinated who was not also extremely capable on the academic terrain. The criteria of coordination which we employ is considerably different from the narrow models which prevail.

The constructs, components, zones, fields, and domains of the Movigenic orientation are not exclusive to the analysis of children with learning failure. They have been employed effectively by teachers of the deaf, blind, orthopedically handicapped, emotionally disturbed, and by hundreds of mainstream teachers. They have also been fruitfully used in a fascinating diversity of contexts. Salesmen for large industrial concerns have found them useful in customer analysis. Several organizations have utilized the models in analyzing committee composition and the evaluation of internal efficiencies and inefficiencies. Counselors and psychotherapists have found them enriching. Track and football coaches have applied the principles in their domains. Dance instructors have reported good results. Three high school band directors have accelerated the learning of half-time marching patterns by applying a Movigenic approach. Ministers, dentists, public-speaking groups, traffic managers, and many others have applied the guidelines to their respective contexts.

These examples are cited to support our contention of expanse. Space and time are crucial variables in *all* facets of the human process.

LEARNING DISABILITIES

In a relatively brief time the concept of Learning Disabilities catapulted from pencil sketches on the cognitive drawing board to the production line of the educational market place to satisfy consumer urgency. Almost immediately it was identified as a category, recently discovered, a previously neglected population deserving of distinctive identity and national concern. It became a small box in the standard Tables of Organization in Special Education, respectfully arrowed and lined to establish its proper position in the corporate structure. A definition was hastily given form, in proper syntax to avoid infringement upon any and all other existing and funded categories (in compromise with the many dissenting voices in those early days) and sufficiently cryptic in trait descriptions to be impressive. An incidence was estimated—sufficiently high to warrant concern but respectfully limited to avoid alarm. Bearing all of the characteristics of category, definition, incidence, and need, Learning Disabilities entered the lobby to solicit legislation and emerged victorious.

The legislative virus became contagious, and state after state came down with an attack of law for children with learning disabilities. The category soon became a budget line item and the search for beneficiaries began.

Among life's many mysteries must be listed the long-standing dichotomy between the zealous efforts of educational reformers to pin down a category, set criteria, pass a law, attain funding, etc., and the magnificent apathy of the local school districts in responding to the urgency of the promoters. Even the most casual survey of learning disability programs across the country will reveal geographic pockets in which learning problems seem to have reached epidemic proportions while neighboring communities have been spared or have built up the necessary antibodies to stand immune. In reality, the incidence of learning disabilities rises or declines in accord with the *implementation conscience* of local leaders and administrators.

Despite encouraging laws, national awareness, Sunday supplement spreads, and embarrassing annual percentiles on achievement tests, the vitality of the movement rests upon the acknowledgment and commitment of local leaders, availability of space, readiness of a teacher to "accept the challenge," and probably, in final analysis, the willingness of an individual principal to "have these children on the premises."

The concept of Learning Disabilities as an educational movement, holding implications for learners of all ages and in all types of learning situations, has not received widespread acceptance. The industrial or commercial worker whose learning disability interferes with his daily efficiency is not yet classified as a matter of instructional concern. Failing college students are routinely considered to be counseling problems and only rarely to be learning problems. Even the most devout enthusiasts at the secondary level must admit that commitment and implementation are far from adequate. The child with cumulative learning failure who manages some measure of success in early grades and gradually becomes less effective as the complexities of the upper grades extend him beyond his capabilities remains neglected.

For all practical purposes, it is safe to conclude that the majority mind of Education has successfully compartmentalized the category within the six to ten year range, showing only a mild tolerance for the intermediate group and a distinct feeling of imposition and negativism for the secondary student. The implementation conscience has been only mildly aroused.

From the earliest days of the movement, I have held a minority position on the domain of Learning Disabilities, arguing against the notion of a category. It is more important to think of the field as a new *concept*—a modern state of awareness of learning failure. Concepts have no incidence figures, set no fixed criteria of qualification, and invite interpretive flexibility. Categories invariably solidify thinking, tend to become methods of exlusion rather than inclusion, and invite further proliferations.

As a concept, Learning Disabilities constitutes an orientation to learning, focuses squarely upon the dynamics of learning, and diminishes the urgency to conduct a depressing search for pathologies and esoteric etiologies. As a category, Learning Disabilities has generated a frantic but seldom fruitful effort to delineate a uniform and specific set of characteristics, focused upon syndromes and antecedents and established a narrow listing of symptoms. The passion for classification has added little to our understanding of learning failure.

I welcomed the designation of the domain of Learning Disabilities as a singular opportunity to concentrate educator attention upon the dynamics of human learning instead of the medical-social diffusions of the past. For the first time in history, it appeared that educators were about to declare a provincial imperative on matters of remedial instruction instead of waiting in the lobby for the x-rays to dry. Regretfully, traditions are too strong and comfortable. The category is cemented, diagnostic seances flourish, and labels are pasted.

Regard for Learning Disabilities as a concept invites a very broad view. My personal definition has been one of describing an individual as being learning disabled whenever he or she is *unable to consistently profit from the curriculum to which he has been assigned.* It must be assumed that his original assignment was prompted by some factor of qualification, in accord with certain criteria and in the belief that the placement would be to his advantage. When he does not learn in the expected manner, regardless of age or type of placement, he becomes disabled in the educational milieu. He can continue to be defeated by inappropriate instruction, suffering in contained submission, becoming progressively more feeble; or he can quit the scene in a hundred different forms of escape. The mandate for a change in instructional approach is signalled by the learner in countless ways. His problem dictates curriculum modification. He may be subjected to a variety of diagnostic studies and described in impressive syntax, but in the end he will be benefited only by change in instructional formulae. His problem is educational and instructional in character, and his solution resides in instructional imagination.

It does not matter whether he or she is six, sixteen, twenty-six, or fifty-six. It does not matter whether the curriculum to which he has been assigned is an elementary classroom, a special class, an internship, an apprenticeship, a business course, a doctoral program, or a credential program—each involves an assumptive course of instruction, demands a particular standard of performance, and leads to a desired objective. It does not matter whether the child is aphasic, minimally brain damaged, emotionally disturbed, deaf, blind, or retarded—if he does not learn in the manner expected, logic dictates a different pattern of instruction.

The focus upon learning, inherent in the designation, makes curriculum modification the heart of recovery. After the parade of diagnosticians has passed and the profound reports have been written, *one lone teacher, trained or untrained, sensitive or insensitive, will face the responsibility of finding a way to instruct the learner so as to benefit rather than detract from his development.* If his educational recovery is dependent upon the exercise of instructional imagination, his future is doomed unless a concentrated national effort is made to develop the teaching competencies which the problem deserves. The massive diagnostic effort has done little to improve the quality of instruction. Lonely and bewildered teachers find little comfort in diagnostic platitudes.

Learning Disabilities, to me, stands as a third major division of a national educational structure. On the one side is the giant landscape of mainstream schooling; on the other side, the historic mission field of Special Education with all of its well-established categories. Between these two massive domains stands a huge Ellis Island called Learning Disabilities, prepared to receive the work-book oppressed, the phonic poor, and the progress-hungry refugees from either side. Both domains have fixed cultures (curricula) representing the collective wisdom of renowned educative minds for several centuries. Practitioners in both domains believe that the curricula are fitting, relevant, and historically secure.

Every specialized curriculum in Special Education is offered with a certain confidence, reinforced by experience, to the category designated for enrollment. A standard program exists. Every teacher in Special Education, however, is aware that one or more children in the class are atypical. These cases are equally deserving of Learning Disability consideration and reformulation of curriculum.

Learning Disabilities is an open domain. It is not exclusive to certain selected populations. It is a constant possibility for perceiving beings who are moving to advance and achieve and to symbolize their experiences. Perception, language, and movement, the three major elements in human learning, must also be placed in perspective if instructional imagination is to be stimulated.

PERCEPTION

For more than two centuries educational programs were carried on with only a passing and casual interest in the character and quality of perceptual functioning among children. The exhortations of historically renowned figures like Rousseau, Comenius, and Montessori were unheeded after their brief moments of prominence; the underlying premise of perceptual function became lost in a clutter of other points of focus.

Educators conceded to the documentations of developmentalists, accepting a perceptual stage as a necessary milestone in the preschool period, but choosing to call the phenomena by many other names once the child entered school. The formal declaration of Perception as a domain of study of experimental psychologists at the turn of the century was regarded by educators as interesting but not relevant to learning.

Direct consciousness of the import of the perceptual process in learning did not occur until the issue of "perceptual disturbance" came into the lexicon of education about thirty years ago. Prior to the brilliant delineations of Strauss and Werner, disorders in perceptual function were automatically associated with mental retardation, to be noted in a long listing of inferiority traits. When the work of these two pioneers awakened the conscience of Education, "perceptual disturbance" finally became a relevant term.

Perceptual disturbance soon became the "in" word among psychometrists, who were delighted with the implications of the new term and fascinated by the ease with which the disorder could be identified. A surprising incidence was found. Where once there were few, there were suddenly many. A few distortions on a drawing task became sufficient grounds to declare an entire domain of human function to be defective. The terms *perceptual handicap* or *perceptual disturbance* have become conventionalized labels to indicate a serious disorder in functioning. In many instances, the term was pronounced in ominous voice to parents and less-sophisticated professional personnel as an intellectual sentence upon the child, condemning him to a very bleak future. Instead of remaining a simple description of a particular difficulty in perceiving, the terms soon took on the character of a dismal handicap linked to some nefarious dysfunction in the central and mysterious nervous system.

The main body of Education has been content to identify the existence of the disorder, confidently associate its presence with the cryptic but popular state of "minimal brain dysfunction," and assign responsibility for study and resolution to the missionary workers in the field of Special Education; while mainstream practitioners, comforted by the compartmentalization, continue about their regular business, unperturbed. The possibility that perceptual disturbance might be found among the nonorganically handicapped child, emotionally disturbed, blind, deaf, culturally disadvantaged, and, yes, even among the mainstream non-handicapped population may require another fifty to sixty years of pricking the conscience of Education. Perception can be disturbed in many different ways. Once again the assumption that diagnosing is equivalent to understanding has led to many unwise declarations.

Without in any way diminishing the remarkable contributions of Strauss and others who followed, I must record that the present state of comprehension of perceptual functioning in children leaves much to be desired. While the delineations of Piaget have been astounding and the documentations of the developmentalists have been impressive, no substantial theory of perceptual functioning in children is available. Experimental studies of various aspects of perceptual development have been diffuse, scattered, and idiosyncratic. An extensive body of literature on perceptual disturbance has faithfully reported its incidence and its presumed etiology, but knowledgeable explanations of its character and nature remain in short supply.

Graphic display of perceptual distortion has been comparatively easy to elicit; but the understanding of the ways in which the graphic distortion interferes with the child's perception of doorways, traffic signals, eating and dressing patterns, play, and the thousands of prosaic perceiving experiences during the course of his typical day is virtually unknown.

While we can easily find evidence to declare a child to be perceptually disturbed, we have not been able to track the mainifestations of such disturbance throughout his routine encounters with his world. Until we are able to delineate the pervasive nature of a perceptual disturbance in *all* casual and formal events, it is difficult to assume that we understand the nature of the phenomenon we are diagnosing.

The simple notion that a child's perceptual deficit has been present long before he gained privileged entry to a psychometric cubicle and will remain with him long after he finishes his drawing effort (until remedied) seems to have eluded the educator's mind. A child's perceptual difficulty is a personal possession, belonging to him, interfering, impeding, and distorting his diverse relationships to his world in hundreds of different ways, minute after minute, day after day. When we triumphantly declare that a child has a *figure-ground* problem because he has failed to properly differentiate the embedded figures in a drawing, we must recognize that the same dilemma follows him wherever he goes. If he cannot attain adequate closure in a geometric form, he cannot attain closure in dozens of other casual events in his life. His perceptual problem is personal and constant. The fortuitous circumstance of psychometry is only a prelude to understanding.

If the prevailing psychometric devices are to be any more than mystical divining rods, they must be interpretively extended to predict and describe the twenty-four-hour nature of a perceptual dilemma—not only its character on the paper. Until we can accomplish this act of interrelatedness and synthesis, our understanding of perceptual disturbance, difficulty, dilemma, problem, or whatever negative descriptor we wish to employ must be classified as very limited.

The current interpretive set on the nature of perceptual function among educators is exceedingly narrow. Evaluative procedures as well as instructional practices are concentrated on the visual mode. While few would argue that this is the only mode utilized by the individual in perceiving his world, comprehension of the nature of the other modes is comparatively sparse. Some authoritative writers have called attention to the auditory mode, but the scarcity of tests, instructional methodologies, and concentrated concern in school programming is a constant reflection of uncertainty. Despite the recognition that tactual, kinesthetic, olfactory, and gustatory perception are vital components in the processing of information, they have received very little attention from perceptual researchers, test constructors, and therapeutic advocates. Each of these modes has some relevance for the totality of the perceptual process, but we know very little about any of them. Only when the primitive character of the child demands attention to these base modes is any consideration given. In practice, among average children designated as having perceptual difficulties, only two modes receive attention: the visual and the auditory. The other four modes are relegated to secondary consideration or totally disregarded in the instructional process. This neglect has made for a huge void in our understanding of the perceptual process.

The failure of investigators to study these modes in the human interaction with the world, of test constructors to bring these to a level of psychometric convenience, and of remedial authorities to devise instructional sequences does not mean that these modes have been eliminated from the human process. Paucity of knowledge is not absolution from concern.

More than thirty theories of perception have been expressed in print; each offered with supporting data and extensive interpretations. None of these attempt to delineate the multimodal nature of the human perceiver.

It is a sad reflection upon the prevailing state of perceptual consciousness among educators that even the existence of this diverse literature on perception remains unidentified and unknown to the majority of teachers who have the responsibility for ameliorating children's perceptual difficulties. Consequently the multimodal neglect among perceptual theorists is equally unknown. Only a small percentage of teachers are aware that the bulk of educational practices, materials, and workbooks currently in use stem from the model of perception developed by Gestalt psychologists. Few teachers can identify the main points of any perceptual theory.

For a number of years I took delight in posing the question, "Which theory or theories of perception form the rationale for your program of perceptual instruction?" to hundreds of teachers responsible for perceptual training programs in the schools. The question proved to be so embarrassing that I discontinued the practice. Only a few had any familiarity with one theory of perception, none with the available body of literature of the topic. The customary reply was to take refuge in a statement of personal philosophy or a casual quote from a current authority. The massive contributions of the many psychologists who have sought to comprehend the nature of perception have never reached most educators' minds.

Regretfully, the era of Perception has long since passed in the field of psychology. The attention of investigators has been attracted elsewhere. It would appear that psychology concluded that the main veins of understanding had been exhausted and that there was little to gain from further study. The topic is rarely considered these days.

This has resulted in a strange state of affairs. The definition of perceptual difficulties continues in the schools. Programs of remediation continue to be organized and desperate teachers continue their quest for comprehension of the problems with which they contend. Educational authorities have not bothered to study and take advantage of what is known about perception, psychologists have turned to other interests, and thousands of children suffer from what amounts to a cultural deprivation . . . neglect of existing knowledge.

Despite the assumption of closure and the accusation of neglect, the obligation to expand teacher's consciousness of the nature of perception remains a necessity for the conscientious instructor and for the development of effective programs. Perception is integral to all learning and cannot be easily dismissed from educational conscience. Where voids exist, empirical generalizations must fill the space. Where variance is evident, synthesized thought must restore equilibrium. Where gaps exist between studies, imaginative interpretations must build the bridge. When opinions are in conflict, clinical confidence must act as mediator. When real life experience is at odds with authoritative literature, the live, dynamic subject must be granted his right to individuality. The understanding of perceptual function is the *sine qua non* of instruction.

My View of Perception

Convinced of the validity of this necessity, I have never ceased to study the human process of perception. My compulsion to understand (admittedly an old-fashioned objective), inevitably led me to the formulation of a perspective on perception which rapidly diverged from conventional views. The full accounting of this divergence must be postponed to some other writing, but a few points of perspective deserve discussion.

The conventional view recognizes the existence of six modes of perception, but holds that each functions in isolation and can be studied separately, stimulated separately, and analyzed separately, perpetuating the practice of focal fragmentation, negating interrelatedness, and dismissing the human gestalt. This is the traditional view of the botanical scientist casually translated in the educational mind.

This view is contradictory to the complexity of human function and contrary to the dynamic unity of the developing child. While the revered paradigms of science require the elimination or at least the control of intervening variables, human complexity defies such exclusion. The profound complexity of human design and human function dictates a quest for synthesis instead of fragmentation. Intervening variables are a constant in the human process. Seeking to eliminate them in the study of human affairs constitutes an unrealistic allegiance to an inappropriate scientific model. The study of human existence and interaction requires a new model for investigation which acknowledges the presence of variables and accepts them as reality factors in all investigations.

Every person is a multimodal being throughout his life. Such a state is a functional necessity in a multivariant world of stimulation. We live in a climate of multimodal demands, and our survival depends upon the integrity of our multimodal matrix—with all modes interrelated and interdependent. The six modes of perception are not designed for scientific or instructional convenience to be separated, one by one, for placement under the microscope or, one by one, for attention by a teacher. They are designed to function in concert, always and forever.

Once you accept the obligation to synthesis, it is no longer appropriate to single out one mode for diagnostic or therapeutic concentration. The idiosyncratic structuring of an individual's perceptual composite in its many states of variance and contrast must be the abiding focus. Being multimodal as a consequence of human design, every human being is mandated to the organization of a perceptual composite—not one mode or another but all modes—interweaving, reciprocating, supporting, impeding, conflicting, and distorting.

The dynamic composition of the perceptual matrix is fashioned in diverse experiences, densities of stimulation, opportunities available, and the contextual environment in which his perceptions remain operative. The individual assigns value, attaches significance, and gives meaning to a multivariant world of stimulation. He thrives in diversity. Perceptual

processing in real life is not conveniently organized into half-hour segments of single-mode stimulation. There is a constancy of all-at-once-ness.

As a consequence of environmental demands and inclinations, parental valuing systems and reinforcements, the expansiveness of certain
curiosities and the perceptual density of his respective context, each person establishes a MODAL HIERARCHY among the six modes, which can
be represented as a rank ordering of preference. The positioning of letters
GOTKAV (Gustatory, Olfactory, Tactual, Kinesthetic, Auditory, Visual)
in idiosyncratic combinations can be employed to reflect this unique ordering of preferences, e.g., AKTVOG, TAKVGO, KVATOG.

The concept of the Modal Hierarchy is intended to interpret the
individualistic aspects of perception. The significance of the first-ranked
mode is that the individual gains most information from his world
through this mode, deliberately converts circumstances to this mode
whenever possible, and "reads his world" through that mode. Each successive ranking implies some reduction in efficiency of function.

Some similarity to this concept will be found in the prevailing educational belief that some learners are "visual learners" and some are "auditory learners." The concept of the Modal Hierarchy extends this thinking
considerably to include the options that some children may be "kinesthetic learners," some may be "tactual learners," some "olfactory learners," and so on. Further, the concept projects the relatedness of all modes
within the learner. While a single child may be properly declared a visual
learner, the state of his visual efficiency will be determined by functional
quality of the ranked ordering of his other five modes. Thus the
visual child with a very low auditory efficiency is less effective in visualiz-
ing situations than the high visual child with accompanying high auditory efficiency. The understanding of the distinctive individuality of each
perceiver grows only when the nature of his hierarchy is comprehended.

Every perception is an act of the composite. No experience can be
purely visual, purely auditory, etc. True, the nature and identity of the
stimulus may be classified as pure; but once the perceiver receives the
stimulation, internally or externally defined, and acts upon it, his composite organization is activated. This may enhance or detract from the acuity
and richness of any single perception. When presented with challenge,
the perceiver not only scans for prior experience in the mode being stimulated but scans his entirety of experiences, seeking assistance and support
from companion modes. All modes make a contribution, major or minor,
to each perception.

This synthesized perspective on perception has distinctive implications for instructional practice. The current practice of defining a problem
in visual perception and scheduling a massed series of activities and
exercises to give concentrated attention to the visual aspects of perception
represents allegiance to fragmentation. To reach optimal effectiveness, a
program of perceptual development must give recognition to the mul-

timodal nature of the perceiver. It must offer multiple and diverse experiences designed to expand acuities and efficiencies in all six modes.

The concept of the dynamic perceiving composite guides an instructor to (a) structure activities which stimulate combinations of two or more modalities in many differing arrangements, (b) heighten the function of the focal mode by attending to contributing factors such as regulation of the luminant surround to enhance listening or control of the acoustic surround to enhance viewing, etc., (c) remain sensitized to the existence and function of the multimodal composite as a constant in the perceiving process, regardless of the precise nature of the stimulus being presented, and to use such sensitivity in determining the quality of response.

MOTOR

The motor issue has become one of the more lively controversies on the school scene during the past ten years. Pro and con arguments centering on the question of relevance have become choice topics for conferences and conventions as well as continuing agenda items in the teachers' lounges of the nation's schools. Reception of the motor message has been mixed and varied, and resolution of the issue is only a distant prospect.

Early enthusiasts interpreted the message as a promise of eternal salvation and elimination of all academic sins. In the fashion of the day it has become a topic to be proved or disproved in a flurry of hastily conceived proposals tapping a variety of federal funds.

In some quarters skeptics predicted an early demise of the notion as soon as the novelty of the premise wore off. Hardened veterans of previous innovations in education magnanimously granted teachers a freedom to indulge their eager fancies for a while, confident that (like hula hoops and yo-yos) the fad would fade, the party would be over, and contrite teachers would recognize the errors of their ways and humbly return to a "solid program of basics" without such foolishness.

Another form of reception was evident among the faithful members of the .99 Level of Confidence Society who, almost immediately, began the chant of intimidation, insisting upon statistical confirmation of the claims and promises. The chant has not subsided, much to the embarrassment of spirited practitioners.

Desperate administrators, confronted with a deluge of public criticism when annual achievement test scores were revealed, clutched at the possibility of shoring up sagging percentiles and pacifying critics with the modern nectar of "enriching innovations" such as experimental perceptual-motor programs. Cautious and conservative administrators decided to wait for returns to come in from outlying districts before conceding that motoric training might have value for a population of children with arms and legs. The message was simply pencilled in on the memo pad as a possible item for some future agenda.

Some physical educationists were alarmed by the possibility of infringement upon their provincial territory, but the main body of physical education has been too busy with the varsity to notice. A small segment of this field welcomed the message being promoted by educators as a solid reinforcement for their own campaigns.

Teachers with a high quantity of kinesthesia in their personal make-up regarded the message as Biblical manna—liberating their motoric souls to conduct programs as they had been disposed all along. Low kinesthetic teachers perceived the message as a stark threat to sedentation and an unwarranted recommendation which would clearly lead to classroom disorder and confusion.

Those who openly espoused the cause of movement in lecture and text were regarded by critics as cultists of nonsense and by adherents as beacons of hope on an educational wasteland. The "language crowd" has consistently passed off such enthusiasm as an occasion of sin to teachers and has ordered that the path of virtue is more properly paved with phonemes and morphemes, with posies of encodings and decodings planted along the edges to brighten the path.

Despite the controversy which has accompanied the delivery of the motor message to the pedagogic mind, the impact cannot be denied. Even the most rabid traditionalists in education must recognize that the motor message is sounding in their midst and will not go away. Some may choose to ridicule its implications, some may argue to reduce its priority, and others may debate its relative significance; but few can deny that it has become a viable issue on the school scene—the foothold has been gained. The coordination problems of the nation's school children are painfully evident and beg for some concern.

To one who has been a staunch advocate of the motor message, the present state of affairs is both gratifying and disappointing. There is joy in the thought that the premise is gaining momentum, but also some sadness of mind when current levels of interpretation and implementation are analyzed.

The majority mind of education has given the message an exceedingly narrow interpretation by concentrating attention to motoric matters at only two levels: (a) the primary learner in the kindergarten and first grade and (b) the failing learner in the eight to twelve year range whose coordination difficulties are blatantly obvious. At all other levels the long sound of $\bar{o}$ remains supreme, and the look-and-listen demand is unchallenged.

The developmental and remedial rationalizations which govern such concentrations constitute only a token interpretation of the spirit and intent of the motor premise. Coordinative efficiency is not age exclusive nor is its absence immediately indicative of some esoteric etiology. It should be a matter of curriculum concern for all levels of education.

To a certain extent, the narrowness of interpretation can be traced to a semantic constraint. Since the word *motor* has been used to identify this new area of concern in the pedagogic mind, it has given rise to a focus upon muscles and athletic skill patterns. The compartmentalized mind of education, long accustomed to fragmenting the learner, has found it convenient to translate the message into a modified and diluted version of physical education programming—pertinent only when obvious difficulty could be defined but inadmissable as an educational generalization. The term *motor,* unfortunately, has invited a traditional definition, a traditional interpretation, and a traditional implementation. The semantic constraint has caused the concept to become a bonus consideration, a "down the hall" proposition, and an item of probable transitory interest. *Screen and schedule* have become the watchwords on the perceptual-motor front.

Movement Consciousness

If the present mushrooming interest in the motor premise is to survive and achieve the curriculum status which it deserves, a much broader conceptualization is essential. The term *motor* should be replaced by the term *movement.* Such recommendation is not an idle quibble over semantics but is, rather, based upon a conception of difference in meaning between the two terms. When the term *motor* is applied, the image is exclusively physical, bringing to mind actions of arms, legs, feet, and hands in some form of coordinated response to external demand. Both definition and image are conventional and narrow. The term *movement* refers to a much broader conception of human action, intertwining perceptual, language, and motor functions into an abiding state of consciousness in the performer, permeating all encounters with his world—physical, social, emotional, and intellectual.

The *motor movement* is presently at what might be called the first stage of movement consciousness—*a state of awareness of possible significance.* Coordination has moved from the athletic field to the classroom. It is only the first step in the acquisition of expanded consciousness. The enthusiastic implementations which have emerged from this first stage of awareness are bound to yield equivocal results. Instead of being disheartened by such findings, movement enthusiasts and critics alike should make a frank appraisal of the limited cognitive investment which has characterized many of these efforts. The study of movement and all of its implications for human response—a prerequisite to formulating a solid rationale—has seldom preceded such implementation.

It is understandable that the fragmented mind of education would read only the list of equipment and ignore the rationale. Weary of theory without practical extensions, educators have simply dispensed with theoretical considerations and plunged into practice, postponing rationale until some later date.

Most perceptual-motor programs consist of an assortment of recommended materials from an assortment of authorities with an assortment of purposes loosely banded together by the thin string of eclecticism. Handbooks of suggested activities are easy to come by, but rationales are scarce. Sadly, the burden of formulating a sustaining rationale has been thrust upon the shoulders of novice practitioners. Lacking the benefit of extended training and study, materials have not surprisingly become more important than concepts and cookbook techniques prized above principles. Screen-and-schedule enterprises quickly became a few trips on a walking rail, a number of exercises at chalkboard, several taps at a suspended ball, a few tricks on a trampoline, a fast turn of the metronome dial, and several other recommended procedures, followed by premature excursions to the psychometry booth to verify results.

At this first level of movement consciousness, the expressions of concern for the coordination difficulties of the child are evident—awareness has been achieved—and some measure of instructional focus is occurring. Programs may be casual and haphazard, instructional finesse may be lacking, and equipment may be assigned greater value than it deserves, but enthusiasm and the joy of discovering a different approach to helping children develop efficiency seem to override such shortcomings. Regardless of the level of sophistication which characterizes any given program it is now clinically clear that children benefit from such experiences. Our present failure to verify such benefits in quantitative form is not the fault of the concept but rather the fault of outmoded psychometric methodologies relying upon insensitive instruments. On-the-spot witnesses of change need no further verification.

Many programs which began in a flush of enthusiasm have advanced to the second level of movement consciousness—*the recognition of motoric or movement individuality.* In this stage detailed analysis of the individual determines the nature of developmental or remedial instruction. Peer comparisons and fixed routines are dismissed from consideration. Matters of postural alignment, personal tempo, modality hierarchies, and zonal preferences become important targets of analysis and instruction. The mechanics, sequence, rate, and timing of individual actions are studied *in persona,* and appropriate strategies are conceived. The criteria of base, thrust, direction, and purpose become prime foci in setting the activity schedule. The quality of performance on the vertical, horizontal, and depth axes takes on significance.

At this level of consciousness etiologies, diagnostic classifications and categorical thinking become secondary to the understanding of the individual's current state of functional comfort and efficiency. Each program is individualized, each response is studied for personal significance, and each outcome is treated as a unique contribution to the individual's movement composite. The program is organized to achieve the highest possible states of awareness and insight into the learner's attitudes toward movement, operational skills, and the social consequences of his current composite. Impediments to efficiency are eliminated one by one, to the growing advantage of the learner in a motoric context.

The first two levels of movement consciousness are instructionally evident in most quality programs on the school scene. They have established the concept of motor programming in the conventional sense—activities of physical action aimed at improving the individual's state of coordination.

Cognitive expansion to the third level is more difficult to achieve. In this stage the instructor must advance his concerns to the study of interrelationships between the dynamics of the learner's motoric function and the prosaic business of academic learning. The movement consistency of the performer in all response patterns becomes the target for analysis. Relationships between gross movement patterning and fine coordinated responses are noted. The concept of fine motor actions emerging from a gross motor base is acknowledged. For example, the child who consistently misjudges the fit of his writing in the prescribed spaces of the workbook is studied for evidence of other instances of inability to properly "fit himself" into diverse common spaces, such as doorways, chairs, or games. The perception of self in space is studied across a variety of contexts.

The unity of the learner is accepted—only the unique patterns of interrelationships and interdependences between all functions in his composite behaviors are in question. The precise nature of perceptual and movement demands in the academic process is matched to an equalized perceptual demand in motoric performance; the commonality of his dilemma is recognized. The conviction that every function is related in some way to every other function in a massive matrix of unique organization guides the instructor in analyzing the composite dynamics of the individual learner. Weakened and strong functions are not merely tallied but are studied for their possible influences upon each other. In a continuously fascinating exercise of inductive and deductive reasoning, the instructor seeks to *understand* the learner's present state of overall efficiency—not only to tally, diagnose, classify, and judge, but to understand.

Synthesis rather than fragmentation becomes the persistent challenge to both instructor and performer. The character of the program shifts from a collection of motor lessons to a strategy of movement experiences, from muscle insights to cognitive modifications, from coordinative improvement to reformulation of self. The attainment of a *thinking body* becomes the crucial objective. Materials and equipment become potential vehicles of personal insight rather than devices to be mastered. The concrete goals of physical activity give way to abstract goals of cognitive expansion in the same context.

The shift from motoric to cognitive objectives with the attendant implications for academic functioning is the prime locus of the current controversy. Operation of programs at the first two levels of movement consciousness may stir some critics to action, but most are inclined to tolerate perceptual-motor programming as an interesting but unessential sidelight. The claim of academic relevance, however, quickly becomes incendiary. Accusations of sacrilege against revered conceptions are shouted across the land.

Early claims of academic relevance were made without due recourse to an expanded consciousness of the movement premise. They were, and are, premature. Models of assessment must be equally expanded. Old wagons do not transport well on superhighways. Present arguments are based upon antiquated models.

When movement consciousness is expanded, the logic of academic relevance is clear. One common illustration can be cited.

A child, lacking lateral confidence, is in a constant dilemma on the academic scene where hundreds of directional demands plead for daily resolution. When a properly conducted perceptual-motor program helps the child to acquire lateral certainty, the frequency of his dilemma will be dramatically diminished. An academic hindrance will be removed, and the child will be free to advance at a much higher level of confidence. The precise impact of such certainty on specific academic function may be difficult to assess, but the methodological problems do not erase the logic of the concept of relationship.

Changes in attitudes toward learning, increased ability to sustain effort, reductions in peer conflict, heightened sensitivity to the world of information, expansions of confidence, and dozens of other interactional modifications which emerge from instructional attention to perceptual-motor efficiency must be counted as evidence of benefit—granting the learner the freedom of time to incorporate and utilize new insights, to test out reformulations, and to embed new levels of capability. Qualitative change must occur before quantitative change becomes evident.

With the attainment of the third level of movement consciousness, there is a full-scale recognition that currently identified gross and fine motor materials belong on the standard shelf of instructional aids to be used along with other academically defined materials in helping children acquire concepts and processes in all subject areas. Counting can be learned with a jump rope just as well as with a box of rods—perhaps even faster, because the *thinking body* is in action. Movement programs may be down the hall at the moment, compartmentalized for convenience, but the true potential will only be realized when such thinking becomes standard to instructional strategy.

Few people are ready to carry the conception of the movement premise into the realm of emotional organization and reach for the fourth expansion of movement consciousness, but the gates are open. The possibility that movement confidence is reflected in approach-avoidance behaviors, concept of self, and internal conflicts is being noted by more and more searching minds. What psychologists call ambivalence is nothing more than a laterality conflict. Withdrawing is nothing more than retreat on the depth axis. Aggressive behavior is nothing more than randomized action on the forward axis. Emotional space is only another of man's domains of operation, subject to a similar form of analysis. The dictate of synthesis demands a singularity of model—once adopted, the permeation of movement in the human process in all domains will yield to understanding.

The probability that *propriotherapy* can become a viable alternative to standard models of psychotherapy in the resolution of personal conflicts is entertained by only a few at the present time; but as the consciousness of movement expands, the realities will become known. Our early efforts along this line have been exceptionally impressive. Adults and children alike have been able to understand the nature of their psychic conflicts clearly in movement terms and to find resolution in a cognitively related movement program.

Nothing has happened during the last decade to diminish either my enthusiasm or convictions regarding the validity of the movement premise. Instead there has been a steady increase in my confidence levels. Conversion from a cognitive model of fragmentation to a new model of synthesis cannot be expected to happen swiftly and smoothly in the educator's mind. There are too many embedded beliefs, beholden to tradition and conventions, to hope for the full realization of the import of an expansion in movement consciousness in reformulating curriculum goals, but such an objective will continue to dominate my future efforts.

The perceptual-motor premise is far more complicated and profound than current interpretations suggest. It is not an issue to be proved or disproved in a few studies and casually buried among the rubble of other educational innovations which have come and gone. For now, a movement program may have to be down the hall, packaged for visibility, offered as an interlude or an interruption in daily curriculum; but with patience and diligence the cognitive expansion will occur to make it a continuity, an integral conception in the understanding of the human learning process. For now, implementations of the concept may appear to be at primer level, but with further exploration and imagination a more sophisticated reading of the human text will emerge. For now, the interpretations may be cast in muscular terms, but with the exercise of logic and dedication to synthesis the cognitive implications will become clearer. In the past ten years we have only scratched the surface of a precious concept of proud heritage in educational thought. Restoration to full beauty will take many years of cognitive labor, inductive polishing, and buffing debate. *We are only beginning to understand.*

LANGUAGE

Most critics and reviewers of the Movigenic orientation have been kind and generous. Some have decided to "wait and see," some have declared the semantics of space to be overly indulged, and a few have been openly laudatory. Most, however, have scored my neglect of language function as a point of weakness in the structure.

The absence of extended discussions of the role of language in the original explications (Barsch, 1967a, 1969) was not due to oversight or neglect, but rather to a desire to clarify a current pressing point of view while postponing my full thoughts on language to some later writing. The final construct of the Movigenic foundation states, *"Movement Efficiency is symbolically communicated through the visual-spatial phenomenon called language."* The brief discussion of this construct which followed was intended to show the culmination of efficiency into symbolic form as a distinctive prerogative of Mobile Man. This was extended in articles (Barsch, 1966, 1967b) which further elaborated the conception of language as a visual-spatial phenomenon, but these either escaped reviewer attention or were considered insufficient. A further attempt to clarify my perspective on language function is on the priority list for future publication. Perhaps my unwillingness to treat language as an isolated phenomenon and succumb to molecularizing practices constitutes grounds for criticism. If this be true, my plea is "Nolo contendere."

The purpose of language is to convey and receive experience. In whatever form it is organized, it represents an emergence from experience. Encountering the world one stimulus at a time and retaining the meaning of each stimulus for its referential value in reducing future errors, in increasing personal complexity, and in building efficiency would be a hopelessly complicated task for the young child. A system for ordering and organizing experience into economically useful units for continuous guidance and adaptation is essential to the human process. Language is such an economy. The ability to invent and use symbols for the representation of experience to self and others stands as a unique characteristic of the human being.

As long as a child's world is limited to oneness and each object or event is in the singular to be directly viewed, heard, moved, touched, tasted, or smelled, there is little need for symbols—the child's world is "too small" to require the economies of symbolization. Only as his world expands does the task of accounting to and for himself and all things around him require the child to employ symbols. The larger his world becomes, the greater his need for language.

Each new human is not required to invent an independent symbol system, although many young children convey that impression during the early stages of language acquisition. The symbol system of his culture awaits him; the world has already been symbolically sorted, organized, and categorized by those who have preceded him. He has only to acquire the "mother tongue," the abiding language of reference. All the nouns, verbs, adjectives, prepositions, etc. plus syntactical structures are available for his progressive acquisition as his complexity of action increases. From the beginning his language is experientially stimulated, contextually defined, and self-expanding. He learns words in time of need. He needs as much language as his mobilities demand. He engages in no drill on word lists and is blissfully unaware of phonemes. Life experiences stimulate vocabulary development. He struggles only to acquire what is symbolically vital to his little expanding world.

This developmental dynamic, so beautifully evident in the young child, remains a constant throughout life. Each symbolic addition is tested for economy and utility in the context of personal reference. Small worlds require few symbols; large worlds require many. The richness of his experience composite will always be reflected in his language fluency. A memorized symbol system unsupported by compelling experience soon decays from lack of utility—a fact of language life which has massive implications for those who plan and conduct language programs.

My characterization of language as a visual-spatial phenomenon is not a casual or whimsical exercise in semantics. It is based upon my conviction that language is a necessary consequence of encounter—a product of experience—purposefully contrived to give symbolic value to a person's perceptions and actions. Language formulation and reception are continuous acts of visualization, inevitable condensations of experience, compacting actions. Experience is never fully replicated, only represented in economic symbols.

Prevailing concentrations on the phonological aspects of language have only served to confuse conceptions of language with conceptions of uttered speech instead of clarifying the dynamics of formulation and their linkage of experience. Casual qualifiers, so readily evident in human commerce, add to the authentication of the visual perspective. Consider the frequency of such phrasing as "the way it appears to me," "the way I see it," "from my vantage point," "my impression is," "in my experience," etc. On the receiving side, consider, "I see what you mean," "I see your point," "that is clear." We "get the drift of a conversation," "see where an argument is leading," "get the picture," and "see what a speaker is driving at." We are "enlightened," "no longer in the dark," and get "glimmers" of meaning. Hundreds of visually oriented references can be tallied daily in casual conversations. What the common man has unconsciously recognized for centuries seems to have eluded many of the contemporary language authorities.

Mastery of the mother tongue for economic utility is only one acquisition in the formation of a linguistic composite. Most learners manage a large variety of symbol systems as their visual space worlds expand. Experiencing the culture, living in the midst of its symbol systems with interactional demands, continues to be the most effective way of acquiring a language. Formalized study of syntactical patterns and the molecules of conjugation, parsing, diagramming, etc. can impede utility rather than advance it.

Every segment of the social, commercial, and professional world has a separate language culture, replete with idiomatic expressions having clear meaning only to those who are members of the tribe. School is a distinctive language culture where idiomatic expressions abound. Any language program should initially acquaint the child with the dimensions of the culture, the school's role as a laboratory of symbol systems, and the particular forms of utility. The study of English as a first or second language is only as small element in the study of communication. My approach to language development in the disorganized as well as in the intact child can best be described as psychological and philosophical, aimed at helping the child to identify himself or herself as a communicator, to become aware of the utility of language and its experiential function. Refinement of pronunciation, syntactical conformity, tense, case and so on is postponed until the child's communicative identity is secure. A vibrant program of activities with ample opportunities for interaction demand expression, in whatever form the child is able—living the language in functional context, giving a diversity of experiences to stimulate the emergence of vocabulary, providing a rich environment of communication without urgency to conformity—are main characteristics.

The adoption of a spatial perspective on language does not require denial or rejection of most traditional and contemporary conceptions, only a reformulation and a variant interpretation consistent with a movement model of reference. It does, however, eliminate the need to pledge allegiance to the *ITPA* and to salute the phoneme.

Opportunities to relate to and learn from deaf adults and children in recent years have reinforced and intensified my convictions concerning the visual character of language. The oral-manual debate which has been so prominent in the field of education of the deaf is in many respects a counterpart to the visual-auditory argument in the field of language development for hearing people. Neither has been resolved by the experts, but the communicators casually go about their daily business of interacting, unperturbed by the symposium clashes and the textbook controversies.

The natural beauty of *Ameslan* (American Sign Language) with its indigenous qualities and idiomatic conceptualizations is a potent reinforcement of the visual-spatial premise. Every teacher who is interested in language development and the plotting of effective strategies for helping children with language deficits, major or minor, in any context, is well advised to incorporate a solid understanding of signed language in all of its present forms into his or her pedagogic and cognitive composite.

My enthusiasm for signed language has led to advocacy of its use in classes for children without auditory impairment. A diligent effort to teach a basic vocabulary or concepts in signs has inserted an exciting dimension into the communication band of the curriculum wherever it has been used. Many children whose progress under traditional language approaches has lagged have suddenly spurted forward in expanded communications once a few signs have been mastered. Acquisition of some signs does not in any way hamper the development of the oral process in the hearing learner. Instead it seems to provide an impetus to expression in oral form.

Language, for me, represents a perceptual-motor emergent. Children perceive and act in accord with their perceptions, attaching symbolic significance to their movements, physically and cognitively. The study of any language is a reflection of the prevailing perceptions and movements of a culture. As the experiences of mankind extend beyond the prior limits of vocabulary, new symbols are added. Since the experience is new it requires linguistic invention ... for conveyance, preservation, and differentiation. In this way the outer fringes of any language are constantly subject to change as experiential referrents expand. This is a phenomenon with which all communicators must contend. Language is a reflection of a space world—limited or expansive—in accord with the dimensions of one's personal world. Enlargement of the learner's space world through diversified experiences compels and advances language development far faster than drill.

THE INDIVISIBLE INSTRUCTIONAL TRIAD

The persisting effort to distinguish between a perceptual problem and a language problem or a perceptual problem and a motor problem in the belief that precise differentiation will isolate a constellation of ailments from an otherwise healthy and integrated being is an exercise in futility. Such belief thrives only in the minds of those dedicated to fragmenting the learner into an assortment of bits and pieces having no relationship to one another.

Consistent with my convictions concerning unity and synthesis, I hold that the three functions constitute an interrelated and indivisible trinity in all learners. One function cannot be ailing while the other two remain integrated. Every child who can be classified as having a problem in any of the three areas, according to current diagnostic practices, will be found to demonstrate difficulties in the other two areas as well, once our sensitivity to functional inefficiencies is heightened and broadened beyond conventional constraints. The absence of convenient measuring devices, the narrowness of conceptions, and the denial of human unity in the professional mind do not cause a dynamic, adapting, mobile being to separate his function. Logic dictates a synthesized approach. Only diagnostic prejudice allows the belief in separateness to flourish.

The integrity of the human learner rests upon his ability to assign meaning and significance to his experiences, to move in accord with his perceptions, and to communicate his intent, purpose, and conclusions. He does not perceive in isolation, move in isolation, or speak in isolation. He is always in context and is always unity. These three elements form the nucleus of all learning.

Every teacher in every setting with every population from infancy to college is simultaneously engaged in perceptual, motoric, and linguistic instruction. Those who teach are constantly seeking to make learners more aware of differences and similarities and details of significance (perception), to motivate a movement of thought and action in a particular space (movement), and to expand their communicative composite (language). The name of the course, the nature of the content, and the sophistication of the learners may vary from group to group, but the nature of teaching does not vary—it is always perceptual, motoric, and linguistic. When the semantic disguises of more impressive terminologies are stripped from the teaching act, the true self of teaching is an indivisible triad. The human learner does not perceive from 9:00 to 9:30, move from 9:30 to 10:00, and speak from 10:00 to 10:30. He is all at once—all the time. Teachers may believe that they are stimulating one area to the exclusion of the other two, but the indivisibility of the triad constantly defeats segregation.

If the psychometric and educative mind can ever be liberated from its bondage to geometric forms in the assessment and interpretation of perceptual functioning, and expanded into a consciousness of a dynamic perceptual composite involving a multimodal constancy, there may yet be hope that the profound human privilege of perception will be understood. If the same mind can be liberated from the constraints of muscles, stamina, and athletic skills in the approach to movement and expanded to embrace a much broader view of movement as a physiologic, sociologic, psychologic, and physical all-at-onceness, there may yet be hope that the magnificence of human mobility will be appreciated. And if the same mind can be expanded beyond the boundaries of phonemes, encodings, and syntax, there may yet be hope that the distinctive gift of communication will be understood.

Such expansions may appear to be only remote possibilities in a climate of fragmentation, compartmentalization, and competition, but journeys without horizons are soon abandoned. One need only have a modest quantum of sensitivity in the presence of a bewildered perceiver to recognize that his dilemma extends far beyond the point of the pencil. One needs only minimal powers of observation to appreciate that the clumsy child is missing more than the ball thrown toward him. Any alerted listener will be keenly aware that a child's desperate search for the right word is far more than a phonemic insufficiency. The empathic educator cannot help realizing that all three functions are one—a single expressive triad—indivisible, in every human being—a profound reflection of the human potential for stature and wisdom, striving for fulfillment.

A FINAL NOTE

These statements of perspective constitute only a small portion of my composite space world—shaped by experience and opportunity, open to debate and criticism, subject to continuous clarification, and constantly emerging. My quest for synthesis continues. . . .

REFERENCES

Barsch, R. H. *The movigenic curriculum.* Madison, Wisc.: Bureau for Handicapped Children, Bulletin No. 25, 1966.

Barsch, R. H. *Achieving perceptual motor efficiency.* Seattle: Special Child Publications, 1967. (a)

Barsch, R. H. The language of direction. *Academic Therapy Quarterly,* 1967, **2,** 223–26, 258. (b)

Barsch, R. H. *Enriching perception and cognition.* Seattle: Special Child Publications, 1969.

Barsch, R. H. *". . . and sometimes y."* Canoga Park, Calif.: Ray Barsch Center for Learning, 1974. (a)

Barsch, R. H. *Each to a different drummer.* Canoga Park, Calif.: Ray Barsch Center for Learning, 1974. (b)

Barsch, R. H. *Listen, my children (Auditory training teachiques for classroom teachers).* Canoga Park, Calif.: Ray Barsch Center for Learning, 1975.

A SELECTED BIBLIOGRAPHY OF WORKS BY RAY H. BARSCH

Barsch, R. H. The concept of regression in the brain-injured child. *Exceptional Children,* 1960, **27,** 84–89.

Barsch, R. H. Explanations offered by parents and siblings of brain-injured children. *Exceptional Children,* 1961, **27,** 286–91.

Barsch, R. H. Evaluating the organic child: The functional organization scale. *Journal of Genetic Psychology,* 1962, **100,** 345–54.

Barsch, R. H. Six factors in learning. In J. Hellmuth (Ed.), *Learning Disorders.* Vol. 1. Seattle: Special Child Publications, 1965.

Barsch, R. H. The concept of language as a visual-spatial phenomenon. *Academic Therapy Quarterly,* 1965, **1,** 2–11.

Barsch, R. H. Teacher needs—motor training. In W. M. Cruickshank (Ed.), *The teacher of brain-injured children: A discussion of bases for competency.* Syracuse, N.Y.: Syracuse University Press, 1966.

Barsch, R. H. The movigenic curriculum. Madison, Wisc.: Bureau for Handicapped Children, Bulletin No. 25, 1966.

Barsch, R. H. *Achieving perceptual motor efficiency.* Seattle: Special Child Publications, 1967.

Barsch, R. H. Counseling the parent of the brain-damaged child. In E. C. Frierson & W. B. Barbe (Eds.), *Educating children with learning disabilities.* New York: Appleton-Century-Crofts, 1967.

Barsch, R. H. The language of direction. *Academic Therapy Quarterly,* 1967, **2,** 223–26, 258.

Barsch, R. H. *The parent of the handicapped child.* Springfield, Ill.: Charles C Thomas, 1967.

Barsch, R. H. Perspectives on learning disabilities: The vectors of a new convergence. *Journal of Learning Disabilities,* 1968, **1,** 4–20.

Barsch, R. H. The consultant for children with special learning disabilities. In K. R. Blessing (Ed.), *The role of the resource consultant in special education.* Washington, D.C.: Council for Exceptional Children, 1968.

Barsch, R. H. *Enriching perception and cognition.* Seattle: Special Child Publications, 1969.

Barsch, R. H. *The parent teacher partnership.* Washington, D.C.: Council for Exceptional Children, 1969.

Barsch, R. H. "*. . . and sometimes y.*" Canoga Park, Calif.: Ray Barsch Center for Learning, 1974.

Barsch, R. H. *Each to a different drummer.* Canoga Park, Calif.: Ray Barsch Center for Learning, 1974.

Barsch, R. H. *Listen my children (Auditory training techniques for classroom teachers.)* Canoga Park, Calif.: Ray Barsch Center for Learning, 1975.

3
William M. Cruickshank

William M. Cruickshank is presently director of the Institute for the Study of Mental Retardation and Related Disabilities, University of Michigan. He is also professor of psychology, professor of education, and professor of maternal and child health at the University of Michigan. Before assuming these professorships at Michigan, he was the Margaret O. Slocum Distinguished Professor of Education and Psychology and director, Division of Special Education and Rehabilitation, from 1946 through 1967, at Syracuse University. Dr. Cruickshank has also been a visiting professor at Texas Women's University, Florida State University, State University of New York at Buffalo, University of Oregon, and Ohio State University. He has been visiting lecturer at Northwestern University, Yeshiva University, University of Uppsala (Sweden), University of San Marcos (Lima, Peru), University of Trujillo (Peru), Kumamato University (Japan), and University of Birmingham (England).

Dr. Cruickshank was born in 1915 in Birmingham, Michigan, and obtained his B.A. degree from Eastern Michigan University. He received his M.A. degree in 1938 from the University of Chicago and his Ph.D. degree from the University of Michigan in 1945. He also studied at Cité Universitaire, Paris, France, in 1944. In 1962, he received an honorary degree from the Universidad National Mayor de San Marcos, Peru, and an honorary Doctor of Science degree from Eastern Michigan University.

Dr. Cruickshank is a member and has served as officer of numerous professional organizations. Among his more distinguished professional memberships, he is a fellow and life member of the American Association on Mental Deficiency, charter member of the American Academy of Mental Deficiency, fellow of the Divisions of Clinical and Abnormal Psychology and Developmental Psychology of the American Psychological Association, and life member of the Council for Exceptional Children.

Dr. Cruickshank has also assumed other major national and international appointments. Among these, he was a Fulbright lecturer and associate director of the Institute San Gabriel Archangel in Lima, Peru, from

1962 to 1963 and in 1968. He is a past president of the International Council for Exceptional Children, the Division of Teacher Education of the Council for Exceptional Children, and the Division of Psychological Aspects of Disability, American Psychological Association, and Priorsfield Fellow, University of Birmingham, England, 1973.

Dr. Cruickshank's publications are internationally recognized. He has contributed numerous book chapters and journal articles. He has also published several books, some of which have been translated into foreign languages. A selected bibliography of works by William Cruickshank can be found on pages 126–27.

FOUNDATIONS AND SIGNIFICANT PEOPLE

I suspect that had I been a teenager of the 1960s, I might well have been a dropout, a runaway, and one disenchanted with the way things were. This last characterization is of the moment, but the other avenues were to a large extent not available to the youth of the thirties. World War II gobbled youth up in the early forties who otherwise might have turned to other forms of personal escape or adjustment. A dominant family structure, a very fixed social attitude, powerful community influences, and World War II either kept me and other young people on a path which was more or less acceptable to the community or required that deviations from that path be sublimated or hidden from view. The depression years, the Puritan ethic, Prohibition, the war years, and the structure of home and community were controlling factors in my early life and that of my peers; and in large measure these have continued to have a pervading influence ever since. These issues, as one looks back over five decades, into the sixth, and to one's youth, can now be seen in a perspective which explains, but not in a perspective which one accepts. They are, however, issues which I have lived and which place me, regardless of age differences, into a position simpatico with my students and with young people with whom I work. To that end, the early frustrations of growing up and finding one's way are not those of completely lost years; but only those of knowing that if the time and situation had been different, greater satisfactions of a personal nature and greater contributions of a professional nature might have been possible.

College

There were great people in my early college and university years who sensed the indecision of a young man and who gave him his tether to roam widely as he needed; who encouraged, but did not control; who set sights, but suggested rather than demanded. The significance of a freshman rhetoric professor in making a student know he *could*, rather than seeing himself as one who *could not*, is an appreciated memory which is long-lasting. The close association which I had with Dr. and Mrs. Francis E. Lord, first as an undergraduate student and later by the former's invitation as a faculty colleague in the early World War II years, provided me with an understanding that faculty members could be human and at the same time humane to students and could by example provide an informal structure on which students could build their lives. There were numerous others in those same years who in their different ways provided me with the guidance which was necessary to turn gross immaturity into positive maturity and leadership. These people who helped to set my sights during undergraduate years are too numerous to name, and they would be unknown to the readers of this book with its special focus. They taught me history and sociology and extended my breadth of thinking. They taught me Greek and French and made me more analytical as well as more appreciative of other communication systems. They taught me music and made me realize the unlimited extensions of the human mind and capacity. They taught me anatomy, kinesiology, and physiology and made me understand the physical bases of thought, aesthetics, and creativity. They taught me many more things than these. They are fondly remembered. Dormitories and classroom buildings are now named after them at Eastern Michigan University.

Universities

At the University of Chicago, however, the list grows longer, for there the names of Professors Franklin Bobbitt, Mandel Sherman, Floyd Reeves, Newton Edwards, John Dale Russell, Guy Buswell, and others who were the lights and leaders in professional psychology and education of that time had an influence on my mind. I learned of the "good life" from Bobbitt; of the social demands and requisites on child growth and development from Edwards; of the responsibilities of leadership from Reeves. There my mind was stretched and pulled as it never was before or since. "Read, Mr. Cruickshank," said Newton Edwards. "Never stop reading; never be without a book. Read, read, read." This advice, written down a few moments later in one of my old notebooks, comes to life again from time to time as a reminder that not all is gained directly from people, but that there are other avenues of education. I read at Chicago, read as I never have again.

Later, at the University of Michigan, professors such as Clifford Woody, William Clark Trow, Irving Anderson, Howard McClusky, Stuart J. Courtis, and others provided a direction which was significant. They opened career avenues for my life. Of even more importance, for I had had much of people, professors, and ideas by that time, were the graduate student associations which were significant. It is always a bit startling to some of my present undergraduate and graduate students to learn of the student associations which helped form my thinking and life, some of which continue today with such colleagues as Dr. William C. Morse and

Dr. Alvin F. Zander, both of the University of Michigan. Others included Dr. Uri Bronfrenbrenner at Cornell University; Dr. William Soskin, University of California at Berkeley; the late George William Bryson of the *Encyclopaedia Britannica;* and many who could easily be added to a long line of significant persons. For nearly forty years Dr. Fritz Redl has slipped in and out of my social and professional life, each time leaving great challenges which had to be intellectualized and explored and then integrated into function. These among dozens of scholars throughout the world with whom I have later been associated, and some with whom I have worked closely, have stimulated me with ideas; illustrated intellectual directions to be followed or pursued; made comments, often as afterthoughts or tangential to an issue, which have suggested fruitful avenues of professional pursuit.

Clinical psychology was an infant art in the late thirties. It was then hardly a science, although the influences of Binet, Goddard, Doll, and others were being felt. The clinical psychology school of the U.S. Army gave me a professional stimulus to continue my efforts in that direction; the hospital experiences of the war itself provided training which could not have been equalled. In the early part of 1941 I had a unique experience which was the beginning of another interest and a new direction in my training, as well another experience with a razor-sharp mind, that of Dr. Samuel J. Beck of the Michael Reese Hospital. Then I was admitted to one of his courses dealing with the Rorschach Test; and although this necessitated my sleeping throughout the period of the course on the stage of the old Auditorium Theater in Chicago, since wartime demands for housing were great, I learned for the first time of at least one way in which man could introspectively penetrate the mind of another.

These early professors, graduate student peers, and more contemporary professional and political leaders throughout the United States and the world, in addition to my immediate family, have indeed made my life. The contribution has been much greater on the receiving end than the giving. Concepts of humaneness to people, concepts of the worth of children, concepts of the ethic of a multiracial society, concepts of structure and its relationship to child growth and development, concepts of equality of people everywhere—all came from those with whom I have had the privilege of associating over the years. Then there are the students. . . .

Students

Under no circumstances are students the only ones who learn in a university or college. It is not easy to pin to a given individual the source of that which has been learned. I am daily reminded, however, that education is a two-way street. The student learns; the professor learns; the student seeks; the professor often can lend his name to help him find. This close interrelationship which can develop between students and a teacher has been a vital aspect of my whole university-centered life, and I anticipate that it will continue. My creed in working with students is to set a sight, attempt to open doors for accomplishment, and then to do everything within my power—within university regulations or sometimes outside or in spite of them—to make that student's success a reality. This effort has not always been the success we—the student and I—had planned, but usually we two have come out to our satisfactions. I believe in lending the name of a faculty member who has made his own reputation to that of a student, if such a joint effort means that an article or book will be published, a professional door slightly opened, and a new career begun. I believe that professors should recruit students as avidly as faculty members are recruited; and I believe that the professor then has an obligation to see that the student's career is launched in the best possible way. The exigencies of mass higher education preclude this individualized approach too often, but it is an effort which appears to me to be the keystone to the future of the professions.

I have been richly rewarded with students who have inspired me and challenged me to be better. To name any is dangerous, for some will be omitted for sure. But my pride in those students prompts me to share this chapter with some of those who can represent those not mentioned here: Dr. E. Donald Blodgett, Dr. Jean Hebeler, Dr. Norris G. Haring, Dr. James L. Paul, Dr. John Garrett, Dr. William Myers (as an undergraduate and masters degree student), Dr. Joseph Cunningham (as an undergraduate), Dr. Daniel P. Hallahan, forty-seven teachers from the National Institute of Mental Health Project for teachers of brain-injured children, Dr. Emory Cowen, Dr. Matthew Trippe, to name only a very few. These former students are as much a part of me as I hope the things they discovered in their relationships with me are a part of them. There is also a present generation of students which is ready to move into the leadership role and will be heard of in years to come. These all are important people, and any faculty member writing in this book or elsewhere would undoubtedly have the same story to tell. It is an important one.

Administration

Early on my career started along three parallel strands, strands which were interrelated to a large degree. One of these—teaching—provided me with personal satisfactions more than others; another—research—gave me an opportunity to test ideas; and the third—administration—made the others possible and provided me with a large degree of ego support, if I am honest.

Administration, on an equally serious note, also made it possible for me to provide a base of professional action for my faculty colleagues and for innumerable excellent students. Without administrative clout, neither professors nor students can progress; this power is what administration has to offer in an institution of higher education. It has always been my private game (now public information) to see what can happen when a door is administratively opened for a student or a faculty member, or when a few dollars are made available. A dream can often come true for a student or a faculty member which a few moments earlier had seemed about to be dashed. I feel that administration has the obligation to be the servant of students and faculty; under any other concept, it is a fruitless treadmill within higher education. Administration can be the stimulator of action programs, or it can be the loadstone around the necks of those seeking their places in society. Administration is exhausting, often worthless for the administrator, and demeaning, except as one can observe through administration that others try their wings and achieve heights for themselves and their professions which otherwise could not have been obtained.

Enough for administration per se. It has been a large part of my life since my late teens in one form or another. It has produced dissatisfactions for me, and probably for many others, while at the same time it has given me the power and position to accomplish much for myself and, I hope, for others on many more frequent occasions. I still wince, however, when I see one of my colleagues or former students moving into administration, for I know too well what he or she will shortly be facing.

Graduate Preparation and the Training School

The war years, to which I have referred already, brought tragedy to many and inconvenience to many more. Although I was one of those who was by comparison modestly inconvenienced, the war years brought me an opportunity to reflect on where I was going and what I was going to do with the rest of my life. An experience with F. E. Lord, as a youthful freshman student, had sensitized my thinking to the problems of exceptional children, although I did nothing about it, even though I was a student in what was then the center of all special education training. My interests were directed elsewhere, and my courage to change directions from what I thought was right was insufficient. These minor brushes with physically and mentally handicapped children and their problems, however, were continued in a very superficial manner at the University of Chicago, where I wrote what was probably the poorest masters thesis ever accepted by that great university. To my knowledge all copies are burned at the moment, except probably the one in the library files there. Perhaps someone will purloin that and securely assign it to oblivion.

That thesis, however, poor as it was, brought me to my first experience with "student recruiting." Somehow the thesis got into the hands of a great University of Michigan professor who wrote and asked me to study with him and to seek a doctoral degree at Michigan. To one who had never really seriously considered going to undergraduate college, this came as a tremendous surprise and a distinct boost. Doors began to open up. Funds were found for me to study on, long before the idea of federal grants was conceptualized! Professors made their ways into my mind and life who by chance or planning (I will never know) began to structure my thinking in the application of the clinical practice of psychology and education with those who were physically, mentally, or otherwise exceptional.

And then, by chance again, as doctoral research became a requirement, I was accepted to do that research at the Wayne County Training School, Northville, Michigan (no longer in existence, but then the world's greatest residential center for educable mentally retarded boys and girls). There I was greeted as an equal by four of the great minds of that day, and by many others as well, for the Training School was a hotbed of professional activity, inquisitiveness, research, and excellence, all under the strong professional direction of Robert Haskell, M.D., who served as a remarkable superintendent for many years. What a vortex of intellectual activity in which a young person could find himself! The great Norwegian psychologist, Dr. Thorleif T. Hegge, headed the Research Department. There were others, but two, as the literature well demonstrates, became particularly significant in my life: Dr. Heinz Werner and Dr. Alfred A. Strauss. These two men, along with their wives, became important persons to me and to my wife, professionally and socially, and so remained until the two died. Strauss the idea man, Werner the laboratory scientist so well epitomized in Sinclair Lewis' *Arrowsmith*. Both were patient; both were thoughtful to suggest and to raise questions which had to be answered. Both were energetic and constantly pointed other directions in which my professional life might go—theirs! The inoculation took well, and their thinking has been mine for more than thirty years.

It was at the Training School, or because of the mutual experiences others had had at the school, that additional professional bricks were put into my career foundation. Dr. Samuel A. Kirk had been there just before me, as had Dr. Maurice Fouracre. The school thus became a conversation piece with these men, which developed into long-term interests in many other matters. Ruth Melcher Patterson, a research psychologist only recently retired from the Columbus State School, showed me much of what research with human beings was all about. Dr. Bluma Weiner, now of Yeshiva University, was organizing her significant professional life at the school at this time also. Dr. Newell Kephart was there. His association, like mine, with Werner and Strauss and their influence on his thinking is well known. Laura Lehtinen was, of course, beginning her career there at that time. These were my associates. Those were good years for me, and I profited from them immensely.

SYRACUSE YEARS, 1946–1966

The war closed; and Syracuse University, through a most remarkable dean, invited me to join the faculty and to begin to develop a center for the preparation of personnel to work with exceptional children. Although some special education had been provided by that university from time to time as early as 1937, 1946 marked the beginning of a major all-university emphasis on these problems. A distinguished faculty, a distinguished student body, and an outstanding series of curricula and a physical facility were ultimately created. Together with the University of Illinois, San Francisco State College, and Teachers' College, Columbia University, Syracuse University was preeminent for twenty years in the broad fields of special education and rehabilitation. These four institutions of higher education set the national pace and provided professors who ultimately staffed dozens of other university and college programs throughout the nation and the world.

Research

Whatever writing or research I have done throughout my professional career has been in addition to administrative and developmental responsibilities. This research has been possible only because of strong staff colleagues who could share some of my responsibilities and who were so strong that they provided their own leadership. Their strength made time for me to work with some students and to pursue my other interests as well—an enviable position for an administrator, for it means that personal desires and aspirations need not be shelved permanently.

Thus, in 1948, with the appearance of my first doctoral candidate (Dr. Jane Dolphin-Courtney), there began a series of dissertations and later personal research which was intended to corroborate much of what Werner and Strauss had done with exogenous mentally retarded boys. My interests, stimulated as I have said by Werner and Strauss, were in the direction of ascertaining what, if anything, they had observed in retarded youth which might be characteristic of intellectually normal but neurologically handicapped children and youth. Thus the task assigned to and accepted by Dolphin was to try to replicate as much as possible the early Strauss-Werner experiments with a relatively homogeneous group of intellectually normal cerebral-palsied children. At that time, 1948, not much was known about cerebral palsy. It was essentially seen as a single entity. The stimulation of Winthrop Morgan Phelps and others was just being felt. As a result, the Dolphin experimental group was not as homogeneous as would be required now, but nevertheless it did constitute an important pilot study for others quickly to follow. Resting her conclusions on a small sample of thirty children with a variety of subtypes of cerebral palsy, she still illustrated statistically significant difference between pairs and between her experimental group of cerebral-palsied children and a carefully matched group of children who were neurologically intact and who were all of normal intelligence as she defined normalcy, i.e., intelligence quotients above 75. This minimum level, however, was essentially the top cutoff point which Strauss and Werner had used with their exogenous retarded subjects. Dolphin found differences between her two groups of children; and she found marked similarities between the responses of her intellectually normal cerebral-palsied subjects and those of the retarded subjects of Werner and Strauss and their associates. Her findings (Dolphin, 1950) illustrated that the perceptual and perceptual-motor problems of neurologically handicapped children are not a function of mental retardation alone, but of some type of neurophysiological dysfunction.

Subsequently, a series of doctoral dissertations by Syracuse students began to provide a more inclusive understanding of the nature and scope of the problem which by now had become an obvious career concern of mine. Not all of these doctoral dissertations were done under my direction; many, as will be noted, were sponsored by other faculty colleagues: Elizabeth McKay, 1952 (Professor L. M. DiCarlo); Alfred Larr, 1955 (Professor L. M. DiCarlo); Merville Shaw, 1955; Matthew J. Trippe, 1957; Thomas J. Qualtere, 1957; Howard Norris, 1958; James Neeley, 1958 (Professor G. O. Johnson); Donald Y. Miller, 1958; Anthony Chiappone, 1963 (Professor G. O. Johnson); Eleanore Westhead, 1965 (Professor G. O. Johnson); James L. Paul, 1966; and John Garrett, 1967. Later, at the University of Michigan, more pieces of the mosaic were filled in through the dissertation efforts of outstanding students such as Daniel P. Hallahan, 1971; John Heckerl, 1971 (Professor William C. Morse); and Charles McNelly, 1973. Obviously, others at other universities have pursued these same issues and pursued them well, but the ones noted here are those which are particularly related to me and to my professional development.

If the findings of Dolphin were correct and if the perceptual disabilities noted in cerebral-palsied children were similar to the exogenous mentally retarded subjects, could other groups of neurologically handicapped children be likewise penalized? McKay's dissertation under DiCarlo's supervision at Syracuse had shown that children with certain types of organic deafness functioned like Dolphin's group. The relationship between this situation and aphasia began to become apparent. Shortly thereafter, Shaw examined a group of heterogeneous children with subtypes of epilepsy. He found that some of the characteristics of perceptual disturbance observed by Werner, Strauss, and Dolphin also are to be observed in some of the subgroups of epileptic children with which he worked. The die was now set, and it looked as if the problem we were studying was of a generic nature and certainly not related solely to a specific medical category.

About this time, 1954, a coincidence occurred which proved important to the field and to me professionally. The Association for the Aid of Crippled Children, Inc., a foundation based in New York City, made available to me a sum of money to begin to study a larger group of cerebral-palsied children. These funds were provided to push further the conclusions which Dolphin had obtained and to ascertain whether or not her findings typified all cerebral-palsied children or whether they were more specific to particular subtypes of the category. The Association announced this grant of money to me in the *New York Times,* and this announcement was read by Dr. Harry V. Bice, then clinical psychologist with the New Jersey Department of Health and its program for crippled children. Dr. Bice telephoned me a few days later, stating that he was also moving to do a piece of research in what appeared to be the same general area. Could we get together and discuss our interests with the possibility of collaboration? He had the children; I had the money, but few available children. This exchange of ideas resulted in a long and mutually satisfying professional relationship and an extensive research study concerned with figure-background relationships in the child. Although we ultimately had to go into eight states to find the population of children which we desired, Dr. Bice's careful clinical records on hundreds of cerebral-palsied children in New Jersey formed the nucleus of a group of intellectually normal cerebral-palsied children which eventually reached approximately 400. Earlier data which Bice had collected indicated that there are not significant sex differences insofar as perceptual disabilities were concerned, and thus it was not felt important to obtain groups of cerebral-palsied children homogeneous by sex.

The significant element with respect to this study was that two major subtypes of cerebral palsy were studied, namely spastic and athetoid. It was found that the great majority of such children can be characterized by the same type of perceptual disabilities as had characterized the children studied by Dolphin and by Werner and Strauss. More than 80 percent of the cerebral-palsied children were so characterized (Cruickshank, Bice, Wallen, & Lynch, 1965). Figure-background relationships were studied, because this psychological phenomenon is so closely related to forced responsiveness to stimuli, dissociation, intersensory integration, and other fundamental factors earlier recognized by those working with problems of organicity in adults. It provided a broad research umbrella to focus in on the problems of childhood.

M.R.–L.D. Relationship

Unwittingly we may have also contributed to a major present-day problem as well. While the research of the 1930s and 1940s had essentially been focused on mental retardation, we were trying to ascertain whether the observed characteristics with that early group also pertain to the intellectually normal. We did make that conclusion, and frequently we stressed the presence of these perceptual factors in the intellectually normal groups. Later this same issue was emphasized by us with the so-called *hyperactive* child. In 1963, when the Association for Children with Learning Disabilities was formed, the mentally retarded child was ruled out of the concerns of that group, perhaps partly because of an exclusion phrase which Dr. Samuel A. Kirk mentioned in one of his speeches to that group and also perhaps partially because of the emphasis we had been putting on the presence of perceptual disabilities in normal children.

Without anticipating the problems to ensue, a line of demarcation was drawn between mental retardation and learning disabilities—a horizontal line separating the two groups at approximately an intellectual level of I.Q. 80. National, state, and local definitions of learning disability reflect this error. In reality the line should be drawn vertically, if indeed there should be a line at all. Essentially what we know about learning disabilities of a perceptual nature in intellectually normal children is based upon the research done with exogenous mentally retarded children. Learning disabilities are characteristic of children and youth of any chronological age and of *any and all intellectual levels*. The artifact of differentiation between the two clinical groups is just that, a recent man-made artifact. It is illogical. We will discuss this later, but state here that the exclusion of the perceptually handicapped mentally retarded child from the specialized teaching and learning situations which are germane to his peculiar learning needs is an unnecessary tragedy, and the situation must be rectified quickly. That professionals permitted this situation to develop is a sad commentary; and a portion of that responsibility I fear is mine. But I do not accept it all, for certain.

The Cruickshank–Bice duo was joined by Dr. Norman E. Wallen, a statistician now of San Francisco State College. Later Karen S. Lynch, utilizing another large population of cerebral-palsied children under our supervision, also joined the research group and assisted in ascertaining the relationship of color, size of figure, and meaningfulness of figure and background, as factors in figure-ground differentiation and discrimination. About this same time, Wedell of England (see Wedell, 1973) corroborated some of my work in studies in which he also employed cerebral-palsied subjects. From the point of view of my own understanding of the nature of perceptual disabilities in neurologically handicapped children, we had sufficient, if not full, data on which to begin to consider seriously some educational and social implications of the findings.

At this time, however, Bice made available to me an unusual amount of his own clinical data for statistical treatment. Bice, for years a clinical psychologist working with cerebral-palsied children in New Jersey, had maintained exceedingly complete records on these children. He made available data on 1000 cerebral-palsied children to whom he had personally administered intelligence tests. He also gave me data on a large number of children to whom he had administered *Bender Gestalt* tests. Wallen, then a research associate, and Dr. Howard Norris, then a research assistant with me, analyzed these data statistically to ascertain what, if any, significance they contained. It was at this time that there was a significant controversy regarding the relationship of cerebral palsy and intelligence levels. The data which we jointly presented indicated unequivocally the high incidence of mental retardation in cerebral palsy and pointed up the fact that, for the most part, multiple handicaps are present in cerebral palsy. The data have been fully described elsewhere

(Cruickshank & Bice, 1966) and need not be discussed again here. Suffice to say that these data, together with those pertaining to perception in cerebral palsy, made it possible to isolate definitively where problems lay and where psychoeducational attacks had to be made.

The Brain-Injured Child

I have sometimes been criticized, perhaps appropriately, for the long-time use I have made of the term *brain-injured* in relation to what is more recently called *learning disabled.* There is a reason for this, if one considers the situation historically. In the period prior to 1960, professional people were struggling to find a term which satisfied the professions as a group. This was difficult, and still is. Strauss had spent much time on this problem also; and indeed, at one point in his struggle to find the appropriate English words, had referred to these children as "cripple-brained," hardly acceptable then or now. Other terms were being used without much success; and in 1960, there were few other than Kephart and me who were publishing in this field. Kephart's use of the term *slow learning* illustrates his effort to find a satisfactory set of words. I took the term *brain-injured,* in spite of its limitations and inaccuracies, primarily because it was unrelated to a specific medical category. It would not have been wise to relate the perceptual problems we were studying to a single category when our data in fact showed them to be a generic problem related probably to all neurological categories. For better or for worse, the term *brain injury* was used, and I employed it in the first of a series of books which we anticipated would appear over a period of time. These volumes did appear in the following order: *A Teaching Method for Brain Injured and Hyperactive Children* (with Bentzen, Ratzeberg, & Tannhauser, 1961); *The Teacher of Brain Injured Children: A Discussion of the Bases for Competency* (edited, 1966); *The Brain Injured Child in Home, School and Community* (1967); and finally, *The Preparation of Teachers of Brain-Injured Children* (with Junkala & Paul, 1968). With this series completed, each volume of which was related in numerous ways to the others, we have turned from the concept of brain injury to those terms more acceptable to current professional thought, even though these latter terms are far from satisfactory.

Interludes into Other Interests

Opportunities came my way during the Syracuse years to engage in professional work which went beyond my primary concern for brain-injured children or with perceptual disturbances. *A Study of Services to Blind Children in New York State* (with M. J. Trippe, 1959) bothered the Establishment considerably, but nevertheless was seen as a significant investigation by forward-looking professionals in that area of physical disability.

I have never felt that one person could be authoritative equally in all facets of work in the field of exceptionality, nor indeed in a single category. I have therefore often gone the route of an editor. Three volumes which began during my Syracuse years continue to maintain a significant position in professional preparation centers, namely, *Education for Exceptional Children and Youth* (coedited with Johnson, 1975); *Psychology of Exceptional Children and Youth* (1971), and *Cerebral Palsy: Its Individual and Community Problems* (1966). These experiences have continued to provide me a way of maintaining a close view of what is going on in the overall field of psychology and education for the exceptional individual. These volumes have made me keep abreast of what is happening in the whole field, while at the same time permitting me to continue in some depth with my special interests in the perceptual problems of children.

Another volume appeared in 1969 which was written as the result of frustration and anger. *Misfits in the Public Schools* (with Paul & Junkala, 1969) grew out of an evaluation of the programs begun under the NIMH grant for teacher preparation with brain-injured children. Although the administrators (to whom the teachers in the program were to report on their return to their school systems) were participants in the training program, the degree of administrative ineptitude, resistance, and adherence to the status quo caused many programs to fail, although highly skilled teachers were available. This administrative irresponsibility culminated in *Misfits,* a volume which focuses not on children or teachers, but on the administrators who know little of education and are the hurdles to effective programming in the public schools. I cannot say that the problem we spoke to is solved; perhaps it has even become worse. The volume provides a springboard for serious thinking and change by those who are disposed to be courageous and to place responsibility for failures where it belongs.

Although one additional Syracuse experience will be discussed shortly, the main events pertinent to this book which took place in my years at Syracuse University have been discussed. The Syracuse years stopped as abruptly as they had begun twenty-one years earlier when, like the problem posed in *Misfits,* it became apparent to me and to many others who left at that time that strong professional programs could no longer be pursued there either within my concept of academic freedom or with adequate administrative support. The University of Michigan opened up a significant opportunity for me as other universities did for many of my former colleagues.

The Status of the Field

In 1964 a family foundation in Philadelphia made available to me a large sum of money for the purpose of assessing any aspect of the field of education for what we were then calling brain-injured children. Teacher competency was paramount. Essentially what was a year-long seminar was organized, although the members met together for only three days toward the end of the experience. Historically, this was an important occasion. It included as active participants William C. Adamson, M.D., Ray H. Barsch, Ph.D., William M. Cruickshank, Ph.D., Elizabeth S. Freidus, Marianne Frostig, Ph.D., William H. Gaddes, Ph.D., James J. Gallagher, Ph.D., Riley W. Gardner, Ph.D., Gerald Getman, O.D., Herbert J. Grossman, M.D., Miriam P. Hardy, Ph.D., Newell C. Kephart, Ph.D., Peter Knoblock, Ph.D., William C. Morse, Ph.D., Sheldon R. Rappaport, Ph.D., Ralph M. Reitan, Ph.D., Charles R. Strother, Ph.D., and Miriam Tannhauser—all persons who at that time were at the cutting edge of work with perceptually handicapped children. Each individual prepared a paper on an assigned topic, in total covering essentially the whole field. These papers were exchanged, and each was subject to critique by each of the personnel in the group. The comments were provided to the member responsible for the paper. The whole group then met for three days to discuss the individual papers and the total problem intensively and to seek areas of common agreement or disagreement. Ultimately the papers were revised and edited and published in a document whose pertinence is as appropriate today as it was in 1966 when it appeared *(The Teacher of Brain Injured Children: A Discussion of the Bases for Competency).* This volume essentially drew together that which was pertinent at the time of the writing. Little if anything presented there has been refuted since.

While refutation has been minimal, if at all, expansion of the field has been great. The appearance of the term *learning disabilities* in 1963 opened a Pandora's box which has resulted in confusion, the phenomenon of the instant specialist, inappropriate definitions of the problem, and a major attempt by many to bring within the definition issues which are far removed from the initial concepts of perceptual disability. Until this situation is cleared up, there will continue to be confusion and inappropriate educational programs for children.

MICHIGAN YEARS, 1966–

Because of the confusion which exists related to learning disabilities and the frustrations which erroneous ideas regarding this problem bring to me and my associates, two new ventures were undertaken in an effort to bring some logic to the problem. Initially it seemed appropriate that if an historical overview of the field were prepared, it in itself might cause people to see the problem for what it is, particularly if such topics as "remedial reading" were not mentioned! Thus, in 1973, the *Psychoeducational Foundations of Learning Disabilities* was published (Hallahan & Cruickshank, 1973). This book attempted not only to bring together the historical perspectives, but also to review in some depth theoretical and experimental data essentially from the areas of visual-motor perception, memory, and attention. The focus of that text was primarily on visual perception and education. No efforts were made to explore, except superficially, issues of auditory perception, language and communication development, or the neurophysiological foundations of the field. Simultaneously, two additional volumes were planned and begun.

While the *Psychoeducational Foundations* brought perspective, and for the thoughtful reader provided a focus on what indeed *learning disability,* specifically defined, is; it was obvious to Dr. Hallahan and to me that more was needed. Once again, resorting to an editorial approach, senior researchers and theoreticians were solicited to participate in a major writing effort which would essentially bring together the multidisciplinary perspective needed in restructuring the field of learning disabilities. Thus, a two-volume set was prepared by an international writing team (Cruickshank & Hallahan, 1975). It concerns itself with both research and theory (Volume 2) and with the psychoeducational procedures resulting from research findings and theoretical concepts (Volume 1). In this writing effort the editors brought together not only psychologists and educators, each of whom wrote in their highly specialized field of expertise, but also a team representing nutrition, physiology, audiology, speech pathology, pediatrics, and other related specialties. Missing, however, from this effort are such specialties as ophthalmology, optometry, and a few others which might have been included if paper and lead shortages and the high costs of publication had made possible a third volume. This may come later.

These three publications—1966, 1973, and 1975—constitute a personal effort to maintain order in a confusing field and to provide a perspective to professional personnel who are logically attempting to provide services in both the school and home situations to perceptually handicapped children with learning disabilities. Sufficient data are at hand now, although research in great quantities is much needed, to turn educational services for these children around full circle, were it not for the inertia of educational systems, the lack of competent university personnel in this field in teacher education programs, and the resulting lack of a corps of well-prepared teachers for these children.

Competencies for Those Who Teach

If one refers to our publication of 1966, to which earlier reference has been made, clear-cut statements of competencies for teachers are outlined. A method of preparing such teachers, possibly needing some modification to insure greater strength, has also been available (Cruickshank, Junkala, & Paul, 1968) for some time. The focus of these next few paragraphs will be on our concern for an adequately prepared teaching corps. Obviously we believe what is said regarding teachers is essential as a basis of knowledge for the professors who prepare them.

The nineteen specialists who participated in the 1966 seminar on teacher competency were essentially unanimous regarding the competencies needed by teachers. While the matter of definition of the problem will be considered later, it was felt that the issue of definition was essential to the teacher's understanding of his or her role. Similarly, much was made of the personality characteristics required of a teacher of these children. Specifically, however, with respect to competencies, we stressed both general and in-depth knowledge on such matters as the relationship of education and medicine, the totality of good elementary instruction, special information regarding reading instruction, mathematical concepts and instruction, and communication and communication disorders. It was also felt by the seminar group that every teacher of perceptually handicapped children with learning disabilities needs to have a firm grasp of problems related to cognition, perception, and motor development of children. We felt that teachers need knowledge in the areas of visuomotor development and audiomotor development, psychodiagnosis and evaluation, handedness, finger localization, and cerebral dominance, and the neurophysiological base of the perceptual disorders. A working acquaintance with issues relating to psychopharmacology was stressed, because teachers often have to work with some children who are medicated. Since most of these children come to the teacher with emotional overlays to an already serious problem, teachers must know about emotional disorders and know something of the values of psychotherapy and pediatric psychiatry. Above all, or at least equal to the other areas, they must know about the dynamics and operation of an interdisciplinary team approach to these children, and how such a team is most appropriately utilized in behalf of the child.

If these are the skills, competencies, and understandings required of teachers, it goes without saying that they must also be the competencies of college professors who purport to prepare teachers. The lack of qualified college faculty members in this field is one of the most serious issues facing the profession, from my point of view.

In 1968 a suggestion to attack this problem was laid before the appropriate federal agency within the United States Department of Health, Education and Welfare. To date that correspondence has yet to receive a response, positive or negative. Since the federal establishment appeared disinterested in this aspect of one of the most crucial problems facing it, other steps were initiated. In May, 1972, prior to the onset of the serious and terminal illness of Dr. Newell C. Kephart, he and I met in Denver to discuss this problem. We agreed that without federal funds, it still might be possible to develop a two-year program for approximately fifty mature college professors who were anxious to develop their skills and their knowledge in this crucial area, and who, after the training, would be able to return to their colleges or universities as much more highly prepared faculty members. Obviously federal funding would have been helpful, but it appeared also that foundations or indeed parent organizations might well assist in this important effort. Unfortunately the exchange of ideas, the conversations, and our plans had to be terminated—at least temporarily—for Dr. Kephart's illness and death precluded further action. This is now a matter of the future, and one in which I hope to have a part. The issue is not dead in any degree; it is temporarily dormant. Perhaps the writing of this personal resumé will be sufficient stimulus to bring it to life again. The need remains an even greater urgency than it was nearly ten years ago.

DEFINITION

One of the problems in the so-called field of learning disabilities is that of definition of the problem itself. Once we knew what this was; but as the problem has become more and more popularized, as hundreds have become specialists, often with less than minimum training, as new terminology has been added in an attempt to clarify the issue, the problem has become more and more confused. In much of my writing I have bemoaned the situation and hoped for clarity. I must admit until recently I have not contributed significantly to the solution of this problem, but have merely commented on the tragedy of a situation which has had too many unfortunate terms appended to it.

I see absolutely no value in the term *minimal cerebral dysfunction,* which became popular in the early sixties as the result of a series of task force reports sponsored by the National Institutes of Health. The term is misleading, for there is little minimal which can be conceptualized regarding the problem. I suppose the term utilized, i.e., *minimal,* was used to differentiate it from the major motor problems in the neurological dysfunction of cerebral palsy. However, even the perceptually handicapped children with learning problems, about which we write, often have both gross and fine motor problems, although they are in no sense similar in degree to those of cerebral-palsied children. The words *cerebral dysfunction,* although somewhat more accurate than the word *minimal,* nevertheless place this issue in a medical context which is not related to the educational arena, in which the predominant therapeutic intervention will take place.

Furthermore, such terms as *hyperactive, hyperkenetic, organic,* and their counterparts—including *brain injured*—are less than satisfactory and are characterizations for the most part, rather than being definitive of the problem per se. *Dyslexia,* a term used to describe a legitimate clinical problem, is inappropriate when it is applied to all of these children, as some are wont to do. The definition by exclusion which has been adopted by the United States Office of Education and its subsidiary bureaus only recognizes the existence of the problem. In several aspects it is erroneous in terms of generally accepted knowledge and understanding of the problem.

The term *learning disability* itself is far from satisfactory. It served an important purpose in 1963 when it was adopted as the banner under which the significant parent organizations throughout the United States could fly. It was not a term adopted thoughtlessly. It was a term agreed upon then by essentially all of the leaders in the field in 1963, including myself. It is positive in its connotation. It puts children's best foot forward. In use, however, it has permitted misinterpretations. Legions of problems have been pushed within its parameters; legions of people have rushed to join the movement and have immediately become specialists in learning disabilities, when indeed their background, orientation, experience, and their problem area often was not that which gave birth to the movement.

Lest I be accused of rigidity and failure to adjust to the times, let me quickly disallow that accusation. I am concerned that children be served. I am concerned that the concept of learning disability as originally espoused meant what we describe here, not what we see today throughout the nation and often the world. The idea held by those attending the 1966 seminar, for example, by those who at the request of parents met in a hotel room in Chicago in 1964 to consider and adopt the term, and by many who have written on this problem since, has been of a much more concise definition and understanding of this problem. There is a difference between children with learning disabilities and children with problems of learning which are the result of poor teaching, emotional problems coincident with the start of formal schooling, some environmental presses, unfortunate parent-child relationships, and similar insults to child development.

The Wepman Committee

Very recently there has appeared a report of a series of national committees concerned with terminology and classification related to exceptional children. This report is the result of a grant made by the United States Office of Education to Dr. Nicholas Hobbs (Hobbs, 1974). Hobbs organized a series of committees to examine the confusing problems of terminology related to the total field of special education. One such committee was under the chairmanship of Dr. Joseph Wepman of the University of Chicago, and in addition consisted of Dr. Ann Morency (University of Chicago), Dr. Cynthia Deutsch (New York University), Dr. Charles Strother (University of Washington), and myself. This committee was charged with looking at the issue of learning disability.

Although the members of the committee came from different orientations and held differing points of view on some matters, we established unanimity in an astonishingly short time. There was no question as to the essential locus of the problem, i.e., neurological; and there was no hesitation to speak of this problem in terms of what it actually is, i.e., perceptual or perceptual-motor. The committee sought to develop a definition by inclusion rather than to perpetuate the definitions by exclusion which in reality describe a situation and do not define a clinical problem. That I had a small part in this is something of which I am professionally proud. It is with the background of this committee's efforts that in this chapter

I have referred to these children as *perceptually handicapped children with learning disabilities.* It is for this reason that the most recent Cruickshank-Hallahan publications have been titled *Perceptual and Learning Disabilities in Children.*

The Issue of Perceptual Dysfunction is Central

Quoting and occasionally paraphrasing from the committee's final draft, I, together with the other members of the committee under Wepman's leadership, define the problem of these children from a psychoeducational orientation.

The committee members, in their report to Hobbs, stated that the term refers to children at any age and noted that the problem is to be found in individuals of *all levels of intellectual capacity.*

This is the first time that a national group has taken the stand that this is a problem not just restricted to children of normal intellectual ability. I find this statement encouraging for the personal concern I have had for years regarding this issue and about which I have spoken and written many times. The committee report stated that these children demonstrate deficiencies in academic achievement (and especially as often, but not mentioned by the committee members specifically, in social adjustment), because of perceptual or perceptual-motor handicaps, "regardless of etiology or other contributing factors." The inclusive nature of the definition is seen in the committee's statement which continues to point out that these children are those who show inadequate ability "(1) to recognize fine differences between auditory and visual discriminating features underlying the sounds used in speech and the orthographic forms used in reading; (2) to retain and recall those discriminated sounds and forms in both short and long memory; (3) to order them sequentially both in sensory and motor acts; (4) to distinguish figure-ground relationships; (5) to recognize spatial and temporal orientation; (6) to obtain closure; (7) to integrate sensory information; (8) and to relate what is perceived to specific motor functions." It might here be observed that insofar as the preparation of teachers and diagnosticians is concerned, there is a total course contained in this definition which should be the core of a curriculum leading to specialization in this field.

The reference point made regarding this group of children is that of perception. It is logical then to speak of these children as *perceptually handicapped with specific learning disabilities.* If this point of view is adopted, much of that which clutters the professional perspective as we now appropriately view it will be dropped. That should also clean up the definitions of those types of childhood learning problems which are not produced by perceptual handicaps and thus also produce clearer thinking for what those issues really are. It is perfectly obvious to me that to move in the logical direction which we here espouse will require changes in definitional laws and regulations at the federal, state, and local levels.

These changes should be relatively easy to bring about if people are willing to see this problem for what it really is.

STRUCTURE AS A TOOL FOR LEARNING

My position with respect to the opportunities for learning by perceptually handicapped children with learning disabilities is known. This position has been described often enough to warrant only a relatively brief exposition as a part of this personal recital. It is a theoretical position, however, which is logical, which has support in terms of the known characteristics of the children affected, and which has educational implications. These implications are closely related to the psychology of the perceptually handicapped.

I make no apologies for the extent to which I have obviously relied on ideas from Werner, Strauss, and Lehtinen. This has been acknowledged, as it was by Kephart and some others, for many years. We took from the famous three that which was subsequently found to be valid with children of higher intellectual capacity than those with whom the original work was done. I extended concepts of structure as far as they appropriately would go, in behalf of the learning potential of the children. And we added to the original ideas of Werner and Strauss those of our own which, through clinical practice and experience, proved to be significant. The concept of relationship structure, first voiced in this regard by Rappaport, was also incorporated into our orientation, because it obviously was a significant concept which had not been considered previously or at least had not been written about.

What have we learned since the early days of Werner and Strauss? We have learned that there are identifiable clinical (perceptual) differences among and between children, and we have learned that some children demonstrate significant perceptual disabilities which prevent them from learning adequately. Referring to the earlier discussion of the definition of this problem to which we strongly adhere and give support, perception is neurological. If there is perceptual dysfunction, there must be neurological dysfunction, *whether or not* with the crude instrumentation available presently to both neurology or psychology, it is possible to identify such a neurological base. This has to be assumed, if perception is an issue. Perception is not a thing unto itself, separate and apart from the neurological system of humans or animals. From the point of view of education, the definitive neurological diagnosis is not an absolute essential. It is enough to know that perceptual disabilities can be identified by competent personnel. These dysfunctions can be described in terms of their impact on adjustment and learning.

We know that it is possible through psychology and education, through audiology and speech pathology, and possibly through other professional avenues, to so exactly describe the perceptual characteristics of a child that a prescription (as described by Peter, 1965) or an educational blueprint (as I have described the problem, Cruickshank, et al., 1961) can be prepared. We also know that it is possible to match this prescription or blueprint with an educational methodology, often on a one-to-one basis, to the end that success experiences can be substituted for failure experiences in the life of the child. Kephart referred to this relationship as the *psychomotor match;* I have described other aspects of this matching concept as the *psychoeducational* match.

We have learned over these years that to meet the needs of these children fully a permissive environment is not helpful, but that planned structure is—structure which is conceptualized and used as a tool of learning, not as restriction or control. Permissiveness requires the capacity to make choices. Children who have had a failure history which often started a few moments after birth (possibly before birth) have not had a sufficient base to make socially appropriate choices on a continuous basis. Permissive environments with these children usually lead to continued catastrophic trial-and-error behavior. Some have spoken of their behavior as *choreiform,* an observation we too have often witnessed, a characteristic which we feel is, at one and the same time, both *internally as well as externally produced.* Structure involves a total concept, as again we have recently described (Cruickshank, in Cruickshank & Hallahan, 1975, Vol. I). This totality includes five major facets *all of which must be employed simultaneously*: (a) environmental structure, (b) spatial structure, (c) programmatic structure, (d) relationship structure between child and adult, and (e) structured teaching materials which are in keeping with the requisites of the psychoeducational match.

A sixth factor is essential. If failure is to be minimized (or prevented entirely from our perspective), then teaching efforts must be initiated at a level so primitive that the child cannot help but succeed. We are not advocating in any degree or sense the concepts of "neurological reorganization" or "patterning" which have been advocated by others. We are stating that initial successful learning may have to be started at levels much lower than that expected of a given chronological or mental age and may in the beginning have to be very mechanistic and segmented. Success, however, has a significant impact on motivation, attention span, and relationships with adults. Multiple success experiences, which can quite easily be provided for and experienced by the child over a period of time, constitute the first steps toward successful adjustment, reintegration into the regular school program, and function within a more permissive social situation—all of these being primary objectives of the educational program.

Obviously the factors which have been mentioned here constitute the operational mechanisms of a program. These must be based upon a thorough working knowledge of what is currently known regarding visual perception, auditory perception, tactile or haptic perception, and, most important, regarding the growing knowledge of *intersensory organization*. Teaching materials, teaching approaches, and experiences for children grow out of an understanding of these features of perceptual disability. This applies to all aspects of sensory input and output, irrespective of the modality under consideration. Although much less is known or understood regarding the issues of hemispheric dominance, midline reference point, localization and finger agnosia, and self-concept and body image, each of these factors has a literature and a content. These areas must be understood insofar as they can be in the light of the present available information. They must be considered when dealing with such mundane learning experiences as peg boards, eye-hand coordination tasks, handwriting, eating, dressing, buttoning, *ad infinitum*. At no time can any of the factors—those which we have here stressed and others which are also reported in the literature—be ignored in the day-to-day thoughtful planning for the child's progress.

The reader will note that the basic theme of what I have here described as my operational orientation toward children with perceptual disabilities and learning disabilities is in considerable degree that which we described as early as 1951 (Cruickshank & Dolphin). I have occasionally been asked if I have changed my point of view regarding the education of these children. The reply is an emphatic "no." The issue is not one of perseveration of an idea or theme, but of rational adherence to a logical concept which has been proven of value to children on hundreds of occasions in practical and clinical settings. It is a concept widely held and replicated in school systems. There is no reason to change fundamental concepts, only a reason to add to the concepts as new research and new data are forthcoming from many sources. Research of a longitudinal nature is needed. We do not need the segmented short-term research on a single aspect of the approach which has unfortunately characterized the literature in the past three or four years. This is not helpful, only confusing.

It is obvious that if programmatic structure is to be achieved for a child, i.e., the psychoeducational match, task analysis must also be employed as a part of a continuous process of assessment (Junkala, 1972). Task analysis, not by any means a new concept, is an absolute essential to all diagnostic teaching. This has been stressed by Kirk and his associates, and is basic to the concept and use of the *Illinois Test of Psycholinguistic Abilities*. It is a concept which is imbedded in the early writings of Werner, Strauss, Lehtinen, and Peter, and which I have stressed in principle since the beginning of my writing activities in this field. Junkala's refinements and clear exposition regarding the emphasis which must be given to this point of view are fundamental and significant. In this concept also is to be found another major strand of emphasis for teacher education.

THE INTERDISCIPLINARY CONCEPT

The therapeutic intervention program is recognized to be essentially one of education—new teaching, not remedial education. We have stated many times that one does not remediate a vacuum. Traditional remedial education has little place in the education of children with perceptual handicaps which have resulted in specific learning disabilities. Every teacher must have background information and understanding regarding perception, cognition, and task analysis in order to assist not only all of the children for whom they have a responsibility, but in particular those children whose perceptual handicaps are not so great as to require specialized clinical teaching. This number, however, is probably less than usually assumed, although no epidemiological studies have been completed on this problem. If a perceptual handicap exists, one can predict that learning disabilities will occur. Therefore, even "mild" problems of this nature should receive early and intensive attention by educators. We state again, as we have many times elsewhere, that general teacher education must include basic understanding of the essential elements related to perceptual disabilities in order that teachers can deal with many if not most of these children in the normal classroom situation before problems in learning become accentuated. These children are likely to be found in every classroom of the nation, many such children in some classrooms.

I first wrote about a logical program of integrating some exceptional children into regular school grades in 1955. The present fad of "mainstreaming" is not a solution to the educational and adjustment problems of these children, first because teachers generally know nothing about their education and nurture, and second because the very nature of the general classroom itself accentuates some children's learning disabilities (Cruickshank, 1974). Tens of thousands of exceptional children are not receiving their just educational due as a result of the current thoughtless adherence to a concept of mainstreaming which violates not only the learning needs of many children, but also their social and emotional needs. Although parents and general educators in large numbers have espoused this concept, the thoughtless application of it to children in need is obviously producing havoc in classrooms and in the children's lives. A backlash of protest is in the making and predictably will be felt. Both general and special educators have only themselves to thank for this unfortunate situation which they allowed to occur. The solution to the education of children with these problems lies elsewhere than in the so-called mainstream.

I prefer at this time to recognize the needs of all teachers for basic information about this problem, as we have here stated. The issue of the clinical teacher and the "resource teacher" is another matter and is of greater concern to me. Whether or not the term *resource teacher* is appropriate is open to question. Gallagher's (1960) concept of *tutorial* relationship between a child and a teacher is a more accurate description of what should happen, whether in a "resource room" or in another setting by any other name. In some school systems the clinical teaching is done in a special classroom for children whose learning needs are more extreme. In any approach, however, the teacher is the central figure, hopefully assisted by an educational aide and a team of volunteers—both men and women.

The educator cannot function alone. Personnel from other specialties are essential in this program. Our experience has convinced us, however, that the typical team approach is not appropriate, i.e., one in which the educator holds the central classroom position and speech therapists, psychotherapists, psychiatrists, and educational specialists (physical education, art, music, etc.) or others draw a child out of the classroom for special treatments from time to time. One of the characteristics of perceptually handicapped children is their often-observed difficulty in relating to adults. To assist the child with this difficulty, a good learning situation must be provided. If the child is asked not only to adjust to a teacher and to an aide, but also to a team of specialists who are attempting to assist or assess him or her, it may be quite a bit more than can easily be accepted. The breakdown which takes place usually will occur in the classroom, because there the child knows that he has an adult present who is used to explosions from him; and he will find security from that adult in his emotional tantrum. Often there is a difference of opinion about a given child's adjustment between the specialist, who has the child alone in a tutorial relationship, and the teacher, who is constantly dealing with a group of children. The fact of the matter is that the specialist sees the child in a situation which is dominated by the adult. It is a compliment to the teacher when the child feels he can explode in the classroom. The child feels enough security with his teacher to strike out emotionally in that setting, something often he does not feel possible in the one-to-one setting with a specialist.

The conclusion is that it is helpful to all if the number of adults to whom the child must adjust is kept to a minimum, particularly during the early months when an attempt is being made to substitute success for failure. This means, in our experience, that the interdisciplinary team must be utilized in a different way.

We have found it is more satisfactory to have the children remain with their teacher for the total school day insofar as possible. Specialists observe a child or a group of children and then feed the teacher ideas, suggestions, or "prescriptions" for special therapeutic interventions which the teacher can carry out as a part of the classroom procedures. To accomplish this change in the function of "specialists," three things are required. First, the specialist must learn how to observe children in a group setting and make definitive decisions as to ways in which speech communication, psychotherapeutic concepts, or other ideas can be integrated by the teacher into the child's life experience. Second, the class day for the children may need to be shortened somewhat in order to provide time within the school day for the specialist and the teacher to converse and to pass ideas, based on the observations, from one to the other. Third, there absolutely must be mutual respect developed between specialists and teachers. They must avoid competing and make a joint effort to seek successful outcomes for children. Nothing will happen except tragedy if specialists talk down to teachers, if specialists or teachers criticize one another to their colleagues, if differences of opinion are allowed to develop to the point where there are continuing tensions. This will not be helpful to anyone involved—child, teacher, specialist, or parents. The appropriate use of team personnel in the manner we are describing will be satisfying both economically and professionally. It will provide a basis for motivation to each of the significant individuals in the educational constellation. This approach has been more fully described in our writing regarding the now-famous Montgomery County, Maryland, program (Cruickshank, et al., 1961) and in subsequent publications (Cruickshank, 1967; Cruickshank, Junkala, & Paul, 1968).

Interdisciplinary teams are not easy to establish, as I only too well know. *Time* is an absolute requisite for success. Founded on trust and faith among and between members, common agreed-upon goals must be conceptualized. Territorial concepts traditionally established by the professions have to be abrogated. Concepts of disciplinary equality must be a primary article in the charter. Recognition of areas of disciplinary *responsibility* does not violate disciplinary *equality*. At the same time, the team members must recognize that the team functioning within an educational setting with perceptually handicapped children has a primary educational focus; and all actions of the team members, collectively and individually, must be toward that goal. Under these rubrics, the children will progress. Many of these children should return to the regular grades, not as mainstreamers appended to a regular class, but as essentially nonexceptional children—children who will often be able to function at age in grade with little assistance.

DIRECTIONS AHEAD

We have written recently regarding the needs in the future for research (Hallahan & Cruickshank, 1973), and what I might state here would, in large measure, be redundant. There are some issues which will not suffer by redundancy, however, and I shall stress them here, whether new or repetitive.

The question of definition of the problem may well be on the road to settlement, although certainly time will be required to reach anything like a universal adoption. That will happen eventually, without question. There is, however, a second major problem, which pertains to the number of children about which we speak. There is an urgent need for both good epidemiological and good demographic studies to be undertaken and completed to provide some accurate notion regarding the scope and nature of the problem. It is my understanding that such studies are being planned at the time of this writing; hence the time may not be too far off when we will have some firm figures. Estimates of the number of children for whom planning must be done varies all the way from the figure of 1 percent of the elementary school population stated (without data) by the United States Office of Education to astronomical figures proferred by groups with vested interests of one sort or another. Local boards of education are hampered by the lack of data. State legislatures are making educational provisions for these children with no accurate data on which to appropriate funds. The national congress, trying to respond to the needs of citizen constituents and professional groups, is rightfully troubled by the unavailability of any hard data. Progress on all fronts is halting and hesitant, because data on which projections can be made are lacking. From a practical point of view, this is a most urgent problem. Until these data are at hand, delivery systems for services to children and their families will be ineffective at all levels of government. We have often stated that research is needed to corroborate everything which we and other professionals say we know. This is not simply a charitable position; it is a necessity. Global, long-term, and carefully supervised psychological and educational studies of various treatment modes are essential to planning for this and subsequent generations of perceptually handicapped children with learning disabilities. Such investigations are needed not only in terms of educational programming and the concepts of structure which we particularly espouse, but in all aspects of the several sensory modalities with special emphasis on the issues of intersensory integration. This will involve basic animal laboratory research, which is now being done, but which must be continued, expanded, and accelerated.

Studies are needed in an area which two decades ago was not seriously considered in respect to the present problem, i.e., studies of a genetic nature. There is sufficient reference to this problem appearing in the literature as now to warrant a major early thrust in this direction. Genetic studies are difficult to do, because of the uncontrolled nature of achievement data in earlier generations related specifically to that of the child presently under consideration. But nevertheless, long-term, extensive studies of numbers of family constellations are needed both to gain new knowledge regarding etiology in some instances and also to possibly prevent the problem in the future.

Three issues then appear to me to warrant immediate financial investments on the part of government, foundations, and personnel: epidemiological and demographic studies, revalidation of that which we know today, and genetic studies related to perceptual and learning dysfunction. There are other areas of needed investigation which I will merely list: research into the valid use of medication to control behavior of young children, research into the issue of biochemical imbalances in children as these may be related to severe perceptual and learning disabilities, research into the possible relationship between hyperactivity (a characteristic of a great majority of the children about whom we write) and the ingestion of artificial food colorings and additives. Research is likewise needed on a much broader ecological front. Why is it that so many children (such a high percentage of children) coming from deprived areas of large cities function behaviorally as if they were perceptually handicapped? Is this due to the foul air constantly sucked into their lungs and bodies within their substandard living arrangements? Is it due to environmental deprivation of another sort, about which Cravioto and DeLicardie (1975) so eloquently write? Is it related to nutritional deprivation at either a prenatal or postnatal age or both? These are not easy answers to come by, but Cravioto has shown a way in which data can be accrued, and his techniques can be applied to other settings.

Research is needed in new ways of diagnosing these problems. The techniques of diagnosis within the field of neurology and psychology are still in their infancy insofar as the history of the profession is concerned, and they can generally be defined as crude, particularly when applied to living organisms, animals or humans. Is there a future for holography as a diagnostic technique, a technique which is very recent and has not been employed with animals or humans? We are not experts in this new field, but our observations of it prompt us to think of its potential in this regard. It is a problem of the future in which holographers, neurologists, and psychologists must join forces to investigate.

SUMMARY

When I look back over my professional life to the period of the late 1930s, the growth in understanding of the problems about which we here write is seen as staggering. Terrible mistakes have been made. Promises to parents have not been kept. There is confusion in the field at this time to an extent which almost makes the total problem often appear beyond the point of salvage. The field has grown too fast on too little data with too few appropriately prepared professional personnel. Many professions are today seen as rushing to make this field their own—education probably where it rightfully belongs, psychology, pediatrics, neurology, the communication fields. The "territorial imperatives" of the professions must cease. There is, to the contrary, a need for a united front by many professions working together as equals on a common problem. There are careers of research begging to be taken up by competent young persons from many professional fields, but they cannot be selfishly pursued to the exclusion of others.

REFERENCES

Bice, H. V., & Cruickshank, W. M. The evaluation of intelligence. In W. M. Cruickshank (Ed.), *Cerebral palsy.* (2nd ed.) Syracuse: Syracuse University Press, 1966.

Chiappone, A. D. A comparative investigation of the associative learning processes between educable mentally handicapped children with and without perceptual disorders. Unpublished doctoral dissertation, Syracuse University, 1963.

Cravioto, J., & DeLicardie, E. Environmental and nutritional deprivation in learning disabilities. In W. M. Cruickshank & D. P. Hallahan (Eds.), *Perceptual and learning disabilities in children.* Syracuse: Syracuse University Press, 1975.

Cruickshank, W. M. (Ed.) *The teacher of brain-injured children: A discussion of the bases for competency.* Syracuse: Syracuse University Press, 1966.

Cruickshank, W. M. *The brain injured child in home, school and community.* Syracuse: Syracuse University Press, 1967.

Cruickshank, W. M. (Ed.) *Psychology of exceptional children and youth.* (3rd ed.) Englewood Cliffs, N.J.: Prentice-Hall, 1971.

Cruickshank, W. M. The false hope for integration. *The slow learning child,* 1974, **21,** 67.

Cruickshank, W. M., Bentzen, F., Ratzeburg, F., & Tannhauser, M. *A teaching method for brain injured and hyperactive children.* Syracuse: Syracuse University Press, 1961.

Cruickshank, W. M., & Bice, H. V. Personality characteristics. In W. M. Cruickshank (Ed.), *Cerebral palsy.* (2nd ed.) Syracuse: Syracuse University Press, 1966.

Cruickshank, W. M., Bice, H. V., Wallen, N. E., & Lynch, K. S. *Perception and cerebral palsy.* (2nd ed.) Syracuse: Syracuse University Press, 1965.

Cruickshank, W. M., & Dolphin, J. E. The educational implications of psychological studies of cerebral palsy children. *Exceptional Children,* 1951, **17,** 1–9.

Cruickshank, W. M., & Hallahan, D. P. (Eds.) *Perceptual and learning disabilities in children.* Vol. 1. *Psychoeducational procedures.* Vol. 2. *Research and theory.* Syracuse: Syracuse University Press, 1975.

Cruickshank, W. M., & Johnson, G. O. (Eds.) *Education of exceptional children and youth.* (3rd ed.) Englewood Cliffs, N.J.: Prentice-Hall, 1975.

Cruickshank, W. M., Junkala, J. B., & Paul, J. L. *The preparation of teachers of brain-injured children.* Syracuse: Syracuse University Press, 1968.

Cruickshank, W. M., Paul, J. L., & Junkala, J. B. *Misfits in the public schools.* Syracuse: Syracuse University Press, 1969.

Cruickshank, W. M., & Trippe, M. J. *A study of services to blind children in New York State.* Syracuse: Syracuse University Press, 1959.

Dolphin, J. E. A study of certain aspects of the psychopathology of cerebral palsy children. Unpublished doctoral dissertation, Syracuse University, 1950.

Gallagher, J. J. *The tutoring of brain-injured mentally retarded children: An experimental study.* Springfield, Ill.: Charles C Thomas, 1960.

Garrett, J. A study of gustation and olfaction in brain injured children. Unpublished doctoral dissertation, Syracuse University, 1967.

Hallahan, D. P. Learning disabilities in historical and psychoeducational perspective. Unpublished doctoral dissertation, University of Michigan, 1971.

Hallahan, D. P., & Cruickshank, W. M. *Psychoeducational foundations of learning disabilities.* Englewood Cliffs, N.J.: Prentice-Hall, 1973.

Heckerl, J. R. Integration and ordering of bisensory stimuli in dyslexic children. Unpublished doctoral dissertation, University of Michigan, 1971.

Hobbs, N. (Ed.) *Issues in the classification of children.* San Francisco: Jossey Bass Publishers, 1974.

Junkala, J. B. Task analysis and instructional alternatives. *Academic Therapy,* 1972, **8**, 33–40.

Larr, A. An experimental investigation of the perceptual and conceptual abilities of children in residential schools for the deaf. Unpublished doctoral dissertation, Syracuse University, 1955.

McKay, E. An exploratory study of the psychological effects of a severe hearing impairment. Unpublished doctoral dissertation, Syracuse University, 1952.

McNelly, C. H. Auditory speech discrimination under various background noise conditions of learning disabled, brain damaged, and normal boys. Unpublished doctoral dissertation, University of Michigan, 1973.

Miller, D. Y. A comparative study of exogenous and endogenous mentally retarded boys on some aspects of the reading process. Unpublished doctoral dissertation, Syracuse University Press, 1958.

Neeley, J. A study of the relationship of figure-background differences and school achievement in cerebral palsied children. Unpublished doctoral dissertation, Syracuse University, 1958.

Norris, H. J. An exploration of the relation of certain theoretical constructs to a behavioral syndrome of brain pathology. Unpublished doctoral dissertation, Syracuse University. 1958.

Paul, J. L. The effects of physical climate on the classroom behavior of children. Unpublished doctoral dissertation, Syracuse University, 1966.

Peter, L. J. *Prescriptive teaching.* New York: McGraw-Hill, 1965.

Qualtere, T. J. An investigation of the relationship between visual figure-background disturbance and performance on *Raven's Progressive Matrices Test* in cerebral palsy children. Unpublished doctoral dissertation, Syracuse University, 1957.

Shaw, M. E. A study of some aspects of perception and conceptual thinking in idiopathic epileptic children. Unpublished doctoral dissertation, Syracuse University, 1955.

Trippe, M. J. A study of the relationship between visual-perceptual ability and selected personality variables on a group of cerebral palsy children. Unpublished doctoral dissertation, Syracuse University, 1957.

Wedell, K. Learning and perceptuo-motor disabilities in children. London: Wiley, 1973.

Westhead, E. Job aptitudes and visual figure-background perception among educable mentally retarded adolescents. Unpublished doctoral dissertation, Syracuse University, 1965.

A SELECTED BIBLIOGRAPHY OF WORKS
BY WILLIAM M. CRUICKSHANK

Cruickshank, W. M. Arithmetic vocabulary of mentally retarded boys. *Exceptional Children,* 1946, **14,** 65–69.

Cruickshank, W. M. Arithmetic work habits of mentally retarded boys. *American Journal of Mental Deficiency,* 1948, **52,** 318–30.

Cruickshank, W. M. Relation of physical disability to fear and guilt feelings. *Child Development,* 1951, **22,** 292–98.

Cruickshank, W. M. The multiple handicapped cerebral palsied child. *Exceptional Children,* 1953, **20,** 16–22.

Cruickshank, W. M. Review of "Studies in reading and arithmetic in mentally retarded boys." *Exceptional Children,* 1956, **23,** 120–22.

Cruickshank, W. M. Realistic educational programs for most cerebral palsy children. *The Crippled Child,* 1958, **37,** 6–7, 22.

Cruickshank, W. M. (Ed.) *The teacher of brain-injured children: A discussion of the bases for competency.* Syracuse: Syracuse University Press, 1966.

Cruickshank, W. M. *The brain-injured child in home, school, and community.* Syracuse: Syracuse University Press, 1967.

Cruickshank, W. M. (Ed.) *Psychology of exceptional children and youth.* (3rd ed.), Englewood Cliffs, N.J.: Prentice-Hall, 1971.

Cruickshank, W. M. Special education, the community and constitutional issues. In D. L. Walker and D. P. Howard (Eds.), *Special education: Instrument of change in education for the '70s.* Selected papers from the University of Virginia Lecture Series, 1971. Pp. 5–22.

Cruickshank, W. M. Some issues facing the field of learning disability. *Journal of Learning Disabilities,* 1972, **5,** 380–88.

Cruickshank, W. M. (Ed.) *Cerebral palsy: Its individual and community problems.* (3rd ed.) Syracuse: Syracuse University Press, 1967.

Cruickshank, W. M., Bentzen, F., Ratzburg, F., & Tannhausser, M. *A teaching method for brain-injured and hyperactive children.* Syracuse: Syracuse University Press, 1961.

Cruickshank, W. M., Bice, H. V., Wallen, N. E., & Lynch, K. S. *Perception and cerebral palsy: A study of the figure-background relationship.* (2nd ed.) Syracuse: Syracuse University Press, 1965.

Cruickshank, W. M., & Dolphin, J. E. The educational implications of psychological studies of cerebral palsy children. *Exceptional Children,* 1951, **17,** 1–9.

Cruickshank, W. M., & Hallahan, D. P. (Eds.) *Perceptual and learning disabilities in children.* Vol. 1. *Psychoeducational procedures.* Vol. 2. *Research and theory.* Syracuse: Syracuse University Press, 1975.

Cruickshank, W. M., & Johnson, G. O. (Eds.) *Education of exceptional children and youth.* (3rd ed.) Englewood Cliffs, N.J.: Prentice-Hall, 1975.

Cruickshank, W. M., Junkala, J. B., & Paul, J. L. *The preparation of teachers of brain-injured children.* Syracuse: Syracuse University Press, 1968.

Cruickshank, W. M., Marshall, E. D., & Hurley, M. A. *Foundations for mathematics.* Boston: Teaching Resources Corporation, 1971.

Cruickshank, W. M., & Norris, H. Adjustment of physically handicapped adolescent youth. *Exceptional Children,* 1955, **21,** 282–88.

Cruickshank, W. M., Paul, J. L., & Junkala, J. B. *Misfits in the public schools.* Syracuse: Syracuse University Press, 1969.

Cruickshank, W. M., & Quay, H. C. Learning and physical environment: The necessity for research and research designing. *Exceptional Children,* 1970, **37,** 261–68.

Cruickshank, W. M., & Shaw, M. C. The use of the marbleboard test to measure psychopathology in epileptics. *American Journal of Mental Deficiency,* 1956, **60,** 3–9.

Cruickshank, W. M., & Trippe, M. J. *A study of services to blind children in New York State.* Syracuse: Syracuse University Press, 1959.

Hallahan, D. P., & Cruickshank, W. M. *Psychoeducational foundations of learning disabilities.* Englewood Cliffs, N.J.: Prentice-Hall, 1973.

Haring, N. G., Stern, G. G., & Cruickshank, W. M. *Attitudes of educators toward exceptional children.* Syracuse: Syracuse University Press, 1958.

4
Edward C. Frierson

Edward C. Frierson was born in Akron, Ohio, in 1933. He received a B.A. degree from Wheaton College in 1955, a M.Ed. degree from the University of Miami in 1959, and a Ph.D. degree from Kent State University in 1964. Currently Dr. Frierson is a lecturer at the University of Tennessee at Nashville and executive director of the Nashville Learning Center, an educational center offering a wide range of services to families in middle Tennessee. From 1964 to 1969, Dr. Frierson was the coordinator of two graduate training programs in the Department of Special Education at George Peabody College for Teachers.

Dr. Frierson is known throughout the country for his lecturing and teaching. He has conducted conferences in more than forty states and has served as visiting lecturer at the University of Vermont, the University of California, the University of Wyoming, and other major institutions of higher education. He has been a consultant to the White House Task Force on Talent Development, a delegate to the White House Conference on Children and Youth, a consultant to legislative study committees on language and learning disorders, and a member of the World Federation of Neurology, Research Group on Dyslexia and World Illiteracy.

Dr. Frierson's service in professional organizations in special education has been diverse. He is a past president of the Division for Children with Learning Disabilities (DCLD) of the Council for Exceptional Children and a member of the Professional Advisory Board of the Association for Children with Learning Disabilities (ACLD). He is a recipient of the ACLD President's Distinguished Service Award. Dr. Frierson is also a past president of the National Association for Gifted Children and was the first director of the Georgia Governor's Honors Program. He has published data and unique case reports regarding gifted children with specific learning disabilities or characteristics of brain dysfunction. He is a lifetime member of the National Education Association and a member of the American Psychological Association, the American Personnel and Guidance Association, Council for Exceptional Children, Phi Delta Kappa, Kappa Delta Pi, Creative Educational Foundation, and American Academy of Political *and Social Science. The Easter Seal Society of Oklahoma awarded him honorary lifetime membership for his meritorious service to handicapped learners.*

Dr. Frierson has published widely in professional and lay journals. He is an associate editor of Exceptional Children *and a member of the editorial advisory board of* Highlights for Children. *A selected bibliography of works by Dr. Frierson appears on page 163.*

INTRODUCTION

I alone know what I think and feel. Everyone knows what I believe because they see what I do. Think about that.

A few years ago I was attempting to justify a procedure which was "hurting" a child. Bill Page, the most remarkable classroom teacher I have ever met, said, "Don't tell me what you believe. I know what you believe because I see what you do. You believe it is all right to 'hurt' a child if you can quote a study, produce a guideline, invoke a policy, or follow a directive from the office. You may think you believe kids are most important, but you really believe research, organization, and authority are slightly more important. If you truly believe your beliefs, you will not cop out of any relationship with kids by following the beliefs of others. You must examine your beliefs so that you can live them consciously."

We all do what we believe, sometimes protesting all the while that it is not we but some outside force, idea, or authority which compels us to behave as we do.

I don't believe in giving grades, but *I have to.*

I believe it is cruel and inhumane to deliberately hurt a weaker person, but *they say* if you spare the rod, you will spoil the child.

I believe kids are different, but in order to avoid confusion and interference, *the school must have a schedule* for eating, using the playground and bathroom that can be followed by everyone.

And so on. We have all heard the words and observed the conflict in behaving. Judging is bad, but we continue to give grades (as if kids were pieces of meat in a butcher shop!). Bullying, threatening, and coercing are bad, but we continue to beat on young, inexperienced humans. Individuals' needs are paramount, but we eat, play, and eliminate on schedule.

What I think and feel about learning disabilities leads me into conflict with much of what goes on in school. What I think and feel about school leads me into conflict with much of what goes on in the field of learning disabilities. How does one leap the ravine between thinking and doing, especially when the doing may be unconventional and unpopular?

My father did it. He made the leap, bringing his behavior into concert with his beliefs. He lived the unconventional results as the pastor of a church with no membership, no affiliation, and no preconceived structure. He led by serving. He continuously explored new meanings in old messages.

My dad never used a note in the thirty-five years I watched and listened to him preach. (I don't ever use them now when I teach, lecture, or keynote.) More importantly, he searched for "deeper truth," as he called it. He wasn't satisfied with clichés, comfortable doctrines, or rituals. As he warned, "There is a danger that if you attach yourself to a stake in the ground (a good idea), however worthy, and begin marching around it, you will soon create a rut. If you march around it long enough, the rut will get deeper and deeper. While you may feel more and more secure, you will soon be completely out of sight!"

How often I have thanked my father for this wisdom. The educational terrain is dotted with those learning disabilities leaders who drove their stakes solidly into the ground only to attract followers who unwittingly trampled promising new paths of understanding into controversial ruts and finally into hollow ringing arguments. When the cant and ritual becomes a thinly veiled charade for understanding, I instinctively "pull up stakes."

BACKGROUND ON A PERSPECTIVE

I am twenty years old in education. The learning disabilities movement is about ten years old. I and the learning disabilities movement both have had somewhat longer histories, of course.

My perspective is that of a teacher; and, as a teacher, I have passed through several stages on the way to becoming the "responsible guy" I am today. After I highlight those stages, I will highlight the learning disability scene as I see it. Finally, I will share my present position as clearly as possible.

THE GOOD GUY—1955–1958

My first year in teaching I did not know much about learning disabilities. I had not had a single course or even a lecture in special education. In essence, I had learned that it was the teacher's job to plan, arrange, motivate, conduct, evaluate, and grade. My experience told me that the teacher wins some and loses some. Therefore, my unwritten goal was to win 'em all—in short, my goal was to be a good-guy!

My teaching was punctuated with dramatic bursts which produced high interest and impossible exams which produced low vocabulary on the part of students. I spiced up dull content with happy anecdotes and urged everybody to do extra credit work when they didn't learn the regular stuff.

Those first years were delightful. As a good-guy, I qualified for and received such student payoffs as being chosen the Homecoming Game announcer who stood on the 50-yard line and presented the queen, the interlocutor of the annual minstrel show, the chaperone for the New York City senior trip, and the most valuable player in the student-faculty basketball game.

In the classroom I was learning that a good-guy does not win 'em all. There were students who would not learn, others who could not learn, and still others whose abilities were an enigma. One of the known characteristics of any good-guy teacher is that he is oblivious to the true characteristics of the many students who do not respond to good-guys.

Good-guys often do the right thing, albeit for the wrong reason. That was one saving virtue of my good-guy years.

There was, for instance, a student named Bill taking up space in my literature class. He sat in the back by his own choice (good-guys don't assign seats!). He never opened a book unless he was asked specifically to do so. It so happened that while he couldn't read at all, he, too, was a good-guy. He would have done anything to be liked.

Bill was the kind of boy who would spot you across the football stadium, would hurry around the end zone to meet you, and would ask, "Can I get you a cup of coffee or something?" Interpreted freely, he was saying, "Since I have to live with you faculty types for the next three or four years, is there anything I can do to make it pleasant for you—other than learn what you are teaching?"

One day as the class labored over *Julius Caesar*, a Shakespearean play that anyone would have to despise after six solid weeks of line-by-line analysis, Bill interrupted, "Aren't you gonna tell 'em about his ol' lady's dream?"

Stunned, I said, "I'm not sure. What do you know about it?"

"Well," he replied, "Mrs. Davis last year thought his ol' lady's dream was the biggest thing. She said Caesar would have been alive if he'd listened to his old lady, but naturally nobody tells Caesar what to do. He'd look like a chicken or something if he got all shook up about dreams and stuff like that."

"Did *you* read *Caesar* last year?" I asked.

"Naw, I just listened. Mrs. Davis knew a lot more about it than you do, but she was awful. This class is more fun."

During the six-weeks test, on a whim, I decided to read the entire test to Bill, giving him just a moment to respond to each item. The test was multiple choice, short answer, and essay. He got no credit for the essay and still outscored eighteen of my thirty-three students. He had clearly performed in the top half of the class under a serious handicap.

Bill's grade card that six weeks had four red *F*'s and one blue *C*. The *C* was in literature. A good-guy had paid off a good guy!

School, in general, of course, is not a good-guy. Therefore, Bill was ineligible to play football although he was a hard and happy 210 pounds. He was kicked out of shop because he couldn't read the shop manuals, yet he held a regular job repairing outboard motors at a marine supply center on a nearby lake.

Bill dropped out of school the next year. The school said he flunked four out of five, again. Although he failed school, Bill was liked by the world.

As it turns out, in those years I flunked four out of five of my encounters with learning disability students, but so what? The world liked me. Just as Bill bought cups of coffee rather than learn, I dished out extra credit, bonus grades, watered-down assignments, and lots of chuckles rather than learn to teach the fringe learners.

I am not apologetic or embarrassed by my first years in teaching. On the contrary, I am proud to say that I created exciting lessons, allowed for a lot of individual differences, was imaginative in presentations, classroom arrangement, and grading schemes. I secured almost universal involvement, had great respect from students, colleagues, and administrators, and covered the material "like the morning dew." I laid it on everyone! I was a good-guy.

The overriding feature of my early teaching was that I assumed responsibility for *everything*. I believed that it was my job to decide what should be taught, how it should be taught, when and where it should be taught, and how the learning should be judged, graded, and reported.

I thought that I "knew kids." I understood my students. I liked them. I knew what was best for them. I did to them what was "for their own good." I determined their needs and tried to meet them. I worked hard.

Today, I reject this posture completely. I regret that I didn't know better. But, I was lucky. I did a pretty good job.

THE GROOVY GUY—1959–1960

"Boy is he groovy," I overheard one of my "clients" say. Now, I was a school counselor and saw clients instead of students. And was I ever groovy!

I had learned how to disclose hidden agendas, to unmask real needs, and to help others truly help themselves. I had profiles, regression coefficients, stanines, and milieu therapy at my beck and call. How could I be anything but groovy?

Fortunately, I was only groovy for about a year. You see, I had become a counselor by taking two elective courses on my way to a master's degree in school administration and supervision. It remained for me to get the full Rogerian treatment and an overdose of conflicting counseling theories and personalities in an eight-week NDEA summer institute.

Under the shadow of Sputnik I, I began to mature in my grasp of interpersonal relationships. As a counselor-trainee, I was observed, taped, and dissected day after day in a real educational clinic setting. No games, no role playing, just honest, day-to-day, gut-rending, real world problems to help solve. The choices were to quit or grow. I grew.

I was profoundly influenced at that point by Bill Techler, Ben Conn, Jay Winslow, Claude Arnold, and later by Don Ferguson, minor area advisor (psychology and counseling) and second reader on my doctoral committee. Most importantly, all counselor-trainees of that late 1950s period were influenced by Carl Rogers, whose concept of "client-centered" therapy was achieving international recognition and acclaim.

I discovered a great truth that year. *Helping others must never be reduced to mere techniques.* I resisted the notion that what a messed-up learner needs is yet another expert to *do* a better technique to him. I said it best at a regional counselors' meeting when I warned, "Don't any of you come to my district and technique our kids!"

My discovery of the limitations and distortions associated with counseling techniques would serve me well as I entered special education. I call the next period my growing years—the years that I grew up in education.

THE GROWING GUY—1960–1969

Walter Barbe altered the course of my life. I really had no intention of leaving the public school, the guidance game, or the sort of "mature-groovy" style that was me (I, if you're an English teacher). It was a fluke that got me into my first special education graduate course. It was the finest educator I have ever known who kept me there.

The story bears repeating because it highlights a rare occurrence in human relationships—the discovery of a person whose greatest satisfaction is helping others find satisfaction. Walter Barbe, the most productive, knowledgeable, creative, dedicated, and stimulating educator I know, got a greater kick out of seeing his students publish, present papers, sit on commissions, direct projects, and generate new ideas than he did when people honored him for doing all those things.

As a director of guidance services and premier counselor (the first that this suburban Ohio district had ever had), I was hit with a horrible problem during Homecoming Week. The English honors class consisting of eighteen girls and four boys—all the neatest girls in the school, but none of the neatest boys—were discussing the foolishness of homecoming dances, parties, etc. As it happened, most of the girls had not been invited to the festivities; and it was suggested by one of them that being in the honors class was a tremendously negative burden to bear. "Who wants to go out with a brain?"

The unmarried honors section teacher disputed the conclusion and, after surveying which girls had not been asked out, posted a list of "Available Girls" to prove that the boys were not asking simply because they didn't want to be turned down. Well, the Army has an expression for what happened when these sharp senior girls saw "the stupidest invasion of privacy one could possibly imagine." One girl rendered the military expression in more acceptable language when she said, "I guess the defecation really made contact with the whirling blade, didn't it?"

At the time of this honors class fiasco, I needed one additional course to complete my certification in guidance. In the Kent State University graduate catalogue, I spotted *Psychology of the Gifted,* a course which would be acceptable. Laughingly, I announced that I would take the course and solve the problems I was facing, which now included demands that the honors teacher be fired, that homecoming be abolished, and that counselors "do something!" other than just "talk it over with you." Walter Barbe, chairman of the Department of Special Education at Kent State University, was the instructor.

As a professional student, I expected the worst, hoped for the best, and took a seat next to the windows about halfway back. (You can always look out the window when it becomes unbearable to look up.) What I got was the freshest breath of educational air imaginable. As a result, I produced my first piece of legitimate educational research—analyzing four significant changes which had occurred in the twenty-two honors students and a comparable group of twenty-two college preparatory students not selected for the honors experience.

I color-coded my data, put tabs on the outside of the report so one could flip to each section, presented forty-four pages of appendix, and typed it all in pica. In short, I did everything but write well. When the paper was returned, there was a scrawled note along the side, "I would like to talk with you sometime about this paper. WBB" But I had my credits, and I did not care to talk.

Several months later, I was on the Kent State campus for a regional guidance meeting. I remembered the note and stopped by the special education office to see if Walter Barbe had remembered. He had. I learned later he remembers everything!

Walter asked me, "What are you going to be?" I knew only one part of the answer: namely, that it wouldn't have anything to do with going to school, Kent State, Walter Barbe, special education, or paying money. You see, between July, 1957, and November, 1959, I had become the father of five (5) children, including two sets of twins. What I did not need and could not afford was to pay for and play the student game again.

Walter concluded, "It seems to me that you cannot afford to go back to school, but you really cannot afford not to. Maybe I can help ... "

For three years I learned about special education. More specifically, I began working with gifted and talented students in every available setting. I designed a seminar experience for rural gifted students, collected data from underachieving gifted students, conducted a unique course in "Understanding Human Behavior" for gifted elementary students, participated in the "One in a Thousand" study comparing highly gifted students (160 I.Q. and above) with moderately gifted students (120 I.Q. to 140 I.Q.), worked with the urban gifted in Cleveland's Major Work Program (tagging along with Dorothy Norris, for several decades the nation's top public school educator of the gifted), demonstrated at national conferences, taught psychology and procedures courses, became involved in The Association for the Gifted (serving on legislative committees, editing a newsletter, and presenting papers at the annual conventions).

Most significantly, I met people. Walter introduced his students to Elizabeth Drews, Calvin Taylor, Paul Torrance, Virgil Ward, Jack Birch, Lou Fleigler, Ruth Martinson, Jim Gallagher, Mary Meeker. I knew Ann Isaacs, Ned Bryant, Joe French, and Charles Bish. I could go on. My education in the area of the gifted was without parallel.

I had the great personal distinction to know Dr. Paul Witty of Northwestern as a friend. One can only guess at the effect on my life that conversations with Dr. Witty had and are still having. As Dr. Witty later told a group of my graduate students about his exchange of letters with Lewis Terman and his objection to the concept *genius* in the title of Dr. Terman's studies, about his disagreement with Leta Hollingworth concerning racial differences in giftedness, about his classes with the legendary John Dewey (a boring lecturer!), you could almost see us growing in understanding.

I spent the summer of 1964 in Georgia serving as resident director of the state's first Governor's Honors Program. With Margaret Bynum, Sam Shearhouse, and Mamie Jo Jones of the Georgia State Department of Education, Ray Hill (of Cartersville, Georgia) and I coordinated the activities of a national faculty and 400 of the most gifted and talented students in the state on the campus at Wesleyan College in Macon. Not only was it the first such program supported entirely by a state legislature, it was the first racially integrated program in the state not requiring a court order.

In 1964, I moved to George Peabody College for Teachers in Nashville, Tennessee. Half of my responsibility was to restructure and coordinate a graduate level training program in the area of exceptional talent and ability—the gifted. From 1964 to 1969, Peabody graduated some outstanding students in the area. Don Crump, Barbara Hauck, and Carol Schlicter have already made significant contributions to the field.

This sketchy synopsis may seem irrelevant to the topic at hand, which is a perspective on learning disabilities. That is because I have mentioned only half of my specific plunge into special education—the gifted half.

Those who know Walter Barbe, my first escort in special education, recognize that he is an even more remarkable leader in the field of reading. He is renowned for his work in reading and learning disabilities even more than for his work in creativity and giftedness. (I used to wonder, too, where he got the energy and time. The secret to anyone producing a significant professional publication *every month* and a major book or series *every year* is to use wisely the hours between 2:00 a.m. and 4:00 a.m. when you seldom have classes, committee meetings, or office distractions!)

My education in reading and learning disabilities took shape under the guiding hand of Dr. Stanley Krippner. No more knowledgeable or fascinating researcher-clinician-teacher exists. Dr. Krippner now directs a dream research laboratory in New York; but during 1960 to 1963, he was the director of the Child Study Center at Kent State University. Stan Krippner's range of competencies included hypnosis, pharmacological management, projective analysis, CNS diagnostics, and other advanced areas. However, he was also the master interviewer, astute clinical observer, patient teacher, and objective advisor.

From diagnosing reading problems, through tutorial procedures, group techniques and classroom reading programs, on into advanced seminar work, my formal introduction to learning disabilities other than the classic "fields" of special education was thorough, imaginative, and demanding.

In addition to the specific reading and language disabilities emphasized in most child centers, Dr. Barbe and Dr. Krippner had introduced a concern for a wide range of disabilities based upon their personal acquaintance with innovators such as Alfred Strauss, Newell Kephart, and others. Kent was one of the first universities to offer a course on brain injury and hyperactivity following Cruickshank's work and using his book as a text. Jim Gallagher had written of his efforts with a brain-injured child, and little-known books such as *The Other Child* (Lewis, 1960) and *Reading, Writing, and Speech Problems in Children* (Orton, 1937) were standard reading.

(As an aside—I have yet to meet the L.D. graduate student who knows that Leta Hollingworth, author of *Children Above 180 I.Q.* (1900), also wrote a text *Special Talents and Defects* in the 1920s and published an account of *The Psychology of Spelling Defects* in 1918. When I quote from these publications, audiences assume that they are contemporary pieces!)

The second half of my responsibilities at Peabody capitalized on my growing experience in the areas of reading disabilities and related school learning problems. I worked with Don Neville, director of the Peabody Child Study Center, supervising practicum experiences for graduate students and offering courses in diagnostic, remedial, and clinical procedures for children with learning problems.

My background in speech (undergraduate major), school administration and supervision (master's degree major), guidance and counseling (nearly fifty hours of post-master's training), special education and psychology (Ph.D. major and minor), had prepared me well for the learning disabilities movement of the 1960s.

In 1965 I was given full responsibility for developing a graduate level training program in learning disabilities. Six universities, Peabody included, were granted program development funds from the U.S. Office of Education for this purpose.

By 1969 I had done in the area of learning disabilities what I had earlier done in the area of the gifted. I had met the leadership people, seen the significant programs, spoken at the key conferences, consulted with the top researchers, and so on. I directed a solid program under the leadership of Sam Ashcroft, chairman of the Department of Special Education. Peabody graduated its first doctoral level students in 1968.

When I left Peabody in 1969 to devote full time to continuing education work with teachers, I was satisfied that I knew where I was and what I wanted to do—carry a practical message to all teachers, not just special teachers. The message would be one that would enable every teacher to accommodate the widest possible range of differences in the classroom—and enjoy it!

THE LEARNING DISABILITY MOVEMENT

By the mid-1960s, the learning disabilities movement had taken on the characteristics of a religious revival period. From conference to conference, evangelical fervor replaced the stupefying symposia convention-goers have come to accept. Prophets emerged with doctrines and dogma which inevitably could lead only to the establishment of "denominations" and the "baptizing" of new converts.

"Do you believe?" was the question asked more often than "Do you know?" Each explanation for learning disabilities was identified by the name of its leading proponent. One could be a Kephart believer, a Cruickshank believer, and so on. The field rapidly acquired the earmarks of comparative religion, and disciples became readily identifiable by their liturgy.

During the revivalist period, with burgeoning state conferences growing into national conventions and letters-to-the-editor pressure mushrooming toward a fulltime Washington lobby, the classroom teacher was left far behind. Learning disabilities was a supra-classroom phenomenon featuring an aggressive parent vanguard, a small professional coterie, and a puzzled special education establishment.

Schools in the 1960s were responding to the Great Society themes which emphasized cultural dissimilarities, compensatory early childhood programs (Head Start, etc.), and equal opportunity curricula. The daily

news featured free speech, riots, war dead, campus take-overs, and her-
alded the moral disintegration of the young via drugs and sexual freedom.

The classroom teacher had his hands full. School "put-down" books
became best sellers. Behavioral psychology and its business ally, management by objectives, swept aside traditional planning and procedures.
School administrators clamoring for respectability and more funds dan-
gled the spectre of achievement test scores over the teacher's salary negotiations.

Amidst this background, the learning disability movement was to the
regular classroom teacher like a Billy Graham crusade to the man on the
street. By and large, it was just a private affair for those already
churchified, massive by some standards, dramatic for a few individuals,
but inconsequential in the general behavior of the populace.

For the academic-minded, revivalist tactics are suspect. The academic seeks data as well as deliverance. So the 1960s saw a somewhat
bimodal distribution of activists. On the extreme right were the hardened
researchers asking new questions, administering new funds, collecting
new bits of datum, and reaching new but not-too-generalizable conclusions. On the extreme left were the clamoring consumers, mostly frus-
trated parents, ready to grab the flimsiest rationale, support the
shallowest charlatan, buy the brightest workbook, and ride the noisiest
bandwagon. Prior to the establishing of the first university training programs in learning disabilities, the objective generalist-translator was a
scarcity.

Interestingly, my approach to the proselytizing period of the 1960s
was placed in perspective by a preacher. As a panel member making an
opening statement to an audience considering drug abuse problems, the
preacher said,

> In my work I have found it is not my point of view that matters most.
> Rather, it is my *point of viewing.* If I could get people to stand momen-
> tarily where I am standing, to hear what I am hearing, to feel what I am
> feeling, to learn what I am learning, then I would be satisfied. For it is
> not what I do or what I think should be done that I wish others to accept
> —not my point of view alone.
>
> When people experience a new point of viewing, the resulting view
> is their own and that is as it should be. I try to share my point of *viewing*
> so that others may find a more satisfying personal point of *view.*

I decided that as the coordinator of a graduate training program in
the area of learning disabilities, I must help students to achieve a personal viewpoint. In order to do that, the students and I together set out
each year to discover and understand the *existing points of viewing.*

Table 4-1 is an example of one summary effort during the late 1960s.
The chart represents where the learning disabilities field has been and
where it still is for many educators. There is nothing sacred or "true"
about this chart. Such a breakdown is merely useful for organizing one's
academic behavior. (See pages 142–43.)

The first column identifies a somewhat distinctive point of viewing. Column two suggests that a diagnostic approach would be incomplete according to this perspective if it did not include the procedure indicated. The third column calls attention to the differences in terminology that might be expected when different frames-of-reference are employed. Column four mentions names of individuals who have contributed to this perspective in the area of learning disabilities.

This list is by no means complete, nor is it intended as an accurate identification of the contributors' perspectives. It is more appropriately a study guide. Such a chart has value as it helps individuals define their own areas of understanding and develop personal goals toward the exploration and understanding of new areas.

The Genetic Point-of-Viewing

Is it possible for an individual to inherit a specific disability in learning? That is, might an individual be completely healthy, wealthy, and happy, and yet have a central nervous system structure that cannot read?

Years ago, individuals were thought to be "word-blind," having a deficit or gap in the area of the brain required for the storing of word patterns. Later, it was found that normal brains do not hold words in a specific place. However, since our brains do vary in structure as do our bones, skin, and hair (no two of us are exactly alike), wide differences in processing words were found to be normal, just as wide differences in skin tanning and hair curling are normal.

One facet of the genetic argument is loaded with true theological dangers. It is speculated that some reading, conceptual, orientation, and perceptual problems may have evolutionary origins. The "emergence" of man thus brings new capabilities but finds them tacked on to old primate nervous systems. Some disabled individuals, according to this view, have not yet acquired their species' specific capabilities—their true humanness.

Differences between boys and girls in visuo-spatial, verbal, and coordinative abilities are interpreted by some to be the result not of abnormality, but of the different selection pressures exerted against men and women in the evolutionary struggle to survive. Since most humans in the world do not yet read, it remains to be seen whether the ability to read is essential to survival, as contrasted, for instance, with the ability to resist the cancer-causing agents we breathe in the automobile exhaust-saturated atmosphere around our reading clinics.

The genetic point of viewing requires a thorough look at family members. One cannot accept the inherited trait explanation for a learning disability on the basis of "a *WISC* and a whim." Familial evidence must be a part of the data used to support the genetic hypothesis. In one case the handwriting samples of four generations proved valuable diagnostically, while in another case the drawings of four impaired siblings were contrasted with that of a fifth who was not disabled.

Table 4–1: *Learning abilities/disabilities—five frames of reference*

Point of viewing	Diagnostic procedure	Descriptive terms	Information	Stink pink
1. Anatomical (genetic)	Family history	Dyslexic Hyperkinetic	Critchley Bannatyne	Naked ape
2. Behavioral (environmental)	Behavior analysis	Nonattending Disruptive	Skinner Haring Lindsley	Behavior shape
3. Biochemical (nutritional)	Metabolic evaluation	Hypoglycemia Anemia	Cott Kretch Davis	Skill pill
4. Constitutional (pathological)	CNS testing EEG	Brain damaged Hyperactive	Orton Strauss Cruickshank	Tumor rumor
5. Developmental (maturational)	Case history	Language-delayed "Late bloomer"	Gesell DeHirsch Piaget	Lag jag
6. Educational (situational)	Achievement testing Diagnostic teaching	Underachiever Educationally handicapped	Holt Page	School fool
7. Functional (inferential)	Motor-perceptual testing "Symptoms"	Cerebral dysfunction Perceptually handicapped	Clements Frostig Kephart	Terrible cerebral
8. Psychoanalytical (clinical)	Projectives Structured interview Psychoanalysis	Phobic Depressed Anxious	Bettelheim Axline	Freud boid

Table 4–1: *Continued*

Point of viewing	Diagnostic procedure	Descriptive terms	Information	Stink pink
9. Modal (integrational)	Optometric exam Audiogram	Visile Audile	Getman Rosner Wepman Kirshner	Minus eyeness Verring hearing
10. Model (linguistic)	Language evaluation I.T.P.A.	Auditory decoding deficit	Osgood Kirk Bateman	Mighty eye tee
11. Neurological (physiological)	Neurological exam	Disorganized Confused dominance	Delacato Fay Ertl	Say hey, fay
12. Personal (anecdotal)	Graphoanalysis Autobiography Drawings	Unmotivated Creative Dependent	Guilford Goodenough	Jerk quirk
13. Psychological (statistical)	Psychometric profile W.I.S.C. Rating Scale	High risk	Wechsler Myklebust	A sigma-enigma
14. Sociocultural (experiential)	Social maturity scale Community analysis	Culturally different Bilingual confusion	Meade, etc. Riessman Doll	Arrived deprived
15. Speculative (miscellaneous)		Sociopathic Delinquent	Krippner Poremba	Etc. bets

Stink Pink is a word game. One player gives definitions for words which the second player must guess. The words must rhyme. A "Stink Pink" is a one-syllable match; a "Stinky Pinky" is a two-syllable match; a "Stinkety-Pinkety" is a three-syllable match. For instance, try this Stink-Pink. A not-so-hot dummy is a —ool —ool. It's "Cool Fool"—you got it.

143

Terminology often reflects a point of viewing. It is as if professionals not only choose up sides, but also choose their words (weapons?) based upon their personal orientation rather than the lucidity of the words. The term "dyslexia" illustrates the point. The genetic, inborn, structural, anatomical point of viewing was originally introduced in the medical literature, especially from ophthamology and neurology. As is the medical custom, a pathological condition was born with the invention of a word formed from the Greek and prefixed and suffixed to satisfy. "Dys"—a medical prefix indicating difficulty or poor condition—plus "lexia"— Greek root meaning "word or pertaining to words"—becomes "dyslexia" —an inborn condition of one having difficulty with words.

Similarly, "hyperkinetic" suggests an inherent neuromuscular disorder resulting in spasms and excessive muscular action. "Hyper," excessive or exaggerated, plus "kinetic," pertaining to motion and the action of forces in producing or changing the motions of masses, becomes "hyperkinetic," the condition of one displaying excessive levels of movement due to inborn neuromuscular forces. The nonmedical literature early described such a child as a "driven child" whose incessant movement and "on-the-go" character was due to an inherited condition rather than to environmental, cultural, educational, or maternal factors.

Each point of viewing has many articulate spokesmen. MacDonald Critchley, president of the World Federation of Neurology, is perhaps the best known and most influential voice of the inborn disorder. His book, *Developmental Dyslexia* (1964), states the case for specific genetic learning disabilities in a clear, research-based style. Critchley, whose home is London, England, is also a country music buff, for years a card-carrying member of the Ernest Tubb Fan Club. As a resident of Nashville, Tennessee, home of the Grand Ole Opry, I appreciate Critchley's point of viewing in a special way.

One benefit of the genetic point of viewing is that it has broadened the concept of "normal." Years ago it was suggested by John Money that if we required the same level of accomplishment with music symbols that we expect of visual language symbols, we would have a national problem of epidemic proportions. We would call it "dysmusicalexia," for it would be inborn—some people just can't carry a tune in a basket!

When we flunk that small number of unfortunates who are born to fail to read, we might just as well flunk those who are born to sing off-key, those who cannot differentiate the tastes of various spices in the soup, those who cannot find a tulip in a flower shop by smell alone, those who don't feel any difference between a cotton, nylon, or polyester sock, and so on. "Normal" includes many children now called "learning disabled." The systematic study of genetic differences changes attitudes, expectancies, and classroom procedures.

The presentation of teaching methods suggested by each of the points of viewing is beyond the scope of this book. In fact, I would challenge you to do as my students do—write yourself a book of procedures.

Constitutional–Pathological Point of Viewing

Do not accept the view that etiology does not matter. The *cause* of a learning disability behavior may very well dictate a remedial procedure far more than the behavior itself. It is tiresome to confront again and again the superficial behaviorist position which discounts the basis of a disability in favor of an observable baseline of behavior brought about by the disability. The brain-damage point of viewing, with its monumental contributions to our understanding of learning disabilities, should be sufficient to temper the behavior winds that have swept up those looking for answers rather than solutions.

The brain can be hurt. Many times the brain can recover from the hurt so that behavior is not altered noticeably. Yet brain damage often produces selective impairments of movement, speech, thinking, emotionality, vision, reading, and so on. Samuel T. Orton published the results of his work in the 1930s, convincingly linking brain pathology with specific reading, writing, speaking, and spelling disorders.

Alfred Strauss, in the 1940s, further associated brain injury and the psychopathology of classroom learning. William Cruickshank's contemporary work leaves no doubt as to the educational importance of the brain-damage diagnosis. In fact, it is clear from Cruickshank's findings that teachers generally are not given experiences in their training which will insure the competencies necessary to instruct brain-damaged learners.

My own intrigue with the "split brain studies in man" resulted in an even greater determination several years ago not to discount what one could learn from any given perspective. R. W. Sperry reported unusual findings in the 1960s associated with ten persons whose brains had been "split" by surgery. Left and right hemispheres had been divided in a dramatic, life-saving move. It is hard to conceive of a more striking instance of constitutional damage—true brain injury.

In an hour-long, dramatized lecture, I sometimes trace the "hemispheric dominance" theories of Orton through the "unity of intelligence" findings of Sperry. The implications for understanding isolated disabilities in visual language and for teaching reading are provocative. Specific illustrations tie together the work of neurosurgeons (á la Orton and Sperry), clinical measurement (á la Wechsler and Durrell), remediation strategies (á la Gillingham and Lehtinen), and classroom realities (á la Fernald and Cruickshank).

The direct result of my presenting the split brain lecture at a conference in Kansas was the saving of a girl's life. I was to learn this fact two years later. A young school psychologist told me his story in the lobby of a convention hotel.

In the month prior to your lecture, I had been observing a little girl whose behavior was baffling her teachers, her parents, and me. She was turning increasingly inward. Almost daily, her verbal communication decreased. She was withdrawing from classmates into a shell.

However, the initial complaint was with her writing. She had begun to write lighter and lighter each day; so that over a four-week period, her papers had become imperceptible. Her writing was also shrinking. A magnifying glass could not even reveal what she had written in the week before your conference speech.

Staffings had produced two strategies for the family and school to follow. The first was a behavior-oriented plan designed to reinforce her speech interactions with classmates and modify her written work. The second was a clinical option based upon a preliminary consensus that some form of autistic syndrome was developing, and its roots would have to be revealed in a play therapy or clinical setting. The parents were prepared to enter into counseling themselves.

I raced home from your "split brain" lecture, which I frankly did not understand all that well. However, the key illustration which you acted out bouncing all over the stage gave me an idea.

I went to the girl's classroom first thing in the morning. I asked her to write her name on a card for me which she did so lightly and so cramped that I could not see anything. Then, I turned the card over and asked her to write her name again, but this time to use her left hand. As she wrote, she labored in the way that most of us do when we use our "dummy hand," as you say. But her clumsy letters were big, bold, and dark!

I almost screamed, "My God! There's something wrong in the left hemisphere of this kid's brain!" Two days later, a tumor was diagnosed which was exerting pressure from the left rear of her brain throughout a generalized area in the left hemisphere.

I can't thank you enough for giving me a different perspective at a time when I needed it!

With those words, he wept openly. My eyes brimmed with tears of thanksgiving—thank goodness, there are many points of viewing.

The Biochemical–Nutritional Point of Viewing

Eventually, the biochemists may tell us more than any other group about basic learning. Certainly, the chemical changes which continuously occur within the brain and throughout the body are critical to learning. The use of medications to affect activity levels, seizures, and emotional states among students is widespread. Research implicating nutritional deficits in certain kinds of learning problems has already provided an alternative to the cultural deprivation and bad mothering conclusions which have been applied indiscriminately to poor people throughout the world.

Recently, health food faddists have been joined by clinicians and researchers demanding that chemical additives be subjected to critical analyses before they are permitted to reach the grocery shelves. One doctor reported that over 50 percent of his patients lost all trace of hyper-activity when restricted to diets containing foods with no artificial color-ing or flavoring. Cott's studies have shown massive vitamin doses to be effective in changing the behavior of schizophrenics as well as learning disabled children.

I guess I am a health nut. I often carry sunflower seeds, pumpkin seeds, raisins, or soybeans in my pocket. I order vegetable soup in place of French fries, and I love to play until I sweat. Notice I did not say *work* until I sweat! I believed Linus Pauling enough to start taking a handful of vitamin C on all trips to prevent catching colds and sore throats—and haven't had one since.

As a point of viewing there is much to learn about nutrition and learning. Most of it makes sense. However, let me share an anecdote.

I had shared a Canadian platform with a distinguished neurologist. After the meeting, he was approached by an anxious mother who waved a newspaper article under his nose and asked, "Do you agree with this? Will it help my son?"

After briefly hearing the nature of the son's learning disability, the neurologist replied, "No, ma'am, it won't help your son, but I can guaran-tee he'll have the most vitamin rich urine in the community. As a matter of fact, he will have more vitamin C in his urine than you'll get in your orange juice!"

In outlining the limitations of the nutritional point of viewing, the doctor admonished, "Everyone agrees that it is bad to overeat, but some people seem now to be saying that it is all right to overeat providing that you buy from the Health Store."

For myself, I can report a gratifying change in an elementary school which removed all Coke and candy bar machines and replaced them with an open snack bar that serves only celery, carrots, cucumbers, peppers, raisins, nuts, and juice. According to one teacher, the favorite single item in this school is a carrot. The same teacher added that restlessness is almost nonexistent, learning is up, and attitudes are noticeably different. The snack bar is always open; and after a two-week deluge of adjustment, the students and teachers take it in stride. Hunger, sleepiness, boredom, and misbehavior are at an all-time low . . . because of a nutrition alterna-tive to the Coke-candy bar syndrome?

The Developmental–Maturational Point of Viewing

In the area of the gifted there existed for many years a myth which stated, "Early ripe, early rot." The idea prevailed that precocious children who did amazing intellectual feats would either burn themselves out at an early age or fall victims to dire problems and become emotionally unstable or even suicidal.

In the area of learning disabilities, there exists a point of viewing which implies that if parents would just relax, the children would eventually grow out of their problems. Examples are common, and it is also common for every school to have its late-blooming academic flowers. There is, however, more to the maturational-lag frame of reference than just a wait-around-and-see attitude.

School readiness studies have repeatedly pointed out that up to one-half of the members of every first-grade class are disadvantaged in that they are behind from one day to six months in just being alive. Except in very innovative schools, all children within a year-wide age range will come to school on the same September day.

Now it is possible to predict with great accuracy which children will fail to learn to read by the end of first grade and which will fail even by the end of the second grade. Correspondingly, we have seen the establishment of "transitional" and "developmental" first grades where high-risk students are not expected to behave like good first-graders.

In those cases where parents have been overanxious and have not understood the plasticity of intellectual development, I have introduced deHirsch's "jello" analogy. Parents are familiar with the process of making jello. After boiling water has been added and the fruit stirred in, the fluid is poured into a mold and placed in the refrigerator. Should you plunge your finger into the mixture shortly thereafter, you will withdraw it covered with colored goo that hasn't hardened yet. You might repeat your gooey experiment several times with the same result.

Finally, you will stick your finger into the mold only to find that the mixture has jelled. It has matured. It is ready.

Perhaps we can say that we have a concoction called a first-grade child. We plunge our fingers into him—first the rhythm band, then the phonics chart, and then the hopscotch mat with numbers. But it all comes out gooey—not because he's sick, damaged, or structurally unsound, but because he hasn't jelled yet for these activities. He's not ready. He may have to "cool it" a while longer.

The maturational point of viewing is a favorite of pediatricians. The typical pediatric case load includes many parent-child relationships which need the "cool it" advice. But when a truly frustrating disability is not responsive to the wait-and-see strategy, the parent-doctor relationship becomes as strained as the parent-child relationship. Enter, then, a new point of viewing.

The Functional–Inferential Point of Viewing

The growing popularity of the learning disabilities movement in the 1960s was due largely to the dysfunction rationale. This rationale rests on the premise that inferences about brain function can be drawn from observing the child's attempts to perform certain specific tasks. For instance, when a child tries to draw a line from an illustrated mouse to an illustrated piece of cheese across paper containing lines of varying widths, the child is revealing indirectly the brain's ability to manage eye and hand under conditions which can be analyzed repeatedly.

With enough imagination, it is possible to create an infinite variety of brain dysfunction measures. Indeed, the ease with which tests of dysfunction are constructed has produced a whole new arsenal of clinical tools which boast of their practical value, their sound standardization, and their quick-scoring format.

So prone are we all to misuse such tests (I still see advertisements promising that "your child can make one year's growth in only six weeks") that I often ask myself the question Carl Haywood first asked, "Perceptual Handicap—Fact or Artifact?" Does poor performance on a test of "perception" constitute a handicap any more than poor performance on a test of "culture," a test of "creativity," or a test of "adjustment"?

Publishing companies that had previously shown little interest in the special education needs of handicapped children stampeded after the dysfunction clientele. So many of us exhibit minimal dysfunctions in so many areas, yet without manifesting lower "intelligence" (pick your I.Q. test and you can be normal too!), that *special* education finally reached commercial proportions ("every classroom needs one . . . "). This is not to discount the existence of motor, perceptual, language, and conceptual disorders which reveal brain dysfunction. Rather, it is to say that the field of learning disabilities hit the commercial big-time with the acceptance of a wide range of dysfunctions where it had been barely a publishing footnote earlier.

Marianne Frostig published tests and classroom worksheets that ushered in an era of classroom remediation strategies. Such strategies began to challenge the goals and procedures of every regular classroom teacher. Newell Kephart broadened the application of his life's work through the *Slow Learner Series*. As a point of viewing, the functional-inferential way of doing things moved the L.D. movement into high gear. For a while, it was the most popular place to stand, though certainly not the safest.

In the southern region, a committee convened by Stan Fridell and Gerald Hasterok found thirty-two separate definitions for learning disabilities and cerebral dysfunction and wisely decided not to generate a thirty-third. Sam Clements summarized the situation for the U.S. Office of Education in the mid-1960s with a report on the terminology and symptoms associated with minimal cerebral dysfunction.

It is instructive to recall here an exchange concerning dysfunction which occurred at an exploratory meeting two years before a division on learning disabilities was organized within the Council for Exceptional Children (CEC).

Eighteen well known CEC members had gathered to propound their views:

First expert:	Why can't we simply accept the fact that learning disability is simply an educational synonym for the clearly established medical syndrome known as minimal cerebral dysfunction?
Second expert:	That would be fine, but I can never get the neurologists to tell me conclusively when they have discovered minimal cerebral dysfunction.
First expert:	Well then, you are talking to the wrong neurologists!
Third expert:	Hold it a minute. It seems to me that around this table we have some persons who are interested in all the kids with central nervous system mess-ups whether or not they have school learning problems. Other persons here seem to be interested in all the kids with school learning problems whether or not they have central nervous system mess-ups. I think that as an educational organization, we simply have to decide at which place we are going to start.

The Educational–Situational Point of Viewing

"Learning disability is a good problem to have," said the M.D. on the platform, "because most learning disabilities disappear at about age eighteen when the child finally leaves school." Hardly a fair comment, but the hearty response of the audience reminded me that school often does compound the problems associated with learning disabilities.

John Holt told of the child who had learned to put her hand up whenever there were three or four other hands in the air. However, he discovered that she never answered a question. When she was unfortunate enough to be called upon, she dropped her hand and mumbled something about not being sure of that one. She had learned to fail to learn.

Schools are preoccupied with organization. Thus, a disorganized child finds himself getting drinks of water at the wrong period, standing in the wrong line, waiting for the wrong bus, looking out the window at the wrong time, speaking to the wrong classmate, and generally seeming disobedient.

Schools are preoccupied with learning subject matter. Thus, a child who is mixed up in chapter one is quite likely to be mixed up in chapters two, three, four, and five. An incomplete project in the first six weeks signals incompletes in the second, third, and fourth grading periods. Disinterest founded on confusion isn't likely to be assuaged by motivational techniques.

Schools are preoccupied with judging children under the guise of evalutaion. Learning disability kids are failures, and no mickey mouse variations in grade cards or reporting systems will change the aura associated with being low man on the totem pole. A few schools have abandoned grade levels, grades, predetermined goals, progress reports, and criterion-referenced learning in general. Failure in such rare settings has an altogether different meaning and feeling.

Some remedial efforts are so strongly tied to traditional school characteristics that we now find it possible to "fail" remedial reading, perceptual training, adaptive physical education, adjustment class, and resource room! In other words, when the school makes a significant effort to help the disabled learner, any learner who still fails to attain the objectives established for him is *really* a bad guy.

It's hard to imagine how disappointing it must be to disappoint everyone who is trying to help you. As long as schools are organization-, achievement-, and judgment-oriented, the problems of the learning disability child will be exaggerated. As I learned in my first survey course in special education, a disability is a handicap only in certain situations. Like school?

The M.D. concluded, "Since we are unlikely to change the central nervous system of the child, the least we might do is help him to be happier during his school years." No doubt, schools could go a long way toward being happier places for disabled learners, but not everyone would agree that we are unable directly to affect the brain. Read on.

The Neurological–Physiological Point of Viewing

Glenn Doman and Carl Delacato really bugged special education and conventional learning disabilities experts with their controversial ideas. Doman's best-selling book, *Teach Your Baby to Read* (1964), introduced a rationale for stimulating learning capabilities that surprised many educators of the handicapped, but was not at all unknown to students of the gifted literature, who were accustomed to early stimulation experiments. Geniuses such as John Stuart Mill and Norbert Wiener, father of cybernetics, were subjected to rigorous training during infancy.

Delacato introduced the neurological organization rationale with its directed, intensive physiological stimulation techniques in his *Diagnosis and Treatment of Speech and Reading Disorders* (1970), a book which has seen several printings. Together, these pioneers established the Institutes for the Achievement of Human Potential in Philadelphia where, according to Doman, "we have seen and treated more brain-injured children than anyone in the world."

In simplistic terms, the Institutes teach that the brain of a disabled learner can be affected directly by stimuli (light, noise, odor, taste, temperature, pressure) and developmental movement patterns which are introduced or applied with greater frequency, intensity, and duration than would normally occur. The theoretical basis for the IAHP approach has often been challenged; the IAHP procedures themselves have been openly rebuked; and Doman and Delacato have been publicly criticized. Nonetheless, the work of these men has been distinct and influential.

It is not necessary to critique the neurological-physiological point of viewing in this treatise. That has been accomplished in the professional literature. What is necessary to say here is that controversy should never be permitted to close the mind. Montagu warned years ago of a condition he called psychosclerosis, hardening of the mind.

For my part, I went to Philadelphia with a group of thirty professionals (pediatricians, psychiatrists, orthopedic specialists, psychologists, and special educators) for a week of intensive training so that I could respond more intelligently to the pressures of a parent group in Nashville and introduce my graduate classes to factual information, not innuendo, concerning IAHP. I have similarly met and studied points of viewing in person with recognized leaders whenever possible. I find I have so much to learn.

Phi Delta Kappan, the journal published by the nation's largest educational leadership fraternity, exemplified the spirit of critical openness by presenting its readers the controversial work of John Ertl. Ertl is the Canadian inventor of an electronic diagnostic device that gives an index of human neurological efficiency. His goal of identifying one's true intelligence by monitoring the electrical energy produced by the brain had been reported in the 1960s by Mensa, a worldwide organization of individuals whose members must score in the top 2 percent on a recognized test of intelligence.

While Doman and Delacato have traveled the world studying primitive cultures in order to isolate developmental patterns that have neurological rather than cultural bases, Ertl has been attaching electrodes to the heads of thousands of persons in order to do the same. Both approaches have produced data that erode further the prestige of traditional tests as a true measure of individual learning potentials. Such tests are more correctly identified as special achievement tests.

The Psychological–Statistical Point of Viewing

The testing game has never been played harder than it is being played in the learning disability arena. Vocational guidance, army classification, college entrance, and school readiness continue to have their day, but the learning disability profile is surging forward to rank near the top on any psychologist's or educational diagnostician's agenda.

The coming of the computer to school districts and research centers is having a profound effect on the learning disability scene. Test scores, coded behaviors, medical data, and the like are punched in, processed, and printed out. The resulting profiles and prescriptions seem to foreshadow a day when a child will enter school with a social security number (to activate the central computer), a dog tag indicating his learning style, an IBM card to record his hourly progress, and TV antennae on his wrist so that he might plug into his daily learning menu as prepared especially for him by the Media Central Learning Dietician.

Diagnostic testing for children with learning disabilities is big business. It is expensive business. It can be monkey business.

I have consistently taken the position that it is wrong to generate test data if there is not a reasonable expectancy of an appropriate response to the data. Why, for instance, should a child be subjected to a battery of tests outside his school when the school personnel have not taken appropriate action on the wealth of diagnostic data contained already in the child's cumulative folder?

Again, why should a child see a specialist who translates diagnostic findings into advice that cannot be carried out in the home and school circumstances in which the child is expected to function? Too often, diagnostic testing meets the needs of the tester rather than the testee.

Statistical analyses do have many valuable applications. The *Wechsler Intelligence Scales for Children* have proven remarkably accurate in identifying learning disabled children. Even more, these scales have differentiated among various types of disabilities. However, it has only been in recent years, through publications such as *Academic Therapy Quarterly,* that classroom teachers have been shown how test tasks relate to school learning tasks with specific suggestions for altering instruction for statistically deviant students.

The diagnostic studies conducted by Myklebust from 1965 to 1969 have provided me with one of my strongest in-service tools, the *Pupil Behavior Rating Scale.* I use it not to diagnose learning disability students, but to diagnose teachers in relationship to such students.

Although Myklebust found that a carefully researched rating scale in the hands of an experienced teacher is more powerful (statistically) in accurately diagnosing learning disabilities than any other single method (e.g., ophthamological examination), I rewrite items to affect *teachers.* For example, when the scale says " . . . mind often wanders from discussions," I have teachers add the phrase, "the way I conduct discussions!"

In this way the teachers always are a part of the problem. Therefore, they can deal with the problem immediately—they can change their parts! They do not have to send the kid out and wait for a profile and a prescription to come back. In my opinion, the more regular classroom teachers who get this message, the more likely we are to accommodate the unique styles of all learners in the mainstream program.

The Behavioral–Environmental Point of Viewing

I contend that teacher behavior must change before student behavior can change. A science of behavior as proposed by B. F. Skinner would specify the changes necessary to elicit more effective student behaviors. Interestingly, controversy has erupted around such an innocuous sounding point of viewing, and some legislatures are presently contending with bills which would make behavioral techniques illegal.

Psychologists have been challenged to face up to the ethical questions that surround the use of powerful "undercover" procedures. Schools, of course, have always used hidden persuaders and gotten away with it.

When learning is defined simply as a change in behavior, then learning disability may rightly be considered as the failure to exhibit a desired change in behavior. Since behavior can be shown to be related to the environment in which it occurs, it is logical to conclude that changing the environment will *ipso facto* modify the behavior. Further, since behavior seems lawfully influenced by its consequences, arranging consequences can be a powerful determinant of future behavior. So far, so good.

The learning disability movement seems determined to borrow the chocolate candy and plastic chips from the mental retardation and emotional disturbance camps and to join the rising chorus of those who say "Labels are lousy, long live behaviorist jargon instead!" So far, not so good.

Labels are fine for jelly jars, I admit. But thank goodness for labels. They make life intelligible. I sure don't want to spread sorghum on *my* biscuits (how could my dad stand the stuff!). What a waste to throw away a ruined biscuit and how senseless to dip a finger into the jar to taste each time before I am able to "relate in a meaningful way" to the contents.

Instead of tossing out all labels, why not face the hard truth that the labels are often meaningful—it is we ourselves who misuse them. It is I who say that sorghum is lousy—the label just says "sorghum."

Since the behaviorist point of viewing is well-represented in this book, let me acknowledge its influence on me by anecdote rather than by analysis.

I was co-hosting a crackerbarrel session at a national conference. My colleagues were Norris Haring and Milt Brutton. After describing a successful clinical experience using programmed reading material, Haring was questioned persistently by a disbelieving teacher:

Teacher:	What material did you use when the child could not do the programmed book?
Haring:	We used no other material.
Teacher:	But you must have. What did you do when the child made mistakes?
Haring:	Our students didn't make mistakes.
Teacher:	Well, when they misunderstood an example, did you make up other similar examples?
Haring:	We don't create reading programs. All we do is see that the students respond correctly to the program we use.
Teacher:	But you must use other materials if all the children are going to be successful.
Haring:	Our job is to see that all students respond correctly to this program; we don't need other programs.

Teacher: I don't see how you can get them all to read.

Haring: We arrange the necessary contingencies so that the students respond correctly—would you agree that *if* the students responded correctly, they would in fact learn to read?

Teacher: Yes, but I don't see how you can do it with only one program.

Haring: Ma'am, we could get a fencepost to read with this program if we could get it to respond just one time!

Since that afternoon, I have been ever more conscious of the "contingencies." I had tried to teach a few fence posts and found that mostly I had entertained them. Of course, I suspected the problem was in the program or in their background, their parents, their development, their handicap, their profile, their chemistry—so what could I do? From that day on, I knew what I could do. I could teach them to read. If Haring could do it, so could I!

The Sociocultural–Experiential Point of Viewing

Each person's environment is different. Therefore, our experience is uniquely different.

When geosociocultural forces combine to produce starkly different environments, we can expect marked learning differences. Where the forces are not so obviously different, we tend to overlook their influence.

Imagine the experiential difference in the formative first five years of life between the Eskimo infant raised on a floating ice cap in a snow block home and an Indian infant raised in the Amazon jungle in a rain-drenched, thatch-roofed home. Or imagine the difference between the suburban teenager in the United States and the newly initiated tribal warrior on the edge of the Kalihari Desert of Africa.

On tests of perception, the Eskimo and Amazon children might differ if certain unfamiliar shapes, colors, or background noises were involved. The conceptual abilities of the warrior and the suburbanite might be comparable, but each would appear retarded in many ways in the other's culture.

Only a rural visitor to downtown Nashville might hear a cricket in the Methodist churchyard—the only grass in a mile radius of cement towers. Every shopper's head would snap around, however, at the sound of a fifty-cent piece striking the pavement. We have ears, but we don't hear everything. We have eyes, but we see what we are accustomed to looking for.

Learning disabilities can be culturally flavored. Margaret Mead, Pearl Buck, and others have helped reveal cultural differences which can be mistaken for ignorance or handicap. And who is to say which abilities are the better to refine? McLuhan and Toffler have speculated that the global village of the present-future may require vastly different abilities than those presently nurtured in schools.

(How about the shocker of the 60s—experientially deprived rats actually suffered from biochemically altered brains and subsequently became disabled learners for whom remediation was ineffective, since ensuing structural changes were permanent.)

The Psychoanalytical–Clinical Point of Viewing

Actually, the learning disability movement has been viewed by some as "the other side of the Freudian coin." For half of this century, learning problems were attributed overwhelmingly to psychodynamic factors. Reading clinics concentrated on motivation, desensitization, sublimating feelings, and the classic passive-aggressive and acting-out syndromes.

Bad mothering, penis envy, and sibling rivalry crept into reports, along with "needs work in phonics" and "needs acceptance." Only in recent years have advice-to-parent columns suggested that a brain-injured, defective, or learning disabled child may cause the parents to be the way they are rather than vice versa. Thank the learning disability movement for getting the monkey off a lot of mothers' backs!

Emotional factors play a major role in learning. I do not mean to dismiss the psychodynamic point of viewing too lightly. However, evidence is increasing which suggests that so-called "mental" illness is much more often symptomatic of physical (including nutritional) deficit than was formerly believed. Furthermore, the psychodynamic therapies have fallen on hard times, with some studies indicating that the chances of getting "well" are no greater if you receive the treatment than if you do not.

The Personal–Anecdotal Point of Viewing

"We have met the enemy and he is us!" The Emerald City appears green because we are wearing green glasses. I must be normal; they are all so different.

No matter how we say it, the message is the same: The differences and problems in the world may very well be in us. We are each one unique unto ourselves.

A perceptual handicap may in one instance be no more than an individual with an I.Q. of 125 sitting at a conference table with three individuals having I.Q.s of 175. In another instance, perseveration, so often associated with mental retardation, may turn out to be a characteristic of creative genius at work (Thomas Edison).

Goodenough (*Draw-a-Person*) and Guilford (*The Structure of Intellect*) point the way toward a highly personal view of learning. It is doubtful that two children have ever drawn a person just exactly alike. It is our mistake that we will give children the same score, attach to both scores the same meaning, and treat the children alike for having gotten that particular score.

Guilford's ideas of intelligence based upon factor analysis have already opened up the field of the gifted by sweeping aside I.Q. and traditional profiles in favor of a mosaic with not less than 120 facets of talent and ability. No doubt the learning disability field will embrace an ever-broadening version of intelligence as well.

Cognitive style is an almost meaningless phrase unless a structure such as Guilford's is used to identify the components of such a style. Historically, of course, style was confined almost entirely to the idea of modalities for learning. A pretty good case continues to be made today for the visile, audile, or tactile oriented learner.

The Modal-Integrational Point of Viewing

Who has not been fascinated by visual illusions? No matter what your brain tells you must be true, your eye refuses to cooperate. You are a victim of what you see, since you are prone to believe it.

The mystery-sound radio contest often asks you to identify a famous person's voice or a common sound magnified many times. Why is it so hard to figure out? You are a victim of what you hear in spite of what you know you should be hearing.

In short, we learn to hear what we hear and we learn to see what we see. Should this basic learning be less than perfect, we will to that extent be less intelligent than we ought to be.

We might trace a learning disability back to the original deficit modality and overcome the disability by developing new sensory efficiency. Then we would reunite the modalities toward an integrated, normal capability. Briefly, this is the developmental modalities point of viewing.

While optometry has been the traditional home of the developmental vision perspective, educating the senses is an old Montessori ideal. Early stimulation is not enough, however. Suppose, for example, that you have four record players playing simultaneously. The first is The Mormon Tabernacle Choir singing "The Battle Hymn of the Republic" accompanied by the Philadelphia Orchestra. The second is "The Stars and Stripes Forever" with the United States Marine Band. Third, Robert Merrill of the New York Metropolitan Opera Company performs his role in "Pagliacci"; and, finally, Boots Randolph of Nashville plays his best-selling "Yakety-Sax." If the record players are all blaring at once, would you be stimulated? Yes! Would you learn anything? Not likely.

The key is structuring experiences for each modality so that it learns to attend, discriminate, arrange, select, reject, associate, recall, classify, and interpret information with other modalities. It is, in essence, teaching the brain to learn. As Getman writes, you can improve your child's intelligence.

The Pick-a-Model Point of Viewing

Just suppose you could not find out about a child's family or identify any clearly inheritable, structural deficit. Suppose you had no metabolic data and couldn't get a complete workup. Suppose, further, that you could find no early records and could get no developmental information from the child's parents. Further, you were unable to learn about the schools the child had attended and the situational factors associated with his performance. A neurological evaluation is not available, no one has ever completed a rating scale, a *WISC,* or a computerized profile. Accept the fact that you have no school readiness data, cerebral dysfunction or perceptual test scores, and the child's neighborhood, geographic, and sociocultural history are unknown to you. Suppose that no drawings, handwriting, cognitive factors tests, or autobiographical forms have been acquired.

What could you do? Would you believe that the most popular point of viewing in the country has not yet been mentioned?

The number one approach in learning disabilities at the present time is the use of a psycholinguistic model in diagnosis, interpretation, remediation, and evaluation. The *Illinois Test of Psycholinguistic Abilities (ITPA)*, based on Osgood's model of language, has won out over other lesser known measures and models. Be of good cheer, you are in the clear.

Miscellaneous Points of Viewing

There are many other places to stand in the learning disability arena. You are welcome to find a comfortable place and settle down.

The maladjustment, delinquency, sociopathic, criminality chair offers some interesting possibilities. Krippner found sociopathic tendencies in several poor readers by the age of twelve—chicken or egg? At several annual meetings of the Association for Children with Learning Disabilities, Chester Poremba has been presenting evidence linking learning disabilities with delinquency in up to 80 percent of the criminal population studied.

One thing seems certain. Long jail terms and forced labor are not likely to alleviate the learning disabilities among juvenile offenders at our penal institutions or among psychodropouts in our educational institutions.

Gifted children with learning disabilities, as well as selective deficits among some super athletes, have been special interests of mine. History has been replete with both.

In any given year, my students and I have had points of viewing charts that contained as many as twenty-one and as few as eight frames of reference. I repeat, there is nothing true about the breakdown presented here. The charts are designed to help teachers appreciate the wide range of possibilities both for understanding a child's unique learning characteristics and for developing ways of teaching a child uniquely. (Each of the perspectives has generated materials, procedures, activities, and techniques which are now exceeded in variety and quantity only by the developmental reading materials which glut the educational market!)

The learning disabilities movement is for real. Learning disability specialists are being prepared in training programs throughout the country. The points of viewing sketched here are among the common denominators in such programs. But education since the 1960s has been changing. New types of buildings, new scheduling plans, new staffing patterns, new media capabilities, and new concerns for the handicapped are evident.

What, then, is the future of learning disabilities to be? Is the answer more specialists and more special classrooms? Will learning disabilities settle down in a niche alongside the mentally retarded, the deaf, the blind, and the orthopedically handicapped, or is there a different future?

LEARNING DISABILITIES AND THE FUTURE

The learning disabilities movement, in my opinion, will profoundly affect *all* of education in the next few years. While I said earlier that the 1960s produced a sort of evangelistic effect among those already evangelized, the 1970s has seen a change of direction, a shift-of-emphasis as it is called in Texas.

The regular classroom is to be the battleground of the next decade. The university, the clinic, the tutorial center, the resource room, and the alternative class have demonstrated sufficiently that changed *relationships* do make a difference for the L.D. child. Therefore, instructional relationships in the regular classroom must change.

Appropriate changes which respect the rights of each student regardless of his learning characteristics come about quite predictably. First, there must be an examination of what we believe about people, school, grading, time, work, responsibility, control, etc. Beliefs examined yield valuable information about prevailing attitudes, which in turn influence our goals. Appropriate procedures, "what to do," depend upon what we are *trying* to do. When the overriding goal of any teacher is to help each child learn, there are many instances where the teacher's behavior must be different from that generally seen in the regular classroom *if* the learning disability child is to succeed.

The ultimate key to success for the L.D. child in the regular classroom is a simple one to state. It is not always easy to know how to carry it out. Success in dealing with learning disabilities, special talents, abilities, handicaps, and problems in the regular classroom *depends upon the extent to which all the kids understand what you are trying to do and participate in deciding, arranging, conducting and evaluating how it is to be done.*

If the teacher thinks "diagnosis" is important, it is the extent to which all the kids understand what diagnosis means and help to design ways to accomplish it that diagnosis will be fully effective. Let the school psychologist come into the class and help the kids set up a "crystal ball center" where you learn things about yourself so you can think about your own future career (e.g., are you coordinated enough to stitch base-balls—production; strong enough to lift cartons of oatmeal—construction; color-conscious enough to arrange flowers—merchandising? etc.) Or how about a "fantastic voyage center" where you can take a trip inside your own head (e.g., with your eyes, try to figure out a visual illusion, find a hidden picture, or pick out pieces to form a certain design without touching them; listen to recorded noises to tell which is the farthest away, how many sounds are occurring simultaneously, and which are the same as sounds occurring in rapid speech). Or try a "space ship countdown" where you can analyze all the learning features of the classroom itself (e.g., the candlepower of the light coming in the window versus the light in the reading tent, the distance noise travels with and without bookshelf dividers, etc.), and check out each child's "comfort margin."

If the teacher believes that contingency management or similar behavioral technology is valuable, it is the extent to which all the students share in his knowledge, understand the purpose of its deliberate use, and help design every facet of its use in the classroom that an honest, human, and democratic program exists. Procedures and techniques which are done *to* kids violate a general philosophical goal of mine. Democratic relationships require the participation of all the individuals affected so that programs may be *of* everyone in the class, *by* everyone in the class, and *for* everyone in the class (resource room, tutoring situation, or home). Unfortunately, the behavior technology being crammed down the throats of school systems seems to condone a belief that classroom management should be *of* the interdisciplinary committee, *by* the teachers, *for* the kids. I reject much of what I see being done to kids, regardless of data supporting the effect, because the basic relationship is wrong.

If the teacher believes that motor-perceptual training or remediation of any sort is helpful for improved school learning or success in life, it is the extent to which all the kids, in fact, accept and value such experience as *equally important* and as worthy of reward as any other training or activity in the class, that such training will be anything other than a monumental "put down." The teacher's intentions are of little consequence. You can "self-concept" a learning disabled kid to death, but his self-esteem will be related not to what we, as teachers, think is important, but what *his* world views as important.

If a teacher believes hyperactivity is a problem that can be solved by the disabled child alone, he will "treat" him like a doctor treats a patient; however, if he believes that everybody has "a tiger in his tank," he will teach all the children that when anyone's "tiger" is awake in a classroom, everyone can appreciate, respond, and relate sensibly to such a reality. It is, therefore, the extent to which all the kids expect and help plan ways to learn things in their classroom at those times when some students are restless, "snarling," and feeling "caged up" as well as ways to learn things when everyone's tiger is purring, sleeping, or "on vacation" that the hyperactive child will find an understanding home away from home (e.g., a classroom with a Learnasium containing handgrips with vocabulary words on them, a ballet bar with math facts on it, a shimmy rope with answer sheets at the top). In such a classroom the kids learn to feed the tigers instead of fight them!

The successful regular classroom of the future will be a classroom of changed *relationships*. Success has little to do with class size, teacher–pupil ratio, money spent per pupil, library volumes, type of scheduling, administrative experience, progress reporting system, or community involvement.

Success for the learning disability child in the school is a matter of attitudes and relationships. When school personnel believe that *the most important factors in school are how the kid sees it, how the kid feels about it, and how the kid goes about it,* the attitudes, goals, and procedures will reflect that belief.

Right now, school personnel believe it, but they don't believe it quite enough! Therefore, they are still looking for a technology, a plan, a program, a strategy to cause handicapped learners to score higher on achievement tests (the god before whom schools have bowed all too long, in my opinion). That posture—achievement is the ultimate responsibility of the teacher—may yield slowly but it must yield.

The better posture—that achievement is the ultimate responsibility of the learner—will cause teachers to (a) spend all the time necessary to learn how each kid perceives, feels, and goes about learning, (b) refuse to diagnose, profile, plan, prescribe, or evaluate without the full involvement of all the kids affected by such activities, and (c) live democratically as a leader insuring that the rights of each student in the classroom are neither greater nor less than the rights of any other student or of the teacher.

MY POINT OF VIEWING FOR THE FUTURE

You know what I believe by what I do. After a long growing period of studying and trying out what other people do—Points of Viewing—I finally grew up in learning disabilities. I have my own point of viewing.

I have reached the totally comfortable position of not knowing what to do about the child with learning disabilities. I *cannot know* until I know how a specific child with learning disabilities sees *his* world, feels about *his* world, and goes about surviving in *his* world.

The way most classrooms are run, the teacher feels responsible for the achievement of the learning disabled child; and, as a result, the teacher analyzes, prescribes, plans, manages, and evaluates what happens. I have found that if all of the kids participate in these activities, not only do they learn, but they also learn how each other sees, feels, and best goes about having a good classroom experience.

With full democratic participation, as a leader I use all the points of viewing as an invaluable means of being a resourceful person to the children. From helping kids organize a "bod squad" which plans motor activities for those restless periods to electing a "decibel-of-the-day" to monitor the noise levels in the classroom, I have found that *when the kids understand* what I am trying to do (help them learn), what I am interested in (all the things that mess up learning or make learning super), and what I believe (everything I am willing to do about differences), the learning disability child achieves.

The future belongs to those who believe in the kids themselves, who trust the kids, and who share responsibility and resource information with them. So, in the end, with all the kids' help, I win!

REFERENCES

Critchley, M. *Developmental dyslexia.* London: Heineman, 1964.

Delacato, C. *Diagnosis and treatment of speech and reading disorders.* Springfield, Ill.: Charles C Thomas, 1970.

Doman, G. *Teach your baby to read.* New York: Random House, 1964.

Hollingworth, L. *Children above 180 I.Q.: Origin and development.* Yonkers-on-Hudson, N.Y.: World Book Co., 1942.

Hollingworth, L. *The psychology of spelling defects.* 1918.

Hollingworth, L. *Special talents and defects: Their significance for education.* New York: Macmillan, 1923.

Lewis, R. S. et al. *The other child: The brain-injured child.* 2nd ed. New York: Grune & Stratton, 1960.

Orton, S. T. *Reading, writing, and speech problems in children.* New York: Norton, 1937.

A SELECTED BIBLIOGRAPHY OF WORKS BY EDWARD C. FRIERSON

Barbe, W., & Frierson, E. Approaching a study of behavioral patterns. *Education,* 1964, **85,** 137–42.

Frierson, E. Creative teaching for gifted children. In J. Dunlap (Ed.), *Man, Language, and Cognition.* St. Louis: Washington University, 1964.

Frierson, E. Determining the needs of the educationally retarded and disadvantaged child. *Education,* 1965, **85,** 461–65.

Frierson, E. The governor's honors program of Georgia. *The Gifted Child Quarterly,* 1965, **9,** 77–78.

Frierson, E. Specific learning disabilities: The responsibilities of special education administrators. *Proceedings, 45th Annual C.E.C. Convention,* Portland, 1965.

Frierson, E. A study of gifted children from upper and lower socioeconomic backgrounds. *Science Education,* 1965, **49,** 205–10.

Frierson, E. Upper and lower status gifted children: A study of differences. *Exceptional Children,* 1965, **32,** 83–90.

Frierson, E. The role of oral reading. *Education,* 1966, **87,** 21–24.

Frierson, E. The education of gifted youth in high school and college. *Education,* 1967, **88,** 25–30.

Frierson, E. The gifted child with specific learning disabilities. In J. Hellmuth (Ed.), *Learning Disorders.* Vol. III. Seattle: Special Child Publications, 1968.

Frierson, E. Gifted children and learning disabilities. *Exceptional Children,* 1968, **35,** 387–88.

Frierson, E. The gifted. In G. O. Johnson & H. Blank (Eds.), *Exceptional Children Research Review.* Washington, D.C.: Council for Exceptional Children, 1969.

Frierson, E. The gifted. *Review of Educational Research,* 1969, **39,** 25–37.

Frierson, E. The dilemma of dealing with differences in a democracy. *Junior High Pressure Points in the '70s.* Danville, Ill.: Junior High School Association of Illinois, 1973.

Frierson, E. Smart Alec says . . . Procedures for teaching the gifted. *The Raspberry Report Card.* Nashville: Edcoa Publications, 1973.

Frierson, E. How to teach a number two—Procedures for children with learning disabilities. *The Raspberry Report Card.* Nashville: Edcoa Publications, 1973–74.

Frierson, E., & Barbe, W. Analysis of topics in selected comprehensive bibliographies. In P. A. Witty (Ed.), *The Educationally Retarded and Disadvantaged. N.S.S.E. Yearbook.* Part I. Chicago: National Society for the Study of Education, 1967.

Frierson, E., & Barbe, W. (Eds.) *Educating children with learning disabilities.* New York: Appleton-Century-Crofts, 1967.

Frierson, E., & Barbe, W. Introduction to learning disorders. In M. S. Auleta (Ed.), *Foundations of Early Childhood Education: Readings.* New York: Random House, 1969.

Frierson, E., & Page, W. *Grading without judgment.* Nashville: Edcoa Publications, 1973.

5
Marianne Frostig

Marianne Frostig, born in Vienna, Austria, in 1906, is founder and Director Emeritus of the Marianne Frostig Center of Educational Therapy, Los Angeles, California. She was executive director of the Frostig Center from 1947 to 1972. Since 1969, she has been a professor at Mount St. Mary's College and the Frostig Center. From 1966 to the present she has been a clinical professor in the School of Education at the University of Southern California. In recent years she has conducted numerous workshops, courses, and lectures for school districts, universities, and professional associations in this country and in many foreign countries.

Dr. Frostig's experience includes a variety of services to children. She was director of rehabilitation programs for the Psychiatric Hospital in Zofiowka, Poland, from 1932 through 1937. From 1945 through 1947, she was an elementary school teacher in California. She served as a school psychologist in the special schools of Los Angeles County from 1949 through 1955.

Dr. Frostig received a B.A. from the New School for Social Research in 1948, a M.A. from Claremont Graduate School in 1949, and a Ph. D. from the University of Southern California in 1955. She is a diplomate in school psychology (American Board of Professional Psychology), a certified clinical psychologist (Board of Medical Examiners, State of California), and holds California credentials as a school psychologist, elementary teacher, and teacher of the mentally retarded.

Dr. Frostig has served on many professional boards and committees. She is a fellow of the American Psychological Association, the American Orthopsychiatric Association, the Society for Personality Assessment, and the International Council of Psychologists. She is a member of numerous other professional organizations, including the Society for Research in Child Development, the American Educational Research Association, the American Association on Mental Deficiency, the Council for Exceptional Children, and the International Reading Association. Several professional groups have given her awards for outstanding professional service in the field of learning disabilities. In 1970, Dr. Frostig was named Woman of the Year by the Los Angeles Times.

Dr. Frostig has published many articles and books in special education. Her educational tests and programs are well known in the field of learning disabilities. A selected bibliography of works by Dr. Frostig appears on pages 189–90.

MY SLOW PATH OF LEARNING

The Beginnings

My fate as an educator was foreshadowed in my childhood. I was the oldest of three children and always ready to teach the younger ones. It also seemed natural for me to lead groups of children in games in the parks while the governesses sat on the benches, chattering. At this young age I learned my first and most important lesson concerning education— children will only cooperate and learn if they enjoy what they are doing.

At the ripe age of fourteen I decided to write a story about my childhood, in which I pointed out what was wrong with education, namely governesses, school, and adult authority in general. An unusually kind teacher, whom I asked to help me, suggested that I should withhold my personal survey until I was over sixty years of age. Only then, she said, does a person have the perspective to write about their experiences. To my surprise, I find that I am now qualified, in respect of years at least, to write about education from a personal perspective; and so I have accepted this assignment.

Before giving an account of an important phase of my early professional life, my social work period, I want to mention some individuals who greatly influenced me at that time, namely Charlotte Bühler, one of the first developmental psychologists, who taught courses (which I was permitted to audit) at the University of Vienna; my uncle, Frederick Silberstein, who directed the Pathological Institute of the University; and Hans Hoff, a young neuropsychiatrist, who later became director of the Neuro-Psychiatric Clinic at the University of Vienna.

At the College for Social Work Training, where I studied to be a psychiatric social worker with children, I was particularly impressed by the teachings of August Aichhorn, who conducted a course in *Heilpädogogie,* i.e., educational therapy. Aichhorn influenced not only all of my subsequent professional work, but my attitude toward other human beings in general. I have never seen anyone more readily able to gain the trust of any youngster with whom he spoke. He gave each child the feeling of being understood by somebody who deeply wished to help him. I learned from him that such surface behavior as hostility, sudden outbursts, refusal to go to school, and other symptoms is usually a defense against underlying anxiety, perplexity, and despair, and that I must not take a child's misbehavior as a personal affront or as directed against me. He also taught me to take into account all the forces in the past and present life of the child and how they are perceived by the child, because these contribute so heavily to the child's development. In other words, Aichhorn was concerned with what we now call "lifespace."

There was just one point on which I did not agree with Aichhorn. At the University Pediatric Clinic where I trained, we were often confronted with children who were victims of encephalitis. Aichhorn held that little could be done for these children because they were brain-damaged. I did not believe him. I observed that my influence over these children was just as great as it was with children who had emotional disturbances, and it seemed to me that I saw improvement in the abilities of some of them. I therefore decided to devote myself to finding ways to help children with brain damage, even if the exploration were to take a lifetime. In so doing, I brought home to myself a new lesson—that we all have to question the statements even of our heroes and the greatest authorities in their fields.

During my social work training I was a temporary social worker for the Jewish Welfare Agency in Vienna and also a fieldworker at the Eggenburg Correctional Institute for Juvenile Delinquents. As a social worker I learned that it is not enough merely to want to help another human being, nor is it always helpful to set about it in the way that accords with one's wishes or standards. One has to be extremely cautious or one can cause more harm than good, especially if acting without knowledge of all of the relevant facts.

For example, I once took upon myself a zealous search for the lost husband of a young woman with a child. But an old lady, not a professional, who devoted herself to helping the poorest people in the district pointed out to me that if I found him I would deprive the mother of her welfare check, which she could get only so long as the child was abandoned. If I really wished to help this mother, the best thing I could do would be to provide a crib for the child, so that both mother and child could get adequate sleep. Thus I learned not to interfere unless I was quite sure that the interference would be of help.

At Eggenburg I learned that even well-intentioned behavior toward a child could be experienced by the child as disrespect. On one occasion a nine-year-old child who had run away explained that the reason for his excursion was that he had been called a bad name by another child. When I found out that the bad name was that of a very well-known scientist, namely Professor Tandler of the University of Vienna, who was expected to visit the institution, I could not help but laugh. Professor Tandler was regarded by the children as a kind of devil because an impending visit by him meant a flurry of activity, extreme orderliness, and the most correct behavior on the part of everyone. My superior's reaction was to explain patiently to the child that he had been called "Professor Tandler" not out of disrespect, but because he wore glasses and looked rather important, so it was really an honor rather than a slur. My reaction of laughter was not helpful to the child and was properly rebuked.

I also learned the necessity of finding out the *causes* of behavior rather than reacting to the behavior itself, and then of planning procedures to remedy or come to terms with the causes. Children who had been committed to the Eggenburg Institution were not punished if they ran away. They were brought back; and the causes of their behavior, whether anxiety, despair, loneliness, or anger and defiance, were explored; so that they could themselves understand the reasons for their actions and be helped to feel better in their environment.

Hellerau Laxenburg

A political revolution in Austria led to the closure of the social work school; the seventy-six people in training there were released from further service. I therefore applied for admission to Hellerau Laxenburg, a school for dancers, musicians, and teachers of gymnastics, specializing in a form of physical education called *rhythmics*. Feeling that the body is the most important possession of any human being, and that it affords the most direct expression of his feelings, I wanted to develop methods involving movement to benefit children with emotional disturbances. I was also interested in learning the use of exercises to ameliorate certain physical handicaps.

To my great astonishment and delight, I found August Aichhorn had taken a position as professor of psychology in Hellerau Laxenburg and that he conducted group psychotherapy with the students. I attended his groups and was privileged to work with him for two more years.

I have mentioned that Hans Hoff was a strong influence during my training as a social worker. This influence continued. He introduced me to the work of Paul Schilder, who was at this time an assistant professor at the Wagner-Jauregg Clinic for Neuropsychiatry at the University of Vienna. I became especially interested in Schilder's discussion of the body image, and what I learned from his books was of considerable help in my work. Some of the children with whom I was conducting movement education or rhythmics had emotional disturbances or physical deficits, especially those in an Adlerian Children's Home. Many of these children showed extreme restlessness and lack of control, but I noticed that their behavior became more calm and controlled as they became more aware of their body movements and mastered them. I thus had a dramatic demonstration of the truth of Schilder's ideas and learned through my own experience the importance of an adequate body image for the optimum development of the child.

A Psychiatrist's Assistant

At twenty-three years of age I married Peter Jacob Frostig, a neuro-psychiatrist in private practice, and left Vienna. For the first years of our marriage we lived in Lwow, a town in Poland. My husband was engaged in writing a textbook, for which he needed information from the English and American literature. Since he read only Polish, French, and German, I undertook the research into material written in English. These years thus gave me a most useful familiarity with much neurological and psychiatric research. Later, my husband administered a small psychiatric hospital with a few hundred patients at Otwock, near Warsaw. When he took the position, there was but one physician on the staff and the care of the patients was mostly custodial. I therefore helped not only in the medical laboratories, but also in the development of workshops in vocational rehabilitation, industrial therapy, and various educational courses for children and adults. By the time we left in 1938, the greatly enlarged staff of the institution used a variety of therapeutic methods; as a consequence, the release rate was high. When the patients were released, they received out-patient care under the guidance of a physician and a highly trained nurse at the nearby city of Warsaw.

My position as director of rehabilitation afforded me most important experiences. The methods which we used were termed *Arbeitstherapie* (work therapy). They were based on methods introduced by the German psychiatrist Simon. To give an example, several patients who had become catatonic, probably because of the long lack of treatment, were trained to pull a wagon with which they delivered food to the different cottages, or delivered bricks to other patients who were building walls, and so on. They were conditioned to react to a signal for pulling the wagon until another signal told them to stop. But this was just the first step.

The next step required the patients to work in pairs carrying baskets to gather leaves and debris from the paths on the grounds. Again a signal was given to get them to move the basket; but this task was more difficult, as they had to react to each other carefully in order to carry the basket correctly. In time the signal was dispensed with and the patients had to direct themselves. Gradually the complexity of the tasks and the degree of independence and responsibility involved were increased.

Reinforcement with tokens was also used. Each patient was paid with tokens which he could exchange for trinkets, smoking materials, and other goods in the hospital store. At the beginning, many patients showed no interest in their tokens and the goods they could get with them, but soon nearly all of them were eager to "go shopping." At the beginning of the therapy program less than 10 percent of the patients worked. After a year more than 90 percent of the patients worked in the hospital. As soon as the patient was able to work in a reasonably self-directing manner, and if no other treatment was necessary, he was transferred to the Out-patient Department in Warsaw. I thus learned more valuable lessons at Otwock—the paramount importance of analyzing tasks and gearing them to the person's capabilities, the necessity for programming work in a step-by-step progression, and the value of reinforcement. I later incorporated these techniques into my educational work. Decades later such techniques acquired standardized terminology and were widely used in the classroom, as various workers applied and built on Skinner's research. "Task analysis," "token economy," and "behavior modification" are now familiar terms and practice.

Another lesson that I learned at Otwock, because of the variety of patients, was that no single approach was appropriate for all patients, and often the individual patient would need a variety of approaches which changed as he changed. This lesson, too, I incorporated into my subsequent educational work.

Some lessons also accrued from working with a big staff in the role of a consultant. Because I had no official title, no salary, and did not wish to derive power from being the director's wife, my authority in teaching the personnel could only spring from the source that is always best in teaching—personal relationship and demonstration. The staff did not receive any extra benefits from the added work the new treatment methods brought with them, except the satisfaction of doing a better job. I learned the importance of modeling as a teaching tool and also about the dedication of which human beings are capable.

A NEW BEGINNING

In 1938 our life in Europe ended. My husband was offered a position in the United States, and I followed after a year. We heard later, when we were in America, that the Nazis had put an end to all our work, murdering the patients and many of the staff in the hospital. Thus I learned, too, of the horrible callousness and cruelty of which man is capable and which must always be opposed by the educator who can promote ideals of cooperation and sensitivity to the needs of others.

It has been comparatively easy for me to report on my early professional years, while it is more difficult to write about the holocaust in Europe and the changes it brought about in my life. But I find it necessary to refer to the latter so that the development of my educational approaches can be understood.

Several circumstances combined to cause my timely emigration to America. Even after moving to Poland, I had visited Vienna frequently; and each year I had met with a young social worker who had a leadership position in the city government. Her reports were increasingly depressing. The health and camping services for school children were terminated. There was a lack of apprenticeships for children leaving school. Many of the young people of Vienna roamed the streets purposelessly. Hunger, misery, and a general mood of despair were rampant. What I saw and heard convinced me that anybody who promised change would be welcomed as a hero and savior, and it was no surprise when the Hitler regime was so easily accepted in March of 1938. Although Poland seemed safe, I was glad when my husband got an invitation to lecture in America; and I hoped to be able to follow him and move to America permanently, not only because of the general atmosphere of alarm in Europe, but because I felt that America was a place where disinterested research could take place and humanitarian work would be supported. I had a very good reason for believing this, which I can only explain by retracing my steps.

In my childhood, the hunger and poverty in Vienna were terrible. One day when I was about fourteen years old, large bales of gray flannel were delivered to our school, and we school girls began to sew dresses for children who needed clothing. We were told that the Quakers in America had contributed this material. Two years later I was working as a volunteer group leader in a home for refugee children. Sufficient food was available only because large amounts of potatoes, carrots, and milk were provided by the same mysterious group. I resolved then that I would one day visit the country where such generous people lived.

My overwhelming desire in America was to be able to introduce educational therapy (*Heilpädogogie*) which I had studied in Vienna, combined with many ideas which I had learned from Montessori through books and through contacts with the Montessori School in Vienna. I also wished to apply my experiences with occupational and work therapy gained in Poland and to extend my first attempt at treating brain-damaged children through perceptual-motor methods. However, for the first six years in this country I was largely engaged in bringing up my two children, an occupation which I thoroughly enjoyed. My daughter was nearly five years old when I came to the U.S.A., and my son was born fifteen months after my arrival. Later, my family was enlarged by the addition of a little refugee girl who stayed with us for more than three years.

My activities were not entirely domestic during those first years in the U.S.A. My husband worked as a psychiatrist in various state hospitals, teaching modern treatment methods to students and physicians. My learning at this time came from the many books I read, the many patients and professional people I met, and the experience of adjusting to living in a new country. I also found time to teach for a semester in a public school when the regular teacher became ill, and I worked for six months as an assistant social worker and for a further six months as an assistant occupational therapist in a mental hospital. These extracurricular activities became possible because my mother had joined us and helped a great deal with the education of the three children. I found at this time that I still had much to learn from my mother in regard to the small miracles that selflessness and adaptability to new circumstances can bring about in rearing young children. Although we had moved from one hospital to the other and the children had hardly found time to grow roots in any one place, the consistent attention they had from my mother gave them the stability they needed. If children receive love consistently, they can survive all manner of external upheavals. This observation has been born out by research on the children of frequently moving army personnel (Kilty, 1974).

THE NEW SCHOOL FOR SOCIAL RESEARCH

My family and I settled in New York in 1945. My husband took his internship to get a medical license for this country, and I attended the New School for Social Research. I was the first undergraduate student ever to attend the school and was allowed to take part in the graduate courses. I was awarded the B.A. degree after nine months—the most exhilarating period I have ever experienced. The school itself was most beautiful. I loved the Mexican paintings, especially those of Orozco, the quiet work in the library, and above all, the courses that I took. The teachers and the occasional lecturers were often very eminent people. I will always remember the lectures of Gardner Murphy, and especially those of Solomon Asch and Lawrence Joseph Stone. Lawrence Stone confirmed what I had learned from Aichhorn: that to understand a child one must look carefully at all the circumstances of his past and present life, and that often circumstances which may at first seem trivial to the observer are at the root of the child's failure to adjust to life. He showed a memorable film about a little boy whose parents were most well-meaning and whose home seemed well-organized, but who was frightened by a very strict old grandfather with whom he had to spend hours of silence and fear each evening. I realized again what Aichhorn had already taught me, that we too often blame parents when we look for adverse circumstances in a child's life, condemning precisely those people who may be the most dedicated to the child and the most eager to help, because we overlook less evident but consequential circumstances.

From Solomon Asch I learned about research methods in sociology and psychology. What was most interesting for me was the insight he gave us into the customs of various Indian tribes and their importance for the tribes' survival. While I had learned from Aichhorn a respect for the individual human being, from Solomon Asch I learned the necessity for understanding other groups and races, especially when evaluating or educating a child.

The most instructive aspect of my learning, however, was the writing of my thesis. I attended the New School for Social Research in the evening and worked during the day or at night. My four-year-old son therefore attended a day care center where, when I was not working during the daytime, I was able to observe three groups of children interacting with each other and with the teachers. The teacher of the three and one-half to four and one-half year-old children was a warm, placid, motherly person, a good organizer who kept her children busy and active. The teacher of four and one-half-year-olds was psychoanalytically oriented, and her training had taken place when Freud's tenets were wrongly understood as giving complete freedom to the child. She gave no directions and the group was bedlam; the children hit each other, misused the materials, and screamed and cried.

The teacher of the five and one-half to six and one-half year-old group was firm and authoritarian, and her children were quiet and busy. I conducted observations and sociometric tests which showed that the youngest group, directed by the teacher who was neither autocratic nor laissez faire, showed far greater social cohesiveness and mutual friendliness than the four and one-half to five and one-half year-old group and nearly as much social maturity as the rigidly run oldest group.

TEACHING SCHOOL IN CALIFORNIA

In 1946 I received my bachelor's degree and returned to California. I taught in the public schools for half a year parttime and then a year fulltime, as a fourth grade teacher. I regard this as one of the happiest times in my life; I loved to work with children who were what one calls "normal," though many lived in adverse circumstances. I made a list of circumstances which I regarded as being highly disruptive in a child's life, such as absence of a parent, strife between parents, chronic lack of physical necessities such as food or sleep, chronic illness of a parent, parental drunkenness, ill health, severe poverty, very circumscribed living space (a large family living in a small trailer, for example), and continuous migration. Many children had attended an average of three different schools in the course of a school year. Of the forty-one children I taught that year, only three experienced none of these adverse circumstances.

It had been stated over and over that large classes are detrimental to the progress of the students, especially in elementary school, although the research is contradictory. But I learned that year how to work with groups of children, especially with respect to structuring a classroom so that instruction could be maximally individualized despite the large numbers attending. To achieve this goal, the teacher has to keep Erikson's theory of psychosocial development in mind. The basis of all later social development is trust. Children with many adverse experiences, such as the children in my classroom, do not trust easily. The first task of the teacher, then, is to gain their trust.

The manner in which this goal is achieved will depend on the personality of the teacher. Trust is mutual. A precondition for the development of the children's trust is that the teacher trust them; and this trust depends in turn on the degree to which the teacher trusts herself to be able to help the children in their learning, to provide the necessary discipline in the classroom, and to gain the friendship of her pupils.

Although the attainment of these goals will differ from teacher to teacher according to the teaching style, I would like to state some ground rules which will apply to many if not all teaching situations:

1. All possible channels of communication between teacher and children should be kept open. Even children in the primary grades can write or draw a note to the teacher indicating that they want to talk to her. A few minutes before and after school, during recess, or during specified times when the children work by themselves (e.g., a free reading period) can be used for individual interviews.

2. Children can learn to run their own classroom, distribute and collect materials (such as scissors, pencils, and so on), collect the milk money, correct each other's papers, and take turns in being the leaders of groups of four to six children. Thus more of the teacher's time is free for more important tasks.

3. To gain the trust of the children, the teacher should convince them that she can help them to success, but not that she is above making mistakes herself or is all-knowing. For example, I must confess that I am still completely innocent when it comes to baseball. In my class was a ten-year-old husky boy who was astonishingly accomplished at this game. He became the baseball coach on the playground, and he felt rather protective toward me because I had not learned even the simplest rules of this game. His group was inspected from time to time by the vice-principal, who reported to me that the children did well and that I could go on with my consulting or small group teaching.

Throughout my teaching experience, my social work education stood me in good stead. Talking is not enough when one wants to help children. Joe needed to be helped to find a pal; Dick needed a referral to a clinic; Tom, who stayed with his brother in a trailer without adult supervision, needed help when his brother got ill; Sue needed some extra food; Jorge needed a Christmas present; and Jesus needed to be helped with a letter to his absent father. I also found the anecdotal writing of notes to be an indispensable help for the understanding of the children in my class.

WORKING WITH THE MENTALLY RETARDED

During the time I taught school I also studied at Claremont Graduate School, where I received my master's degree. At Claremont I worked with Dr. Florence Mateer, first as a student and then as assistant in a summer course. I still use the materials Florence Mateer developed for children with mental retardation. She was a great teacher with much experience and a deep understanding of children. I admired her and learned much from her. She was a master at task analysis long before this phrase had become a byword in education. By step-by-step matching of numerals, of objects, of numerals, pictures, and objects, she developed number concepts in even the slowest children.

Later, when my husband decided to begin a practice in Los Angeles, I continued my studies. I obtained my teaching credentials, my school psychologist credentials, my license as a clinical psychologist, and finally, a Ph.D. in educational psychology.

In Los Angeles we moved into a little house on a hill with meadows and a lake nearby. The house had a front yard with two enormous Deodor firs and in the back a tiny garden with grass, flowers, and fruit trees. My children and I were delighted that we could remain in a country-like atmosphere.

We moved into our new home in the fall of 1947. Since it was too late to find work as a teacher in a public school for the first semester, I told my former teacher, Charlotte Bühler, that I was looking for some children for educational therapy and asked for her help. She recommended one little patient; very soon I had ten children in my care, and there was too little room for them in our small house. I then heard about Belle Dubnoff, a teacher who was interested in educational therapy and had a big house to work in. We decided to work together and were in partnership for the next three-and-a-half years. Belle was a very gifted teacher, and it was a pleasure to work with her.

WORKING WITH JUVENILE DELINQUENTS

During the first years in Los Angeles, I also worked parttime as a counseling psychologist in Juvenile Hall and in the camps for delinquents in Los Angeles County. The experiences gained in this work were of great significance for my later undertakings.

In one of these institutions I was assigned to a class of sixteen- to eighteen-year-old girls who had been diagnosed as dyslexic. These girls were not only unable to read, they seemed unable to do anything constructive. They were unhappy, angry, and felt defeated. Most of these youngsters did not fail because of disabilities in visual or auditory perception or in associational functions. Even those girls who seemed to have shown early retarded development in these functions had by now acquired the basic skills necessary for beginning reading. They could not learn to read because they were afraid of failure. They were bored by the task, ashamed to learn what young children already knew, and were not motivated to put forth any effort. Thus, the first task of the teacher was to make reading meaningful.

It was necessary to avoid anxiety; the word "reading" was deleted from the vocabulary of the teacher. The girls were only asked what they wanted to learn. Was there anything they wanted to know more about? One volunteered that she wanted to know how to plant a garden. The others agreed. From a Sears Roebuck and other catalogues, we gained much information necessary for planning a garden—for instance, the cost of seeds and plants and how to order them, as well as how to plant and care for them. The catalogues also provided us with pictures. The girls cut out pictures and wrote the information they had gained below the pictures. Repetition of their vocabulary was a natural process, as the same basic information had to be gathered by all the girls. One girl, for instance, had decided on planting cucumber seeds and wrote down the cost, while another one wrote down the same information about melon seeds, and so on. As they combined and compared the information, they were exposed repeatedly to the same words and noted them down; and they acquired without great difficulty a basic reading vocabulary. After a second similar project most of the girls were able to read simple commercial books.

In Juvenile Hall and in the other correctional institutions, I learned that children with learning difficulties, whether they were aggressive and hostile or downtrodden and depressed, had to regain their self-respect before they could engage in learning. As their self-respect grew, they became more and more capable of achieving new skills. Learning and gaining self-respect was a spiraling process: As skills increased, self-respect increased, and vice-versa.

One of my tasks in Juvenile Hall was the testing of children. In my children I found the same indication of previous or still existing perceptual deficits, especially disturbances in the body image and in spatial orientation, that I had previously noticed in Vienna as well as in the hospital in Poland. Although these children ranged in age from nine to fifteen years, their drawings of figures were frequently immature and even grossly distorted. The figures might have enormous heads or arms originating in the head. Some drew multiple limbs or figures without arms or trunks.

Many of the children could not draw a simple geometric shape such as a diamond or even a triangle. They had difficulties in copying a letter. Sometimes they reversed letters; often they could not solve simple spatial puzzles. They were usually also far behind their age-mates in academic achievement.

At this time I read the papers of the Gestaltist school, especially those of Kurt Goldstein (1948), who had written about the brain-injured soldiers he had observed and treated during and after the first World War. I also read a book by Strauss and Lehtinen (1947) and another one by Heinz Werner (1948). In these books there were discussions of the perceptual and conceptual functions and dysfunctions which I had observed in the postencephaletic children in Poland and which I observed now in Juvenile Hall. I concluded that many of these children might be suffering from a neurological dysfunction. This, I thought, might be a clue for helping children with learning difficulties. As there might be a connection between the perceptual disturbances and their learning deficits, I decided to find out what this connection might be. These observations were the beginning of our attempts to construct the Developmental Test of Visual Perception and training materials for visual perceptual difficulties.

THE DEVELOPMENTAL TEST OF VISUAL PERCEPTION

Developing the *D.T.V.P.*

After a few years I had to give up the work with the delinquent children because the number of children in our little school increased, and the work there began to take up all of my time. All of the children in our clinic school had difficulties in school learning. These children, as those in Juvenile Hall, had been referred to us with different diagnoses, but again I found in many of them the same disturbances which I had noticed in Vienna and in Poland in the institutions for juvenile delinquents. Methods and materials designed to pinpoint and possibly ameliorate disturbances were needed. The work of Strauss and Lehtinen (1947) and Strauss and Kephart (1955), the various ideas of Montessori (1965), and the studies of Werner (1948), Wedell (1960), and Cruickshank, Bice, and Wallen (1957), guided me in the choice, application, and development of such methods, and were basic to the development of the *Frostig Developmental Test of Visual Perception.*

The *Marianne Frostig Development Test of Visual Perception*

For the many children with perceptual dysfunctions, the perceptual training seemed to be a most significant aspect of their program. We assumed perceptual dysfunctions on the basis of observation and later by the few available tests, but we were little satisfied with these methods of evaluation. My observations indicated that children would often score very low on the *Bender* (Koppitz, 1964) or other tests, even when they had no difficulty in form discrimination, because they had difficulties in reproducing the figures. The *Bender* test seemed not to differentiate reliably between children with sensory motor problems and those with perceptual deficits, nor did this test differentiate the different kinds of perceptual disturbances.

I had noticed several visual perceptual difficulties in my little clients. Many of the children could not perceive a part of the visual field as distinct from the rest. This had also been observed by such scholars working with handicapped children as Cruickshank (1957), Wedell (1960), Strauss (1947, 1955), Werner (1948) and others, and had been termed a *deficit in figure-ground perception.* Children with these deficits showed their difficulties on the Gottschaldt test (1926, 1929), which is unfortunately little known in the United States and not standardized. The children could not solve puzzles requiring them to find hidden figures, nor could they outline a figure when it was intersected by another figure. They typically had difficulty in locating a word in the dictionary or finding a name in the telephone directory or a particular item of information on a page. They also exhibited other behavioral deficits, especially lack of attention. It was often difficult to say which was primary, the lack of attention or the perceptual deficit, but perceptual training seemed to improve both.

Other children had greater difficulties in categorizing shapes. They would, for instance, not recognize the squares on a page when they were presented in different colors or sizes, or they could not recognize familiar words in an unusual print or in a new reader. We interpreted this difficulty as a difficulty in the *constancy of their visual perception of form and size*.

The third deficit we observed was an inability to perceive the direction in a drawing consistently, especially the direction of a symbol. This resulted in a confusion between symbols such as *b* and *d*. We termed this ability *the perception of position in space*.

Another deficit observed in some of the children was a difficulty in spatial orientation. They could not perceive the relationship of one symbol to another as well as to the observer. When these children had to copy a pattern, they would be stymied. They also had great difficulties when various tasks were presented on a page. They were confused when a page was crowded. In math, they had difficulty with long division and multiplication, because they would use the wrong numerals in solving problems. The term chosen for this disability was *disturbance in the perception of spatial relationships*.

In addition to these deficits, many children had difficulty in copying, drawing, and tracing. These skills also had to be assessed, so that a differentiation could be made between the deficit in perceptual and in perceptual-motor abilities, and the appropriate training administered.

Over a period of several years, my colleagues Phyllis Maslow, Welty Lefever, John Whittlesey, and I worked on developing a test with which to evaluate these five abilities: eye-hand coordination, figure-ground perception, perception of form constancy, perception of position in space, and perception of spatial relationships.

We were assisted in the development and standardization of the test by many people, especially school psychologists, principals, and teachers from the school districts of Hermosa Beach, Glendora, and La Puente in Los Angeles County. Our only outside funding was from the Rosenberg Foundation, who awarded us two grants totaling $15,600.

The final standardization sample comprised over 2100 children between the ages of three and ten years. These children were all from the Los Angeles County area, from school districts and nursery schools representing white suburban middle-class populations. The geographic and ethnic restrictions of the sample were in part determined by our awareness that children, regardless of their background, were expected to meet the demands of school systems which reflected white middle-class goals and expectations. Restrictions of the sample to the local geographic area also permitted us to train and personally monitor the administrators, scorers, and recorders of the tests.

The dining room, living room, and recreation room of my personal living quarters became filled with test booklets, data recording sheets, and people. A mother of one of our school children volunteered to help with all the coordinating duties, and her services were invaluable. The carrying out of all the standardization procedures became a truly cooperative enterprise, enhanced by the feedback we received during the period 1961 to 1964 from users of the experimental edition of the test. With the publication of the standardization monograph (Maslow, et al., 1964) in October, 1964, Consulting Psychologists Press of Palo Alto took over publication and distribution (Frostig, Lefever, & Whittlesey, 1964).

The test has engendered a great deal of research; I have commented on the assumptions underlying some of this research in a paper entitled "The Future of Perceptual Training" (1974). The ten years of work since publication of the test have, however, in general supported my basic contentions that visual perceptual abilities are critical for a child's adequate adjustment and classroom learning, especially at the age of beginning school entrance, and that these abilities can be trained.

From the very beginning of my work, my coworkers and I began to develop materials and methods for training visual perceptual abilities. Materials were also developed by the teachers who trained and worked in our clinic school. While the test was being standardized, these materials and methods were being collected, organized, and field tested. David Horne assisted with the writing of the Teacher's Guides, and Bea Mandell made the original drawings; my daughter, Ann-Marie Miller, later worked on revising the guides, especially for preschool children (Frostig, Horne, & Miller, 1966, 1972). But without the organizational work of Phyllis Maslow little would have been accomplished. The publication of the training materials (Frostig & Horne, 1964, 1973) by Follett Publishing Company of Chicago actually preceded the test publication by a few months.

I regarded and still regard the understanding of the variety of visual perceptual functions, their evaluation, and remediation, as an important aspect of the training of handicapped children; but the evaluation and amelioration of these disturbances is only one aspect of the total treatment.

THE PSYCHOLOGICAL PROFILE

The entire treatment plan depends on the range of symptoms and on the characteristics of each child—his assets, his deficits, and the environment to which he has to adjust. Neither learning difficulties nor behavioral disorders are the same in all children. They may exhibit defiance, hostility, anger, or despair and listlessness. Some are irritable and restless, while others withdraw. Commonly these children suffer from the rejection of their parents, siblings, and school teachers. They often cannot satisfy the demands placed on them. As a result, they become more and more angry, rebel, and finally give up. Before positive results can be achieved, home visits, parent counseling, or a change in the school placement are frequently necessary.

I often marvel at the resiliency of the human organism. Children improve as the pressure diminishes, whatever the method of diminishing this pressure might be. They feel better because learning is made easier by such measures as providing perceptual training, eyeglasses or rest periods during work, a different reading method, or putting them in a situation where they can be of help to others. The feeling of being loved, of being important, of having found a new friend, often changes their attitude toward living and working. Teaching of lagging skills as well as compensatory methods are both important. Gradually the whole picture may change, and the children find that they are able to succeed better both at home and at school, even when they continue to be handicapped by their own deficits or by an uninterested school teacher, a nagging parent, or a fussy sibling.

Visual perceptual training must therefore be combined with the training of other abilities. My emphasis on integrative training has become greater during the years; but from the beginning on, our approach was multifaceted. The phrase "the total child" has become hackneyed from constant use, but it is still a most important concept; and educational therapy must be concerned with all aspects of the child's development and with his total environment. Such concern remains a hollow phrase without charting the psychological profile.

Multifaceted remedial training must be based on multifaceted evaluation. Our next objective was, therefore, the establishment of a test battery which would permit charting the child's psychological profile which would highlight his assets and deficits. We wanted to include all the main groups of abilities which a child develops up to the stage of formal operations. We therefore included sensory-motor abilities, which develop maximally during the first year and a half of life; language functions, which develop maximally between one year and one-half and three and one-half years; perceptual abilities, which develop maximally between four and seven and one-half years of age; and higher cognitive functions, which show the maximum development during the school years. We decided to use formal tests to evaluate the child's cognitive and communicative abilities and observations, interviews, and various projective tests to explore his social and emotional development.

For research as well as for teaching purposes, we assembled a test battery which consisted and still consists of the *Frostig Test* (Frostig, Lefever, & Whittlesey, 1964) to evaluate visual perception, the *Wepman*

Test (1958) to evaluate auditory discrimination, and the *Illinois Test of Psycholinguistic Abilities* (Kirk, McCarthy, & Kirk, 1968) to evaluate higher cognitive functions.

Later the *Frostig Test of Motor Skills* (Orpet, 1972) was added to evaluate some of the child's sensory-motor skills. This latter test developed, as did the *Frostig Developmental Test of Visual Perception,* from observations of children; it also reflected previous factor analytic studies (Guilford, 1958; Nicks & Fleishman, 1960) which had established several attributes of movement: coordination, agility, flexibility, strength, speed, balance, and endurance. Because there was no standardized test battery which specifically explored these attributes, Dr. Russell Orpet constructed and standardized the *Frostig Movement Skills Test Battery* over several years. It was published by Consulting Psychologists Press in 1973. It contains twelve subtests, can be administered in approximately thirty minutes, and was normed on 744 Caucasian elementary school children from kindergarten through sixth grade. Factor analysis of the standardization data supports the existence of five factors: hand-eye coordination, balance, strength, flexibility, and visually guided movement.

The basic tests are supplemented by other instruments chosen according to the individual needs of the child, such as projective tests, articulation tests, and aptitude and achievement tests.

A diagnosis of the assets and disabilities of each child is essential before individual programs can be outlined. The test results must be the basis for suggestions for the teacher in regard to the remediation of deficits which cause the school failure and the methods in teaching academic skills and subject matter which will make use of the strengths of the child. Suggestions should also include those procedures which will be useful in the transfer of newly acquired basic skills to specific academic tasks.

The teacher should also realize that the initial standardized testing provides necessary but not sufficient information for the choice of the optimum program. Evaluation must be continuous. Observation, nonstandardized and sometimes additional standardized achievement test results, and interviews with parents, teachers, and others in the child's environment, and especially with the child himself, may be necessary.

Our next task was to develop educational methodologies. As the results of the evaluations revealed great differences among the children's abilities, disabilities, interests, and learning styles, we concluded that education would have to be highly individualized. Specific methods would therefore have to be developed to teach the children as well as to motivate them. We also had to find ways to systematize our approaches and at the same time to present the tasks so that teaching and learning would not become boring. Individualization, motivation, methodology, and systematization became our four key concepts. Many papers, two textbooks, and a monograph, as well as several chapters in various books (see Selected Bibliography), were published to describe the teaching methods and to discuss their choice and adaptation to the needs of an individual child. Special materials developed at the Frostig Center are now available commercially.[1]

PSYCHOTHERAPY WITH PSYCHOTIC CHILDREN

Some of the children at the Frostig Center showed extremely severe forms of developmental disturbances. These children had usually been diagnosed as suffering from childhood psychosis or from autism or from schizophrenia. David Horne was my coworker in my exploration of methods which would specifically help these children.

I had always worked with some children mainly from an educational point of view and with others more in the role of a counselor and psychotherapist. The first children who had been referred to me had been children with severe emotional disturbances. Many of these had adjusted well in public school and even later to the demands of adult life, in spite of the initial guarded prognosis.

As our clinic grew in size and complexity, my time for individual therapy became more and more restricted, and a staff of psychotherapists working under the direction of a psychiatrist was engaged. Among these therapists was one who showed an uncanny ability to relate to psychotic children. David Horne's patients improved to an astonishing degree, in spite of the initial seriousness of their illness. David and I decided to study the progress of these children. We postulated that these children were severely retarded in various psychological functions and that we had to find means to establish their developmental status and to study the approaches by which the therapist could improve the children's abilities to communicate with their environment and to master it. Our working hypothesis was that these children, regardless of their diagnosis of schizophrenia, childhood psychosis, or autism, had severe deficits in sensory-motor functions, language development, perception, and thought processes, as well as emotional and social aberrations. We observed unusual responses to stimuli, including overreaction and oversensitivity and a lack of response.

Many of these children seemed lost in an inner world and separated from their environment without any adequate methods of communication. We tried to change these symptoms through a patient, loving, cheerful, and gentle attitude of the therapist as well as through a gradual change in the stimuli we presented and through a gradual enlarging of the range of the child's activities and responses. The more specific lags we hoped to remediate through more specific methods. We decided to code the interaction between the therapist and the child by indicating the main

[1]Developmental Learning Materials, 7440 Natchez Ave., Niles, Illinois 60908.

characteristics of the child's responses. Whenever we observed deviations in movement, language, perception, or thought, we coded these characteristics as well as the form of the therapist's intervention. The treatment was an educational one in its broadest sense. A film on the treatment of the children documented our work. In this film, *The World Outside,*[2] David Horne functioned as a therapist as well as a narrator and even helped with the details of the production of the film.

The conclusion which we drew and which is documented by the film is that the severely emotionally disturbed child has to learn to become aware of himself as an acting, directing person; he can do this only if he forms a relationship to the therapist which gives him the necessary feeling of security.

The child must also learn to relate to inanimate objects. Horne states in the film that toys became his prime weapons in overcoming the children's withdrawal. Language was another indispensible instrument in making the child aware of his actions. The therapist would say, for instance, in a voice which expressed enthusiasm and joy, "Oh, John puts the small block on top of the big one. John has made a tower!"

It is not possible to describe here all the various methods which were used with these children. We tried to convey to them that living can be full of joys.

I am rather appalled by the adverse conditioning methods which are now used with so many of the so-called autistic children. I am even more appalled that these methods are publicized to the degree of indoctrination of masses of people who do not have the professional education for adequate judgment. To indoctrinate people by presenting to them controversial and unproven methods of treatment (Caldwell, n.d.) seems to me to be grossly unfair. Films which are commercially available and which document the results of behavior therapy with psychotic children seem to me to indicate that many therapists use a great deal of relationship therapy in addition to behavior modification methods and that these therapists often have obtained very good results. I am less impressed with the results of behavior therapy which uses aversive conditioning or which is solely based on the giving of tangible reinforcers. These methods seem to train in new behavior step by step, but teach only what Kephart (1971) would have called "splinter skills," isolated skills, such as reading a certain number of words, looking at the therapist when told to do so, stopping certain unwanted behavior, learning to indicate the need to go to the toilet, and so on. These children learn to substitute socially acceptable behaviors for formerly disruptive ones, but I have not seen any child who became self-directive, happy, and adaptable through conditioning methods *alone.* These children seem to remain automatic in their actions, anxious, and unable to direct their own lives. The children in our sample,

[2]S/L Film Productions, 5126 Hartwick St., Los Angeles, California 90041.

with the exception of a very few severely disturbed, brain-damaged ones, have become self-directing individuals who have learned to communicate and cooperate well with others.

While such activities as the development of tests and of the methods to rehabilitate disturbed children and children with learning difficulties were priorities during certain phases of my life, I also devoted much of my energy to the development of a setting in which diagnosis and treatment of children with learning difficulties would be feasible. Since the first little client had entered my home, I had hoped and planned for a place and an organization suitable for my work, which would also provide space for teacher training and research. Growth of our enterprise was slow but steady. I saw first a few children in my home; then I moved to the home of Belle Dubnoff; then, to the first rooms in an office building. A few years later I had the first building I could call my own. Because of the growth of the ancillary services, the additional training facilities for teachers, and the involvement in the community, this building and ancillary buildings were soon too small, and the present new building was built by a lay board. As the conversion of the center into a nonprofit organization became feasible, the name no longer characterized the multiplicity of activities; and so it was changed from the Marianne Frostig School of Educational Therapy to the Marianne Frostig Center.

Administration of this enlarged facility took more and more of my time. The teaching of children and psychotherapy, which had formerly been my main tasks, were now nearly impossible. I therefore decided to resign from my post as director of the institution and to retire to a life of research and teaching. But I wanted first to set up a training program for teachers, so that educational therapists could learn, carry on, and add to the approaches and methods developed at the center.

I had formerly taught at different colleges and at the University of Southern California, and these experiences stood me in good stead in my new project. In association with Mount St. Mary's College, teacher credential, master's, and postmaster's programs for specialists in teaching the learning handicapped have been established. No publication, no honor, no achievement has ever given me such satisfaction as the training of teachers. The establishment of the formally approved graduate programs was the fulfillment of my fondest dreams.

The center's role in teacher training is not restricted to the programs which we carry on in conjunction with Mount St. Mary's. There are also workshops and lectures given at the center and other workshops and lectures in different other locations in this country and abroad. Not only do students come to us from all parts of the world, but I and other staff members have travelled to many continents to provide training. It is deeply gratifying to realize that our work contributes to a worldwide effort to help children develop their capabilities to the fullest.

IN THE PRESENT AND IN RETROSPECT

It is a clear day. From my desk in my apartment in Santa Monica, I can look out across the ocean and watch the sailboats on the shimmering water and see the mountains of Catalina Island in the distance. If I look from another window I can see the San Bernardino Mountains standing clearly against the sky, and far in the distance the snow-covered peak of San Jacinto. As I look at this beautiful scene, I feel myself to be exceedingly fortunate. I remember the dangers of war and persecution that I was able to escape through the kindness and help of many people—I owe my life to them; and I feel the deepest gratitude to the many who have helped me so devotedly in my quest to help children with learning disabilities. Most particularly I am indebted to my coauthor, coworker, and friend of many years, Phyllis Maslow, to my esteemed teacher and friend, Welty Lefever, to John Whittlesey, Russ Orpet, and to the countless others who have shared with me the joy of undertaking a common humanitarian task.

Life has its distinct phases, not only during childhood. A human organism is made aware of these phases, of their beginnings and endings, through markers erected by society, such as baptism, school entrance, confirmation, school leaving, and so on. The redirection of one's life which is introduced by these events emphasizes the biological changes. They are the symbols on a clock which is wound but once, and whose hands will never point again to the symbol they have passed. We should not regret this unceasing march of time. The completion of one phase means always the beginning of another, with new experiences and opportunities. Perhaps this applies to death itself.

I have recently ended another phase by retiring from my position as executive director of the Marianne Frostig Center. This "retirement," by freeing me from the burdens of administration, permits me to concentrate my energies on the exploration of the results of teaching methods which are designed to match the ability patterns and experiences of individual children. The study of test results and observational notes provides the clues to the needs of the children. Thus I am still learning and am still teaching others what I learn. Not only am I able to enjoy my relationship with children and teachers at the Frostig Center with a new freedom, but I am also able to accept invitations to lecture abroad as well as in this country and gain new experiences and perspectives. I feel about the present as I have about most of the past: Life is a beautiful gift.

My work and my total life experiences have shaped my philosophy of education. My own experiences, and the reports concerning the cruel wars and the famines in Indo-China, Pakistan, Africa, Europe, and in other places on this earth, have convinced me that the main task of the educator is to develop a more compassionate generation. The attainment of this goal can only be possible when the teacher furthers moral as well as cognitive development. The main task of the teacher must be to develop methods to help children to guide their actions by their thoughts and deepest feelings rather than by their impulses, to see the consequences of their actions, and to solve problems intelligently and compassionately. Cognitive education has to be integrated with an education of attitudes marked by sensitivity to the feelings and experiences of others.

At this time in the history of mankind, there is danger to the very survival of the human race. I regard education as a prime means to avoid such disaster, provided the millions of educators try to do their part in this respect. If their experiences match mine, they will find that in thus making their lives useful to others, they will find great happiness for themselves.

REFERENCES

Caldwell, B. M. Child development and social policy. Unpublished report on research supported in part by grants from OCD, the Carnegie Corporation, and the Rockefeller Brothers Fund.

Cruickshank, W. M., Bice, H. V., & Wallen, N. E. *Perception and cerebral palsy.* Syracuse: Syracuse University Press, 1957.

Frostig, M. The future of perceptual training. Paper presented at Leadership Conference, University of Michigan, Ann Arbor, November, 1974.

Frostig, M., & Horne, D. *The Frostig program for the development of visual perception.* 1964. (Rev. ed.) Chicago: Follett, 1973.

Frostig, M., Horne, D., & Miller, A. *Pictures and patterns: Teacher's guides and workbooks.* 1966. (Rev. ed.) Chicago: Follett, 1972.

Frostig, M., Lefever, D. W., & Whittlesey, J. R. B. *The Marianne Frostig Developmental Test of Visual Perception.* Palo Alto, Calif.: Consulting Psychologists Press, 1964.

Goldstein, K. *Language and language disturbances.* New York: Grune & Stratton, 1948.

Gottschaldt, K. Uber den Einfluss der Erfahrung auf die Warhnehmung von Figuren. I. *Psychol. Foroch.,* 1926, **8,** 261–317. II. *Psychol. Forsch.,* 1929, **12,** 1–87.

Guilford, J. P. A system of psychomotor abilities. *American Journal of Psychology,* 1958, **71,** 164–74.

Kephart, N. C. The slow learner in the classroom. (2nd ed.) Columbus, Ohio: Charles E. Merrill, 1971.

Kilty, W. Personal communication. Re: Research on children of frequently moving army personnel. 1974.

Kirk, S. A., McCarthy, J. J., & Kirk, W. D. *The Illinois Test of Psycholinguistic Abilities.* Urbana: University of Illinois Press, 1968.

Koppitz, E. M. *The Bender Gestalt Test for Young Children.* New York: Grune & Stratton, 1964.

Maslow, P., Frostig, M., Lefever, D. W., & Whittlesey, J. R. B. The Marianne Frostig Developmental Test of Visual Perception, 1963 standardization. *Perceptual and Motor Skills, Monograph Supplement,* 1964, **19,** 463–99.

Montessori, M. *Dr. Montessori's own handbook.* New York: Schocken, 1965.

Nicks, D. C., & Fleishman, E. A. What do physical tests measure? A review of factor analytic studies. Technical Report I, prepared for the Office of Naval Research by Yale University Departments of Industrial Administration and Psychology. New Haven: Yale University Press, 1960.

Orpet, R. *Frostig Movement Skills Test Battery.* Palo Alto, Calif.: Consulting Psychologists Press, 1972.

Strauss, A. A., & Kephart, N. C. *Psychopathology and education of the brain-injured child,* Vol. II. *Progress in theory and clinic.* New York: Grune & Stratton, 1955.

Strauss, A. A., & Lehtinen, L. *Psychopathology and education of the brain-injured child.* Vol. I.: *Fundamentals and treatment.* New York: Grune & Stratton, 1947.

Wechsler, D. *Wechsler Intelligence Scale for Children.* New York: The Psychological Corporation, 1973.

Wedell, K. Variations in perceptual ability among types of cerebral palsy. *Cerebral Palsy Bulletin,* 1960, **2,** 149–57.

Wepman, J. *Wepman Test of Auditory Discrimination.* Chicago: Language Research Associates, 1958.

Werner, H. *Comparative psychology of mental development.* Chicago: Follett, 1948.

A SELECTED BIBLIOGRAPHY OF WORKS BY
MARIANNE FROSTIG

Frostig, M. Visual perception in the brain-injured child. *American Journal of Orthopsychiatry,* 1963, **33,** 665–71.

Frostig, M. Corrective reading in the classroom. *The Reading Teacher,* 1965, **18,** 573–80.

Frostig, M. The needs of teachers for specialized information on reading. In W. M. Cruickshank (Ed.), *The teacher of brain-injured children: A discussion of the bases of competency.* Syracuse: Syracuse University Press, 1966.

Frostig, M. Testing as a basis for educational therapy. *Journal of Special Education,* 1967, **2,** 15–34.

Frostig, M. A treatment program for children with learning difficulties. In M. Bortner (Ed.), *Evaluation and education of brain-injured children.* Springfield, Ill.: Charles C Thomas, 1967. Pp. 223–42.

Frostig, M. Education of children with learning disabilities. In H. Myklebust (Ed.), *Progress in learning disorders,* Vol I. New York: Grune & Stratton, 1968. Pp. 234–66.

Frostig, M. Visual modality, research and practice. In H. Smith (Ed.), *Perception and reading,* Vol. 12, Pt. 4. Newark, Del.: International Reading Association, 1968.

Frostig, M. *Move-Grow-Learn.* Chicago: Follett, 1969.

Frostig, M. Jim (a child with familial language disorder). In A. J. Harris (Ed.), *Casebook on reading disability.* New York: McKay, 1970.

Frostig, M. *Movement education: Theory and practice.* Chicago: Follett, 1970.

Frostig, M. The analysis of cognitive and communicative abilities. *Journal of Special Education,* 1971, **5,** 151–53.

Frostig, M. *Selection and adaptation of reading methods.* San Rafael, Calif.: Academic Therapy Publications, 1973.

Frostig, M. The future of perceptual training. Paper presented at Leadership Conference, University of Michigan, Ann Arbor, November, 1974.

Frostig, M. The role of perception in the integration of psychological functions. In W. M. Cruickshank & D. P. Hallahan (Eds.), *Perceptual and learning disabilities in children,* Vol. I. Syracuse: Syracuse University Press, 1975.

Frostig, M., & Horne, D. Changes in language and behavior in psychotic children during successful therapy: Method of evaluation and findings. *American Journal of Orthopsychiatry,* 1963, **33,** 734–37.

Frostig, M., & Horne, D. An approach to the treatment of children with learning difficulties. In J. Hellmuth (Ed.), *Learning disorders,* Vol. 1. Seattle: Special Child Publications, 1965. Pp. 293–305.

Frostig, M., & Horne, D. The Marianne Frostig Center of Educational Therapy. In M. V. Jones (Ed.), *Special education programs within the United States.* Springfield, Ill.: Charles C Thomas, 1968. Pp. 122–48.

Frostig, M. & Horne, D. *Frostig program for the development of visual perception.* (Rev. ed.) Chicago: Follett, 1973.

Frostig, M., Horne, D., & Miller, A. Beginning, intermediate, and advanced *Teachers Guides to Pictures and Patterns.* (Rev. ed.) Chicago: Follett, 1972.

Frostig, M., Lefever, D. W., & Whittlesey, J. R. B. *The Marianne Frostig Developmental Test of Visual Perception.* Palo Alto, Calif.: Consulting Psychologists Press, 1964.

Frostig, M., & Maslow, P. Language training: A form of ability training. *Journal of Learning Disabilities,* 1968, **1,** 105–15.

Frostig, M., & Maslow, P. Reading, developmental abilities, and the problem of the match. *Journal of Learning Disabilities,* 1969, **2,** 571–74.

Frostig, M., & Maslow, P. Treatment methods and their evaluation in educational therapy. In J. Hellmuth (Ed.), *Educational Therapy,* Vol. 2. Seattle: Special Child Publications, 1969.

Frostig, M., & Maslow, P. Visual perception and early education. In L. Tarnopol (Ed.), *Introduction to learning disabilities: Educational and medical management.* Springfield, Ill.: Charles C Thomas, 1969.

Frostig, M., & Maslow, P. Visual perception, integrative functions, and academic learning. *Journal of Learning Disabilities,* 1972, **5,** 1–15.

Frostig, M., & Maslow, P. *Learning problems in the classroom.* New York: Grune & Stratton, 1973.

Frostig, M., & Orpet, R. Cognitive theories and diagnostic procedures for children with learning difficulties. In B. Wolman (Ed.), *Manual of child psychopathology.* New York: McGraw-Hill, 1972. Pp. 820–43.

Maslow, P., Frostig, M., Lefever, D. W., & Whittlesey, J. R. B. The Marianne Frostig Developmental Test of Visual Perception, 1963 standardization. *Perceptual and Motor Skills, Monograph Supplement,* 1964, **19,** 463–99.

Sands, R., Frostig, M., & Horne, D. Educational therapy in learning difficulties: The role of the pediatrician in prevention, diagnosis, and therapy. *American Journal of Diseases of Children,* 1964, **107,** 155–59.

6
James J. Gallagher

James J. Gallagher was born in 1926 in Pittsburgh, Pennsylvania. He received a B.S. degree from the University of Pittsburgh in 1948, a M.S. degree from the Pennsylvania State University in 1950, and a Ph.D. degree, also from Penn State, in 1951. Since 1970 Dr. Gallagher has been director of the Frank Porter Graham Child Development Center and Kenan Professor of Education at the University of North Carolina at Chapel Hill.

Dr. Gallagher's career has included a variety of professional and administrative posts. From 1951 to 1952 he was director of psychological services at Dayton Hospital for Disturbed Children, Dayton, Ohio. From 1952 to 1954 he was assistant professor and assistant director of the Psychology Clinic at Michigan State University. During the years 1954 through 1967 he served on the faculty of the University of Illinois and was associate director of the Institute for Research on Exceptional Children at that university. He was on leave from the University of Illinois from 1966 through 1967 in order to serve as visiting adjunct professor at Duke University and from 1959 through 1960 in order to become senior investigator for a National Science Foundation fellowship at Stanford University, studying mathematics and improving research capabilities. In 1967 he became Associate Commissioner of Education, U.S. Office of Education, and chief, Bureau of Education for the Handicapped, a post he held until 1969. From 1969 to 1970 Dr. Gallagher was Deputy Assistant Secretary for Planning, Research, and Evaluation, U.S. Office of Education, Department of Health, Education and Welfare.

Dr. Gallagher has served many professional organizations. He is a past president of the Council for Exceptional Children and of The Association for the Gifted, a member of the Professional Advisory Board of the Association for Children with Learning Disabilities, a member of the National Advisory Committee on Classification of Exceptional Children, and a consultant to national and state leadership training institutes on the gifted *and talented. In addition, he has contributed in various capacities to numerous other state and national panels, committees, and boards.*

Dr. Gallagher has written much in the areas of child development and special education. A selected bibliography of his many works appears on page 208.

CHANGING VIEWS OF CHILDREN
WITH LEARNING DISABILITIES

The offer to relive a part of one's professional career through this chapter is very tempting. With very little effort it could be such a personal odyssey that all that emerges is a stupifying ego trip. In order to protect against that as much as possible, I've tried to order my recollections in terms of sequential changes that have taken place in my attitude towards children with learning disabilities, over the twenty-five years that I have been involved with them. This period of time can be characterized as representing the systematic abandoning of one set of hypotheses after another in search of a closer approximation to the reality of the causes and potential remedial programs that could benefit these children.

DOES LEARNING DISABILITIES STEM FROM MENTAL
HEALTH PROBLEMS?

Although I had previously met children with unusual patterns of development in an internship in Southbury Training School for the Mentally Retarded in Southbury, Connecticut, my first organized and systematic hypothesis about causes and cures for these youngsters was developed in the graduate program in clinical and child psychology at the Pennsylvania State University. During that period, the emphasis in training was a rather peculiar blend of neo-Freudianism and the client-centered therapy of Carl Rogers, with a dash of Clark Hull and B. F. Skinner thrown in for seasoning. In each of these theoretical positions there was an underlying assumption that if a child has serious learning problems in school, such problems stem in large measure from interpersonal relationships that have failed in the family. Therefore, academic problems are a symptom of interpersonal relationship problems and indicators of problems in the self-concept of the individual himself. These assumptions then led to the remedial strategy of play therapy and parent counseling with a relative disinterest in specific remedial work on the academic problem itself, since it was seen as only a symptom of the major problem.

In spite of the persuasive arguments of a good set of professors, I never was totally convinced of the complete legitimacy of that approach, although it obviously holds for individual cases. I think my skepticism was born out of listening to the experiences of my mother, who had extensive experience as a teacher of the educable retarded and who personally demonstrated to me that a youngster can change from being unhappy to being extremely happy in the educational situation by means of improving his or her competencies in dimensions seen as important to the child. Thus, teaching the child to type, which was one of my mother's unique and special skills, enhanced the self-image of many mentally retarded youngsters and literally turned many behaviorally disruptive children into extremely enthusiastic, cooperative, and happy students. So it was clear to me that it was not necessary to hypothesize, in every case, a deep underlying emotional cause of learning problems; and, further, if one directly attacked the learning problem, there would be a possibility of major change in the emotional status of the child. It suggested a conclusion that the emotional and academic areas are linked together, and substantial improvement in either could carry over and benefit the other.

My own feelings about the relationship between one's self-concept and learning problems is amply summed up in a *New Yorker* cartoon that had a man at a party expressing himself to a companion, "The problem is not that I feel inferior, I *am* inferior." Children who are not performing up to teacher expectation in the classroom are all too well aware that they are not doing well. Such observations can indeed lead to low self-concept and feelings of inferiority. These feelings of inferiority probably cannot be erased by merely discussing them, since they are not misperceptions of the child but adequate perceptions of an unfortunate set of characteristics. Therefore, the appropriate remedial effort should be focused on dealing with the correctly perceived deficiency and relying upon the child's own ability to perceive his increasing competence as the best medicine for improving self-image and feeling comfortable.

During the three years that followed my doctorate degree, in which I worked in child guidance clinics in public and university settings, these kinds of youngsters that are now called "learning disabled" appeared from time to time; and I dealt with them as best I could from a kind of remedial reading strategy which sometimes worked and sometimes didn't.

DOES LEARNING DISABILITIES STEM FROM EARLY BRAIN INJURY?

The next major shift in my attention to the problem presented by these youngsters came with my move in 1954 to the University of Illinois, to become a member of the staff of the Institute for Research on Exceptional Children. The Institute was at that time, and for the thirteen years that followed my arrival, under the direction of Dr. Sam Kirk. Upon my arrival at the Institute Sam mentioned that there was a possibility of a major research project on brain-injured children that could receive funds from the state mental health program, *if* he could deliver to them both a proposal for and a director of such a project. I expressed my own interest in the project. The proposal was made and accepted, and thus began a four-year research project that was carried out at the Dixon State School for the Retarded in Dixon, Illinois. This project focused on the identification and tutoring of brain-injured mentally retarded children.

The reasons for this special attention to brain-injured children reflected the professional climate of the time. We were in the mid-1950s—in the midst of the strong influence of Alfred Strauss, who had brought forth a series of clear statements and positions in collaboration with Laura Lehtinen and Newell Kephart (Strauss & Lehtinen, 1947; Strauss & Kephart, 1955). These described the presumed etiology of youngsters with special learning problems. That is, early brain injury was assumed to be the cause of the differential development of these children. Laura Lehtinen reported a series of remedial programs that provided clear directions as to how to remediate the deficits of these children.

Also, Sam Kirk was particularly interested in the problem, since he had just obtained initial results from his preschool stimulation program (Kirk, 1958). His results suggested that children with demonstrated organic injury profited less from remedial efforts in his nursery school stimulation program than did children without such identifiable problems, even if both groups were of the same approximate ability level.

The Dixon project was designed to provide a tutorial program that was individually tailored for youngsters who were brain-injured and mentally retarded. The tutorial approach was based upon the earlier experience of Kirk that these organically injured youngsters, because of their particular developmental patterns, might not respond well in group instructional situations. The Strauss Syndrome, as the pattern of characteristics eventually would be labeled, is composed of perceptual difficulties, attentional problems, and hyperactivity. It also seemed to dictate a tutorial strategy in which a teacher would work with one child at a time and could tailor the material to the youngster. He or she would more likely have success experiences from academic exercises and would allow the tutor to gain more control over the educational environment, which would thus reduce the child's tendencies toward distractability and frenetic activity.

Under the direction of Paul Benoit, who led a staff of three other tutorial specialists hired to work in the project at Dixon State School, a population of over forty youngsters was identified as organically injured and mentally retarded. The procedural plan for the project was that extensive diagnostic testing would be done on each youngster. On the basis of that testing, a series of tutorial lessons would be devised to help the youngsters improve development in those areas in which they were markedly deficient.

The staff dutifully followed the Strauss principles and planned to work in small tutorial rooms provided for us by the Dixon State School in a new cottage just constructed. The rooms would be bare except for a table and a couple of chairs—even the windows would be screened off, making the environment as free of distracting stimuli as possible. The only stimuli would be the specific tutorial lessons that the teacher was presenting the youngster. At that time there were extreme strictures against having colorful pictures or bulletin boards on the walls or allowing the child to be distracted, even by jewelry worn by the teacher.

Thanks to the cooperation of the director of the institution, Bob Wallace, it was possible to set up a careful experimental design matching the youngsters in mental level and dividing them into experimental and control groups. The experimental group received one hour of tutoring a day, while the controls received the usual institutional program. After two years, the experimental group was removed from treatment and the previous control group was taken on as tutorial subjects in an experimental transposition to see (1) whether the experimental children could retain the gains they had made and (2) whether the control children could respond at a higher level of development under the tutorial program than they had in the two years they had merely been control group subjects. A final examination of both groups was taken a year later, after the tutorial program was abandoned.

It was this basic experience which caused me to have growing doubts about the validity of the Strauss Syndrome and of the accompanying remedial strategies, per se. One of the early products of the program was the publication of a child development monograph (Gallagher, 1957) which tried to review the literature on comparing brain-injured versus nonbrain-injured children across a number of variables. Matched groups (on mental age) of brain-injured and nonbrain-injured children were compared on their performance on an extensive battery of tests given to the brain-injured children in the basic tutorial experiment. That study and the review of the literature suggested that the differences in the groups rested less in the perceptual-motor skills (see Cruickshank et al., 1961), which were regarded as the central key towards remediation, and more in the behavioral and attentional domain. The brain-injured children in our study received consistently poorer ratings by teachers on the observable dimensions of attention, hostility, aggressive behavior, etc., than did their familial counterparts.

We were also impressed by the great diversity of developmental patterns and characteristics of the brain-injured youngsters in the tutorial program. Some of the youngsters did show the Strauss Syndrome and behaved much as was expected, but others showed so little sign of the specific syndrome of hyperactivity, attentional, and perceptual disorders that we went back and reexamined the neurological reports which diagnosed the youngsters as brain-injured in the first place. In this regard, we had not only the diagnosis of the medical staff at the institution but specific examinations by consulting neurologists and EEG patterns that were specially read for this project by University of Illinois medical school staff. There was little doubt in our minds that the great majority of youngsters in the project were clearly brain-injured, whereas for the rest of the youngsters a good case could be made for their neurological involvement, given the degree of sophistication of neurological diagnosis at the time of this study (in the middle 1950s). We also noticed that the presumed distractibility of these youngsters quickly went away, if it ever was there, with the consistent personal interactions with the tutor.

In regard to our original procedural plans, a very human thing happened. The tutors were scheduled to have roughly forty to forty-five minute tutorial sessions with each youngster and would see six youngsters a day in this pattern. The tutors were originally supposed to take out of the desk in the tutorial room only the special material and exercise that they were going to use with the particular youngster. After the tutoring session they were supposed to carefully replace these materials out of sight, bringing forth the new set for the next child, who would be arriving in fifteen minutes. Those who have taught youngsters realize how impractical this was. Eventually, the teachers found that they could not put all of the materials back; and a lot of the materials would be lying around the tutorial room when the next child came in. To the surprise of the tutors, this did not seem to interfere with the tutoring session, nor did the child seem to be unduly distracted by the presence of various other irrelevant materials or information around him. It seemed as though the direct and specific instruction of the tutorial settings was sufficient to counteract whatever distractible traits the youngster had. This result confirmed in our own mind the wisdom of the tutorial strategy approach.

In our search for the elusive perceptual-motor problems that we were convinced were present in these children, we devised a number of tests on which we expected the brain-injured youngster to do poorly. In one such test we had a series of cards with pictures of common objects like a shoe, a spoon, or a house. We then took identical photographs and put strips of adhesive tape over the pictures, breaking up the gestalt or the wholeness of the pictures. According to the Strauss and Lehtinen theory, such a destruction of the total gestalt would cause the brain-injured youngsters to be unable to identify the objects. Our first surprise was that the brain-injured youngsters going through the set of pictures could identify almost as many of the broken-up pictures as they could the undisturbed pictures. This suggested to us that visual perception was not the basic problem.

As pointed out earlier, a minority of the youngsters did show the Strauss Syndrome in reversing geometric figures, plus in a certain amount of general hyperactivity. Even then, such perceptual-motor problems seemed to relate neither to the academic performance of the child nor to successful remediation. It was possible to remediate these perceptual-motor problems, but the gains did not seem to carry over to other dimensions. In short, the demonstrated perceptual-motor problems of these youngsters did not seem to be the central issue, but merely an observable side-issue to the educational problems of the learning disability child.

The overall results of the project (Gallagher, 1960, 1962) revealed an improvement of the I.Q. score of the experimental group over the control group of between five to ten I.Q. points, with a couple of youngsters gaining as much as twenty or twenty-five I.Q. points. The younger the child, the more responsive he was to remediation. We also showed a lesser ability of the control group to respond to remediation during the third year, when they received special tutoring. The weaker response was attributed to the more advanced age of that group by the time they reached the tutorial sessions two years later.

In the end we reached the conclusion that the basic problem of children with learning disabilities lies not so much in visual perception as in a general pattern of behavior in which the child shows a disoriented and disorganized approach to his environment. It is the inability to pay attention, to focus on relevant stimuli, and to strain out irrelevant stimuli that differentiates the learning disabled youngster. The learning disabled child seems to be a victim of irrelevant stimuli, all of which have similar power and influence to distract the child. (For opposing views which stress importance of perception see Frostig and Horne, 1964, and Cruickshank, et. al., 1961).

The Frontiers of Learning—Lake Como

While working with the Bureau of Education for the Handicapped at the U.S. Office of Education in the late 1960s, I had the opportunity to attend a unique conference financed by a forward looking business executive in the Westab Corporation (Miller, 1969). This five-day conference, held in a villa on the banks of Lake Como in Italy, explored the frontiers of learning of what we knew about the human brain. Invited were outstanding researchers in the neurological and biological fields from Europe and United States, with a few psychologists and educators added to explore how such new knowledge could be effectively translated for education. The result of this memorable experience was based upon the notion that:

> For the first time, science seems to be within reach of understanding not only in the physiochemical workings of the brain and nervous system, but also the mysteries of consciousness, memory, learning, and other mental processes. This new knowledge could open an entire new era in man's history. Obviously it could have immense implications for all education [p. 1].

The conference itself revealed that we are in the midst of an era of major discoveries regarding the functioning of the central nervous system; in particular, an understanding of the fundamental processes of memory and learning. At the same time, the conference inadvertently revealed something else. In my opinion, we remain some decades away from the easy translation of that knowledge of the nervous system to effective education. Laboratory experiments on memory carefully designed to eliminate extraneous stimuli are difficult to translate to classroom learning, which takes place within a mass of such extraneous stimuli.

It soon became clear that there is a new body of research not yet executed that will have to be inserted between the laboratory knowledge and the classroom before the full educational benefits of these scientific discoveries are realized. The initial notion that brain injury or dysfunction causes children to have special learning disabilities is probably correct, but currently irrelevant for educational remedial purposes.

If there is etiological evidence that the child has received damage to the central nervous system, it is of interest to the neurobiologist, but hardly to the educator. The educator and the remedial psychologist must focus on the problems that such injuries create in a developing organism (see Dunn, 1968).

LEARNING DISABILITIES IS AN INFORMATION PROCESSING DEFECT

The next hypothesis is that the children described as learning disabled have an essential breakdown in the information-processing mechanisms (see Chalfant & Scheffelin, 1969). Specifically, many learning disabled children do not have effective use of the internal organizers of information which code and simplify incoming information. An essential need of the human being is to cluster information in conceptual bundles so that it is more easily retained and more easily retrieved upon demand. Chomsky (1957, 1965) has described and McNeill (1970) has discussed one type of internal organizer, the Language Acquisition Device, which sorts information on symbolic language. This allows the youngster to identify certain grammatical and syntactical rules which enable him or her to cluster the information sufficiently. The child with learning disabilities, who is described as distractible, is in effect a child who possesses limited ability to organize and cluster such information.

If this latter hypothesis is true, then the remediation of choice is the building of such internal organizations or the production of some substitute for them to allow the learning disabled child the same kind of options that are given to the normal child of the same age and level of development.

Early diagnosis can deal with one of the most frustrating of issues—the development of secondary problems (see Gallagher & Bradley, 1972).

The chronic frustration and lack of success that the child feels in not being able to handle expected tasks can well lead to a series of secondary symptoms which can be alternatively referred to as boredom, lack of motivation, uncooperative attitude, etc., all of which refer essentially to the child's response to chronic failure in situations where he is expected to succeed.

Information-Processing Models: The *ITPA*

One of the major influences in the field of learning disabilities in the 1960s was the work of Sam Kirk, who began to discover a number of children who showed major discrepancies in development. Kirk attempted to explain these children by use of the *Illinois Test of Psycholinguistic Abilities* (Kirk, McCarthy, & Kirk, 1968). A flood of research was generated based on the test. This great expansion of research effort proved once again the value of a new idea and a measuring instrument that is easily used.

Coming out of the Institute for Research on Exceptional Children were a variety of research projects and doctoral dissertations which used the *ITPA* to explore the possibility of unique patterns of development in children who were reading disabled (Kass, 1962), culturally disadvantaged (Ryckman, 1966), speech handicapped (Ferrier, 1963), visually handicapped (Bateman, 1963), and mentally retarded. Other studies, such as a distinctive dissertation on the cross-modal transfer of information (Hurley, 1965), were similarly inspired. All of these studies seem to reach a similar basic discovery: In the various special population studies, there were some children with major developmental discrepancies, but not very many! Three- to four-year variations in development were a clinical problem of a relatively rare group of children that Sam Kirk had discovered. At the same time, the knowledge of these children generated much excitement about learning disabilities and its prevalence. The field of learning disabilities expanded daily far beyond the small clinical group that generated the initial effort.

Federal Involvement

My next major contact with these children and their special needs came in a dispute over whether children with learning disabilities really belonged under the general federal definition of "handicapped" children. This was a matter of more than theoretical interest. The growing federal budget for handicapped children had opened the door for substantial increases in resources for handicapped children, and those that were included in the definition were eligible for these services and resources.

Since learning disability children were not specifically named (as were, for example, the mentally retarded), there was a question as to whether they could be included. One argument was that they fit under the phrase "Other Health Impaired," on the grounds that they were brain-injured. Under that assumption, they were included. This was not an argument that appealed to the very active and growing Association for Children with Learning Disabilities, which wished to change the definition specifically to include the words "learning disability."

The reason for the reluctance of others to accept the ACLD suggestion centered on the issue that has always plagued the professionals in the field, namely, the definition. *Who* are learning disabled children and *how many* of them are there? The most expansive of the ACLD advocates were suggesting that as many as 20 percent of the general population could be called *learning disabled*. This scared advocates of other handicapped children, who felt that huge numbers of these vaguely defined children would swoop down and use up the resources designed for all handicapped children.

At any rate, there was some legislation passed that specifically identified children with specific learning disabilities and allowed money to be spent on model centers, training, and some research. However, the legislation also effectively stopped a major diversion of funds for the handicapped into the programs for these children, for the time being.

When major sums of public money are being spent on education, the solution is usually partly political and partly professional. So it was in this instance. The full acceptance of learning disabled children as a part of the handicapped category probably awaits a clearer professional portrait of just who it is that we are talking about.

Parenthetically, it is likely that the fuss over who is handicapped and who is not was the final straw in the categorical-noncategorical struggle. Lawmakers and educators both recognized that there could not be a continual adding of more and more vaguely defined categories into the "handicapped" domain, and pressure began to be generated for a less rigid set of subdivisions within the entire handicapped area. We in special education are currently living with the results of breaking the internal categorical boundaries which the learning disabilities controversy helped to stimulate.

CURRENT APPROXIMATIONS OF THE TRUTH

After this journey of two decades, what remains is some kind of current status statement as to where my own thinking is, regarding questions now being asked about the general area. The first of these questions would naturally be, "What is a learning disabled child?" In my view these are youngsters who exhibit outstanding discrepancies in their individual development which lead to serious academic problems (Gallagher, 1966). It must necessarily be pointed out that while all children with development discrepancies and academic problems are learning disabled, not all persons with academic problems are learning disabled. The learning disabled child may have internal discrepancies in development that are often as much as four to five years between their highest and lowest measurable skills at the time the child is of school age. These are the youngsters that can be considered to have "specific learning disabilities." Furthermore, they are relatively rare, certainly less than 1 percent of the school population. Further, they are the special responsibility of special education, since no regular education program should be expected, unaided, to meet their quite special needs.

The second question is, "Why are there such wide variations in incidence figures of learning disabled children?" This great variation seems to be due to certain professionals' starting their counting from the manifestations of educational problems rather than from the specific characteristics of the child. If one starts from the position that all children who are not learning appropriately in school are learning disabled children, then one can identify huge proportions of the school population, ranging from 10 to 20 percent. Such a population, however, would include a miscellaneous collection of problems revealing no common entity. In some cases there will be children who cannot read because of inadequate educational background or early training, together with children with minor behavioral problems. It would include many youngsters who ought to be handled within the framework of a good regular education program with some minor adaptations to their specific needs.

A third major question needing response is, "What is the current treatment of choice?" For these specific learning disability cases, there seem to be few alternatives to the tutorial approach on an individual basis. A child with an auditory input problem or vocal expressive problem is not going to cure that problem spontaneously without very specific treatment. In some cases this will mean a deliberate plan to bypass the deficit and allow other, more adequate skills to take over. These are clinical decisions to be made in each case based on estimates of degree of remediability.

The treatment picture is complicated considerably by the presence in many learning disability programs of children who have milder difficulties and who turn out to be essentially remedial reading cases. For these children, parttime small-group remediation strategies may well be possible.

The tutorial approach is extremely expensive, and alternatives need to be explored so that more children can receive the benefits of that very small cadre of skilled clinical educators now available. The great similarity of training programs for learning disability and/or emotionally disturbed children has been remarked upon by many others. This essentially provides the opportunity for joint training efforts that can be beneficial to everyone concerned.

It should be clear that we still have major gaps in our knowledge about both the nature of these special children and what needs to be done about them. What we are missing in particular is a developmental portrait of the changes in the learning disabled children over time. The information-processing model devised by Kirk (Kirk, 1966) is essentially a cross-sectional model which views the child at a particular point in time but does not speak to the issue of whether there are expected changes in the developmental pattern from age four to age eight to age twelve.

In a practical sense, there is the question once posed to me by a knowledgeable teacher, "What happened to the wall climbers?" In other words, we commonly observe large numbers of *hyperkinetic* children who wear out parents and teachers alike with their relatively uncontrolled and very active behavior. However, one does not see many such individuals at age seventeen or eighteen, and a very legitimate question is, "What happened to them?"

One of the likely explanations is that brain injury results in delayed control and integration of functions of the central nervous system. Therefore, the ability to do tasks that normal children are able to accomplish at a younger age in terms of behavioral inhibition and control comes *eventually* to the youngster with neurological injury, but comes at a later age. A related problem for these children is that if they are behaviorally uncontrolled during the period of primary grades, then the skill base for their school learning is never established. The academic problems are compounded for that youngster in education, even after he or she has gained control over these impulses.

"What explanatory model seems most useful at the present time?" It seems likely that the information-processing model, if we can modify it for progressive changes in development, is the most useful educational model at the present time. The concept of minimal brain injury for these children is *not* useful because of the difference between our concept of *disease* model and *disorder* model. In the disease model, useful in some phases of medicine, the discovery of the cause of the disease is tantamount to discovery of the proper treatment. Discovery of the cause of measles brings forth a vaccine to cure measles. However, in a disorder model the cause does *not* relate directly to treatment, and learning disabled children represent a disorder in the same way that a hearing problem is a disorder. Therefore, discovering the physical cause of the problem, for example, brain injury, does not tell the educator what to do or how to do it. Such discoveries may be very important for eventual insight into brain structure and function, but the educator wants and needs an educational diagnosis stressing the *current* strengths and weaknesses the child may have in information processing.

THE FUTURE

It should be clear to the reader that a developmental information-processing model is merely one more approximation to the truth about the cause and remediation of the problems of such children. Undoubtedly its place will be taken by other models which explain and predict the phenomena with more accuracy. The important thing is that such attempts continue. Newton once said, "If I see farther than others, it's because I stand on the shoulders of giants." Any scientist must bear homage to the legacy of past scientific and clinical workers. Such pioneers as Alfred Strauss and Sam Kirk will certainly eventually turn out to be partially wrong in their conceptualizations of the problems of these children. By taking a courageous position they allow the next generation of scientists to determine where their ideas are incorrect and what can be added to gain that highly desired closer approximation to the truth. In this sense, scientists working on this problem are part of the river of history: They are affected by the currents of the past and lead to the currents of the future.

In this regard, there is a continuing fundamental disjunction between the needs of science and the very human needs of the scientist. Each person working in scientific endeavors, I suspect, harbors some form of fantasy whereby his or her insights are so precise and so perceptive that they will survive the ravages of time and remain fixed in a changing kaleidoscope of facts and ideas and, by so doing, immortalize that scientist. Such fantasies are doomed.

The mature scientist accepts the inevitability that his ideas will be discredited and changed by additional facts and truths unknown at the time of his or her major work. It is in that spirit that we need to view the complex problems of the child with learning disabilities. Much remains to be discovered about these puzzling youngsters. We depend on the next generation of scientists to provide more effective and precise answers to these puzzles.

REFERENCES

Bateman, B. Reading and psycholinguistic processes of partially seeing children. *CEC Research Monographs,* 1963 Series A, No. 5.

Chalfant, J. C., & Scheffelin, M. A. *Central processing dysfunctions in children. NINDS Monograph,* 1969, No. 9. Bethesda, Md.: U.S. Department of Health, Education and Welfare.

Chomsky, N. A. *Syntactic structures.* The Hague: Mounton, 1957.

Chomsky, N. A. *Aspects of the theory of syntax.* Cambridge: M.I.T. Press, 1965.

Cruickshank, W. M., Bentzen, F., Ratzeberg, F. H., & Tannhauser, M. T. *A teaching method for brain injured and hyperactive children.* Syracuse: Syracuse University Press, 1961.

Dunn, L. M. *Minimal brain dysfunction: A dilemma for educators.* In C. Haywood (Ed.), *Brain damage in school children.* Arlington, Va.: Council for Exceptional Children, 1968.

Ferrier, A. An investigation of psycholinguistic factors associated with functional defects of articulation. Unpublished doctoral dissertation, University of Illinois, 1963.

Frostig, M., & Horne, D. *The Frostig program for the development of visual perception.* Chicago: Follett, 1964.

Gallagher, J. A comparison of brain-injured and non-brain-injured mentally retarded children on several psychological variables. *Monographs of the Society for Research in Child Development,* 1957, **22,** No. 51.

Gallagher, J. *The tutoring of brain-injured mentally retarded children.* Springfield, Ill.: Charles C Thomas, 1960.

Gallagher, J. Changes in verbal and nonverbal ability of brain-injured mentally retarded children following removal of special stimulation. *American Journal of Mental Deficiency,* 1962, **66,** 774–81.

Gallagher, J. Children with developmental imbalances: A psychoeducational definition. In W. M. Cruickshank (Ed.), *The teacher of brain-injured children: A discussion of the bases for competency.* Syracuse: Syracuse University Press, 1966.

Gallagher, J., & Bradley, R. Early identification of developmental difficulties. In I. Gordon (Ed.), *Early childhood education.* Chicago: University of Chicago Press, 1972.

Hurley, O. L. The interrelationships of intersensory integration, visual sequential memory, spatial ability, and reading ability in second and third graders. Unpublished doctoral dissertation, University of Illinois, 1965.

Kass, C. E. Some psychological correlates of severe reading disability (dyslexia). Unpublished doctoral dissertation, University of Illinois, 1962.

Kirk, S. A. *Early education of the mentally retarded.* Urbana: University of Illinois Press, 1958.

Kirk, S. A. *The diagnosis and remediation of psycholinguistic disability.* Urbana: University of Illinois Press, 1966.

Kirk, S. A., McCarthy, J., & Kirk, W. *Illinois Test of Psycholinguistic Abilities.* Urbana: University of Illinois Press, 1968.

McNeill, D. The development of language. In P. Mussen (Ed.), *Carmichael's manual of child psychology.* (3rd ed.) New York: Wiley, 1970.

Miller, J. (Ed.) *Frontiers of learning.* Columbus, Ohio: Mead Laboratories, 1969.

Ryckman, D. Psychological processes of disadvantaged children. Unpublished doctoral dissertation, University of Illinois, 1966.

Strauss, A., & Kephart, N. C. *Psychopathology and education of the brain-injured child.* Vol. II. New York: Grune & Stratton, 1955.

Strauss, A., & Lehtinen, L. E. *Psychopathology and education of the brain-injured child.* Vol. I. New York: Grune & Stratton, 1947.

A SELECTED BIBLIOGRAPHY OF WORKS BY JAMES J. GALLAGHER

Gallagher, J. J. A comparison of brain-injured and non-brain-injured mentally retarded children on several psychological variables. *Monographs of the Society for Research in Child Development,* 1957, **22,** No. 51.

Gallagher, J. J. *The tutoring of brain-injured, mentally retarded children—An experimental study.* Springfield, Ill.: Charles C Thomas, 1960.

Gallagher, J. J. Productive thinking. In M. L. Hoffman & L. W. Hoffman (Eds.), *Review of child development research,* Vol. 1. New York: Russell Sage Foundation, 1964.

Gallagher, J. J. Children with developmental imbalances: A psychoeducational definition. In W. M. Cruickshank (Ed.), *The teacher of brain-injured children: A discussion of the bases for competency.* Syracuse: Syracuse University Press, 1966.

Gallagher, J. J. New directions in special education. *Exceptional Children,* 1967, **33,** 441–47.

Gallagher, J. J. Organization and special education. *Exceptional Children,* 1968, **34,** 485–92.

Gallagher, J. J. The future special education system. In E. Meyen (Ed.), *The Missouri Conference on the Categorical/Noncategorical Issue in Special Education.* Columbia, Mo.: University of Missouri, 1971.

Gallagher, J. J. The special education contract for mildly handicapped children. *Exceptional Children,* 1972, **38,** 527–35.

Gallagher, J. J. New educational treatment models. *Annals of the New York Academy of Sciences,* 1973, **205,** 383–89.

Gallagher, J. J. Preventive intervention. *Pediatric Clinics of North America,* 1973, **20,** 681–93.

Gallagher, J. J., Benoit, E. P., & Boyd, H. F. Measures of intelligence in brain-damaged children. *Journal of Clinical Psychology,* 1955, **12,** 69–72.

Gallagher, J. J., & Bradley, R. Early identification of developmental difficulties. In I. Gordon (Ed.), *Early childhood education.* Chicago: University of Chicago Press, 1972.

7
Gerald N. Getman

Gerald N. Getman brings the perspective of an optometrist to the field of learning disabilities. Born in Larchwood, Iowa, in 1913, he attended high school in Rock Rapids, Iowa. His professional training was received at Northern Illinois College of Optometry, where he was awarded the degree of Doctor of Optometry in 1937 and the honorary degree of Doctor of Ocular Sciences in 1950. He has engaged in additional postgraduate study and research at the Ohio State University (with Professor Samuel Renshaw), Yale University (with Dr. Arnold Gesell), and Temple University (with Dr. Emmett Betts), and continued study since 1937 through the Optometric Extension Program.

Currently Dr. Getman is a member of the faculty at Southern California College of Optometry in Fullerton, California. He and Mrs. Getman are presently living in Irvine, California, having moved in early 1975 from Pennsylvania. Dr. Getman, in his clinical assignments at the optometric college, provides visual care services to preschool and primary school children, with special emphasis on the visual problems of children who demonstrate learning problems. As a faculty member he is involved with the Children's Clinic in the Orthoptics and Visual Training section. He is also involved with the outreach program of the college in conducting teacher workshops in the college's school consultancy program.

Until moving to California, Dr. Getman was chairman of the Section on Children's Vision Care and Guidance of the Optometric Extension Program and consultant for Children's Visual and Perceptual Development at the Gateway School in New York. He continues as a member of the editorial advisory board of the Journal of Learning Disabilities *and the board of consultants for* Academic Therapy Quarterly. *He has delivered many lectures and conducted numerous seminars and workshops both in this country and abroad.*

Dr. Getman's interest is not confined to the practice of optometry. He has served in a variety of capacities with institutions and organizations dealing with exceptional children, including Purdue University Work-

shops on the Brain-Injured Child (with N. C. Kephart, A. A. Strauss, and L. Lehtinen), the Glen Haven Achievement Camp for Retarded Children (with N. C. Kephart), the Summer Achievement School for Slow-Learning Children, Wisconsin State College at Stevens Point (with R. H. Barsch), the South Dakota Association for Retarded Children, the American Montessori Society, the Association for Children with Learning Disabilities, the Pennsylvania State Department of Mental Retardation, the Committee on Vision of Children and Youth of the American Optometric Association, and the 1970 White House Conference on Children. He is a member of several optometric and professional education associations and has received numerous special awards and honors for his distinguished service in optometry and special education.

Dr. Getman is the author of numerous publications in the fields of optometry and special education. Many of his instructional programs and materials are widely used in teaching exceptional children. A selected bibliography of works by Dr. Getman appears on page 237.

No matter what one's specific interests are, or what major forces drive a person through time and situations, when the need comes to recapitulate forty-five years of one's own development, it suddenly becomes an overwhelming task. First of all, one must realize all the nonspecific interests lying hidden by the disciplinary label worn and widely recognized as the author's primary field of endeavor. Second, the major forces are seldom those which others would even think of as being pertinent, because they can seem so alien to the author's visible activities and efforts. The eagerness to participate in a volume such as this one is counterbalanced by the stress and concern over being objective and coherent throughout a very complex accounting of so many years of one's life. Yet the needs so succinctly expressed by the editors in the preface make it imperative one try to meet the challenge offered.

A unique man by the name of Skeffington (who has been my intimate friend and valued mentor for more than forty years) has often said: "If one is to fully interpret an author, an understanding of the author's background is more significant than his present position." The one question I have been asked more often than any other in the past twenty years illustrates this. As soon as someone is reminded that I have always been an optometrist, the question: "But what does that have to do with children and their learning problems?" is voiced in all sincerity. The answer to this question has been feebly given in most instances, because there is no possibility of a simple answer in the moment of time the questioner has available to hear an answer. I am inclined to believe this situation is more common than we realize with many others who are now finding themselves interested in the learning problems of children; it is so expressed in the preface by Kauffman and Hallahan, when they suggest the reader study each author's vitae before reading his or her contributed chapter.

There is always the tendency to stereotype every person by disciplinary label and to assume that this label denotes a uniformity and equivalence in performance and thought. I grew up in a very unusual intellectual climate, one not at all common to most optometrists in the 1930s. As a result, my early preparation was unusual and had strong influences upon the directions I have taken in the intervening years.

213

EARLY PREPARATION

My father was truly a self-educated man, with no formal schooling beyond the sixth grade. Like every other who had the driving desire to become fully informed, his attitudes of curiosity and his thirst for more and more information in his chosen subjects set a pattern of influence during all my early years. My earliest memories of him let me still see him sitting for hours under a floorlamp, surrounded by dictionaries and reference books. He would study late into the night trying to find answers to his questions and explanations for the visual performance of the patients he was seeing in his optometric practice in the early 1900s. The frustrations of his ignorance and the futility of the search for answers not yet available were influences I did not recognize then but have in the recent years when I have found myself in like situations. My father was one of the first of the "functional optometrists" who realized that the measurable structure of the eye, and its refractive labels, did not begin to fully explain all the variations in visual performance his patients would demonstrate to him.

For example, two patients of the same age and ocular refractive measurements, needing the same lens powers in their glasses, would perform on visual tasks in a completely contrasting manner. One would wear his glasses only for highly demanding visual tasks such as driving in heavy traffic, going to a movie, or watching a baseball game. The other would not be able to find the floor in the morning until he had first put his glasses on his face. Or a patient showing the need for a minimal amount of lens power in his glasses would not be able to perform any of his daily duties without his glasses. Further, a patient who needed a very common lens prescription would insistently report he could not hear another person on the telephone or carry on a personal conversation unless he had his glasses on his face. Finally, there were all the children who consistently demonstrated spectacular improvements in all classroom visual performance when given a low lens power for use in all study tasks. None of the classical texts, none of the classical theories, none of the classical lecturers provided any of the explanations for these responses from hundreds of patients over many, many years of clinical practice.

Another very subtle but very significant paternal influence upon the philosophies I hold today was not even recognized by me until very recently. My father was a druggist in the late 1800s and the early 1900s before he became an optometrist. Those were the times (before druggists became pharmacists) when all prescriptions were made up from the essential and generic ingredients. It was also the era when every druggist had to be able to recognize ingredients by the texture, the color, the taste, and the odor of the chemicals. Even more important, every prescription was evaluated by the clinical results in each individual to whom it was given. One of my father's notebooks dated 1894 has come to my attention. This notebook contains many of the 1975 "recipes" for excessive sweating, skim blemishes, corn removers, and shampoos. There are also formuli for "fever rx," "Bill Baker's Liniment," as well as "Horse Tonic," "Mrs. Tony Bruggeman's Skin Ointment," and "Blaine's Hog Remedy." No recipe went into this little notebook until it had been clinically proven to the satisfaction of my father and the local physician. These observable and demonstrable results with the patient (either human or animal) were later to determine the use and development of every clinical procedure in my father's optometric practice—and in mine as a result of his rigid demand that *every* patient had to show improvements, or the remedy was suspect or discarded. I will never forget my father's constant inquiry of me: "Yes, but *why* do you think your patients are more comfortable and effective in their visual activities?" Neither have I forgotten his admonition that what the patient told me, or demonstrated to me, was primarily correct even if there were no scientific proof or explanation for the response. My father's faith in the validity of the patient, and the validity of the patient's answers **if** we could ask the proper questions, has been a strong factor in my own development of clinical skills.

The importance of the individual, as proven to my pharmacist father at the turn of the century, and the fact that drugs which could be commonly applied to animals must be individually prescribed for humans have undoubtedly led me away from the statistics on multitudes and toward the clinical results on one patient at a time. Many investigators in the 1960s and early 1970s, emphasizing and enthusiastic about studies of large numbers of children for statistical purposes, have tended to overlook the individualities of each child (and adult) and have sought averages, means, standard deviations, and correlations in areas of performance and behavior which I feel are not subject to such treatment. I cannot feel confident that individualities are fully considered or explained in what are termed *standard deviations*. There can be no doubt about the need to validate clinical procedures and educational techniques, but even these must be analyzed for their influence upon individuals and the single individual's peculiar responses to the methods. My father's insistence that a tiny bit of strychnine is not a tiny bit to every person holds the same message today, and I feel it is applicable to all we do with children in most of their developmental guidance. The rigidity and exactitude of the druggist's individualized recipes are more important to me now as a lesson for our care of individual children than the gross applications of common methods to large groups of children who have been categorized by age and by custom. Thus, my perspective has always been biased toward the individual instead of the group. Add to this the validation of approaches which comes from their repeatability whenever an individual's peculiar needs and processes are incorporated, and it becomes more difficult for me to accept broad statistical treatments of masses of children and some of the conclusions so based.

Probably the greatest influence of my father's drive for understanding the visual behavior of the patients he saw came in the challenge he passed on: Since he could not find some of the answers he wanted so badly in his lifetime, I should continue the search. I have been tremendously more fortunate than he was. He came into the optometric profession before it was a distinct discipline and had only a handful of colleagues. I entered the profession at a time when there was a strong national movement by many within the discipline to find these answers. Dr. A. M. Skeffington, whom I mentioned earlier, was another driven by his need for answers. With the organizational skills of Dr. E. B. Alexander, he established the Optometric Extension Program. This organization (later to become an international foundation) has spearheaded almost all of the significant clinical research and study conducted within the profession since 1928. It has also carried the responsibility of disseminating this information to every practicing optometrist who desires more clinical expertise and background knowledge.

My father was one of the original supporters of this movement and led me into opportunities even before I entered the professional college. As the last of four optometrists in the same family, I was led into a pattern of continuing search and study upon graduation. This pattern of four to eight national postgraduate educational congresses every year and monthly local study group sessions exposed me to others in my profession who were as eager and curious as I. Out of this came opportunities completely singular and unique in every respect.

FIRST PROFESSIONAL INFLUENCES

The first of these extrafamilial influences came from an annual national conference on vision training where the influences of practice and learning on visual performance were probed and discussed by the leaders in the profession. It was here that so many of us in my profession were first introduced to the concepts of how the human learns to improve his skills in any of his action and information systems. These conferences provided the opportunity for each participant to report his clinical innovations for the extension of his patients' visual skills and to receive feedback and encouragement from his colleagues' use and adaptation of the reported procedures.

From these conferences in the late '30s and early '40s, a number of us moved to two- and four-week sessions in the Department of Experimental Psychology under the guidance of Professor Samuel Renshaw at Ohio State University. Renshaw's vocational and avocational life was completely occupied with his explorations and observations of the visual system in humans. He provided about fifty of us with a laboratory in which we could explore almost any aspect of visual performance we could question. Here, over a period of twenty years, in the company of the best minds in my profession, the lessons of individual differences and individual processes of visually interpreting the lighted world were not only reinforced, but broadly elaborated and extended. Here, colleagues with comparable, and even identical, end organs (eyes) were subjected to every investigation we could design. In spite of any measure of similarity in the structure of the eyes themselves, the differences in the visual performance were frequently spectacular. Year after year, with the unstinting assistance of the best informed and most experienced of my clinical associates, the methods and processes by which the individual made his interpretations, and his judgments and actions based upon these interpretations, taught me how to observe performance that consistently exceeded that one would expect on the basis of obvious structure or classical measurements.

Further opportunities within this laboratory setting (in the early 1950s) to observe children from nearby schools and institutions allowed us to extend our studies into performances and behaviors not usually associated with, or expected among, children already carrying negative diagnostic labels. These experiences, and the introduction to several Down's syndrome children in my own practice, quickly reduced my awe of such diagnostic labels. Too many of the classical diagnostic signs as detailed in the textbooks ceased to be relevant when more critical observations of the children's *abilities* were made. Further, as more critical tests of functional vision were developed and applied, and more than letter recognition on a distant wall chart or static measures of the eyes were considered, these children frequently were capable of giving responses not previously elicited—or expected! This was my first introduction to the parents who were being disregarded and even ridiculed because they insisted these children ought to be able to learn more if the proper approaches could be found and utilized.

At about this same time, the most significant of all experiences occurred. An invitation came to visit the original Yale Clinic of Child Development to make some observations of very young children recognized as precocious and especially alert. The staff of the clinic, especially Miss Glenna Bullis, had become extremely interested in the early appearance of visual skills and their possible relevance to reading readiness. My interest in children was known to Dr. Arnold Gesell. I then undertook more than four years of study. This situation provided a view of the opposite extreme from the Down's syndrome children with whom I was already working and provided a frame of reference in which I could make better judgments of the skills those children ought to have developed for more adequate progress in the total learning process. Within the opportunities for study at each end of this spectrum, I found the Down's children also gave me greater insights and understanding of the superior children and the skills they had achieved. These years of working with Miss Bullis, under the guidance of Dr. Gesell, strengthened and enhanced my already deepening convictions that averages of height, weight, number of teeth, and frequency of cavities could be established by the collection of data from large groups of children—but the performance and intellectual growth of each child was as individually distinct as the dawn of each new day. The full understanding of the child and his peculiar needs would have to come from scoring instruments which would compare the child with himself, rather than comparison and contrast with ten thousand other children. As time continues to pass, and as I continue to work with children of every size, kind, and unjustified diagnostic label around the world, I become more and more convinced there is no average child; and no child who can demonstrate that he is a standard deviation from the mean.

MY OWN PHILOSOPHY

Actually, all of the above is but a scant and brief accounting of the major influences upon the philosophy of child development I now hold. It is obvious that my approach to children with learning problems stems from my developmental bias. Even here, given all the pages needed in which to recollect and describe, it is impossible to present all the influences and reasons for my present posture. There is, however, one more influence of the utmost significance which must be included here, else the early question about what optometry has to do with learning problems will still go unanswered. This is the influence my profession has had upon my personal development. Much of this is already implied in what has been written above, but there is one aspect needing discussion before going on to other details of my personal perspective of children's learning problems.

The reader needs to have some differentiation between the optometrist who practices as a structuralist and the optometrist who practices as a functionalist. If the reader is aware of the differences, he will have a more complete understanding of the relationships I enjoy with education, as well as the growing cooperation between hundreds of my colleagues and the teacher who needs to know more about children's visual skills than he or she is usually being told by some clinicians.

Briefly, the structuralist measures the eyes and makes his clinical decisions upon what he finds only in the end organs—the eyes. He makes his judgments on the philosophy that what the eye is determines what the eye can do. In contrast, the functional optometrist will make the same measurement of the eyes, but then goes on to much more careful explorations of what these eyes can do because of, or in spite of, what they measure. Thus, all the emphasis by the functionalist is turned to ability rather than to defect or disability, as is the method of the structuralist. From this perspective, then, the functionalist has had to develop a philosophy which will account for abilities regardless of structure. This philosophy includes the old and well-proven physiological "law" that function will determine structure and its operation more than structure determines function.

In full retrospect, with the careful consideration of all of the influences of time, growth, and experience, it becomes more and more apparent to me that the individual differences to which I refer so frequently are determined by *what the individual does with what he has.* This viewpoint demands that all of us who consider ourselves to be functionalists go beyond the sheer anatomy and physiology of the eyes into the developmental and learning systems characteristic of the human. Once into this, it seems inescapable that we turn to learning processes, the how and why a human does anything for his own benefit over and beyond the basic survival actions. The moment we functionalists came to these conclusions, we found ourselves in the same areas of interest held by the developmental educator. Thus, how a child learns to use his visual system can be compared with and related to how he learns to use any other information-receiving and processing system.

This conclusion led to one more inescapable conclusion: Vision is a very complex process which includes much more than the eyes. Certainly the visual process originates when light reflected from objects, or brightness contrasts like print, strikes the retina and is then transmitted as neurological beeps to the entire central nervous system. However, the completion of a visual act involves the entire organism and all the relevancies and interrelationships which exist between all information systems. Thus, being a functional optometrist has led me into the exploration and observation of all learning processes and puts me into the academic world—NOT as an educator, but as a clinician who has to understand the total function of the one learning system upon which our culture now places the tremendous load of the printed page.

As I review these years since 1937, in which I have practiced my profession, it becomes very obvious that no person develops a philosophy in isolation; one cannot learn in a vacuum. Greater opportunities came my way than usually come to an individual—first, in the daily practice of my profession where I cared for so many children having school problems and where results were judged by gains in scholastic achievement. Mine is not one of the clinical disciplines where pain and disease are the critical factors to be eliminated. My major clinical responsibilities were the improvements in visual performance on the critical and demanding tasks of the classroom, where vision had to be the dominant information system if the child were to succeed. Thus, diagnostic criteria and clinical results could not be achieved without extensive communication and discussion with those holding similar interests and engaged in similar professional pursuits. During these years, the almost unlimited opportunities to present my philosophy (and all the clinical observations upon which it has been based) to optometrists, physiologists, behavioral scientists, and educators have tested me and my position in every conceivable manner. The approval and the criticism, the applications and appraisals in other optometric offices, the challenges and corrections, the translations and interpretations by others, all have made me carefully examine and reexamine my perspectives again and again. If my clinical recommendations did not assist my colleagues and were not consistent with their clinical experiences, the feedback from literally hundreds of them gave all of us the essential opportunity to re-evaluate every concept being clinically utilized. In this manner, my philosophy has grown almost entirely out of the tried and proven clinical practices where positive results had to be achieved or the patient sought assistance elsewhere. With hundreds of my colleagues supporting and correcting my progress, there came convictions of validity, always evolving out of successes in many optometric offices. Like the most successful teachers, I have been the ultimate pragmatist.

Not only have I had this important and valuable input from my own discipline, but constant input has also come to me from hundreds of classroom teachers who have been able to utilize the portions of our optometric clinical procedures appropriate to the classroom and to the teachers' level of understanding. These years of constant presentation to children, and to those responsible for their progress, has allowed us to replace "armchairizing" with actual practice and observable results. My father's influence set the stage for a pattern of investigation and observation. The years of clinical practice; exploratory research with Renshaw, Gesell, Betts, Kephart, and many others; the constant personal guidance and questioning of Skeffington; and the support and challenges of my colleagues in optometry and friends in education have brought me to a philosophy and a breadth of perspective no person could have achieved by himself. I have not had the restrictions so characteristic of those whose disciplinary responsibilities have deprived them of full exposure to the shakers and makers in other related disciplines.

This personal history should clearly establish the fact that I have not been trained as an educator. I have come into the field of concern for children with learning problems from the clinical side—and this is not the usual route of the academician. This has been both an advantage and a disadvantage. It has been a hinderance at times where closer communication with educators has been desirable but difficult because of our old prejudices about birds of a feather flocking together. On the other hand, it has been a great advantage in every meeting with those whose primary interest and concern lie with the child and his learning problems. The greatest advantage to me has been in the clinical background I could express to others, so they, too, could look more closely at children and less intently at programs.

With children as my primary object of regard, it has been easy to see the values of the divergent views now held regarding programs and issues of philosophy. The very diversity of the inherent learning characteristics of children has proven the values of almost every program which has been applied in the past twenty years. When we have been able to see the children's disinterest and distraction as a realistic critique of the materials placed in front of them, we have come away with a much better understanding of children and their needs. The children's reactions have not meant the materials should be discarded, but have challenged us to adapt the materials so they could be more adequately utilized by the children.

From this particular vantage point, it has been possible to better understand why some materials and programs could not be applied carte blanche. I do not think I am unique in feeling the discomfort and aloofness of those who have become so enchanted with their programs and proposals that they found it difficult to really hear what was being said about their products. It is here that diversity and confusion has hindered our overall progress toward better solutions for *all* children in *all* classrooms. There would be NO progress without the diversity and conflict of philosophies. Only thus can we compare, contrast, and refine what we need to know—but, when these diversities operate to close minds and to halt revisions of old postures, the children and our efforts both suffer immensely.

EDUCATIONAL ENVIRONMENTS

The editors of this volume have requested each of us to describe the specifics of the most conducive school environment and the most effective milieu for children with learning problems. This is subject enough for an entire book, and much of it is already in the literature in better form than I could possibly present it. There are two or three points, however, which I must make—and these will sound redundant because of my child-centeredness. There is ample evidence that most classrooms contain more learning restrictions than they do learning contributions from structure, lighting, seating arrangement, and equipment such as desks and chalkboards—yes, and even in the newest of the audio-visual and closed circuit TV equipment. I will be discussing all of this indirectly later, but I must emphasize our desperate need to gain a better understanding of the physiology of learning and the functions of the entire child as these pertain to the expected acquisition of skills in subject matter universally placed before the child in our present schools.

It is very important here to refer all readers to the research and contributions of D. B. Harmon (1951, 1958; Rappaport, 1975) in his studies of classroom environment and its influence upon children's well-being and their scholastic achievement. This extensive work was done in Texas schools in the early 1940s and involved 160,000 primary school children. Our adult preoccupation with subject matter and teaching materials and the advent of World War II probably have contributed to the neglect of the Harmon data. Immediate information can still be obtained from the *Medical Women's Journal*, March 1942, and from *The Co-ordinated Classroom*, American Institute of Architecture File No. 35-B. The introductory paragraphs to this latter publication provide an insight to its contents.

The human organism strives to grow, develop, and function as an integrated whole. In each of its responses to the forces or restraints in its environment which stimulate it, it performs organically by seeking physical balances with those forces and restraints which meet certain functions on inherently determined systems of co-ordinates. These responses have a large share in determining the organism's later developments, efficiencies, and well-being.

The work environment of the immature organism (the child) must be equally co-ordinated with the organism itself, if we would have the child arrive at an optimum maturity, fully capable of using its resources and developmental experiences in meeting its needs in an efficient, acceptable, and satisfying manner.

Probably the most significant part of the classroom environment is the teacher. It is not my prerogative to critique the teaching skills of the teacher or the training being given to teachers in this chapter. Again because of my clinical background and bias, I do feel obligated to comment that the most effective milieu in every classroom is the teacher's attitude and respect for the children with whom he or she must work each academic day. This is another point I will be discussing later, but my abhorrence of the diagnostic labels which so negatively influence the teacher's attitudes and behavior toward any child having difficulties demands that I speak out against these labels at every opportunity. If we could learn to describe the children's abilities instead of the constant overemphasis upon their "disabilities," the entire milieu would become more supportive and positive. Likewise, the children would become more cooperative and interested and would be much more available and receptive—AND productive!

MY CURRENT PERSPECTIVES

My personal development, my clinical training, and my rich wealth of exposure to many of those people who have made the greatest contributions to our better understanding of children and their needs have all contributed to the perspectives I now hold regarding all children—not just those who so vividly demonstrate learning problems that they get our primary attention. The following are the several convictions I now hold —almost as absolutes—in an area of concern as variable and mercurial as human performance.

First. The validity, ability, and completeness of the individual child must be considered above and beyond any and all diagnoses of deviation from the "norms." The continuing predeliction to categorize children and then devise methods and techniques to suit the category is totally inconsiderate of children. This categorization has been going on for too many years in our standard educational system, and we are now reaping the sorry harvest of thousands of children who cannot read, spell, write, or cipher as well as their native intelligence would predict. Almost every periodical one picks up contains articles about the lowering standards and skills among the children in the standard classrooms. Yet we go on with the same categorizations and groupings of children and the same old methodologies which have less and less relevance to the individual children who come to the classroom far more sophisticated, because of the space age culture, than the children of ten or twenty years ago for whom most of the materials were designed.

I know that some will immediately take issue with me on this because of the old idea that there can be little individualization of materials in groups of thirty or more children. There are now many teachers with whom I have worked—those who know child development—who now tell me and show me how they can individualize for both small and large groups of children. It can be done if the teacher is trained to use the teacher's manual as a guide and reference source instead of a lesson plan book. Having written a couple of these manuals and having surveyed hundreds of them, I know that these can only apply to a small percentage of the children in *any* classroom. They have to be adapted, developmentally reduced, or developmentally extended for the rest of the children. All prepared and commercially produced materials have some value, or they would never reach the market. There are few really bad materials, but there is extensive bad use of materials because the individualities of the children are ignored; or all the teaching is done according to the categories already laid upon the children.

Second. There *must* be an immediate recognition that diagnostic labels are a definite hinderance to the understanding of a child's personal needs. The stigma which usually results so influences the adult's attitudes and views of the children that each child's abilities are either overlooked or ignored.

I have a personal dislike for a phrase now much too commonly used and have been waging a personal vendetta against it for almost fifteen years. This is a vendetta I do not expect to win, but neither do I expect to cease or even reduce my attack. It is my personal opinion that we have harmed more children than we have helped with the label "learning disabled." This phrase immediately suggests to many who share responsibility for these children that they are incapable of learning. This is almost NEVER true!! Certainly, these children do not learn to read, write, spell, and do arithmetic *as we wish they would* for the social success in a symbol oriented culture . . . but they can, and do, learn many other skills if given the proper opportunities. Not infrequently, they even learn many of the academic skills under the physiological circumstances matching their abilities instead of their "disabilities." More often than not, because these children have been labeled as *dis*abled, they are actually deprived of opportunities in which they could learn. The adult who reads this label unconsciously sets an attitude of not expecting any learning progress from these children. Either unwittingly, unintentionally, or because of previous records and reports, the adult deprives the child of the situations he should have.

Back in 1919, a man by the name of Nicholson was discussing a very similar situation. He wrote: "When a tradition once becomes established by the hallmark of acknowledged authority, it takes more than cold facts to uproot it from men's minds—it takes much time." This is exactly the situation which now exists with the phrase *learning disabilities* and its hallmark of the authority of a national organization. The common language of the educators and clinicians who thrive on categorization will continue to hinder our approach to many thousands of children for a long time to come. Undoubtedly these children learn differently and with less ease and speed than other children, but the vast majority of them are NOT disabled and incapable of learning.

Third. I firmly believe we must find a different approach to the research conducted to determine the validity and propriety of methods, techniques, therapies, and materials being thrust upon the children demonstrating learning problems in the academic world. It is my conviction that we are not yet asking the proper questions in many of the projects designed to evaluate the progress of the children being subjected to many of the procedures now available. This need is as great in every clinical area of approach as it is in every area of academic approach.

It would be easy for me to give several examples in educational programs, but since I am not an educator I will stay in my own field of experience and expertise. There has been much written about the values —or lack of values—of perceptual training in the area of vision. In almost every single critique, either favorable or unfavorable, there has been an attempt to directly correlate reading skills with the clinical procedures used. Much of this error stems from the old concept that the eye is like a camera and that 20/20 sight acuity is proof that there are no problems in the visual system. The conclusion has then been drawn that since most of the children with learning problems could demonstrate 20/20 sight acuity, vision has nothing to do with reading ability. This conclusion contains another glaring error because there has been no differentiation between sight and vision. This was touched upon earlier where the differences between the structuralist and the functionalist were presented. This error continues to occur because the structuralist stops his mediation with sight acuities while the functionalist fully explores visual performance. It is becoming of greater interest to me that this error of non-differentiation is being committed by the clinicians who are supposedly best informed on the visual system and less and less often among the educators who are on the firing line when it comes to coping with the problems of the children in learning difficulties.

Further, many of the research studies have been so poorly designed that there has been little or no relevance to the primary question. For example, children have been exposed to extensive "visual-motor-perceptual" programs incompletely described in the teacher's manuals and then immediately tested upon reading programs, as if simple gymnasium or playground routines could be directly translated into reading skills. Only a few of the proponents of visual-motor-perception training procedures have even suggested there might be a relationship here. Many of us who have been studying child development for thirty-plus years have become convinced there is a relationship between the comprehension and appreciation of visual space and the symbols which will be used to express this space. We have contended that if the child does not achieve the mastery of *visible* space through primary movement and exploration and the resulting skill of *visual* interpretation of space, the symbols cannot have the comprehensive values they should have when the child is expected to read these symbols for information he needs. Thus, the research must be done on the visual skills achieved, not on the reading skills which the child will still have to learn for himself under the guidance of an alert and well-trained teacher who can assist the child in the translations of his movement skills into the symbolic skills. The research design must explore the more basic developmental skills instead of the abstracted and projected skills which come later as extensions of the total learning processes.

Let me be very precise on this. I have already emphasized that I am a pragmatist and not a statistician. I am fully convinced that proper research and study should be done, but it needs to be done by those with much more familiarity with the total processes involved and the concepts being applied. This has not been the case in too many of the recent reports. It is also essential that the research be done from the same philosophical base as that utilized in the design of the procedures in question. For example, if the research design is based upon the structure of the eye, while the perceptual training program is based upon the total function of the visual system, there cannot possibly be any valid correlations drawn. My personal desire for validating studies grows each day, but my optimism over its occurrence does not. Until research design is carefully improved, and until we treat children as other than categorical masses, the statistics will continue to confuse us rather than guide and support us for the benefit of children. I am constantly reminded of the several well-known, and highly respected, educators who frequently state that almost nothing which has ever been statistically proven is in use in classrooms today—that most experienced teachers plan each day on the basis of the individuals in their charge and the positive responses received from the individual children, regardless of the "proven" or "unproven" values of the procedures. This situation does not invalidate research and statistical data. It seems to me that it does validate the needs and peculiarities of every child.

I am deeply committed to the idea that if a particular method will allow two or twenty children to acquire a concept that they can utilize and apply in the further extension of their knowledge, it is a valid and correct method, even when data can be presented to show this method did not bring the desired results with hundreds of children in controlled and rigidly structured studies in other classrooms. When a method works with a child, averages, means, and standard deviations lose all meaning and relevance. Somehow the experts in statistical analysis will have to devise instruments which distinguish the single child from the masses; and the research design must be based upon *how a child achieves his answers* rather than *how many answers are correct or incorrect.*

Fourth. The more classrooms I visit, the more consultations I conduct, the more groups of children I guide in visual perceptual procedures, and the more individual children I observe as a functional optometrist, the more convinced I become that we must listen *and hear* Socrates' statement that "we teach a child nothing—we can only arrange conditions for learning." All adults (parents, teachers, clinicians, and therapists) seem to have the habit of imposing information upon children as if our knowing it will automatically let them know it. The evidence of our lack of success is accumulating with more and more high school graduates falling lower and lower in their SAT scores and college entrance examinations.

It certainly appears that we have become so enchanted with methods and materials that we have forgotten the children. We assume the materials will convey the information we wish the children to have if they will give enough time and attention to the materials. One only has to survey a few of the commonly used primary materials to discover that these contain inherent confusion and misinformation greater than the messages they are supposed to convey to the children. If the children fail to acquire the information the materials are supposed to contain, and if the manufacturer's statistics show other children profited from these materials, we are quick to blame the children. We accuse the ones who "fail" of inattention, of lack of motivation, of being uncooperative or lazy. If his school records have already labeled him as "learning disabled" we accept his "stupidity" and pass on to the children who "passed" the materials. We too frequently fail to assess the materials for their inherent content or to see if the information is presented in a manner appropriate to the children's needs and developmental abilities.

If we are to arrange conditions so the children can learn, in clinic or classroom, on playground or at home, we must begin to explore *how* children learn rather than *what* they learn. *Every* child who survives infancy has numerous learning systems available to him. These systems, which have been called *sensory systems* in the past, are much more than mere receptors for stimuli. These are actually information-processing systems and are available to every child to some degree. Instead of testing these modalities for defect or "normalcy" we must begin to explore them for their operational characteristics and for the manner in which *each* child learns to use *each* of these systems. Instead of appraising a child's "strengths and weaknesses" in academic subjects, we must begin to appraise his learning system skills and find the ways he can use to integrate and interrelate these systems. In this fashion, the systems with the greater skill can be utilized by the child to enhance and extend the systems with the lesser skills. None of this is impossible, and many developmental optometrists and many developmental educators have been assisting children in this manner for years. A careful analysis of the Montessori procedures will show how she accomplished this for the children she cared for at the turn of the century. A careful consideration of the concept being detailed here will allow us to better understand William S. Gray's 1948 statement: "No child gets meaning from a word in any of his word perception training. He must at all times bring meaning to the word if he is to be successful in the reading process."

Further, and of greater importance, we must realize that it will be the knowledge of *how* each child learns that will allow us to individualize the entire educational program for however many there are in a classroom. Groupings would then be arranged on learning abilities and learning system skills, instead of pass or fail scores on standardized academic tests which may, *or may not,* be appropriate to the children's needs. One day, perhaps, we can get to the task of fitting the programs to the children instead of continuing to expect our children to fit themselves to our programs. We *must* begin to learn how to "arrange conditions so the child can learn."

Fifth. In the previous four expressions of my personal perspectives, I have implied something which I feel must be more definitively stated. There has been the repeated reference to our need to appraise *how* a child learns, instead of putting so much emphasis upon *what* he has learned. If we are to accomplish this, there must be much more consideration given to the physiology of learning—the functions of the learning systems and the manner in which every child (regardless and in spite of his negative and frequently irrelevant diagnostic labels) learns how to use his learning systems. There is much evidence now accumulating that a child acquires more knowledge through the use of his own learning systems than he does through exposure to information presented to him by others. There must be sound reasons for the clichés like "experience is the best teacher" and "doing is understanding." We will have to gain much more knowledge of the physiology of taction, audition, language, kinesthesis, and vision before we will be able to so arrange conditions that each child can apply his system skills to the tasks we place before him in every learning program. We have spent too many years in the psychology of learning, almost as if all learning took place in the brain and as if there really were a mind–body dichotomy. We give lip-service to the "total child" and continue to piecemeal him according to clinical bias or academic convenience. We can no longer ignore the interrelationships of the learning systems; and, if we are to fully appreciate these interrelationships to the benefit of children, we will have to gain a better understanding of the physiological *purposes* of each of the systems. We must know why the system operates as it does for the acquisition of knowledge.

We must begin to ask such questions as: "What is taction *for?*" "What is audition *for?*" "What is vision *for?*" Up until recently we have been satisfied to answer: "Touch is for feeling." "Audition is for hearing." "Vision is for seeing." The sort of questions I am suggesting can lead us into the understanding of why we touch and what does feeling have to do with reading or writing or arithmetic. We need to know why we hear and what does hearing have to do with the classroom subjects. We certainly must get a much better understanding of why we see and what vision has to do with all of the activities related to learning programs. These explorations will then lead us into the tactual aspects of vision, the tactual aspects of audition, the visual aspects of taction, the visual aspects of audition, and the auditory aspects of vision, etc., etc., until we begin to recognize the influences of each system upon the related functions of every other system.

Since this must sound like double-talk, let me be more specific. We all know that a child cannot spontaneously say words he cannot hear. We must also realize that a child cannot comprehendingly hear words he cannot comprehendingly say. A most vivid example lies in the perseveration of baby-talk past the usual developmental time. The child who lisps or the child who is still using baby-talk very frequently does not hear that others are speaking differently than he does, and he does not begin to hear the differences until he clarifies his own speech patterns.

It is very difficult to interpret a word visually which one cannot say. Every detail of the word may be fully visible and well-printed; but if one cannot fully pronounce the word, the total construct of it cannot be seen, and the symbolic unity of the word will not be appreciated nor understood. To experience this, one only has to look at a word printed in an unknown foreign language. One only sees a series of letters, and this series will not take on the construct, or gestalt, of a word unless it can be fluidly pronounced. Both the auditory and the speech systems play a large role in the development of the visual system. The visual system, likewise, plays an even greater role in the development of the auditory and speech systems.

To take this one step further, consider the age-old concept of "eye-hand coordination" upon which we have built so many of the primary learning programs. Eye-hand coordination is much more than *just* the use of eyes and hands upon the same task, and it is much more complex than the act of copying or tracing geometric patterns. In the very early years (before the age of two in most instances), the child learns the visual characteristics of textures through his primary experiences of touching and manipulating textures of objects. These can only "look" rough or smooth if they have been thoroughly explored for the "feel" of rough or smooth. With still further experiences and practice, the child learns to "see" corners and angles, edges and surfaces, directions and sequences of lines as a result of his "feeling" all of these characteristics.

Every teacher and most adults observing children know the child who cannot stay within lines while coloring or who cannot make the expected corners or angles while drawing. Many of the presently popular tests of reading readiness and visual-motor-perceptual development contain portions where a child is expected to copy geometric forms and patterns. If the child cannot complete these according to established norms, he is immediately diagnosed as "unready" or "immature" or as a "visual-motor-perceptual problem." None of these tests indicate *why* the child fails. In some instances, the eyes are suspected, and the conclusion is reached that this child cannot see. Yet reports are returned to parents and teachers that this child has "perfect vision and 20/20 acuities." In other instances, the observer decides the child does not have "fine motor control" and that he has faulty motor skills. Yet he may well be the most skillful model builder in the entire neighborhood. In the majority of these situations just described, it is not an *either/or* condition—*either* poor eyes *or* faulty motor skills—but is a developmentally based problem wherein the child has not yet learned what each of these systems is for in the total process of serving each other in symbolic tasks. Since he cannot feel the printed corner, he does not adequately see it. He may not adequately see the directions of the lines, so he may be inaccurate in the drawing of them.

Early in this chapter, I referred to the importance of primary movement and the significance of perceptual-motor procedures in the preparation for symbolic skills. It is impossible for me to express fully my personal perspective of the learning problems being demonstrated by so many children without some further comment on this. In this discussion, movement within each of the noted systems has been implied in the words: talking, looking, feeling, and exploring. It is very natural that I, as a functional optometrist, would make special issue of these action words. It is a well-established fact that none of the information systems can receive and act upon stimuli unless each of the systems is also free to move and act within its own physiological design. For example, it has been clearly shown that if the movement system of the hand is rendered inoperable with a specific drug for this purpose, the sensory system also becomes inoperative. However, the reverse is not true. If the sensory system is rendered inoperative with the proper drug, the movement system is not similarly influenced. This experience is known to all who go to the dentist and have a sensory system blocked but not the action system. A point is being made of this because those of us in functional optometry are so very aware of the influence of any of the drugs which are sometimes used to "put the eye at rest" for a refractive examination of the eyes. These drugs actually have a paralytic effect upon the motor components of the visual system, and thus, the sensory system will be so influenced as to interfere quite radically with the information-processing actions of the visual system. In this instance the systems *within a system* can be so influenced that there is detriment to the interrelationships with other information systems. Further, this is another instance where we must be much more than casually aware of what a system is for, as well as how the system operates within the total learning process.

ONE PERSONAL PREJUDICE

Any person who has lived and worked within a particular discipline for as many years as I have is entitled to a prejudice or two as long as a degree of objectivity is managed and maintained at all times. Because I have spent most of my professional career in the study of the visual system and its contribution to the total learning process of the humanoid (both young and old), I must also express my conviction that there is not enough recognition of vision as the primary learning system. Neither has there been enough consideration of its operational purposes in either the design or the application of the learning programs we present to children. Many authorities have emphatically referred to the importance of the visual system and its role in the reading process. Because of space I will quote only four here and would refer the reader to any modern library on the subject of vision and reading. Birch (1962) states:

> One can postulate that reading disability may stem from the inadequate development of appropriate hierarchical organization of sensory systems and so, at least in part, be the product of failure of visual system hierarchical dominance. In such cases, concurrent stimulation in sensory modalities such as the visceral or proprioceptive will function not as essential background to the organization of the visual percept but as a displacement stimulus resulting in the disorganization of visual response, and the appropriation of the visual stimulation to the nonvisual pattern of arousal and behavioral organization. It is clear from this point of view that one of the essential features in the development of so-called *reading readiness* is the organization of a hierarchical set of relations among the sensory systems wherein the telereceptors, particularly the visual, become hierarchically dominant. Failure for such dominance to occur will result in a pattern of functioning which is inappropriate for the development of reading skill [p. 164].

It is apparent that Birch puts all emphasis here upon reading readiness and reading skill because he was writing a book on reading problems. There is good reason to assume he could just as well be writing about all the other symbolic tasks our children face, and his emphasis upon the interrelationships between systems adds emphasis to previous paragraphs here.

Duke-Elder (1942) stated:

> The most salient factor in the evolution of man was the ousting of smell as the dominant sense and its replacement by vision; and to equip the eyes (the visual system[1]) with the power to form the basis of man's physical dexterity. For man's intellectual supremacy the whole nervous system has been reorganized [p. 242].

[1] I have added the parenthetic phrase to Duke-Elder's statement, because of our broadened concepts of "the eyes" since 1942.

Here Duke-Elder is referring to the same relationships between vision and movement also emphasized here.

M. D. Vernon (1952) states:

> It appears that our normally accurate sense of spatial orientation and our accuracy of movements are dependent upon the maintenance of the habitual relationship of the main co-ordinates of the visually perceived field with both the kinesthetic and labyrinthine sensations [p. 91].

Again, the emphasis is upon the interrelationships of the systems.

Even more directly, Skeffington (1962) wrote the following:

> The problem of the "slow learner" and the "poor reader" remains with us. It would seem possible that some generally overlooked factor might have some bearing on the problem. As far back as the midnineteenth century, Helmholtz noted that all that comes to the individual from his outside world are "signs" out of which, as he summons past experiences, he can get meaning.
>
> The act of reading is essentially the process of "matching" the visual signs with the already available auditory-speech organization within the person. The child is delivered to the school with a reasonably good working vocabulary. He uses words and sentences to express himself and to communicate. These youngsters have adequate tools of language stored within them, and can use them. They can be chatterboxes, or they can be grave, reserved types; yet a percentage of them will be the despair of the conscientious reading instructor. Their reading (if it can be called that) is laborious and profitless to them ... and to the teacher. It is a mechanical process that can be likened to the conditioning processes of Pavlovian tradition.
>
> Speech is learned readily by most humans. Reading is another story. Gesell has laid out in detail how the early eye-guided movements of the hand are the "dress-rehearsal" for the day when it will be necessary to follow the lines of the printed page, in full control of the elements of "reach, grasp, and release."
>
> Speech is learned, and so is vision. Vision is usually acquired well and fully, in every aspect of the world around the child, until the culture faces him with the printed page and demands of him the supremely difficult task of matching that visual configuration with a far more developed speech-auditory system [pp. 1753–56].

Skeffington's comments bring us to another aspect of this entire problem, but he especially emphasizes the close relationship between language development and vision development.

As one becomes more deeply involved and exposed to our present educational programs (whether for special children or those in the standard classroom), one thing becomes very obvious. These programs are so language-oriented that there is more emphasis upon speech and hearing than any of the other functional entities of children, which is understandable because the speech of children is so easily appraised.

There are writing programs available to every teacher, but most of these are more concerned with the size and shape of letters and words than with the skills of writing for expression of thoughts and for communication. Many of the reading programs are more concerned with word recognition and word fluency than with the use of reading for the acquisition of information of importance to the child. The increasing failure of children to reach acceptable scores on universal reading tests has kept our attention upon the task of reading instead of the purpose of reading. The comments of Birch, Duke-Elder, Vernon, and Skeffington (and too many others to include here) should alert us to the more critical evaluation of the role of vision in every educational program. We must now question *why* and *how* the child learns to see and *why* and *how* the adequacy of the visual learning system can determine how much a child does or does not learn in the symbolic tasks of the present classroom. The increasing employment of the vision specialist who works in close cooperation with the language specialist, the reading specialist, and the movement specialist is a most encouraging sign.

If we are to achieve the ultimate results of this cooperation of specialists in support of the classroom teacher, there will have to be a complete re-evaluation of the roles of the disciplines who can stand in support of the teacher. Those who are adequately trained in the physiological purposes of vision, audition, language, taction, and movement will have to come into the arena of attack upon the learning problems now spreading among our primary school populations. The classroom teacher cannot be the completely informed expert in all these areas. However, the classroom teacher can be the expert in the presentation of the materials appropriate to the needs of his or her group. As the teacher fulfills this role, and the support specialists make their contributions, every classroom can become an environment in which the individualities of each child will be fostered and enhanced.

Just before Hugh Downs left the *Today Show*, he interviewed Rev. Ivan Illich, whose book *The Celebration of Awareness* (1971) had just been published. Downs selected a passage from Illich's book which I feel is very appropriate to the situation I am discussing here.

> The speed of change (in educational programs) will come from the loss of credibility in educational systems as they now exist. Learning is the result of wanting ... not the result of teaching! Let us rule out the technologies which are making children increasingly more passive! The crisis is so critical, the future is very bright.

From my personal perspective, I see great and very positive changes in the near future. Arnold Gesell always told me that confusion is the most dynamic of the intellectual states because confusion is the realization that something other than status quo exists, and the human characteristically attempts to do something productive about confusion. The confusion now visible to most who are not satisfied with the status quo is being demonstrated by the widening search for valid answers—and the even greater search for the right questions!! One of the exciting evidences of this search is a program being undertaken by a group of educators and clinicians to establish joint courses of study at the undergraduate *and* graduate levels. These proposed courses will not be another rehash of the educational systems which Illich feels are now really losing their credibility, but will be a new curriculum incorporating the most reliable information on the learning processes of the child and the roles of the physiological systems therein. Here will be the matching and interweaving of academic and clinical philosophies followed by the validation which can only come out of classroom application. The first move in this program will occur in the fall of 1975, and the involvement of the several disciplines willing to contribute cooperatively will be an immediate part of the program. I am tremendously excited about being able to participate in this venture.

This reference to *mutual*-disciplinary efforts needs a word or two of further comment. The interrelationships between the disciplines which can contribute to the attack upon the problems we face is really not taking place. There is much talk of the *team* effort and the team concept, but it is little more than conversation. Internal jealousies and the old game of one-up-manship still prevent the unity of the team so frequently suggested as the ideal we must achieve. Most authorities with whom I work have unhappily concluded the team concept, as now held, will not work, because too many of those who should become involved cannot give up any of their personal identity within a team unit. In contrast to this almost universal barricade to the progress we should all be making as maturing professionals is the desire and willingness of many to contribute so the educational team *can* devote its expertise to the academic problems. It appears to me after many experiences in both failing team efforts and successful consultation activities that the time has come for those who do not wish to contribute to step aside and allow those who can and will contribute to do so. It is even more imperative that those who are not trained and currently prepared to contribute or those who do not wish to contribute no longer prevent others from making whatever input is possible. At this point of urgency in the problem, there is *no* final authority and no one discipline in a position to control all the others. Neither can any single discipline set itself as the final judge of what is, or is not, appropriate for children having learning problems.

Just as there must be a recognition of the interrelationships of the information systems within the total child, there has to be a recognition of the interrelationships of the sources of information now available. Just as none of the information systems of the child can be considered in isolation, neither can the information sources be considered in isolation. This concept is not new by any means; but although it is frequently expressed, it has yet to be very frequently implemented because of the reluctance of so many in some disciplines to either listen to or read the philosophies of other disciplines. I learned long ago that I eventually profit most by directing myself to read and examine the writings of those with whom I do *not* agree. If we can all begin to do that, new and positive vistas will be opened to such as those of us contributing to this book—but more especially to every child we will be influencing, either directly or indirectly.

"The crisis is so critical, the future is very bright." I totally agree with Illich and have a deep conviction that our new awarenesses of children as individuals and our rapidly increasing knowledge of the *total* learning process will bring changes that completely violate the old rule that changes within our educational system always take twenty-five or thirty years to happen. Nicholson wrote that changes demand more than facts —they demand time, but we are all well aware that there is a right time for the full bloom of every idea. This is the right time! The changes so many of us seek and work for are on the near horizon, and many of these changes will not wait for another decade to pass. As I review the past decade and what we have accomplished in behalf of children, I have strong feelings that many of our present goals will be reached before the '70s have run out.

Then comes the sobering thought that all the new answers will raise more questions than we now have. There is much comfort, however, in the hope and belief that the answers we reach between now and 1980 will make the new questions less awesome than some of those we have faced in the '70s. There is now a momentum in favor of children which will not be halted, and I would not trade any of my thirty-five years of experience with children and teachers, nor any of my present perspectives based upon children's performance, for anything in this world.

REFERENCES

Adler, F. H. *Physiology of the eye.* St. Louis: Mosby, 1953.

Ayres, A. J. The visual-motor function. *American Journal of Occupational Therapy,* 1958, **12,** 130–38.

Ayres, A. J. The role of gross motor activities in the training of children with visual-motor retardation. *Journal of the American Optometric Association,* 1961, **33,** 121.

Barsch, R. H. *Achieving perceptual motor efficiency.* Seattle: Special Child Publications, 1967.

Not all of these sources were cited in the chapter. While the references provided here by no means represent a complete listing of relevant material, they are provided to justify consideration of the points I have raised or developed in my personal perspective.

Birch, H. G. Dyslexia and the maturation of visual function. In J. Money (Ed.), *Reading disability: Progress and research needs in dyslexia.* Baltimore: Johns Hopkins Press, 1962.

Cannon, W. B. *The wisdom of the body.* New York: Norton, 1932.

DiMeo, K. *Visual-motor skills response characteristics and prereading behavior.* Winter Haven, Fla.: Winter Haven Lions Club, 1968.

Duke-Elder, W. S. *Textbook of ophthalmology,* Vol. 1. St. Louis: Mosby, 1942.

Educator's checklist of observable clues to classroom vision problems. Duncan, Okla.: Optometric Extension Program Foundation, Section on Children's Vision Care and Guidance, 1968.

Educator's guide to classroom vision problems. Duncan, Okla.: Optometric Extension Program Foundation, Section on Children's Vision Care and Guidance, 1968.

Gesell, A., Ilg, F., Bullis, G., Getman, G. N., & Ilg, V. *Vision: Its development in infant and child.* New York: Hoeber, 1949.

Getman, G. N. Developmental vision. Duncan, Okla.: Optometric Extension Program, December, 1950 to September, 1951 and October to September, 1961.

Getman, G. N. The primary visual abilities essential to academic achievement. Duncan, Okla.: Optometric Extension Program Foundation, 1964.

Getman, G. N. *How to develop your child's intelligence.* Irvine, Calif.: Research Publications, 1967.

Getman, G. N., & Hendrickson, H. H. The needs of teachers for specialized information on the development of visuomotor skills in relation to academic performance. In W. M. Cruickshank (Ed.), *The teacher of brain-injured children: A discussion of the bases for competency.* Syracuse: Syracuse University Press, 1966.

Getman, G. N., Kane, E. R., Halgren, M. R., & McKee, G. W. *Developing learning readiness.* New York: McGraw-Hill, 1968.

Gibson, J. J. *The perception of the visual world.* Boston: Houghton Mifflin, 1950.

Harmon, D. B. The coordinated classroom. American Institute of Architecture, File No. 35-B, 1951.

Harmon, D. B. *A dynamic theory of vision.* Austin, Tex.: Author, 1958.

Hebb, D. O. *The organization of behavior.* New York: Wiley, 1949.

Illich, I. *The celebration of awareness.* New York: Doubleday, 1971.

Katz, D. *Gestalt psychology.* New York: Ronald Press, 1950.

Kephart, N. C. *The slow learner in the classroom.* (2nd ed.) Columbus, Ohio: Charles E. Merrill, 1971.

Kluver, W. *Cerebral mechanisms in behavior.* New York: Wiley, 1951.

Lancaster, W. B. The story of asthenopia: Important part played in Philadelphia. *Archives of Ophthalmology,* 1943, **30,** 167–78.

Linksz, A. *Physiology of the eye,* Vol. 2. New York: Grune & Stratton, 1952.

McQuarrie, C. W. *A perceptual testing and training guide for kindergarten teachers.* Winter Haven, Fla.: Winter Haven Lions Club, 1969.

Orem, R. C. *Montessori for the disadvantaged.* New York: Putnam, 1967.

Polyak, S. L. *The retina*. Chicago: University of Chicago Press, 1941.

Pratt, C. C. The role of past experience in visual perception. *Journal of Psychology,* 1950, **30,** 85–107.

Rappaport, S. R. A pioneer in vision and educational environments: Salute to Darell Boyd Harmon. *Journal of Learning Disabilities,* 1975, **8,** 332–35.

Renshaw, S. Psychological optics. Duncan, Okla.: Optometric Extension Program, 1959.

Sherrington, C. *Man on his nature*. Cambridge: Cambridge University Press, 1951.

Skeffington, A. M. What "learning lenses" mean in the beginning school grades —and why. *Optometric Weekly,* 1962.

Skeffington, A. M., *et al.* Postgraduate papers. Duncan, Okla.: The Optometric Extension Program, 1928–1969.

Smith, K. V., & Smith, W. M. *Perception and motion*. Philadelphia: Saunders, 1962.

Strauss, A. A., & Kephart, N. C. *Psychopathology and education of the brain-injured child.* Vol. 2. New York: Grune & Stratton, 1955.

Strauss, A. A., & Lehtinen, L. E. *Psychopathology and education of the brain-injured child.* Vol. 1. New York: Grune & Stratton, 1947.

Sutphin, F. E. *Perceptual testing and training handbook*. Winter Haven, Fla.: Winter Haven Lions Club, 1964.

Teacher's guide to vision problems (with checklist). St. Louis: American Optometric Association, 1957.

Vernon, M. D. *Visual perception*. Cambridge: Cambridge University Press, 1937.

Vernon, M. D. *A further study of visual perception*. Cambridge: Cambridge University Press, 1952.

Wiener, N. *Cybernetics*. New York: Wiley, 1948.

Witsen, B. V. *Perceptual training activities handbook*. New York: Teachers College Press, 1967.

A SELECTED BIBLIOGRAPHY OF WORKS BY GERALD N. GETMAN

Gesell, A., Ilg, F., Bullis, G., Getman, G. N., & Ilg, V. *Vision: Its development in infant and child.* New York: Hoeber, 1949.

Getman, G. N. Studies in perceptual development. *Optometric Weekly,* 1954.

Getman, G. N. Studies in visual development. *Optometric Weekly,* 1954.

Getman, G. N. View, review, and preview. Optometric child vision care and guidance. Optometric Extension Program, Post Graduate Courses, 1963, Series 8, No. 1.

Getman, G. N. The primary visual abilities essential to academic achievement. Duncan, Okla.: Optometric Extension Program Foundation, 1964.

Getman, G. N. The visuomotor complex in the acquisition of learning skills. In J. Hellmuth (Ed.), *Learning disorders,* Vol. 1. Seattle: Special Child Publications, 1965.

Getman, G. N. *How to develop your child's intelligence.* Irvine, Calif.: Research Publications, 1967.

Getman, G. N. Vision, audition and problems of learning. A series of papers released by the Optometric Extension Program, Duncan, Oklahoma, to its members, 1968–1969.

Getman, G. N. Critique [of Cohen]. *Journal of Learning Disabilities,* 1969, **2,** 503–4.

Getman, G. N., & Hendrickson, H. H. The needs of teachers for specialized information on the development of visuomotor skills in relation to academic performance. In W. M. Cruickshank (Ed.), *The teacher of brain-injured children: A discussion of the bases of competency.* Syracuse: Syracuse University Press, 1966.

Getman, G. N., Kane, E. R., Halgren, M. R., & McKee, G. W. *The physiology of readiness: An action program for the development of perception for children.* Minneapolis: Programs to Accelerate School Success, 1964.

Getman, G. N., Kane, E. R., Halgren, M. R., & McKee, G. W. *Developing learning readiness.* New York: McGraw-Hill, 1968.

Getman, G. N., & Kephart, N. C. *The perceptual development of retarded children.* Lafayette, Ind.: Purdue University, 1956.

8
Samuel A. Kirk

Samuel A. Kirk was born in Rugby, North Dakota, in 1904. He obtained his bachelors degree in psychology and his masters degree in experimental psychology from the University of Chicago, and his Ph.D. in physiological and clinical psychology from the University of Michigan.

Dr. Kirk is presently professor of special education at the University of Arizona and professor emeritus at the University of Illinois. From 1952 through 1967, he was director of the Institute for Research on Exceptional Children and professor of Special Education and of Psychology at the University of Illinois. From February to June of 1964, he was director of the Division of Handicapped Children and Youth, United States Office of Education. He was chairman of the Graduate School of Milwaukee State Teachers College from 1946 through 1947, where he was also director of the Division of Education for Exceptional Children from 1935 through 1947. He also served as a Major in the U.S. Army from 1942 to 1946. From 1931 to 1935, he was a research psychologist and remedial teacher at Wayne County Training School in Northville, Michigan. From 1929 to 1931, he was resident teacher at Oaks School for Mentally Retarded Children, Cook County, Illinois.

Dr. Kirk has received numerous awards. He received an honorary degree from Lesley College in 1969. In 1956 he received the Phi Sigma Nu Award of Merit. He became honorary vice-president of the British Association of Special Education in 1962, and in the same year he received the First International Award in Mental Retardation from the Joseph P. Kennedy, Jr. Foundation. He was the recipient of the New York State Association for Retarded Children's Award in 1963. In 1966 he received the J. E. Wallace Wallin Award from the Council for Exceptional Children, the Saint Colleta Award from the Caritas Society, and the Award of Merit from the Association for Children with Learning Disabilities. The American Association on Mental Deficiency honored him with its Training Award in 1969. In 1971, he received the Award of Merit from Cardinal Stritch College. In 1975 he received the International Milestone Award from the International Federation of Learning Disabilities.

Dr. Kirk has numerous professional affiliations and is a former president of the International Council for Exceptional Children and vice-president of the American Association on Mental Deficiency. He is a diplomate in Clinical Psychology and a fellow of the American Psychological Association, the American Association on Mental Deficiency, and the American Academy for the Advancement of Science.

Dr. Kirk has published more than 160 articles, chapters, tests, and books. A selected bibliography is included on pages 268–69.

Several years ago some of us—Drs. Cruickshank, Myklebust, Kephart, Frostig, and myself—were asked to reflect and comment on our contributions to special education and particularly on the field of learning disabilities. I began my address by stating that the committee had inadvertently asked me to confess my sins. At that time I stated:

> My first sin is accepting the reputed posture of an expert in mental retardation and learning disabilities. In this field, such a posture today is usually reserved for those who can show that they have taken a sequence of courses in a field and can obtain a certificate from agencies such as the State Department of Public Instruction. I must confess to you that the two areas of special education in which I have never had a college course are "Mental Retardation" and "Learning Disabilities." In these two areas, according to our present criteria for trained professional personnel, I must admit that I do not qualify, and I also have a sneaking suspicion, although I have not investigated too thoroughly, that my colleagues on this panel may be in a similar embarrassing predicament. (Kirk, 1970, p. 199).

This somewhat facetious comment actually explains to some extent why the field is so diverse and why it was necessary for those who have pioneered in the field to originate their own approaches. Under these circumstances each evolved his own approach without contact with others, and inevitably a discipline with a number of approaches was produced.

In this report it will be necessary for me to (1) explain the various experiences and people who influenced my career, (2) describe the related experiences that led to a more definitive point of view, (3) discuss the agencies that have recently influenced the field, (4) assess the current status of operations in the field, and (5) present a prologue of possible developments of the field. The reader should be cautioned that any of these discussions must necessarily be biased by my own present point of view.

241

EXPERIENTIAL INFLUENCES

My experiences have been relatively limited, including teaching and research at two residential schools, teaching and research in a teachers college, and graduate teaching and research in two universities. The details of these experiences and their influences follow.

Initial Experience at The Oaks School

My professional career in special education began, like that of many others, through the accident of a particular job. In 1929 I had completed my bachelor's degree in psychology at the University of Chicago and had begun studies toward my master's degree. As part of my graduate work I took some courses at the Institute for Juvenile Research in Chicago and was initiated into psychological testing. I also learned a little about problem children by sitting in on some case conferences for mentally retarded and delinquent children. Through this contact with the Institute for Juvenile Research, I applied for a position in an experimental school near Chicago. It was a school for delinquent mentally retarded boys, ages eight to sixteen. This experimental school was sponsored and administered by the chief psychiatrist, Dr. Paul Schroeder, in charge of the Institute for Juvenile Research. During the beginning of the Depression I was happy to be offered any position at all and was very happy to become "Resident Instructor," even though at that time I had had no experience or training in education. My job was to manage fifty deliquent mentally retarded boys and to provide recreation and extra school work in the late afternoons and evenings and on Saturdays and Sundays. In the mornings I attended graduate classes at the University of Chicago; in the afternoon I drove to Oak Forest, Illinois, in a T-model Ford, to work with these delinquent retarded boys.

At this school I taught in the afternoon and served as a recreational worker after school. In the evenings I helped the nurses put the boys to bed and see that they stayed there. In reading the clinical folders of one of these children from the famous Institute for Juvenile Research, I noticed that the boy was labeled "word blind," a term I had never heard before in my psychology courses. He was ten years old, a nonreader, and had a recorded I.Q. of 82. This clinical folder referred to Marion Monroe's monograph on reading disabilities, Hinshelwood's book on congenital word blindness, and Fernald's kinesthetic method. After reading these references, which I found the next day in the university library, I arranged to tutor the boy at nine o'clock in the evening, after the boys were supposed to be asleep. This boy, who was eager to learn, sneaked quietly out of bed at the appointed time each night and met me in a small space between the two dormitory rooms and, actually, in the doorway of the boy's toilet. By making this arrangement we both knew we were violating a regulation, since the head nurse had directed me not to allow the boys out of bed after nine. In the same vein as the Boston Tea Party, and knowing the consequences of civil disobedience, I decided to take a chance and violate the directions since the cause was good. I often state that my first experience in tutoring a case of reading disability was not in a school, was not in a clinic, was not in an experimental laboratory, but in a boy's lavatory.

Monroe had advocated the phonic method of remedial reading, and fortunately I had learned to read by a phonic method myself. This skill assisted me in being acquainted with the approach and also with the ability to use it. I used the phonic method advocated by Monroe; with nonphonic words I used the Fernald kinesthetic method. I found that through these methods the boy could learn to read.

In seven months' time this boy was reading. I sent him to the Insitute for Juvenile Research twenty miles away for testing and learned that he was now reading at the third-grade level. Because it was believed he could now succeed in school, a parole was obtained for him from the judge of the juvenile court. I was also invited to go to the Institute for Juvenile Research in Chicago to confer with Dr. Marion Monroe on the method I used to teach the boy in such a short period of time. Following this conference, Dr. Monroe was kind enough to tutor me in diagnosis and remediation of severe cases of reading disabilities. Incidentally, her diagnostic concepts of the late 1920s are still being used. These include (1) a two-year discrepancy between the Binet mental age and reading level, (2) the reading potential index of (C.A. + M.A. + arithmetic computation)/3 to determine reading potential, and (3) the analysis of reading errors from oral reading, word recall, and word discrimination.

During the two years I worked at this experimental residential school and was studying for my master's degree at the University of Chicago, I tried to incorporate courses to help me in teaching, taking courses in juvenile delinquency and experimental psychology, especially in the field of learning. Courses in handicapped children did not exist in universities in the 1920s and '30s. During summer sessions I took courses in teaching reading and by luck enrolled in a course on handicapped children with Dr. J. E. Wallace Wallin, who was a visiting professor at the University of Chicago for that summer quarter. He had published a scholarly and authoritative book on *The Education of Handicapped Children* in 1924, one of the earliest in the field of education. This book and Dr. Wallin's lectures were inspiring and very helpful. Actually it was the only course in handicapped children that I had during my undergraduate or graduate work.

My graduate work in psychology at the University of Chicago was in basic psychology. The Department of Psychology was famous for having had the original behaviorist, John B. Watson, and for the "functional school of psychology" under Harvey Carr. The functional school of psychology attempted to apply theory and research to practical problems. Most of the studies in learning, for instance, dealt with factors that influence learning and factors that facilitate or interfere with forgetting. This school of psychology was the predecessor of Skinner's school of operant conditioning. Using the principles of learning and forgetting emphasized by the functional school, we were able to organize instructional materials similar to modern methods of programming. At that time psychoanalysis was becoming popular, but the behaviorists rejected such an approach and dealt with symptomatic treatment in learning.

During a summer session of 1930, I enrolled in a course with Dr. Stevenson Smith, the director of the Child Development Laboratories at the University of Washington, Seattle. He scoffed at psychoanalysis, stating that you don't psychoanalyze a child who is biting his nails. You consider the cause of fingernail-biting resulting from a habit which needs breaking by symptomatic training. File the nails short so that they will not be rough and you will aid the child in overcoming the fingernail biting. Five years later at the Wayne County Training School, I did just that. I filed the nails of forty fingernail biters and assisted most of them in breaking the habit.

My master's thesis dealt with the Fernald kinesthetic method. I used six boys at the Oaks School, teaching them to read five words one day using the Look-and-Say method, and five words the next day using the manual tracing method. I continued this for thirty days. In contrasting the Fernald method with the Look-and-Say method, I found that the number of trials for learning was the same, but that retention over twenty-four hours was greater when the manual tracing method was used (Kirk, 1933).

Professional Experience at The Wayne County Training School

By the time I completed my master's degree in 1931, the great depression had hit. Jobs were not to be found, even for Ph.Ds. Applications for jobs often did not even merit a reply. At about this time the Wayne County Training School at Northville, Michigan was looking for a psychologist with a master's degree who was trained and experienced in reading and reading disabilities with mentally retarded children. With my meager experience with the mentally retarded, my experience of tutoring three children with reading disabilities, and my studies with Marion Monroe, I was recommended for the job. Apparently, in spite of unemployment, there was a shortage of people who had done some research and remediation of mentally retarded reading cases. For this reason I was offered the position.

My work at the Wayne County Training School was half-time teaching and half-time research. At this county residential training school, I found that the children had many disabilities—reading disabilities, language disabilities, perceptual disabilities, and behavior disabilities. I was fortunate to have the opportunity to teach and conduct research on children with a variety of disabilities and a variety of problems.

At this time, in the early 1930s, there was great emphasis on brain theory and its relationship to aberrations of behavior—mirror reading, mixed eyedness and handedness, and strephosymbolia. Pathological brain dysfunction was proposed to explain many of these aberrations. Samuel T. Orton's theories of cerebral dominance and strephosymbolia and the work of Lee Edward Travis on cerebral dominance and stuttering were in the forefront at that time. It became obvious to me that to understand all those language, perceptual, and reading disability problems, it was necessary to understand the workings of the brain. Thus, at the University of Michigan, I concentrated on courses in physiological and experimental psychology and in neurology. I did my doctoral dissertation by testing the handedness of rats and training them to discriminate between an *F* and a mirrored *F*. After surgically producing brain lesions and retesting the rats after postoperative recovery, I made autopsies to determine the degree and location of brain lesions and their relation to perception and handedness and to determine whether I could change dominance and create a strephosymbolia in rats. My digression into such obstruse areas as "Hemispheric Cerebral Dominance and Hemispheric Equipotentiality" (1935) and "Extrastriate Functions in the Discrimination of Complex Visual Patterns in the Rat" (1936) may seem esoteric, but was elemental in directing my future thinking. I realize now that studying physiological psychology and neurology and conducting experiments with the brains of rats bear no relationship to what I did then, to what I have done since, or to what I do now for children with learning disabilities. It is for this reason that I have not been concerned with such terms as "brain dysfunction" or "brain damage" or even with terms such as "strephosymbolia," "word blindness," "alexia," or "dyslexia." I feel that it is more parsimonious to give a designation in behavioral terms by stating, for example, that the child has not learned to read.

At the Wayne County Training School I had the rare opportunity to spend half-time teaching mentally retarded children, supervising graduate students from the University of Michigan who were interning in the research department, doing research, and also studying at the University of Michigan for a Ph.D. in psychology. This opportunity was afforded me and others by an unusual superintendent, Dr. Robert Haskell, a psychiatrist who had a high respect for science and research. He established a research department in the institution and treated it as a "sacred cow." As a psychiatrist and an administrator of a children's institution, he felt that his institution needed to conduct research and to advance knowledge. The research department was a result of this belief. He employed Dr. Thorleif G. Hegge, a recent emigrant from Norway, who had a Ph.D. in psychology from Goetingen, Germany, and who had spent a year in the research department of the Vineland Training School. Dr. Haskell, knowing of the Vineland Training School in New Jersey which had become famous through the research contributions of Dr. Henry Goddard and Dr. Edgar Doll, wanted the Wayne County Training School to become famous through research. He appointed Dr. Hegge as director of research and asked him to develop research promoting the academic abilities of mentally retarded children and particularly of mentally retarded children who had not learned to read. The department was manned primarily by psychologists and graduate students in psychology, speech, and social work from the University of Michigan.

The research department at the Wayne County Training School has, indeed, made its mark through developments in mental retardation and in learning disabilities, as attested to by the many famous people who were offered an opportunity to develop their ideas as employees of that institution. Among these are Alfred Strauss, Heinz Werner, Sidney Bijou, Newell Kephart, Boyd McCandless, William Cruickshank, and Bluma Weiner. It is interesting to note that these people developed their ideas in an institution for the mentally retarded rather than in a university. Many of them later accepted appointments in universities after their contributions were known. Unfortunately, today few residential schools offer such outstanding opportunities; few serve as centers of research and development.

During this period, in the early 1930s, my efforts were influenced by Marion Monroe's achievements in the diagnosis and remediation of reading disabilities, which were an outgrowth of her work with Samuel T. Orton at the University of Iowa. I have always felt indebted to her for teaching me how to administer the *Monroe Diagnostic Reading Test,* which analyzes reading errors in a variety of reading situations. The analysis of reading errors was difficult, since every word had to be analyzed. This included vowel and consonant errors as well as reversals, substitutions of letters and words, and repetitions. These error scores were converted into standard scores relative to the child's grade level and portrayed on an error profile. Errors above one standard deviation were considered excessive and below one standard deviation, superior. Remediation was then designed to correct the deficient errors in reading with the assumption that when the errors were corrected, the reading level would increase. I mention this test because I used it successfully for many years and taught many students how to analyze errors in reading. Many years later I used the same approach in profiling abilities and disabilities as revealed by the *Illinois Test of Psycholinguistic Abilities.*

My remedial methods were greatly influenced by both the Fernald kinesthetic method and the Monroe's phonic method. I used both methods in teaching mentally retarded children with reading disabilities. The Hegge, Kirk, and Kirk *Remedial Reading Drills* (1936) evolved from trial-and-error teaching of children with reading disabilities. They evolved at about the same time as the Gillingham method, both influenced indirectly by Samuel T. Orton and Marion Monroe. The Hegge, Kirk, and Kirk remedial exercises were programmed in 1933 and 1934, using the principles of learning from the Chicago school of functional psychology. Recent emphasis on the principles of programmed instruction promoted by the school of behavior modification denotes much the same approach.

My experience at the Wayne County Training School served not only as unique clinical practice in teaching difficult children, but also as an opportunity for research and writing. Dr. Hegge had been trained in the German school of accuracy and careful interpretation of data. He made it a policy to go over every paper meticulously, sentence by sentence, and comma by comma. In addition, my wife, Winifred Day Kirk, who was also a graduate of the University of Chicago functional school of psychology, made contributions as a team member in the research department while attending the University of Michigan, departments of psychology and of education. We have been publication partners since.

For four years at the Wayne County Training School, I taught difficult cases, organized and helped develop the remedial reading drills, and conducted and published research. During my last year at the school I was appointed mental hygienist, in which capacity I was in charge of the mental health of the boys, while a woman psychiatrist was in charge of the girls. In this position I learned a little about psychoanalysis and, although not being analyzed myself, I tried psychoanalysis on the boys. After analyzing dreams and making Freudian interpretations of behavior over a six-month period, I gave up psychoanalysis with the conclusion that I was either a poor analyst or psychoanalysis was not a suitable procedure for the problems of mentally retarded youngsters. The techniques that I then used were primarily milieu therapy and behavior modification.

Experience at the Wayne County Training School left me with the feeling that much more could be done with handicapped children than most people believed. The excellent case histories and diagnoses by clinics and schools in Detroit and by the staff of the residential school were for me an education in case analysis and procedures. The case conferences added much to my recognition that many children who were diagnosed as hopeless could be rehabilitated. One boy with whom I worked had an I.Q. of 56 on the Binet, was declared delinquent, and could not read; the only thing he could write was his name—and that he wrote backwards. As an experiment, I tried to teach him to read and found that in two years time he reached the fourth grade level (at the age of fourteen). Although he could score seventh grade on the *Gray Oral Reading Test,* his comprehension scores were at the fourth grade level. I worked with him a third year, but could not increase his comprehension scores substantially. At sixteen he tested in the borderline range of intelligence and was consequently paroled to his grandmother. Later I learned from a follow-up study that he had not only become a self-supporting citizen, but was also supporting his grandmother and his sister.

Teacher Training at The Milwaukee State Teachers College

In the fall of 1935, with a brand new Ph.D., I was offered the position of director of the Division of Exceptional Children at the small Milwaukee State Teachers College, later to become the Milwaukee branch of the University of Wisconsin.

Fortunately, the Peter Principle was not known at that time, and I accepted a college position as head of the department without really being prepared for teacher education. The college concentrated on a high-level teacher education program, conducted primarily by a faculty of master teachers with master's degrees. The president, to comply with the accreditation boards, was forced to hire some Ph.D's, whether or not they knew anything about teacher education. I was one of them.

This small teachers' college, with a carefully selected student body of 1200, served as a postdoctoral training center for me. The teacher education program consisted of three years of liberal arts education with majors and minors in academic subjects. The fourth year was devoted entirely to teacher education. Students did practice-teaching for half of each day from September to June and met in small groups with a faculty member for two hours each afternoon for didactic instruction. Each faculty member had a maximum of twelve students to supervise and to teach. All faculty members were required to share any area of expertise which they had with students assigned to other instructors during the afternoon periods of didactic instruction. My connection, in addition to my responsibilities for the students in the Division of Exceptional Children, was primarily with the Kindergarten–Primary Division. Their instructors taught my students for the first nine weeks of the year in primary education, while I reciprocated by lecturing to the Kindergarten-Primary students on child development and on problems in teaching reading. To fulfill my obligation it was necessary to visit classes for normal children, study the school curriculum, observe techniques of instruction, and apply what theoretical knowledge I had in learning and child development to the program for primary grade student teachers. By combining my theoretical training in psychology and observing programs and techniques of education, I obtained postdoctorate training in the education of regular children from the professionals in the field.

Parenthetically I must state that, although I did not take college courses in handicapped children (except the one from Professor Wallin), I did audit three courses in speech pathology, two courses in the education of the deaf, one summer session workshop in the education of the visually handicapped, and one workshop in cerebral palsy offered in a graduate medical school. All of these were audited after I had my Ph.D.

Development of Concepts for Training Intelligence

In 1939 I attended a lecture by Harold Skeels, who had been working in Iowa on the well-known Iowa studies. He described how he had placed young children singly on various wards of an institution for mental defectives. With early stimulation by ward girls, these children increased significantly in I.Q. He also introduced me to a translated article by Alfred Binet which was entitled "The Educability of Intelligence." In this chapter Binet did not accept the concept of the constancy of the I.Q. Instead, he designed curricula in Paris to educate intelligence. This chapter impressed me greatly, since from my experience at the Wayne County Training School I had developed a marked bias in the favor of the educability of intelligence. This chapter published by Binet in 1909 has been recently reprinted (Kirk & Lord, 1974).

In 1941, in collaboration with the directors of special education in the Milwaukee Public Schools, we organized a class of young mentally retarded children who were causing great difficulty to classes in public schools. Actually they were not as young as I had wanted, but were six and seven-year-olds with I.Q.s in the fifties and sixties and histories of behavior problems in school in addition to the inability to learn. In those days children were not placed in special classes until they had shown difficulties for several years in regular classes. We placed these twelve children in a special class in one of the public schools in Milwaukee and organized a curriculum for preschool education adapted to their needs. The curriculum was organized around Thurstone's primary mental abilities which isolated seven factors in intelligence. These seven factors did not differ markedly from ordinary readiness activities such as language training (reception and expression), quantitative thinking, space relations, and so forth. The teacher selected for this class was particularly interested in organizing games for the development of such functions in children (Kirk & Stevens, 1943).

This class was not evaluated very thoroughly. The principal felt that it was the best behaved class in the school, since these children were always working when he came to their class. We devised a great number of educational games that interested these children, all designed to develop the primary mental abilities.

Unfortunately we did not continue this research. With the incursion of World War II, I was commissioned in the Army and dropped the program between 1942 and 1947.

RESEARCH ON HANDICAPPED CHILDREN AT THE UNIVERSITY OF ILLINOIS

After World War II the state of Illinois appropriated funds for the expansion of public school programs for the education of handicapped children. Under the inspiring leadership of Ray Graham, the state director of special education, numerous special classes were organized throughout Illinois. Special class teachers were not available, but through Graham's encouragement, the University of Illinois became interested in preparing professional personnel in special education as well as in elementary education. I was invited to join the faculty of the University of Illinois to develop a program of teacher education at the undergraduate and graduate levels in all areas of special education. In the fall of 1947 I initiated teacher preparation programs for teachers of the mentally retarded and teachers of the deaf. I resisted the organization of other teacher training programs because it became obvious to me that a large state university was an inadequate place to train teachers, but an ideal place for research and graduate programs. Therefore, I restricted undergraduate teacher education and attempted to develop a doctoral program and research activities.

The problems we faced in developing a doctorate program were the lack of a precedent in other universities and the difference between a doctorate in special education and a doctorate in educational psychology or clinical psychology. The pattern finally established for a doctorate program in special education (Kirk, 1957) included:

1. Requiring a masters degree;
2. Requiring two years of teaching experience in some branch of special education;
3. Obtaining advanced work in social foundations in education, statistics, basic psychology of learning, child development, physiological psychology, and social psychology;
4. Studying the relationship of basic disciplines to special education in advanced seminars (For example, the seminar in problems of mental deficiency included units to answer questions of the contributions of biological, psychological, sociological, and educational science to mental deficiency);
5. Having basic knowledge in three areas of special education, and
6. Preparing a doctoral dissertation in the field.

This type of program logically led to university positions for the graduates because of the emphasis on basic academic knowledge and research. Before federal fellowships, the G.I. bill and research assistantships in the Institute for Research on Exceptional Children supported the doctoral students.

Research on Early Education

To continue previous research, and with the encouragement of the progressive state director, I applied for a grant from the Institutes of Mental Health to try a project on "The Effects of Preschool Education on the Intellectual and Social Development of Young Mentally Retarded Children." This project was also supported by the state Department of Public Instruction, the state Department of Social Welfare and the University of Illinois, in addition to the National Institute of Mental Health. I shall not review this study here but only state that it was an experiment both in the community and in an institution, with contrast groups in each locale. The results were published in 1958 in a book entitled *Early Education of the Mentally Retarded*. This was the hardest book I have had to write, since a project of this kind, where many of the variables cannot be controlled, is very frustrating to an experimentalist. Some people call this kind of field research "dirty research," but sometimes dirty research done as well as possible may have much more effect than the small experimental projects we conduct in psychology. Together with the Skeels study, this experiment had some effect on the development of Head Start and similar projects. These two studies helped to convince Congress many years later to pass a bill and appropriate funds for preschool education of handicapped children (Kirk, 1968).

The experiment in preschool education of mentally retarded children gave us an opportunity to study the effects of intensive training in the educability of intelligence at the preschool level. The experiment was considered successful. Six of the fifteen children in the institution were permanently paroled because of intellectual growth, and one later graduated from college. None of those not receiving preschool education was paroled. Actually they tended to drop in I.Q. The same type of result was obtained in the community group (Kirk, 1958).

It is interesting to note that after the results of the study were published, there was a revival of interest in the Skeels study. Dr. Skeels, who had been criticized for this 1939 report, and who was then working for the U.S. Public Health Service, was urged to do a follow-up study of his cases. He did so and published it in a monograph which is probably one of the best longitudinal studies of such programs ever published. All of the children of his experimental group were self-supporting twenty-one years later, while only half of the contrast group were self-supporting. Five of the contrast group were in institutions (Skeels, 1966).

While working in the preschool it became obvious to us that the term "mental retardation" had very little meaning as far as a program for these children was concerned. We were forced to observe the behavior of the children and to organize programs for their particular needs. For each child we asked the questions "What deficits exist?" and "What do we do about these particular deficits?" The label "mentally retarded" did not help us very much. One child with marked nystagmus as a result of rubella was diagnosed as legally blind and severely mentally retarded. This child could see, but it took her a long time to recognize and identify objects and pictures visually. We had few tests for preschool children at that time (1949), so we used our "clinical" observational insights to delineate the areas of development that required remediation in each child. We decided that with her nystagmus and visual problems, which prevented prolonged view of any object, this child had difficulty in recognizing objects and pictures. We consequently initiated an intensive training program for developing speed of perception, one of Thurstone's primary mental abilities. We used a tachistiscope to develop this ability. Less than one-half hour a day of tutoring in addition to the preschool experiences made it possible for this girl to progress rapidly in speed of perception. Her central dysfunction of speed of perception improved to a point where she was responding to pictures at one-twenty-fifth of a second. She was later placed in regular grades rather than a class for the mentally retarded, since her I.Q. had risen from approximately 50 at age four to about 85 at age six. At the age of ten she was doing adequate third-grade work in a regular class, in spite of all of the problems she had had earlier. There is a tendency to assert that the early diagnosis of mental retardation was false, but this would be denying the change that can take place as a result of adequate remediation.

Another child with the same label of "mentally retarded" had a recorded I.Q. on the Binet of 37. We were convinced that this I.Q was invalid, although she was unable to talk at the age of five. This child should have been classified as a learning disabled child, since she had a specific disability that was amenable to training. She was given intensive training in auditorization and speech. The remedial training for this girl was not visual perception but auditory perception and verbal expression. She made progress in development similar to the girl with the disability in speed of visual perception. By the age of eight she was testing in the 80 and 90 I.Q. range on intelligence tests and was in a regular school program.

As we analyzed and worked with many of these children, mostly on a trial-and-error basis, we found that most every child had some peculiar block or impediment to his or her development. We wasted a lot of time trying to pinpoint basic disabilities in these children and in organizing a general preschool program which included an individualized remedial program for each child's unique impediment to development. Our experience in these preschools led us to question the diagnosis and the label "mentally retarded" with many of the children and to have less respect for the I.Q. and its constancy.

The Development of the *ITPA*

Observations of these children's abilities and disabilities led us to treat them as children with specific learning disabilities that required remediation. Our clinical guesses, as evaluated by the results of remediation, were again on a trial-and-error basis. We had no objective measures that would assist us in delineating these abilities and disabilities. Because of this situation we began to develop tests that would help us determine linguistic, perceptual and memory abilities and disabilities of young children. This task proved to be very difficult, but eventually, after ten years of work, we produced an experimental edition of the *Illinois Test of Psy-*

cholinguistic Abilities. After it was used for seven years, it was revised and published in 1968 (Kirk, McCarthy, & Kirk).

The *ITPA* became popular from the beginning because it is an intraindividual test, comparing a child's own abilities and disabilities for the purpose of organizing remediation for deficits. The time was apparently ripe for working with individual children, instead of classifying them into groups for instructional purposes. Since its appearance, the *ITPA* has served as a research and clinical instrument for many studies; it has been translated and standardized in a number of foreign languages.

Unfortunately, this test has also spawned many illusions and false hopes. Some people have taken the *ITPA* as *the* instrument for the diagnosis of all ills and educational problems. In spite of our numerous warnings, it is used for junior high school students, even though it is intended for young children. Many also use it to diagnose problems to which the *ITPA* does not apply. Furthermore, many people want to use it without taking the time to learn how to give it; and many people give the *ITPA* routinely and use it very mechanically. Although it is an instrument that is very beneficial for the diagnosis of certain disabilities within a restricted age range, some people desire to use it without the necessary preparation or clinical judgment. This problem, of course, is common in many areas of learning disabilities. We misuse tests and sometimes materials by taking remedial methods developed for one type of child and using them for a child for which they are not suitable.

The Institute for Research on Exceptional Children (IREC)

The organization and results of the preschool had three major effects. One was the popularization of the notion that preschool education is a preventative measure. A second result was the organization of the *Illinois Test of Psycholinguistic Abilities,* and a third effect was the feasability of joint ventures by the university and state departments of education and of welfare. Pooling the resources and personnel of these three bodies led to the organization of the Institute for Research on Exceptional Children.

This Institute was organized at the University of Illinois in cooperation with the two state service agencies. With a relatively small but high quality faculty, it served for many years as a research and training institute. The initial faculty, James J. Gallagher, Bernard Farber, Oliver Kolstoe, Lawrence Stolurow, Herbert Goldstein, Merle Karnes, and Clifford Howe, serving between 1952 and 1962, produced volumes of research in many areas of exceptionality. (See Kirk & Bateman, 1964.)

There have been other spin-off research institutes for handicapped children, but few have had the effective cooperation and coordination of the university and the state agencies. Much credit must go to the active ingredient of such state officials as Ray Graham, whose interest and personal effectiveness were of paramount importance, and to president

George Stoddard and dean Willard Spalding, both of whom were quick to grasp the significance of the proposal for a research institute which was prepared by Graham and myself.

The value of cooperation between research personnel and service organizations cannot be overemphasized. Any state Department of Public Instruction should be happy to have a research team based in a university. Some of the research done by the University of Illinois Institute for Research on Exceptional Children was (in addition to more basic research) an effort to answer practical problems faced by the state, such as "Is preschool education for handicapped children worthwhile?" or "Is it feasible and profitable to organize classes for trainable children in public schools?" (a controversial topic in the early 1950s). Or "How are children with high I.Q.s adjusting and progressing in the regular grades?" These and other problems were partially solved through the pooling of resources, physical and financial, of the university and the state departments. The result of these pieces of research led the state Department of Public Instruction to introduce bills and to obtain state appropriations for public school services for trainable mentally retarded and for gifted children. Similar cooperative research was conducted in the Institute in cooperation with the Department of Public Welfare. In general, the service organization paid for the service aspects of the research, while the university, through federal or state grants, supplied the research personnel.

This type of organization should be considered by federal and state agencies if they desire relevant research. A description of the organization of the Institute for Research on Exceptional Children has been published by Kirk and Spalding (1953).

ORGANIZATION OF AGENCIES FOR LEARNING DISABILITIES

Prior to 1960 states did not provide subsidies to school districts for other than the traditional type of handicapped child, the mentally retarded, the deaf, blind, speech handicapped, and crippled. Any school system which provided services for severe reading or language disabilities conducted these services without state or federal help.

The studies with the *ITPA* and the effects of preschool education demonstrated to most of us in the late 1950s and early 1960s that labels for children have little educational significance and that the measurement instruments that we have been using were primarily classification instruments. The term "brain-injured," for example, used by Strauss, had become a useless label, since some brain-injured (cerebral-palsied) children were obtaining Ph.D.s and M.D.s, while others with the same label were extremely low in intelligence. Furthermore, teachers wanted to know what to *do* with children, instead of receiving a label or an I.Q. in the clinical reports.

One reason the *ITPA* became popular so rapidly was the fact that others, too, were feeling dissatisfaction with merely labelling a child as "mentally retarded" or "brain-damaged." Perceptive psychologists and educators were becoming disenchanted with the medical model and were ready for a means of diagnosing a child in terms of what could be done to help him. My early articles clarifying the difference between classification and diagnosis and the need for assessment of children for remedial purposes fell on receptive ears, and I discovered a great demand for further elaboration at meetings and conferences.

The Role of Parents' Organizations

During the period of rapid organization of special services for handicapped children, one group of parents felt neglected. Many children, who were not developing in some area, were referred to departments of special education only to be rejected because upon diagnosis they were found not to be deaf or blind or mentally retarded or crippled. But they were *not learning*. At the same time a new category was postulated by Strauss—the brain-injured child. Associations of parents were formed locally, and private classes for brain-injured children were organized. Some, not favoring the label "brain-injured," resorted to other terms, like "perceptually handicapped." After many such local and state organizations were formed, they decided to hold a national conference. This conference was held in Chicago in April, 1963, and was interestingly called "The Conference on Exploration into Problems of the Perceptually Handicapped Child." A number of us who were interested were invited to speak at this conference.

Before my address to them, several approached me with the admonition that they needed help in the selection of a name for their proposed national organization. To present my point of view at this meeting I stated:

> I have felt for some time that labels we give children are satisfying to us, but of little help to the child himself. We seem to be satisfied if we can give a technical name to a condition. This gives us the satisfaction of closure. We think we know the answers if we can give the child a name or a label—brain injured, schizophrenic, autistic, mentally retarded, aphasia, etc. As indicated before, the term "brain injury" has little meaning to us from a management or training point of view. It does not tell me if the child is smart or dull, hyperactive or underactive. It does not give me any clues to management or training. The terms cerebral palsy, brain injured, mentally retarded, aphasic, etc. are actually classification terms. In a sense they are not diagnostic, if by diagnosis we mean an assessment of the child in such a way that leads to some form of treatment, management, or remediation. In addition, it is not a basic cause since the designation of the child as brain injured does not really tell us why the child is brain injured or how he got that way. Recently I have

used the term "learning disabilities" to describe a group of children who have disorders in development, in language, speech, reading, and associated communication skills needed for social interaction. In this group I do not include children who have sensory handicaps such as blindness or deafness, because we have methods of managing and training the deaf and the blind. I also exclude from this group children who have generalized mental retardation (Kirk, 1963; see Kirk & Lord, 1974).

The various parents' associations later met to organize a national association. After much debate they decided on the name of *Association for Children with Learning Disabilities* (ACLD). Since that date the term "learning disabilities" has become the general term for a heterogeneous group of disabilities of varying degrees of severity. This term and its use and misuse will be discussed later.

The Federal Role

Under the Eisenhower and Kennedy administrations, federal appropriations were made to subsidize the preparation of personnel for handicapped children and to support research. Under Public Law 88–164, signed by President Kennedy in October, 1963, provisions were made to award fellowships to students and to provide supporting funds to universities to prepare professional personnel for children with mental retardation, sensory handicaps, serious emotional disturbance, speech handicaps, crippling conditions, and other health impairments that required special education. No specific mention was made of "learning disabilities," a term which at that time had not been in general use.

Having been appointed as the director of a newly created Division of Handicapped Children in the federal Office of Education, I interpreted "other health impaired" to include learning disabilities, under the assumption that learning disabled children have a central dysfunction which interferes with their development. Four colleges and universities obtained grants in 1964 to train personnel in learning disabilities. A few research grants in learning disabilities or related areas were also awarded. This development of federal subsidy for the preparation of personnel in learning disabilities has continued since that date with varied and limited funding.

The funds that were allotted for training and research for learning disabilities were relatively meager compared to comparable allotments in other areas. As a result, parents' groups and professionals interested in learning disabilities requested Congress to include learning disabilities in the programs for the handicapped. In considering this request, Congress heard many interested people give contradictory definitions and prevalence figures for the learning disabled, ranging from 2 to 30 percent of a school population. To clarify such issues for Congress, the National Advisory Committee for the Handicapped, of which I was chairman, defined *learning disabilities* as:

Children with special (specific) learning disabilities exhibit a disorder in one or more of the basic psychological processes involved in understanding or in using spoken or written language. These may be manifested in disorders of listening, thinking, talking, reading, writing, spelling, or arithmetic. They include conditions which have been referred to as perceptual handicaps, brain injury, minimal brain dysfunction, dyslexia, developmental aphasia, etc. They do not include learning problems which are due primarily to visual, hearing, or motor handicaps, to mental retardation, emotional disturbance, or to environmental disadvantage.

The committee estimated that from 1 to 3 percent of school children are likely to have a specific learning disability. On the basis of the report by the committee, Congress passed the Learning Disability Act of 1969, which authorized training, research, and service in learning disabilities. No appropriation of money was made for these services, however, and the federal funds available are still token appropriations in relation to the size of the problem.

ASSESSMENT OF SOME CURRENT PROBLEMS

Although there are numerous problems in diagnosis, remediation, administration, and other areas in learning disabilities, I shall discuss only a few of these problems: (1) the concept of learning disabilities, (2) educational retardation versus specific learning disabilities, (3) mental retardation versus specific learning disabilities, (4) the responsibility of regular elementary education, and (5) the status of research in learning disabilities.

The Concept of Specific Learning Disabilities

Although I did not originate the term "specific learning disabilities," it has been attributed to me because (1) I used the term in 1962 in my book on exceptional children when I defined it as "a retardation; disorder, or delayed development in one or more of the processes of speech, language, reading, spelling, writing, or arithmetic resulting from a possible cerebral dysfunction and/or emotional or behavioral disturbance and not from mental retardation, sensory deprivation, or cultural or instructional factors," (p. 263) and (2) I later (1963) suggested the term as the least objectionable to the parents' groups organizing ACLD.

But like Pandora's box, the term, the concept, and the field produced a wide variety of activities not originally intended. A term and a title intended to encompass a heterogeneous group of disabilities—dyslexia, aphasia, apraxia, agraphia, acalculia, and various forms of auditory, visual, or haptic perceptual problems—is bound to lead into many directions. The common thread among all of these disabilities is, of course, the difficulty the child has in learning academically, socially, logically, or linguistically.

Since that time we have had a bandwagon effect with learning disabilities. To some, most children have a learning disability. The prevalence figures given by different groups in congressional testimony have ranged from 10 to 30 percent. It appeared for a while that a third of the school population could be classified in this category. It has even been suggested that mentally retarded children be labeled "general learning disabilities" and that we label the others "specific learning disabilities." Parents have brought their children to learning disability centers for diagnosis because their children were not obtaining straight A's in school.

Another problem created by the term is its confusion with learning in general. Mentally retarded children have learning problems, hence the move to label them "general learning disabilities" instead of "mentally retarded." Indeed all exceptional children—the deaf, the blind, and others —have learning problems. But these children are not children with a *specific learning disability,* that is, a learning disability in one area when all other functions are intact. Many fail to heed this major criterion of a learning disability: namely, major discrepancies between the deficit area (or disability) and other areas (or abilities). A child who is not deaf and who is not basically mentally retarded but does not talk could be a child with a specific learning disability; but a deaf child who does not talk is not.

Educational Retardation versus Specific Learning Disability

A major problem that has evolved in the schools is the confusion between educational retardation and specific learning disabilities. It is a fact that on any test given, 17 percent of the children will fall below one standard deviation of the group. In many if not most school systems, this initial figure is used in selecting children for programs for children with learning disabilities. In a recent survey of learning disability programs in twenty-one states (Kirk & Elkins, 1974), it was found that the emphasis was primarily on reading problems—children who were on the average retarded in reading one year below their mental-age reading-grade expectancy, and who had similar retardation in arithmetic and spelling. We stated:

> It is obvious from the data presented in this report that most state projects have selected reading, spelling, and arithmetic as the areas that are considered the major focus for remediation under the learning disability program. It would appear from the data that the majority of children in the projects, although underachieving to some degree, would not qualify as specific learning disabled children, since (a) many of the children were retarded equally in reading, spelling, and arithmetic and

were therefore not specific but general in academic retardation, and (b) a substantial proportion were minor or moderate in their degree of underachievement.

One can raise the question of whether underachievement in reading, spelling, and/or arithmetic regardless of degree or circumstances can be considered a specific learning disability and come under the federal appropriation and intent of the Learning Disabilities Act of 1969. There are, however, many circumstances that result in underachievement in school children, among which are (a) disadvantaged environments, (b) lack of motivation, (c) inadequate instruction, (d) lack of school opportunities, and (e) deviations in learning ability such as are found in mentally retarded and slow learning children. Underachievement is also found in sensorially handicapped children, i.e., the deaf, blind, cerebral palsied, etc.

There are a number of reasons for this confusion and development. First, funds became available for children with specific learning disabilities and not for the slow learning child or the underachieveing child. By labelling these children as "learning disabled" they could now obtain services in the regular grades or through resource rooms. Secondly, many teachers who were not trained in learning disabilities, but in remedial reading, speech, mental retardation, or school psychology became learning disability specialists overnight or by taking a general course or two in summer sessions. They were able to cope with the problems, since most of the children in the program required some attention in developmental reading or other areas and did not have specific learning disabilities that required specialized instruction. This does not mean that all learning disability programs are working with children with minor problems of learning in school, but it is my opinion that this is true in all too many situations.

The emphasis on mainstreaming and especially on the provision of consultants to regular teachers is also a reason for emphasis on helping children with minor learning problems (and in some cases undoubtedly neglecting the children with severe and specific learning disabilities). This was the case with speech correctionists in the school many years ago, when the emphasis was on the number of cases served and primarily on the correction of minor articulation disorders in the first and second grades. Children with severe language disorders that took a great deal of time of the speech correctionist were not served.

Another problem that has entered the arena is the changing definitions for *mental retardation*. In 1962 the American Association on Mental Deficiency defined *mental retardation* as those children who tested one standard deviation below the mean on a standard intelligence test. This meant that children with I.Q.s of 84 and below were mentally retarded. In 1973, after several court cases challenged the assignment of such children to special classes, the AAMD changed its criterion to two standard deviations, or an I.Q. of 68 and below, as the psychometric definition of mental retardation. Consequently, in some school systems the borderline group of children with I.Q.s of 68 to 84 or 90, who are educationally retarded in the schools, are found in learning disability programs. Undoubtedly some of these have specific learning disabilities, but the majority are probably not children with specific learning disabilities.

Mental Retardation versus Learning Disabilities

The federal definition of learning disabilities, quoted earlier, states, "They do not include learning problems which are due primarily to visual, hearing, or motor handicaps, to mental retardation, or to environmental disadvantage." This definition has been misunderstood because of the lack of attention to the word "primarily." In addition, parents' groups and other people want their children to be normal and are glad to accept the exclusion, in a way not meant by the definition.

It would be ironic to exclude all children labelled "mentally retarded" from remedial programs for their disabilities. As indicated in my previous discussion of the first child I worked with and of our experience in the preschool, the learning disability children I worked with were all classified as mentally retarded. All the children I taught at the Wayne County Training School were classified as mentally retarded. In all of these cases my purpose was to show through the results of remediation that these children should have been classified as learning disabled instead of mentally retarded, since they were normal in some respects but had specific disabilities.

The differentiation between the learning disabled child and the mentally retarded child is that the mentally retarded child is relatively retarded in all abilities, while the learning disabled child is retarded or defective in some abilities but relatively normal in other abilities. The learning disabled child is characterized by *discrepancies* in growth or in abilities and disabilities. We have demonstrated with cases (Kirk & Kirk, 1971) that of two children who have an I.Q. of 70, one could be retarded in all abilities, while the other is markedly retarded in some abilities and normal in other abilities. These show up clearly when their abilities and disabilities are profiled, as on the *ITPA*. A child who is markedly retarded in reading, but has achieved in language and in arithmetic, has a discrepancy in achievement and can be considered a specific case of learning disability (reading disability); while another child who has had inadequate school experiences may be underachieving in reading, spelling, arithmetic, and language. He would not be considered a case of specific learning disability but rather of general educational retardation.

One of the criticisms of the federal definition has been the exclusion clauses, particularly relating to the words "primarily environmentally disadvantaged." This has been falsely interpreted by some to exclude children in disadvantaged areas from consideration in learning disabilities programs. The National Advisory Board of ACLD discussed this problem and recommended the following addition to the federal definition: "Children with specific learning disabilities who also have sensory motor, intellectual, or emotional problems, or are environmentally disadvantaged, should be included in this definition, and may receive multiple services."

The Responsibility of Regular Elementary Education

As mentioned earlier, the field of learning disabilities may become the dumping ground for all school problems—the slow learner, the underachiever, the emotionally disturbed, the corrective reading case, and others who are failing to achieve in school up to the expectations of their parents and teachers. The employment of itinerant, resource, and consulting teachers who can assess these children's problems and organize remedial programs in the regular grades has been used as the solution to these school problems. Funds appropriated for learning disabilities are being used to support this development.

It is my opinion that this current practice for helping the underachiever in the schools through funds appropriated for learning disabilities is transitional. Unfortunately, elementary education has failed to assume responsibility for children who are underachieving and who need adequate instruction rather than special education. I make this statement because many of the children who are currently in learning disability programs are children who are underachieving because of poor instruction, inadequate backgrounds, lack of motivation, and other factors, and not because of a psychological disorder that is serving as an impediment to learning. This should be the criterion of a specific learning disability.

There are a number of reasons for the development of current school programs for underachieving children under the label of "learning disabilities." The same transitional program occurred with other handicapped children, especially with the mentally retarded. Schools have been going through the same cycle of (1) organization of special classes in public schools, (2) expansion of programs to include many who may not be mentally retarded but problems to the regular teacher, and then (3) a return to earlier concepts and practices for those who are strictly mentally retarded.

It should be recalled that in the 1920s children referred to classes for the mentally retarded were required to have I.Q.s below 70 to be eligible. This standard was established by the Wisconsin state superintendent of public instruction in 1927. After World War II, when special classes were subsidized by state funds, elementary teachers welcomed the movement. Like the trend today in learning disabilities, teachers referred great numbers of children who were behavior problems, underachievers, and of below-average intelligence to special education programs. Directors of special education who judged progress in terms of the number of special education classes that could be organized in a school system found reasons to enroll these elementary education cast-offs in classes for the mentally retarded. The AAMD psychometric criterion of an I.Q. of 84 and below as the definition of mental retardation aided this expansion. In the inner cities with these definitions and criteria and with tests standardized on middle-class whites, classes for the mentally retarded enrolled a disproportionately high number of minority group children. This practice tended to break the camel's back, because the minority groups objected to having such a high proportion of their children inaccurately labelled "mentally retarded."

In conforming with our usual tendency to overreact, we began to abolish all special classes for the mentally retarded under the recent slogan of "mainstreaming" and consequently mainstreamed those who should never have been in a special class for the mentally retarded as well as those who could have profited from such an organization. I maintain that today learning disabilities is going through the same cycle of overexpansion, except that few authorities have advocated special classes for the learning disabled.

One of the reasons elementary teachers have difficulty coping with the problems of underachieving children is that their preparation in college did not provide training in the management and education of underachieving children. Before World War II, elementary teachers were prepared in teachers' colleges that specialized in teacher training as their sole responsibility. After World War II, with the extreme shortage of teachers, universities organized programs for the preparation of elementary teachers, while the teachers' colleges converted their programs into universities.

As a former member of a teachers' college faculty, I was appalled at the programs that evolved in universities. Universities generally required Ph.Ds for their faculty and could not find personnel who had had experience in teaching elementary children. In addition, the tradition in universities was to promote people on the basis of the "publish or perish" principle. Consequently there was little reward for faculties which concentrated on teacher education. Teacher preparation in elementary education in universities was clearly a second-order priority. It is for these reasons that elementary teachers trained during the postwar period found themselves unprepared to cope with children who deviate slightly from the large majority.

I do not wish to leave the impression that I am condemning the present practice of giving teachers special help for the atypical child, help for children who are slow learners, underachievers, and conduct problems. Although many of these children cannot be considered specific learning disabilities, they do need services to help them compensate for their lack of achievement.

The learning disability movement has made a definite contribution to regular education by introducing into the regular grades many procedures not ordinarily taught to elementary education students. These include looking at children from an intraindividual point of view, instead of only comparing one child with another, and emphasizing techniques of individualization of instruction, including visual and auditory aids to learning, learning stations, programmed learning, task analysis, and behavioral objectives. These techniques are not unique to special education, but of necessity have been used with handicapped children.

The general program today is to offer help to elementary teachers through consultation, itinerant teachers, or the resource room. It is hoped that in time, and through inservice training, regular elementary teachers will assume responsibility for the large number of minor problems, so that the learning disability specialist can concentrate on the hard-core learning disabled children.

THE STATUS OF RESEARCH

It is unfortunate that relatively little research in learning disabilities is being conducted at the present time. This is probably due to a large number of factors, including:

1. Most people in learning disabilities are service-oriented and are devoting all of their time to service activities.

2. College personnel have been employed in most colleges and universities to prepare teachers and specialists in learning disabilities. Federal subsidies of training programs have encouraged teacher training, rather than research.

3. Few research personnel in special education are being trained by universities. Such people seem to come from related disciplines like psychology. Many of them conduct basic research which in many instances does not have immediate application.

4. Commercialization of materials and methods in these days seems to take precedence in most instances over research since the latter has few rewards except possibly promotion in rank in a few universities that value this activity.

A major societal reason for the paucity of relevant research in learning disabilities, in my opinion, is that we have not created the vehicles that will encourage and sponsor research year-in and year-out. Much of the research that is reported is short-term masters and doctors theses, which are rarely continued after graduation. These tend to be sporadic, piecemeal, and discontinuous. Unless a professor or a research institute sponsors programmed research utilizing doctors dissertations as part of larger programs, not much results from such piecemeal research on any permanent basis.

It is interesting to note that in the past major and lasting research has emanated from service institutions: The Vineland Training School, The Wayne County Training School, the Central Institute for the Deaf, and others. In most of these installations, the researcher was able to select from his or her service activities relevant problems for the field and was allowed time off to conduct research. In the field of mental retardation the federal government has appropriated funds for the development of research. It is also supporting the research and training of personnel under university affiliated programs. There is no such research and developmental support for learning disabilities.

It is my opinion that relevant research on learning disabilities will not be accomplished until we, as a society, create or institutionalize research in such a way that we encourage the probing of problems on a continuous basis. This may be accomplished by:

1. Organizing research in a cooperative institute between a university and a public school system. This system must be institutionalized by definite agreements between the president of the university and the board of education. There are cooperative relations between a university professor and a local school principal or teacher in some places, but these tend to be temporary and fleeting, and dependent upon the stability of employment of the personnel. A change of positions by the professor or the teacher tends to terminate continuous research.

2. Providing basic and continuous funding for research. Our present system of relying on a grant from Washington for a one to three year period tends to limit the research project to a short-time basis. The employment of personnel on soft funds is also temporary. Much of the sporadic, piecemeal, noncontinuous research that is now being accomplished is the result of our system of temporary grants, temporary research personnel, and lack of cooperation between research and service personnel. In universities it is necessary to allot a minimum of continuous research funds for research, especially for personnel, and to organize research in cooperation with a service organization.

3. Providing time for research, if significant research is to be accomplished. The pressure for teacher training in colleges and universities has not only directed personnel to teaching at the expense of research, but has led to the selection for university faculties of individuals interested and competent in teaching, rather than those interested and competent in research. The selection of faculty on hard money who are interested and competent in research, and who will be given the time for research (not necessarily excluding some graduate teaching) should be a prerequisite.

EPILOGUE

Any discourse on the ills of society, or in this case on the hectic development of programs for learning disabled children, should include a statement of goals or projections for the future. I shall try to comment on a few of the goals as I see them. These goals include: (1) regular elementary education, (2) learning disability specialists, (3) teacher preparation for learning disabilities, (4) amelioration of disabilities in children diagnosed as mentally retarded, and (5) research.

1. Regular elementary education should assume the full responsibility for the minor problems of underachievement. This can be furthered through inservice education and the introduction of programs for understanding exceptional children into the curriculum for elementary education. Since most of the teacher education programs in the schools include instruction in reading, there is no reason why a school system cannot have remedial reading teachers and reading supervisors to assist the teacher. There is no reason why elementary education cannot deal with children who are underachieving due to lack of motivation, poor instruction, inadequate backgrounds, etc. In other words, elementary education should assume the responsibility for children who *do not* have basic psychological impediments to learning that require remediation.

2. Today learning disability specialists are devoting a great deal of time to consulting with regular teachers on minor learning problems. It is hoped that when elementary education assumes its responsibility, the learning disability specialists will devote their time to the training of the hard-core or severe cases of learning disability that require intensive instruction for the amelioration or compensation of the basic psychological disorder impeding the learning process. This goal can be accomplished by an itinerant or resource teacher with sufficient time and a caseload small enough to assure results.

3. Teacher preparation for specialists in learning disabilities should maintain similar standards as are held by clinical members of ASHA, namely a masters degree and sufficient clinical experience. Unfortunately, many of the learning disability specialists in the school today have had very little training and experience in learning disabilities. Many have taken a few courses in summer school or are certified by the state department because of a degree in one area of special education. What is needed is for universities to maintain high standards of training, regardless of the certification standards of the state department of public instruction, which by necessity must lower standards to meet demand. Ideally a two-

year graduate program is needed to prepare a learning disability specialist. It will require two years of clinical practice and instruction to learn the skills of assessment and the procedures for the remediation of different kinds of learning disabilities.

4. Much more work should be done with children diagnosed as mentally retarded. It is unfortunate that mentally retarded and disadvantaged children are not considered in programs for the learning disabled because of the misunderstanding of the federal definition. Personnel in learning disabilities have either forgotten or have not known that Strauss', Kephart's, Cruickshank's, and my own work dealt with children who were diagnosed as mentally retarded, but who were treated by us under the concept of learning disabilities. Our programs were designed to ameliorate the psychological disorders of the children who otherwise had potential, in order to remove the diagnosis of mental retardation. I personally would like to see a great emphasis on this group of children with discrepancies of development, instead of the current emphasis by learning disability personnel on minor reading problems in the school. Reading specialists and regular teachers are in a better position to deal with these minor problems.

5. Comments have been made in the text on the need for research and on the organization for research in learning disabilities. In addition to these comments I would like to see greater emphasis on idiographic research, or on the study of an n=1. Our concentration on nomothetic research with control groups and the use of computers to test significances and correlations is not developing in us the insights necessary to advance the field. It is possible that we are not ready for nomothetic research, and that we could learn more if we made intensive studies of single cases of severe learning disabilities. Research of this type seems not to attract the attention of researchers, because it is believed that we cannot evolve laws of behavior from a study of one case. I am not sure that we are proving anything from the studies that are supposedly using control or matched groups.

REFERENCES

Hegge, T. G., Kirk, S. A., & Kirk, W. D. *Remedial reading drills.* Ann Arbor, Mich.: George Wahr, 1936.

Kirk, S. A. The influence of manual tracing on the learning of simple words in the case of subnormal boys. *Journal of Educational Psychology,* 1933, **24,** 525–35.

Kirk, S. A. Hemispheric cerebral dominance and hemispheric equipotentiality. *Comparative Psychology Monographs.* Baltimore: Johns Hopkins Press, 1935.

Kirk, S. A. Extrastriate functions in the discrimination of complex visual patterns. *Journal of Comparative Psychology,* 1936, **21,** 145–59.

Kirk, S. A. A doctor's degree program in special education. *Exceptional Children,* 1957, **24,** 50–52, 55.

Kirk, S. A. *Early education of the mentally retarded: An experimental study.* Urbana, Ill.: University of Illinois Press, 1958.

Kirk, S. A. *Educating exceptional children.* Boston: Houghton Mifflin, 1962, rev. 1972.

Kirk, S. A. Behavioral diagnosis and remediation of learning disabilities. In *Proceedings of the conference on exploration into the problems of the perceptually handicapped child.* Chicago: Perceptually Handicapped Children, Inc., 1963.

Kirk, S. A. Statement before the Select Subcommittee on Education of the Committee on Education and Labor, House of Representatives (90th Congress) on H. R. 17829, a bill to authorize preschool and early education programs for handicapped children. July, 1968.

Kirk, S. A. Reflections on learning disabilities. Paper presented at the Seventh Annual International Conference of the Association for Children with Learning Disabilities. Pittsburgh, 1970.

Kirk, S. A., & Bateman, B. D. *Ten years of research at the Institute for Research on Exceptional Children.* Urbana: University of Illinois Press, 1964.

Kirk, S. A., & Elkins, J. Characteristics of children enrolled in child service demonstration centers. Final report supported in whole or part by the U.S. Office of Education, Department of Health, Education and Welfare, Project No. H-12-7145B, Grant No. OEG - 0 - 714425, the Leadership Training Institute in Learning Disabilities, University of Arizona, June, 1974.

Kirk, S. A., & Kirk, W. D. *Psycholinguistic learning disabilities: Diagnosis and remediation.* Urbana: University of Illinois Press, 1971.

Kirk, S. A., & Lord, F. (Eds.) *Exceptional children: Educational resources and perspectives.* Boston: Houghton-Mifflin, 1974.

Kirk, S. A., McCarthy, J. J., & Kirk, W. D. *The Illinois Test of Psycholinguistic Abilities.* Urbana: University of Illinois Press, 1968.

Kirk, S. A., & Spalding, W. B. The Institute for Research on Exceptional Children at the University of Illinois. *The Educational Forum,* 1953, **18,** 413–22.

Kirk, S. A., & Stevens, I. A. preacademic curriculum for slow learning children. *American Journal of Mental Deficiency,* 1943, **47,** 396–406.

Skeels, H. M. Adult status of children with contrasting early life experience. *Monographs of the Society for Research in Child Development,* 1966, **105,** No. 3.

Wallin, J. E. W. *The education of handicapped children.* Boston: Houghton-Mifflin, 1924.

A SELECTED BIBLIOGRAPHY OF WORKS BY SAMUEL A. KIRK

Hegge, T. G., Kirk, S. A., & Kirk, W. D. *Remedial reading drills.* Ann Arbor, Mich.: George Wahr, 1936.

Kirk, S. A. The influence of manual tracing on the learning of simple words in the case of subnormal boys. *Journal of Educational Psychology,* 1933, **24,** 525–35.

Kirk, S. A. The effects of remedial reading on the educational progress and personality adjustment of high-grade mentally deficient problem children—Ten case studies. *Journal of Juvenile Research,* 1934, **18,** 140–62.

Kirk, S. A. A study of the relation of ocular and manual preference to mirror reading. *The Pedagogical Seminary and Journal of Genetic Psychology,* 1934, **44,** 129–205.

Kirk, S. A. Hemispheric cerebral dominance and hemispheric equipotentiality. *Comparative Psychology Monographs,* Baltimore: Johns Hopkins Press, 1935.

Kirk, S. A. Reading aptitudes of mentally retarded children. *American Association on Mental Deficiency,* 1939, **44,** 158–62.

Kirk, S. A. *Teaching reading to slow-learning children.* Boston: Houghton Mifflin, 1940.

Kirk, S. A. A project for preschool mentally handicapped children. *American Journal of Mental Deficiency,* 1950, **54,** 305–10.

Kirk, S. A. How Johnny learns to read. *Exceptional Children,* 1956, **22,** 158–60.

Kirk, S. A. *Early education of the mentally retarded—An experimental study.* Urbana: University of Illinois Press, 1958.

Kirk, S. A. Remedial work in the elementary school. *National Education Association Journal,* 1959, **48,** 24–25.

Kirk, S. A. *Educating exceptional children.* Boston: Houghton Mifflin, 1962, rev., 1972.

Kirk, S. A. Diagnostic, cultural, and remedial factors in mental retardation. In Sonia F. Osler & R. E. Cooke (Eds.) *The biosocial basis of mental retardation.* Baltimore: Johns Hopkins Press, 1965. Pp. 129–45.

Kirk, S. A. The *Illinois Test of Psycholinguistic Abilities: Its origin and implications.* In J. Hellmuth (Ed.), *Learning Disorders,* Vol. 3. Seattle: Special Child Publications, 1968. Pp. 395–428.

Kirk, S. A. Ethnic differences in psycholinguistic abilities. *Journal of Exceptional Children,* 1972, **39,** 112–18.

Kirk, S. A., & Bateman, B. D. *Ten years of research at the Institute for Research on Exceptional Children.* Urbana: University of Illinois Press, 1964.

Kirk, S. A., & Dunn, L. M. Impressions of Soviet psycho-educational service and research in mental retardation. *Exceptional Children,* 1963, **29,** 299–303, 305–11.

Kirk, S. A. & Johnson, G. O. Are mentally handicapped children segregated in the regular grades? *Journal of Exceptional Children,* 1950, **17,** 65–68.

Kirk, S. A., & Johnson, G. O. *Educating the retarded child.* Boston: Houghton-Mifflin, 1951.

Kirk, S. A., & Kirk, W. D. The influence of the teacher's handedness on children's reversal tendencies in writing. *Journal of Genetic Psychology,* 1935, **47,** 473–77.

Kirk, S. A. & Kirk, W. D. *Psycholinguistic learning disabilities: Diagnosis and remediation.* Urbana: University of Illinois Press, 1971.

Kirk, S. A. & Lord, F. *Exceptional children: Educational resources and perspectives.* Boston: Houghton-Mifflin, 1974.

Kirk, S. A., & McCarthy, J. J. *The Illinois Test of Psycholinguistic Abilities*—An approach to differential diagnosis. *American Journal of Mental Deficiency,* 1961, **66,** 399–412.

Kirk, S. A., McCarthy, J. J. & Kirk, W. D. *The Illinois Test of Psycholinguistic Abilities.* Urbana: University of Illinois Press, 1968.

Kirk, S. A., & McCarthy, J. M. (Eds.) *Learning disabilities: Selected ACLD papers.* Boston: Houghton-Mifflin, 1975.

Kirk, S. A., & Stevens, I. A preacademic curriculum for slow-learning children. *American Journal of Mental Deficiency,* 1943, **47,** 396–405.

Kirk, S. A., & Weiner, B. B. (Eds.) *Behavioral research on exceptional children.* Washington, D.C.: Council for Exceptional Children, 1963.

9
Thomas C. Lovitt

Thomas C. Lovitt was born in 1930 in Hutchinson, Kansas. He is currently professor of special education at the University of Washington. He received a B.A. degree in music education from the University of Kansas in 1952 and attended the Eastman School of Music during the summer of 1956. In 1960 he received a M.A. degree in music education from Kansas University and in 1966 a Ed.D. degree in special education, also from that university.

Dr. Lovitt began his professional career as a musician with the Kansas City Philharmonic and music instructor at a number of colleges and universities in Kansas and Missouri. In 1962, he began his career in special education as a teacher in North Kansas City, Missouri. From 1963 through 1964 he was a special education instructor at the Children's Rehabilitation Unit at the Kansas University Medical Center and a remedial reading instructor in Kansas City, Missouri. After a year of full-time graduate study at Kansas University (1964–1965), he became a graduate assistant in mental retardation and an administrative assistant in the learning disabilities program (1965–1966). From 1966 to 1968 Dr. Lovitt was the coordinator of the learning disabilities program at the University of Washington, and from 1967 to 1969 he served as training coordinator for the learning disabilities demonstration project. Since 1967, he has coordinated the Curriculum Research classroom at the Experimental Education Unit. During the academic year 1974 to 1975, Dr. Lovitt was a visiting professor with the psychology department at the Universidad Nacional Autónoma de Mexico, Mexico City.

Dr. Lovitt is active in many professional organizations, including the Council for Exceptional Children, the Council for Children with Behavioral Disorders, Phi Delta Kappa, and the American Educational Research Association. He has presented numerous papers at meetings of professional societies and is well-known as a researcher and writer, particularly in the area of behavior modification or applied behavior analysis. He has served as an associate editor for Exceptional Children, Journal of Learning Disabilities, *and* Journal of Applied Behavior Analysis. *A selected bibliography of works by Thomas C. Lovitt appears on pages 303–4.*

At the outset, I would like to thank Kauffman and Hallahan for asking me to write this chapter. I was honored and pleased to find myself in such distinguished company as the other contributors to this book. The idea of the editors to invite several persons to provide personal accounts of their development as it relates to the field of learning disabilities is highly original. I hope that such an approach to the dissemination of information will prove helpful to those individuals concerned with the instruction of children with "learning disabilities."

I must admit that being asked to write "my story" as it relates to "learning disabilities" was an ego trip for me. Being invited to write about oneself, knowing that those words will be published, and, what is more, published along with the self-analyses of persons I have long respected, is heady wine indeed.

Once I began to outline my writing plan I felt, along with the exhilaration of writing my own story, a compulsion to be candid, because my career was shaped by positive and negative experiences alike. In this respect I do not believe I am alone, for most of us are rather hedonistic in that we continue to do those things that are reinforcing, while we do fewer of those things that are punishing. Therefore, most of us have not progressed from one happy scene to the next. Yet to tell the whole truth and nothing but the truth is, of course, impossible.

There are many reasons why it is impossible to trace accurately the whole course of one's own development. For one thing (and thank heaven for this), we tend to repress some of our more unpleasant and less benign experiences, while we highlight and even amplify some of the more pleasant interludes of our lives. Another difficulty in tracing our lives is that we cannot always remember from whom we received which inspiration, or from what experience we came up with which revelation—if there have, in fact, been inspirations and revelations. Since most of us have not spent lifetimes dispensing reinforcers to those who further our development, it is difficult to trace the exact origins of many thoughts and ideas that have, in turn, precipitated action. Notwithstanding these hazards of writing about one's development, I will make an effort to be as candid as possible in presenting my case.

Throughout this chapter I will point out a number of people who significantly contributed to my development. Most of them were significant in that they encouraged me to continue in the direction I seemed to be going. A few persons were significant in that they threw roadblocks in the path that either they or I thought I was traveling. In either event, they were influential people. When it comes to the first type, I will try to identify them vividly. When it comes to the second, I will be as ambiguous as possible.

Apart from being candid, I am aware of a further responsibility in writing this chapter. That responsibility is to represent the behavior modifiers, precision teachers, and other operant people who happen to be practicing in the field of learning disabilities. Although when referring to this methodology, I prefer the terms *applied behavior analysis* and *direct and daily measurement* to many of the other labels, I will try to carry the banner high for this set of colleagues who proclaim "our" methodology, by whatever appellation.

THE OLD MAN WITHOUT A HORN

I arrived in special education via a circuitous route. I did not, as did many of my colleagues, come into the field through elementary education, speech therapy, psychology, or even sociology or anthropology. I came in through music. My first two degrees, both from the University of Kansas, were in music education. I was apparently studying to become a band director in some small town in western Kansas.

My experience in music began in the fourth grade when I started taking trumpet lessons. I continued playing the trumpet through high school; and when a choice as to what major to elect in college became imminent, I decided to continue with music. When it came to making a decision as to where to study music, I knew of only three schools: The University of Kansas, Emporia State Teachers College, and Wichita State College. I decided to enroll in the state university at Lawrence. Coming from Burrton, Kansas, I was certain this was the biggest school in the world.

When I completed my undergraduate degree I went into the Air Force. During that four-year stint I fought the battles of Lackland in San Antonio, Andrews Field in Washington, D.C., and Lowrey in Denver. Throughout this period, I played in field bands; and wherever I was stationed, I continued to take trumpet lessons.

When I was discharged from the service, I enrolled for a short period at the Eastman School of Music in Rochester, New York. During that summer I ran out of money and heard of an opening for a trumpet player in the Kansas City Philharmonic. I auditioned and was offered the position as the second trumpet player. I eagerly accepted the offer and remained with that orchestra for six seasons.

During those symphony years I also played with the Lyric Opera Company in Kansas City and with various dance bands and other groups. In fact, during that time, I played for anyone who called; I played every type of engagement from Italian weddings to Bar Mitzvahs.

In addition to playing, I taught for many years at the Kansas City Conservatory, now affiliated with the University of Missouri. For short periods of time, I also taught at the University of Kansas, Kansas State College in Pittsburg, and Central Missouri State College in Warrensburg. For a number of years after I stopped playing in the symphony I continued to give private lessons and to play various jobs around Kansas City.

I have briefly reviewed my career in music, because the music profession had a significant influence on my special education career. Often I have used analogies from the world of music to conceptualize or describe some learning or developmental matters with children. But apart from furnishing me with illustrative material, there are some rather specific behaviors I acquired in the music business that have not been extinguished, even though I switched fields.

One important behavior I learned from music is the idea of "doing-it-every-day." Many times in our hurry-hurry world we seek quick solutions to complex problems and expect rapid development of highly technical skills. The advertising business has certainly fostered this idea, with commercials that promise quick mastery to many problems, ranging from learning to play the guitar to speaking French.

The musicians I knew, particularly those who played in symphony orchestras, had studied for many years in order to become competent performers. They followed rigorous and demanding schedules of practice and study throughout most of their lives.

It is important to keep in mind the notion of steady and prolonged work when attempting to help others develop complex skills. Rather than arranging crash courses in remedial reading, for example, teachers should schedule reading every day over a period of many years. They should take every step to increase the probability that pupils will become competent in all the many behaviors of reading and will, as a result, be highly proficient. They must be complete readers, not superficial skimmers who could be likened to those language students who take crash courses two months before visiting a foreign country.

A second behavior I learned in music was the principle of immediate feedback. Many times when this term is used in psychology or education classes, it is just an abstract concept—one of the many learning principles that students must learn.

To a musician, however, immediate feedback is a continual reality. Once the trumpet player blows air thorugh his horn or the violinist pulls his bow across a string, something happens: the tone is sour, mediocre, or gorgeous. If he is conscious at all, he receives immediate feedback. Moreover, if he is a dedicated performer, he can, if necessary, make some adjustments in his playing so that the next tone will be more pleasant, if improvement is needed.

In teaching skills to youngsters, it is important to give them immediate feedback as to the quality of their performance and to inform them as to the extent to which they are approaching a specified criterion. Along with providing feedback, it is important for teachers to assist pupils in using this information. I will comment further on this later.

Another noteworthy behavior I brought from music into special education has been the importance of natural consequences. Natural consequences are those which are indigenous to any particular environment. They may be contrasted to synthetic consequences which have been brought into an environment.

In music there are many natural consequences. Perhaps the most important natural consequence that an independent musician learns is that if he plays well he is employed. Although there is a certain degree of politics in music, the practice of granting reinforcement contingent on performance is carried out to a greater extent than in most other trades or professions.

Homme (1963) and Ferster (1967), I believe, first proposed the notion of using natural consequences in psychology and education. They suggested that clinicians and teachers should use the consequences currently available in a person's environment rather than employ synthetic consequences in their efforts to effect change.

In the Curriculum Research Classroom, where I work, when it is necessary to arrange consequences for children in order to assist them to develop certain behaviors, we routinely arrange natural consequences. It has been our belief, which is to some extent supported with data, that when natural consequences are used, the probability is great that the initial effects on behavior will be satisfactory and that once the behavior is developed, generalization to other situations is likely to occur.

Another feature I brought with me from music to special education is the notion of continuous measurement, for the professional musician is evaluated each time he plays. Accordingly, predictions about his performance on future occasions are made from several past performances.

This practice of continuous measurement is one of the key components of applied behavior analysis. Those of us who abide by the dicta of this methodology support the belief that a great deal of data should be obtained from an individual in regard to the behaviors he is being required to develop and that decisions regarding those behaviors should be based on those multiple impressions, rather than on a few pieces of data.

Another pedagogical feature from the music business that has greatly influenced my relationships with students is the strategy of one-on-one teaching. As I have mentioned earlier, I gave trumpet lessons in many locations for a number of years. All of those lessons were one-on-one: one pupil and one teacher. At one time I estimated that I had given 12,480 private lessons over a period of 6,240 hours.

Teaching can be extremely refined in a one-on-one situation—that is, of course, if the teacher is a good one. The pupil has more opportunities to respond in this type of situation; hence, the teacher has more opportunities to provide feedback, to serve as a model, and to give reinforcement. The opportunities for these transactions in class situations are greatly reduced.

In the situation where I have worked in Washington, we have taken children labeled as "learning disabled," primarily because of reading problems. With these children we have arranged brief, one-on-one teaching situations throughout the year. Generally, these children have gained from two to three years in reading during a twelve-month period. I am convinced that these gains were not due to the super techniques we used, for as I will explain later, our procedures are very simple. I believe the primary reason the pupils have thrived is that they were in situations where they could interact individually with a teacher. Other factors that have certainly contributed to their progress have been that the exact behaviors of concern were dealt with, and they read daily for many days. We did not give them a quickie "blitz" treatment.

Another trait learned from music that has served me in special education was learning about criticism: the ability to criticize and be criticized. In music, particularly when he gives lessons, the teacher must learn to be critical of others. He must tell his students when they are not performing appropriately. It is the poor teacher who allows too many flaws to go unattended.

For most people, of course, this is no problem; they are more than happy to criticize. The real skill in being critical is to know how much criticism can be dispensed before the recipient perceives of the criticism as punishment. Most of us have been in experiences where we have received more criticism than we could take, and we therefore removed ourselves from the situation. Thus, the skillful teacher is able to identify the student's tolerance for negative feedback.

This skill is particularly necessary for teachers of "learning disabled" children, for many of these children have experienced failure for several years. Because of these failures, they have received a great deal of negative criticism. Consequently, many have become immune to criticism, both positive and negative, and tune out the feedback attempts of teachers. With these children, teachers must initially provide small amounts of criticism (along with ample doses of reinforcement), then gradually increase the dosage. The rationale is that the more feedback a person receives, the more opportunities he has for correction, hence the more opportunities he has to develop.

Regrettably, I cannot say that my musical training taught me to discriminate feedback levels accurately enough to be able to schedule the appropriate amount. But I did learn that there were individual tolerances and those levels were likely to change from one day to the next.

Another behavior I generalized from music was the notion of directness. This attribute, along with continuous measurement, forms the heart of applied behavior analysis. In the music profession people are very direct; they are concerned with specific behaviors.

In Kansas City, for example, if an agent wished to hire a very dependable trumpet player who could read music and play extremely good jazz, Bill Traumbauer's name came up. If the agent was looking for an excellent first violinist to lead a chamber group, one who could play at sight any of the literature for such a group, Hugh Brown was generally the first choice.

The agents who called Bill and Hugh for those specific assignments were not concerned that Bill's primary interest was not the symphonic literature, or that Hugh was not a jazz violinist. Their performances were evaluated in those situations where each professed to be an expert. Their performances were directly evaluated.

This concept of directness was also apparent in the type of instruction that was provided in music. If a pianist aspired to become a concert artist, he received instruction from pianists who knew the concert literature and he practiced on those materials. It is unlikely that he would engage a jazz tutor or practice that type of music.

As I have said earlier, I translated this notion of directness into special education. For example, I would recommend that if a teacher desires to evaluate a child's progress as he reads from a Lippincott text, he should obtain measurement as the pupil reads from a Lippincott text, not from his performance on an achievement test. Accordingly, if the teacher wants to teach the child to read a Lippincott book, his instruction should be directed toward that book, not toward another text.

LIKE THE REST OF THE CLAN, BACK TO THE SCHOOLS

I came from and married into a family of teachers. My mother taught high school English for many years, and my father taught everything in a country school for a short period. My father-in-law was an English professor in a Kansas college for many years, and my mother-in-law taught elementary school music for several years. My wife is an elementary school music teacher, and my daughter is preparing to teach special education.

I had thought, when I began playing in the orchestra in Kansas City, that I had escaped the teaching business. Although I gave private lessons —so in a way, I was in the teaching business—I was not totally committed to pedagogy. But along the way there were several circumstances that pushed me out of music and into special education. I will first recount two of the earlier incidents.

One of the negative forces was the Sante Fe Opera. For two seasons I had played first trumpet in the orchestra for this fine organization and had planned to return for a third. But for some reason (perhaps they wanted to upgrade the orchestra), I was not invited to come back. I was, to say the least, deeply disappointed.

The second factor that drove me out of the music business was Dallas. Actually it was not the fault of Dallas; it was that I went there to audition for a job. I had heard, through the national trumpet grapevine, that there was an opening for the position of principal trumpet player in the Dallas symphony. I called the business manager of the orchestra and arranged for an audition. I flew into Dallas one night and auditioned the next day. When it was over they thanked me and said they would call if they needed me. They never called.

Although I cite these two incidents, I was at that time becoming generally discouraged with the music profession. It had become obvious that if I opted to continue in music I would remain forever in Kansas City as the second trumpet player. So I began looking for other reinforcers.

During this period when I was being encouraged to leave the music profession, I was also being lured into special education. While I was obtaining my master's degree I had taken courses from the late Mark Hahn and the late E. Thayer Gaston. These men were excellent music educators and had established at Kansas University one of the nation's finest training programs for music therapists. During the courses with these gentlemen there were many discussions about the uses of music with exceptional children. I seriously considered taking all the required courses in order to become a music therapist once I had completed my master's degree.

I believe that during this period I first began to consider working with exceptional children. Up to that time I was very naive about the types of exceptionality. In Burrton there were no classes for the "mentally retarded," much less for the "learning disabled." We knew that Dorothy Dawson and Margaret Cavin were smarter than the rest of us and there were always a few who never quite got the message, but that was the extent of our sophistication in identifying exceptional people.

Another man who steered me into special education was Jack Edwards. In order to earn a master's degree, an educational psychology course was required. I elected to take the survey course in special education that Jack taught. Although it was a large class with no intimate involvement with the professor, I was fascinated by the course. That class stimulated me a great deal to think about special education. I became particularly interested in those individuals described as "mentally retarded" and "emotionally disturbed."

After I had finished my master's degree I continued taking courses for two reasons. One was that I had decided to work toward a specialist's degree in music therapy. The other motive for taking courses was that I received some G.I. Bill money for going to school.

One of the classes I took during this period was a course in mental retardation taught by Bill Johnson. Bill was, and still is, the director of pupil services for the North Kansas City school system. From time to time he is engaged by the University of Kansas to teach specific classes in special education. Occasionally during his lectures, Bill proselytized for the need of male teachers in special education. So at the end of the semester I asked him if there was a need for male special education teachers in North Kansas City. He informed me that there was and encouraged me to apply for a position. In a few days I arranged an interview and was hired for the coming year.

It was during this period that I met another influential person insofar as my career was concerned. Dr. Norris Haring had just assumed the directorship of the Children's Rehabilitation Unit (CRU) associated with the University of Kansas Medical Center. During his first semester in Kansas City, my wife and I enrolled in his course on the emotionally disturbed. This was an exciting class, for he described the research he and E. Lakin Phillips had just completed in Virginia. During some evenings he lectured from the galleys of what was later to become a classic book in special education, *Educating Emotionally Disturbed Children* (Haring & Phillips, 1962). It was also during this time, immediately before I began teaching in North Kansas City, that I met three men who would later be my companions throughout the doctoral program, and become my very good friends and professional colleagues: Dick Whelan, Gene Ensminger, and Jerry Chafin.

During the summer prior to my teaching, I arranged a practice teaching situation at the CRU. I taught under the tutelage of Joyce North. Her class was a group of very heterogeneous children. About all they had in common was that they had extremely limited educational and social repertories. Joyce was, and continues to be, one of special education's best teachers. From her I learned several techniques for managing the obstreperous behaviors of youngsters.

In North Kansas City I was assigned a class of twenty children; that was the limit for Missouri special education classes at the time. Although it was called a class for the "mentally retarded," there were some children of many types in the group. There were several youngsters in the class who could not read well, could not spell as well as they should, and were a bit naughty; they were "learning disabled." There were also children in the class who had more serious handicaps.

My class was in Norclay Elementary School, in the heart of North Kansas City. There were six special education classes in the building, four of which were for intermediate age youngsters and two of which were for those of primary age. I was assigned one of the intermediate classes; the children were eleven and twelve years old.

The principal of Norclay was Floyd Lesley. Bill Johnson could not have selected a better principal or school for educating so many special children. Floyd was always involved with children and teachers in a very positive way. His behavior led me to believe that the primary responsibility of the principal was to reinforce teachers for good teaching and that interactions with other administrators were secondary. Unfortunately, I have learned many times since that most principals reverse those priorities.

In spite of the fact that I had been exposed to good teaching during the summer before I began my work in North Kansas City, I knew very little about how to instruct children. Of course, now the contingencies were changed. In North Kansas City I was the teacher, not a student. I did not know how to arrange seats, collect lunch money, or make coffee for the teachers' lounge, much less how to program basic skills for children. Fortunately, throughout that year I was surrounded by two master teachers: Ethyl Parks and Frances Washam. They reinforced any behavior on my part that approximated good teaching and responded with helpful advice to all my queries about instruction. Throughout the year I learned a great deal about arranging programs for exceptional children from them.

During this year of teaching I had my first experience with the concepts of I.Q. and M.A. When I received the list of pupils for my room I began to calculate their mental ages. Since I knew their chronological ages and their I.Q. scores, from either Stanford-Binet or a Wechsler test, I was able to determine their M.A.s. After I had determined each child's M.A., I selected reading and arithmetic books. For example, if a child's M.A. was 7, I chose a second-grade reader and arithmetic book for him. Thus, by a few lightning calculations I had grouped my children!

When the children came to school and I began working with them in their assigned texts, I was greatly disappointed. My placement attempts were grossly inaccurate. In general, I discovered that about one-third of the children were placed too low, one-third about right, and one-third too high.

Granted, I had used the M.A. concept and I.Q. scores very literally. But because of this initial experience and because of many subsequent encounters with those abstractions, I have learned to attach little credibility to them as aids to programming.

The next year I taught a demonstration class at the Children's Rehabilitation Unit. Norris Haring had asked me to teach a class for junior high students at CRU, and I eagerly accepted the opportunity.

The children in this class were, as they say, "severely involved." Although there were only six or seven in the class, several maladies were represented. Because the children in this class were so unique, it was impressed upon me once again how totally different the learning styles of children can be. I also learned that since many parents of exceptional children have shopped from one school, clinic, therapist, and physician to another in search of help for their youngsters, some of them have become very aggressive. They have amassed a repertory of skills to obtain their just rights that are quite sophisticated. They can, therefore, easily overwhelm an inexperienced teacher. It became obvious that if one is to be effective with exceptional children, at least a modest understanding of the whole family is necessary.

Teaching at the CRU was an exciting experience. There were many impressive dignitaries who toured the facility. It was also stimulating to work with people like Norris Haring, Gene Ensminger, Jerry Chafin, Dick Whelan, Mary Mira, Diane Renne, and many others. In addition to the inspiration during the day at the CRU, we had many invigorating evenings at Jimmie's, a fantastic pub on State Street.

During this year I took a few classes, most of which were good; but one was memorable. This was a course in mental retardation taught by Jack Cawley. He is an excellent teacher, a true professional. I was, and continue to be, impressed by Jack's knowledge of the literature and programs for the mentally retarded.

The next year, 1964, I was awarded a fellowship. Thus I was able to attend school fulltime in order to finish the necessary course work for my doctorate.

It was during this year that I first became acquainted with operant conditioning. The stimulus for reading on this topic was an independent study I undertook with Haring. He asked me to read and report on every operant conditioning study—applied and basic—that had been published.

Throughout one semester, for one day a week, I went to the Linda Hall Library in Kansas City, and read the operant lore. During that year I became acquainted with the research of Baer, Bijou, Orlando, Staats, Ferster, Lindsley, Goldiamond, and others. That semester I read every piece of operant research that I could locate. Although this assignment required many hours of reading, it would require many more hours today in order to read all the operant literature than it did in 1964.

I remained at Kansas the following year as an instructor in special education. During that year, two more men contributed significantly to my education: Jim Smith and Ogden Lindsley. I am deeply indebted to Jim Smith for many assists along the way, but his first contribution was to organize my doctoral program. Prior to Jim's coming to Kansas, I had been taking courses for a few years and had, in fact, taken about everything that was offered in special education. When I showed Jim a copy of this array of courses he said something like, "That's interesting, but do you have a program, and if so, when do you plan to graduate?" He helped me form a plan for finishing my course work and for scheduling written and oral examinations that I was able to follow and complete.

During this period Jim gave me another big boost that significantly broadened my interests. He had been asked to write a chapter on speech and language for a CEC monograph. This was to be one chapter, along with others that dealt with the various categories of exceptionality. Jim asked me to assist him with this project.

Working on this chapter gave me an opportunity to interview personally several eminent people in the speech and language field. Locating experts in this area was rather simple, for at that time, some of the finest scholars engaged in speech and language research were in the Kansas City area: Harris Winnitz, Dan Boone, Bill Deitrich, Bill Shelton, Margaret Byrne, June Miller. I asked these individuals and others throughout the country to identify the most significant research dealing with speech and language since 1960. The articles that Jim and I abstracted in that chapter were those recommended by this group.

Up to that time I had not studied the literature on speech and language. Because of this experience, however, I was convinced that research on these topics should be seriously considered by everyone in special education, regardless of his specific interest.

I was also greatly influenced by Ogden Lindsley during this last year at Kansas. When I first knew him he was direct from Harvard. Although he was exploding with ideas about how to revolutionize education with the system that came to be known as "Precision Teaching," he was still very much a scientist, able to communicate the merits of the experimental analysis of behavior.

Og was particularly helpful to me after I had finished my course work. I woke up one morning and was smitten by a common doctoral malady. I thought, "My God, now I have to write a dissertation." I had never really thought about designing and conducting research while I was taking courses, so when the time came I tried to be creative. For a few days I jotted down some ideas for research and submitted them to my committee members. I had thought, apparently, that if a committee member would reinforce one of my ideas, I would further develop that thought and proceed to carry out a reasonable piece of research.

One afternoon during this "creative" period, I strolled into Og's little brick house on Eaton Street across from the K.U. Medical Center, and we began talking about research. I talked about the need to do some, and he talked about what it was. Although he gave me many ideas, he was of the persuasion that a researcher should study what most interested him, not what someone else told him to investigate.

During our discussion he asked about my background and my current interests. I mentioned that I had most recently been a student, before that a teacher, and before that a musician. Og was most interested in the latter point and mentioned that he had played the bass drum in a Rhode Island high school band. He mentioned also, and perhaps more significantly, that he had done some research with music.

Thereupon, he took from his file of reprints the monophonic and stereophonic study that was eventually published in the *Journal of Music Therapy* (Morgan & Lindsley, 1966) and asked me to read it. This was an ingenious study wherein the two modes of music were presented simultaneously to the subjects. The subjects could, by either responding at a predetermined rate or by not responding, obtain their preferred mode of music. The apparatus used to obtain these preference data—the conjugate reinforcement system—was designed by Lindsley.

I was fascinated by the prospect of doing research with music or other narrative forms and using the conjugate device, so I asked if I could begin. Og and Eric Haughton, who was then a doctoral student, proceeded to arrange the conjugate reinforcement apparatus in the kitchen of the brick house: the relay racks, cumulative recorder, power supply, and conjugate servo.

The first study I did with this system was an investigation to determine the relative preferences for five types of narration. The second investigation sought to compare the reinforcing effects of two stories.

Another conjugate reinforcement study that I conducted was my doctoral dissertation. In addition to being interested in conjugate reinforcement at this time, I was fascinated by compressed speech. Jerry Chafin had collected most of the research up to that time on compressed speech, so thanks to him I was able to study this topic. After reading several articles I talked with Og about the possibility of combining the two interests: conjugate reinforcement and compressed speech. We designed a study whereby the preferred rates of speech of retarded and normal boys were determined. This research was eventually published in the *Psychological Record* (Lovitt, 1968).

While conducting the conjugate studies I learned a great deal about direct and continuous measurement. Throughout these studies a response was a button press that was directly recorded by a cumulative recorder. This type of recorder also provides a continuous, moment-by-moment display of the response.

I also learned during this period what it is like to be an independent researcher. During that time I arranged for my own subjects, brought them to the lab, ran the sessions myself, analyzed the data, drew figures and tables to represent the data, wrote up and described the data, and wrote for grants for further investigations.

During my last year at K.U., Haring had moved to Seattle. I had agreed to join him at the University of Washington the following year. In the summer of 1965, before moving to Seattle, he was responsible for having me invited to Seattle to present a paper at a learning disabilities conference.

This was only my third opportunity to deliver a paper and my first chance to put together some of my ideas about "learning disabled" children. I therefore welcomed the invitation and invested a great deal of time developing a paper on the assessment of learning disabled children. I must give credit to Stephen Sulzbacher, then a graduate student, for his help in assisting with this paper. He was a valued critic throughout the many stages of its development.

In that presentation I tried to make the case that the traditional form of diagnosis—that is, achievement tests and other inferential measures— is a fallacious way of assessing behaviors. It is deceptive for two reasons: the measures are often indirect, and they are invariably infrequent. I presented an argument for an alternative method of assessment that employs direct and daily measurement. In that paper I relied heavily on my conjugate research, since that was the only data I had, together with the assessment strategy of Lindsley's that was published in the *Journal of Education* (1964).

This paper was revised and published in a 1967 issue of *Exceptional Children* (Lovitt, 1967). I have received more reprint requests for this assessment article than for anything else I have written. In addition, the paper has been reprinted in six collections of readings. I just finished reading the article; and although I still agree with the general message, that direct and daily measurement is the best method for assessing behavior, the article now appears incredibly naive. Read from the vantage point of a teacher, it is lacking immediate suggestions that can be put into action. In order to translate the ideas in that article into practice, the teacher would have to be a highly skilled extrapolator, indeed.

A SEATTLE MOTEL

In September 1966, I took the family to Seattle. I had been appointed an assistant professor in special education at the University of Washington. I moved into an office in the Experimental Education Unit (EEU), which was at that time in a motel about ten blocks from the main campus.

The EEU was made up of about six classrooms, all of which were arranged on the basis of David Premack's reinforcement strategy (Premack, 1959). That is, each classroom included two sections, the high and low probability areas. In one room (the low probability room), the pupils sat at desks and worked on their reading, writing, and arithmetic assignments. The other room (the high probability room) was used as the free time area. A variety of games, toys, and other activities that were relevant to the various ages of the children were placed in that room.

Daily data in regard to each child's performance in every academic area were kept. On the basis of these data, the children were awarded minutes of free time. Data were also obtained in regard to when and how the free time was spent.

Harold Kunzelmann, the first principal of the EEU, was largely responsible for organizing all the classes. For several years, as the principal of that school, he worked tirelessly to establish one of the few data-gathering schools in the country, and probably the finest. A great deal of credit for the success of this school should also be extended to some of those first teachers at the EEU, for they obtained data on behaviors that had not, prior to that time, been carefully monitored. Those teachers attempted to measure daily virtually every aspect of the elementary school curriculum.

For the first few months I was at the EEU I did a lot of looking and talking. I was fascinated by the classrooms and wanted to learn as much as possible. My interests, however, were still with conjugate reinforcement. A few months after I arrived in Seattle, I assembled the apparatus in the kitchen area connected with Karen Curtiss' classroom. I began to use the pupils from her class for conjugate studies. In one of the studies, I attempted to determine preferences for various types of music and stories. I also conducted several studies in regard to the interactions of dyads. For some of these latter investigations I collaborated with Robert Burgess, a sociologist and valued colleague of mine at the University of Washington.

Since the EEU, including the classroom of Karen Curtiss, was extremely visible (several visitors came through each day), I was constantly asked to explain my research. Many of the tourists wanted to know how my research could help children. They were concerned with the immediate application of my findings in helping children read, write, and cipher. I had some answers for those queries that generally required an analogy to current classroom practice. Although some of the visitors seemed impressed by the apparatus and apparently agreed with the logic of my educational analogies, I often felt that they were underwhelmed by my explanations. I must confess that I became less and less convinced of the worth of these investigations.

Partially as a result of these nagging visitors and the fact that a classroom was available for research, I became more and more interested in the basic academic skills of children. I began to watch the children in this room more carefully as they responded to the various programs and to talk with Karen about the measurement of academic behaviors and the scheduling of techniques to develop those behaviors.

Since we were both interested in arranging situations to investigate the effects of certain teaching procedures precisely, we conducted several studies with these children. In fact, when all the basic academic subjects of the children were scheduled, we were able to arrange at least one research project with each child. In addition to being an excellent teacher, Karen is a meticulous researcher. She saw to it that the research studies were conducted every possible day and took every precaution to insure that they were reliably managed.

Because of this experience in arranging several studies within a single classroom, I began to think more and more about establishing a classroom whose primary purpose would be to conduct educational research. In a few years I was fortunate enough to be associated with such a class, the Curriculum Research Classroom.

Although we conducted many studies in Karen's classroom, two of them were, I believe, of greater significance than the others. In one of these we investigated the effects of a boy's verbalizing his arithmetic problems before he made a written response. This research was published in the *Journal of Applied Behavior Analysis* (Lovitt & Curtiss, 1968). In this research we attempted to demonstrate that a common teaching procedure, one that has been used with children for many years, could profitably be subjected to experimental analysis. This study also showed that antecedent events, as well as subsequent events or reinforcers, can significantly influence behavior.

Another investigation that we conducted in this classroom also appeared in the *Journal of Applied Behavior Analysis* (Lovitt & Curtiss, 1969). Through some conditions of this research, a pupil was allowed to specify his own contingencies. That is, in several academic areas he could determine how many minutes of free time he would earn for a certain number of correct answers. This study helped to demonstrate that another dimension of reinforcers is available: allowing children to determine certain aspects of their school routine. It also stimulated some teachers and researchers to consider the teaching of independence as a distinct curricular offering.

Apart from this experience of conducting research with a small group of children, I had a second valuable experience during those first years at the University of Washington. Haring had received a federal grant concerned with the training of teacher consultants. Our first task was to train four persons to use contingency management procedures and to obtain direct and daily measurement of classroom performances. Following the training period, the consultants were assigned to four elementary schools where they were to instruct the teachers in those schools in the use of management and measurement procedures. I was the training coordinator for this project.

This was my first experience working with all the personnel of a school: teachers, principals, and ancillary staff. I learned several things during my two-year tenure with this project. I learned, for example, that if a school is to change certain of its practices, everyone's views in that school must be considered. We had erred in this regard. I also learned that teachers are as unique as children. This uniqueness was most apparent in our attempts to influence them to measure the important behaviors of children. We discovered that some teachers were motivated to learn, whereas others were extremely resistant to change. We learned that many environmental circumstances must be rearranged before some teachers will measure the performances of children. I have John Kidder, who worked with me on this project, to thank for his patience in determining the instructional levels of, and reinforcing events for, teachers and in maintaining their behaviors once they began to measure pupil performance.

Although this project was conducted a few years before the mainstreaming vogue, it was apparent to us that if regular teachers were taught certain behavior analysis techniques, they would be able to educate many children who would otherwise be sent to special classes. This seemed to be particularly true of the children who were referred to us as "learning disabled."

One of the studies that we conducted during this project took place in a sixth grade and was published in *Behaviour Research and Therapy* (Lovitt, Guppy, & Blattner, 1969). This study, supervised by Tal Guppy, the consultant, and managed by Jim Blattner, the teacher, showed that the spelling performances of most children in a class could be improved when a simple but systematic free-time contingency was arranged.

I had a third rewarding experience during those first Seattle years. For two years, beginning in 1967, my wife taught a group of "learning disabled" children in a suburban Seattle district. This period was frustrating and yet rewarding for me.

Although prior to that assignment, Polly had had several successful experiences with children, she lacked some of the special skills needed to educate a crew of very difficult youngsters. The range of capabilities and disabilities of the children assigned to her group was extremely wide; the population was certainly not as homogeneous as the administrators of the district had apparently assumed by referring to them as "learning disabled."

Every night during this period we talked about the children in her class: about Eric's reading problem, Paul's fighting on the playground, Sue's reversals, John's swearing. We did not theorize, for she demanded solutions for her problems. She became very much disenchanted with me and other experts who criticized teachers but did not help them. She was quite unimpressed by the verbal artists who talked about "getting teachers to change."

Although there were several evenings during this period when the tension ran very high, in regard to practical solutions, the most memorable night was one occasion when Og Lindsley, Eric Haughton, Harold Kunzelmann, and I were in our home talking about the wonders of precision teaching. We were discussing the fact that when teachers finally get off their duffs and become systematic, the education of children will be greatly improved. In the background of this lofty conversation, Polly kept asking first one of us and then another for some specific suggestions about current problems in her room. We all managed, however, to ignore her. Finally, when she had had enough and demanded to be recognized, she poured a full glass of Budweiser on my head. I will have to admit that I was a tad piqued by this unreasonable play for attention. But that experience and many others during that two-year period forced me to make increased efforts to stay in contact with the day-to-day realities of the public schools and to try to investigate and recommend techniques for solving current problems that can be readily implemented by teachers.

Along with these positive experiences during the motel years, there was one negative reinforcer, which pertained to grantsmanship and labeling, that significantly shaped certain of my behaviors. My primary assignment at Washington was to coordinate the program in learning disabilities. Haring had written the first grant in this area and was awarded about five masters' fellowships. The next year I wrote the grant and was awarded seven masters' fellowships.

The following year I wrote another grant. The response to this grant was a site visit. A team of federally sponsored visitors came to Seattle to inspect our learning disabilities program. Their primary concern was the manner in which I defined, or did not define, the population of children considered to be "learning disabled." When I was pressed for a definition, I spoke of children who did not read very well, who had difficulty with spelling and arithmetic, and who were perhaps a bit naughty, relative to their peers. This definition did not seem to correspond to the one the government people wanted. Ours was apparently not consistent with that of one of the many task forces engaged by the government to grapple with the problem. Their definitions were arrived at only after several professionals had spent many hours and the government had spent many dollars. Following that site visit, we received three or four fellowships.

The next year I again wrote the grant. When the officials received this application, which was still vague in respect to defining "learning disabilities," I received a phone call and a letter. By this time they were openly perplexed about my cavalier approach to the matter of defining "learning disabilities." Shortly thereafter we were again site-visited. This set of visitors continued to probe into the matter of definition. I maintained that "learning disabilities" were generally confined to basic skill deficits; and like other presumed categories in special education, "learning disability" is a label relative to specific regions, schools, teachers, and many other factors. I also presented my belief that our current categorizing structure was ill-conceived, since the labels had neither led to better grouping for children, which would reduce heterogeneity, which would in turn facilitate teaching, nor to specific ecucational techniques, which would in time obviate the condition associated with the label and promote educational development. I continued to try to make the point that it was more important to diagnose the exact school-relevant behaviors of children, to keep daily data, to schedule simple and direct teaching techniques, to continue monitoring the behaviors, than it was to try to define "learning disabilities." In fact, during the period of these discussions, I expressed the belief that no worthwhile function could be served by our special education labels. At the end of this chapter I will comment on my current viewpoint in respect to labeling.

It could be because of my unwillingness to modify my position on the matter of definition that after this last site visit our learning disabilities grant was transferred to the interrelated area. We were awarded two or three fellowships from our new benefactor.

During that year a newcomer joined our special education faculty. He was most anxious to coordinate a fellowship program; I was, by that time, eager to get rid of one. As a result, one of those rare, amiable academic transfers took place when I handed the reins of the much-maligned and often site-visited learning disabilities program. The new faculty man was given identity, and I was federally stripped of my label.

Being rebuffed by the federal people proved to be a blessing, because I no longer had to attend to the tiresome administrative trivia that program directors are saddled with. And I no longer wasted time as another quixotic rhetorician in search of the LD label. Being now disfranchised, I was able to intensify my research with "learning disabled children."

CURRICULUM RESEARCH ALONG THE CANAL

In 1968 the EEU moved from its motel to a grand new facility behind the university medical center along the Montlake Ship Canal. The EEU is a single level building made up of fourteen classrooms and many offices and therapy rooms. It, along with separate edifices that house the Clinical Training Unit, Residential Unit, and Medical Research Unit, comprises the Child Development and Mental Retardation Center.

The space that I was provided with when we settled into the Unit and have continued to occupy has almost perfectly served my ideas for conducting curriculum research. The facility includes a small classroom, two offices inside the classroom, and four small cubicles adjacent to the classroom. On both sides of the class are corridors that are separated from the class by one-way mirrors.

Each year we enroll seven different children into this class. These children are, of course, learning disabled, because in their regular schools they had more difficulty than the other youngsters with reading, writing, spelling, and ciphering, and they were, from time to time, a bit naughty. These children have been from nine to twelve years old and come from middle-class homes. Most of them have been boys.

In this classroom we schedule a rather complete academic program for the children. They read, write, spell, do arithmetic, and have social studies, history, art, music, shop, and physical education. However, since the pupils were referred to us because of basic skill deficits, most of our emphasis is placed on these behaviors: reading, spelling, arithmetic, and writing. In these areas we identify specific skills to teach and keep daily data in regard to the progress of the youngsters in each skill.

In most of the basic skill areas, e.g., reading, we identify a research theme. Although the pupils perform at different levels in the various areas, the general procedures are the same. For example, this past year in reading, we investigated the effects of being able to skip material on oral reading rate and its comprehension. In spelling we studied the comparative effects of the selection of study words by the teacher or by the pupil on the rate those words were learned. In arithmetic we studied the influence on performance of various types of feedback. Other research themes were identified in the areas of penmanship, math story problems, and story writing.

Ordinarily, two fulltime teachers have been assigned to this class. They have been graduate students in special education. In addition, other graduate students have worked parttime in the class. I would like here to note briefly a few of the more significant studies that have been completed in this classroom and take this opportunity to register my thanks to the several teachers and students who have assisted with the research.

One of our first studies that was, I believe, of some importance was conducted primarily by Mary Schaaf Kirkwood. As a part of her master's thesis we investigated the effects of several types of reinforcement contingencies on oral reading. For some children the contingencies were placed on correct rate, for others on error rate, for some on both. In this study we learned a great deal about the specific effects of reinforcement. We also learned about the use of traditional and applied behavior analysis research designs as they relate to reading research.

Marie Eaton, also a teacher in the Curriculum Research Classroom, conducted some important reading research that eventually led to her doctoral dissertation. In a series of studies in which the pupils read orally and answered comprehension questions, the effects of several types of pre-viewing were determined. In some instances the teacher read the story aloud before the child read it; other children were required to read the story silently before they read it orally. Other types of pre-viewing were also investigated. In this set of studies our purpose was to assess thoroughly some procedures that have long been recommended by publishers of reading materials, but have not been seriously subjected to experimental analysis. Another study that Marie and I designed was a comparison of two types of measurement: the pre–post achievement test method versus direct and daily measurement. We compared the two systems on the basis of three functions of data: placement, evaluation, and communication (Lovitt & Eaton, 1974).

Cheryl Hansen, the current head teacher of the Curriculum Research Classroom, has conducted several significant reading studies. One of these was concerned with the matter of placement. A procedure was devised and tested whereby pupils were assigned to specific readers for purposes of initial reading instruction on the basis of their oral reading and comprehension performances. This study appeared in the proceedings of the fifth annual Conference on Behavior Analysis in Education held at the University of Kansas (Hansen & Lovitt, 1974). A second study that Cheryl managed demonstrated that when pupils were allowed to skip pages in their readers, contingent on their performance, their oral reading and comprehension abilities improved.

In addition to our reading research, several arithmetic studies have been conducted. In the early days of the Curriculum Research Classroom, Kidder was very helpful in identifying various types of math facts and produced sheets of materials designed to aid in obtaining reliable math data.

Some of the most important math investigations in our room were directed by Debby Deutsch Smith, who worked in this classroom for several quarters throughout her doctoral program. One of the studies she managed dealt with the effects of various teaching aids on arithmetic performance. In another study we investigated the influence of a withdrawal contingency on performance. The material for Debby's doctoral dissertation was also obtained in this classroom. For this research, she assessed the influence of feedback, modeling, instructions, and various reinforcement procedures on several arithmetic skills. Data from this research were presented at the fourth and fifth annual Conferences on Behavior Analysis in Education (Smith & Lovitt, 1973, 1974).

Colleen Blankenship, a recent teacher in this classroom, also directed several arithmetic studies. In one investigation we analyzed the effects of several types of feedback on the arithmetic abilities of children. We have also conducted some preliminary research in regard to story problems. Since no applied behavior analysis research had been done on this topic, it was necessary to first define various classes of story problems, then write several problems of each type, then identify some instructional techniques that could alter performance, and then arrange experimental situations to evaluate the effects of these techniques.

Once again, I must acknowledge Jim Smith, this time as a contributor to our research classroom. During Jim's first year at the University of Washington he conducted several interesting studies in this class. One of Jim's research interests was to evaluate the effects of instructions, that is, telling a pupil what to do. He was convinced that systematic reinforcement could change behavior, but he also believed that consistent and carefully administered instructions could alter behavior. This interest led to a study which demonstrated that two aspects of a boy's speech could be altered by simple and consistent instructions. This research appeared in *Exceptional Children* (Lovitt & Smith, 1972).

Jim contributed in many ways to our classroom that year, for he shared my belief in the importance of a research classroom in conducting research and training researchers. Toward this end he offered many valuable suggestions about how to improve our situation.

During this period with the Curriculum Research Classroom, along with being able to conduct research on a continuous basis, I had two opportunities to analyze the current state and forecast the future of applied behavior analysis as it relates to curriculum development and exceptional children. The first was in 1970 and began with a call from Grace Warfield, editor of *Exceptional Children* (Lovitt, 1970).

Grace asked me to edit a special issue of *Exceptional Children* that dealt with behavior modification. I leaped at the opportunity and began immediately to assemble what I thought would be the classic collection of behavior modification articles. Although the issue, for many reasons, fell far short of my initial desires, I learned a great deal from that experience and am deeply indebted to Grace for her patience. For one thing, I learned a fair amount about editing and how to put together a magazine. The most important experience that came from putting together that issue, however, was that I stepped back and looked at behavior modification in its current state and predicted its future. It was important for me at that time to attempt to assimilate the research of many investigators over a long period of time and to identify new behaviors and locations where this methodology could be applied.

The other significant experience of this type came very recently. I was invited, along with several others, to prepare a position paper for the NIE. These papers were to provide direction for that organization in respect to future funding priorities. My particular assignment was to suggest which research relating to curriculum for "learning disabled youngsters" should be encouraged by the National Institute of Education. In addition, I was asked to write this report from the viewpoint of an applied behavior analyst and to recommend that methodology as a research strategy.

I took this opportunity to consider the needs of "learning disabled children," if not children in general, and make some suggestions about future educational research in their behalf. In this paper I made some general research recommendations pertaining to such matters as generalization, retention, and establishing performance criteria. I also made some specific research recommendations in each of the basic skill areas; some of those are repeated in this paper.

Writing this paper also afforded me the opportunity to evaluate objectively the applied behavior analysis methodology as it relates to curriculum research. In doing so I thought I detected, at least from my vantage point, several flaws in our system. In general, it seems to me that our system has become too constraining, and as a result has inhibited some creative research and perhaps has contributed to the preservation of an archaic system of education.

As a result of writing that paper I also thought about the places where educational research has been conducted and how this factor affects the dissemination and generalization of research information. I will comment more upon this point later.

I would like to end this section by very briefly summarizing the development of my research and by describing my current beliefs in regard to educational research. My investigations have, first of all, shifted from basic to applied research in the past few years. I first began in Kansas City and Seattle with the conjugate reinforcement research and then conducted some rather complex studies in an experimental class. During the past few years in the Curriculum Research Classroom our explorations have attempted to focus on problems of immediate concern to teachers.

I have become more and more convinced that education in general should be simplified. Therefore, it should be the researchers' responsibility to discover direct and simple ways to teach the fundamental behaviors and then to pass those techniques on to teachers.

Education has gone in the other direction during the past generation or so, for the business of teaching has become very complex—particularly in those systems wherein individuals must go to particular sites to learn to teach, receive instruction from personnel accredited by those institutions, use only certain educational materials and techniques, and employ a certain type of educational jargon.

Not only have these sophisticated teaching systems complicated and restricted the business of teaching, but publishers also have contributed to the process. Their major strategy to restrict and complicate education has been to program obsolescence. Through their advertising, they try to convince teachers that they must constantly buy fresh, modern materials.

Rather than contributing to this idea of restricting the number of those who practice teaching, thus making education more expensive, educational researchers should make every effort to simplify instruction and thus turn over the business of teaching to anyone who has something to teach and wants to teach it.

This idea has stimulated many of our investigations. We have investigated some very straightforward techniques—some, in fact, that have been used for years. The difference, many times, between our use of a technique and the way it has been employed by others is simply that we have attempted to be more consistent day after day in order to judge its effects more precisely.

Many visitors have looked in on our classroom and have inquired about our procedures. When told what we were doing, some were clearly disappointed; they had thought we were developing totally new and very sophisticated methods. They were amazed that we were using techniques they had employed when they taught in Boise or Spokane.

I believe this notion of using simple and direct teaching methods is particularly relevant to those children called "learning disabled." I maintain that many of these are the victims of complex diagnosis and instruction. Many have been shuffled from one clinic to another and have been subjected to innumerable techniques to attenuate their reversals, eliminate their strephosymbolia, and deal with their dyscalculia.

As an example of simple teaching, it has been my experience that often, when the teacher takes time to diagnose a child's problem thoroughly and carefully analyzes his pattern of responding, the remedial technique that should be used will be obvious and simple. I hasten to add that when I suggest that a child's behavior should be thoroughly diagnosed, I do not suggest that a battery of tests should be given. I mean that the behavior that has prompted concern should be scrutinized. If the teacher is concerned because of a child's reversals, that behavior should be studied. If he is concerned with reading in a Ginn basal reader, that behavior should be investigated. The teacher should not rely on indirect assessments that are all too often irrelevant.

Informed by these thorough observations, the teacher should design and administer an instructional technique that is child-specific. He should not necessarily depend on a technique that another teacher has devised, or one that is available from a publisher that may not be designed for the immediate problem.

Too many teachers, particularly teachers of the "learning disabled," have "solutions in search of problems"; they eagerly await pupils who display "learning-disabled-behaviors" so they can use their special techniques. Many times these treatments are not directly related to the problems of the youngsters. They may even at times cause side effects that, when compounded with the original problem, necessitate stronger solutions than would have been required in the first place.

SO WHAT NEXT?

There have been many recent significant social developments and forces that will assuredly influence many educational practices in the future. I would like to note briefly those which I believe are particularly relevant to the future education of the children in our schools. After I have mentioned some of these social forces, I will recommend some changes in our system of education that I would like to support, particularly as they relate to "learning disabled" youngsters.

One of the significant social–political forces of the immediate past that will assuredly influence educational style might be labeled "governmental disenchantment." Two prolonged events that have yet to be totally resolved portray this mood: the Vietnam War and the Watergate affair. Although these disasters have influenced people variously, most of us have been affected in one way or another. To a great extent, people now realize a need to decentralize power, to encourage more countercontrolling agencies; we are aware of the necessity for supporting honest representatives. Such attitudinal and behavioral changes on the part of the citizenry will certainly be reflected in the manner in which they view and support their school systems.

A second force that began to express itself a few years ago and that is continuing to gain momentum is the women's and minority rights movements. The effects of these groups have already become evident in education. Many curricular offerings have been modified to represent more equally the contributions and potentials of these groups. The teaching and administrative staffs of many school systems have been realigned to equalize the representation of many factions.

A third social factor that is becoming very important in determining educational policy is unionization. More and more school systems are becoming affiliated with unions. It is now common practice for teachers to bargain as a group for higher wages, reduced class sizes, more paraprofessional help, more preparation time.

Another important group that has particularly affected the education of exceptional children and will continue, I am certain, to exert great influence, is the parent movement. Parents of exceptional children have learned that when they have organized their efforts, their collective voices have much more often been heard.

Still another force that has effected, and will continue to effect, change—a force closely aligned with the efforts of parent groups—is the child advocacy or legal movement. Lawyers, parents, and other interested citizens have discovered that one of the most effective ways to alter educational practices is through the courts. There have been many incidents in which educational changes have resulted when suits were filed against teachers, schools, even entire school districts. The success of such litigations will certainly stimulate additional action.

A sixth social–educational factor with bearing on future educational policies is the accountability movement which, although it may have peaked a few years ago before it became widely acclaimed, may still leave its mark on our educational future. Two or three years ago the concept of accountability was loudly proclaimed in higher education and was implemented in a few school systems. Some schools were totally influenced by this concept and signed on with private firms in performance-contract operations. The notion of accountability was also implemented by some teacher-training institutions and state departments of education, which attempted to put the notions of accountability into practice by granting degrees and professional advancements on the basis of measured competencies.

Yet another force, albeit a minor one, is the legion of educational critics. The conditions of the late '60s and early '70s spawned a rather large and extremely vocal group of critics such as Goodman, Illich, Herndon, and Holt, who have criticized virtually every aspect of the schools, from the training of teachers and the structuring of the curriculum, to challenging the very notion that schools should be the place where education takes place.

Irrespective of these social forces, the economy will certainly influence the extent and type of education children will receive in the future. This factor can override every other force for social change. People can all agree that a given educational system is good, but unless the funds are available to support it, a less expensive system is certain to be adopted.

There are many evidences that the inflation of the past few years has greatly influenced educational practice. For example, people in many cities have indicated by their votes their unwillingness to pay the price asked by their school districts. As a result, many schools have curtailed their services. They have increased class sizes, disengaged many ancillary services, shortened the school day, and eliminated many special programs. These events, many of which are in opposition to those promoted by special interest groups, have greatly affected the education of our children.

Another indication of the continuing effect of the economy is the manner in which the state and federal governments have dispensed funds for educational purposes. No longer is every special or exemplary program supported simply because it is special or exemplary. Obtaining dollars for these programs has become an extremely political and highly competitive undertaking.

It is anyone's guess which educational practices will ultimately be actualized, for the groups that are attempting to influence education are many and the aspects of education they wish to change are highly diverse. As a matter of fact, some groups are advocating procedures that are in direct opposition to those of another group. For example, the accountability people and the unions are in great disagreement over the matter of hiring and promoting teachers on the basis of data. Furthermore, the priorities of the special interest groups that have obtained legal assistance are not always in accord with the views of the unions *or* the accountability people.

Either because of these forces for educational change or in spite of them, there are a few aspects of educational practice I would like to consider here. As to some, I am recommending a total change. In respect to others, I am suggesting only a shift of emphasis—that is, certain of the procedures I advocate are currently in operation, and I would simply recommend that they be given higher priority.

My first recommendation is that more teachers should measure more behaviors of more children more often. In recent years many teachers in various parts of the country have used direct and daily measurement procedures to monitor several behaviors of children. Certainly the precision teaching system of Ogden Lindsley and the responsive teaching system of Vance Hall should be given great credit for this recent increase in the number of teachers who measure. But the proportion of teachers in the country who gather data in regard to the daily performances of their children is extremely small.

The advantages to teachers who measure behaviors on a daily basis are many. First of all, they can be apprised of the current strength of the behavior. Furthermore, they can ascertain the effects of teaching procedures, they can communicate exact accomplishments to parents, they know when performance goals have been reached. It is even more imperative in the case of exceptional children that direct and daily measurement be obtained in reference to their important behaviors. Since by definition their performances are excessive—too high or too low—their behaviors should be monitored with the greater precision. In fact, as is the case with individuals who are critically ill, the more serious the problem, the more intensive the measurement system should be. The rationale for such a strategy is, of course, that when the behaviors are continuously and accurately monitored, instructional treatments can be involved until the individual begins to recover. Then the treatments can either be stabilized or withdrawn.

A second recommendation, and this one also applies to regular as well as exceptional children, is that more one-on-one teaching should take place. Special education has often based its case on smaller class sizes. The implication sometimes follows that children in special classes will receive more individual attention than they would in regular classes. This, however, is often not true. Many special education teachers use a group instructional approach, whether they are assigned ten, five, or even two youngsters.

Many teachers and well-intentioned citizens clamor for smaller class sizes. They believe the quality of education will improve because of this reduction. What they should be demanding is more one-on-one teaching, irrespective of class size. Accordingly, we should direct some of our research toward efforts to discover ways to increase the one-on-one time of the teachers.

In regard to this point, I realize that I am speaking well beyond my data, for I certainly have no hard evidence to support the idea that tutorial experiences are better than those derived from groups. To make such a statement I have again drawn upon my trumpet teaching days when I, generally, worked with one pupil for thirty uninterrupted minutes. I learned that the problems and capabilities of the trumpet students were very different. Their tolerances for feedback and their desires to improve were unique. Although I was not always sensitive to these differences, at least I had the opportunity to be so. A sensitivity for these individual differences would have been less possible in a group setting.

I believe that other learning situations are similar to this one back in my studio. Children are extremely individualized in their abilities and motivations to learn to read, spell, play the guitar, or write stories. Therefore, I strongly recommend, especially for exceptional children, that we search for more approaches that will enable teachers to spend more time with individual children. Along with this recommendation goes, of course, the hope that the teachers who serve our children are genuinely capable of teaching; allowing inept teachers to interact at a personal level with children would simply be counterproductive.

In recent years there has been some research on the ability of people other than professional teachers to teach. The work of Fred Keller (1968) has, for example, stimulated a fair number of programs and research projects wherein college students have taught other college students. There have been other investigations attempting to assess the abilities of paraprofessionals and children to teach children. Research of this type should be encouraged. When the data are all in regarding one-on-one teaching, I would hypothesize that in many instances, and of course varying with the teacher, one minute of tutorial help is worth twenty minutes of group "teaching."

A third recommendation is that self-education should be taught. Our current educational system teaches individuals that the circumstances associated with learning—books, tests, schedules, grades—must be arranged by someone else and must take place in schools.

Pupils should be taught to manage their own lives so that they will become more productive and independent, so that they will not always be dependent on other agencies to change their behaviors. Pupils should be taught to identify their own needs and arrange instructional situations which are in response to those needs, which include much more than desires to stop smoking or lose weight, or even to learn a foreign language or to type. They encompass the necessities for maintaining sound mental and physical health as well. Although there are a few self-made persons who have arranged their own environments and developed some skills on their own, most people, in order to acquire new behaviors, rely entirely on formal teaching agencies.

Recently there have been several studies directed toward various aspects of pupil management. At the fifth annual Conference on Behavior Analysis in Education, for example, one of the priority topics was research on this subject. This subject has from time to time been a research interest of mine, one that I would like to give more attention to in the future.

My next recommendation is that more research concerned with children with "learning disabilities"—in fact, research concerned with all children—should be conducted in schools, homes, or other places where children naturally reside. There is still a need for educational research in university settings, to be sure, but the emphasis upon more investigations conducted in the schools themselves should, I believe, be strongly encouraged.

I make this recommendation primarily because of the age-old absence of a rapproachement between schools and other applied settings and research situations. Researchers have bemoaned the fact that schools have not implemented their findings, while teachers have accused researchers of being impractical. And although this controversy has raged for many years, the gap between the two contenders has not been significantly decreased; teachers have not been greatly influenced by research, and researchers have not been overly sensitive to the needs of the schools.

It appears to me that if research situations were to be established in schools, the problems that are particularly indigenous to those specific situations could be investigated. Further, I believe that if the total school had some voice as to just what procedures or practices were researched, the dissemination of subsequent findings to the teachers in that school would be greatly facilitated. Teachers would, I believe, be motivated to put into practice some new procedure they had initially suggested should be evaluated. It is even more imperative that research situations be established in schools where exceptional children are housed. Since traditional techniques have not always been effective with these youngsters, more innovative techniques must be arranged and evaluated.

By suggesting that research should take place in schools, I mean that long-term research programs should be sponsored in schools. In the past there has been a great deal of research in the schools, but invariably this research has been fragmentary—one investigation is conducted and then the researchers pack up and leave. I am suggesting that research should be conducted in schools the year round, and this research should be directed toward the problems of the schools. Further, this research should be systematic in that the results of one investigation should lead to another study.

My last recommended change in educational practice pertains to labeling. Earlier on in this chapter, I confessed that during the whole of my involvement with the learning disabilities program I was much opposed to labels. I could see absolutely no useful end that was served by the terms "mental retardation," "emotionally disturbed," or "learning disabilities." I still do not. However, I am now inclined to believe that the labeling *process* should not be abandoned, but instead we should develop a classification system that is functional.

Categorizing schemes have greatly assisted other sciences. The system used by biologists to classify plants and animals, for example, has enabled them to study those organisms with far greater effectiveness. The development of other sciences has been furthered because of their organizational systems.

In contrast, the system of classification we have used in special education has not served us well and might be likened to a grocer who chose to classify his stock according to color. In the white section he placed together the eggs, milk, flour, salt, bread, onions, paper towels, oysters, toothpaste, white wine, and vanilla ice cream. In the yellow, red, and blue sections the items were equally divergent. The purchaser could not shop for items according to any useful dimension. Furthermore, the grocer would have to design unusual shelves and storage spaces for each section —he would, for example, have to provide refrigeration units for all of the sections. There are other even more obvious drawbacks to such a system of classification.

But even though this system would undoubtedly prove to be nonfunctional, the grocer would be ill-advised to abandon classification systems entirely and simply stock his groceries on the shelves at random, for even greater shopping and display problems would then arise. Our grocer, we would all agree, would be better advised to reclassify his stock along other dimensions until both he and, more importantly, the purchasers, were served.

I listened one afternoon to Israel Goldiamond (1974) as he talked about the labeling and classification system used in the mental health field (their system for classification has proved to be as nonfunctional as ours). He suggested that people should be classified on the basis of what they were trying to learn, rather than on the basis of what they had trouble learning or on the basis of some physical or mental abnormality such as manic depression that might or might not be related to learning.

I first thought about this notion when I was taking a Spanish class at the university in preparation for my sabbatical year in Mexico. The instructors and students treated me like a student of Spanish. I was not labeled a "language deprived student" simply because I had not studied Spanish in Burrton, Kansas. I was not labeled as "learning disabled" because I occasionally reversed some sounds or letters. I was neither labeled "gifted" nor "emotionally disturbed" because I was a university professor. I was simply a student of Spanish.

I later thought about this notion in the context of special education and concluded that if this labeling concept were practiced, particularly in schools where instruction is individualized and where direct and daily measurement is used, teachers could then label each student not only by the behaviors he is acquiring, but by his current levels of acquisition in each of those behaviors. If, for example, a pupil was learning to read in the Lippincott C text and his correct and error rates for a given day were 76 and 2, and he was also learning add facts and his corresponding rates on one day were 33 and 4, he could be referred to as a "Lippincott C (76/2) and an Add Facts (33/4) Child." Using such a labeling system, one that reflects what is being learned and the extent to which it is learned, the pupil's labels could change each day.

Whether or not this system of classification would assist in the education of children certainly remains to be demonstrated. But most assuredly, two positive changes would result from its use. The first would be that since all the behaviors a person is trying to develop would be included in the label, labelers would readily see the many facets of the subject's development, and would be reminded that most people (children at least) are trying to learn several different things at the same time. The second would be that since a performance score would be supplied along with every identified behavior, the labelers would be dramatically apprised of the cardinal fact that people learn certain things more quickly than they do others. They would be aware of the tremendous range of individual human differences.

By using such a labeling system, based on development rather than on despair, teachers could take advantage of the self-fulfilling prophecies that teachers of special education are so concerned about. If pupils do behave according to their labels, for whatever reason, then those labeled as readers would read, those labeled as painters would paint, and those labeled as trumpet players would learn to play the trumpet.

REFERENCES

Ferster, C. B. Arbitrary and natural reinforcement. *Psychological Record,* 1967, **17**, 341–47.

Goldiamond, I. Lecture presented at the University of Washington School of Medicine, Seattle, Washington, March, 1974.

Hansen, C. L., & Lovitt, T. C. Reading round one: Matching the child to the book. Paper presented at the Fifth Annual Conference on Behavior Analysis in Education, University of Kansas, October, 1974.

Haring, N. G., & Phillips, E. L. *Educating emotionally disturbed children.* New York: McGraw-Hill, 1962.

Homme, L. E., deBaca, P. C., Devine, J. V., Steinhhorst, R., & Rickert, E. J. Use of the Premack principle in controlling the behavior of nursery school children. *Journal of the Experimental Analysis of Behavior,* 1963, **6,** 544.

Keller, F. S. "Good-bye teacher ..." *Journal of Applied Behavior Analysis,* 1968, **1,** 79–89.

Lindsley, O. R. Direct measurement and prothesis of retarded behavior. *Journal of Education,* 1964, **147,** 62–81.

Lovitt, T. C. Assessment of children with learning disabilities. *Exceptional Children,* 1967, **34,** 233–39.

Lovitt, T. C. Operant preference of retarded and normal males for rate of narration. *Psychological Record,* 1968, **18,** 205–14.

Lovitt, T. C. *Exceptional Children,* Guest Editor, Behavior Modification, 1970, **37.**

Lovitt, T. C., & Curtiss, K. A. Effects of manipulating an antecedent event on mathematics response rate. *Journal of Applied Behavior Analysis,* 1968, **1,** 329–33.

Lovitt, T. C., & Curtiss, K. A. Academic response rate as a function of teacher and self-imposed contingencies. *Journal of Applied Behavior Analysis,* 1969, **2,** 49–53.

Lovitt, T. C. & Eaton, M. Oh! that this too solid flesh would melt: Direct and daily measurement hath cometh (The erosion of achievement tests). In N. Bartel & S. Axelrod (Eds.), *The handbook for special education research.* Washington, D. C.: Council for Exceptional Children, 1974.

Lovitt, T. C., Guppy, T. C., & Blattner, J. E. The use of a free-time contingency with fourth graders to increase spelling accuracy. *Behavior Research and Therapy,* 1969, **7,** 151–56.

Lovitt, T. C., & Smith, J. O. Effects of instructions on an individual's verbal behavior. *Exceptional Children,* 1972, **38,** 685–93.

Morgan, B. J., & Lindsley, O. R. Operant preference for stereophonic over monophonic music. *Journal of Music Therapy,* 1966, **3,** 135–43.

Premack, D. Toward empirical behavior laws. 1. Positive reinforcement. *Psychological Review,* 1959, **66,** 219–33.

Smith, D. D., & Lovitt, T. C. The use of modeling techniques to influence the acquisition of computational arithmetic skills in learning disabled children. Paper presented at Fourth Annual Conference on Behavior Analysis in Education, University of Kansas, 1973.

Smith, D. D., & Lovitt, T. C. The influence of instructions and reinforcement contingencies on children's abilities to compute arithmetic problems. Paper presented at the Fifth Annual Conference on Behavior Analysis in Education. University of Kansas, 1974.

A SELECTED BIBLIOGRAPHY OF WORKS BY THOMAS C. LOVITT

Eaton, M., & Lovitt, T. C. Achievement tests versus direct and daily measurement. In G. Semb (Ed.), *Behavior analysis and education—1972*. Lawrence: University of Kansas Press, 1972. Pp. 78–87.

Haring, N. G., & Lovitt, T. C. Operant methodology and educational technology in special education. In N. G. Haring & R. L. Schiefelbusch (Eds.), *Methods in special education*. New York: McGraw-Hill, 1967. Pp. 12–48.

Haring, N. G., & Lovitt, T. C. Experimental education: Basis for strategies of service, research and training. In M. B. Rosenberg (Ed.), *Educational therapy*. Vol. III. *Educational programs*. Seattle: Bernie Straub Publishing and Special Child Publications, 1973. Pp. 121–43.

Lovitt, T. C. Assessment of children with learning disabilities. *Exceptional Children*, 1967, **34**, 233–39.

Lovitt, T. C. Free-operant preferences for one of two stories: A methodological note. *Journal of Educational Psychology*, 1967, **58**, 84–87.

Lovitt, T. C. The use of conjugate reinforcement to evaluate the relative reinforcing effects of various narrative forms. *Journal of Experimental Child Psychology*, 1967, **5**, 164–71.

Lovitt, T. C. Free-operant assessment of musical preference. *Journal of Experimental Child Psychology*, 1968, **6**, 361–67.

Lovitt, T. C. Operant conditioning techniques for children with learning disabilities. *Journal of Special Education*, 1968, **2**, 283–89.

Lovitt, T. C. Operant preference of retarded and normal males for rate of narration. *Psychological Record*, 1968, **18**, 205–14.

Lovitt, T. C. Relationship of sequential and simultaneous preference as assessed by conjugate reinforcement. *Behavior Research and Therapy*, 1968, **6**, 23–30.

Lovitt, T. C. Behavior modification: Where do we go from here? *Exceptional Children*, 1970, **37**, 157–67.

Lovitt, T. C. *Exceptional Children*, Guest Editor, Behavior Modification, 1970, **37**.

Lovitt, T. C. Self-management projects with children with behavioral disabilities. *Journal of Learning Disabilities*, 1973, **6**, 138–50.

Lovitt, T. C., & Curtiss, K. A. Effects of manipulating an antecedent event on mathematics response rate. *Journal of Applied Behavior Analysis*, 1968, **1**, 329–33.

Lovitt, T. C., & Curtiss, K. A. Academic response rate as a function of teacher- and self-imposed contingencies. *Journal of Applied Behavior Analysis*, 1969, **2**, 49–53.

Lovitt, T. C., Guppy, T. C., & Blattner, J. E. The use of a free-time contingency with fourth graders to increase spelling accuracy. *Behavior Research and Therapy*, 1969, **7**, 151–56.

Lovitt, T. C., Eaton, M., Kirkwood, M. E., & Pelander, J. Effects of various reinforcement contingencies on oral reading rate. In E. A. Ramp and B. L. Hopkins (Eds.), *A new direction for education: Behavior analysis.* Lawrence, Kansas: Department of Human Development, 1971. Pp. 54–71.

Lovitt, T. C., & Esveldt, K. A. The relative effects of math performance of single versus multiple-ration schedules: A case study. *Journal of Applied Behavior Analysis,* 1970, **3**, 261–70.

Lovitt, T. C., & Esveldt, K. A. A contingency management classroom: Basis for systematic replication (four studies). In N. G. Haring & A. H. Hayden (Eds.), *The improvement of instruction.* Seattle: Special Child Publications, 1972. Pp. 311–68.

Lovitt, T. C., & Hurlbut, M. Using behavioral analysis techniques to assess the relationship between phonics instruction and oral reading. *Journal of Special Education,* 1974, **8**, 57–72.

Lovitt, T. C., & Kidder, J. D. Experimental analysis of children with learning disabilities. In R. Jones (Ed.), *Perspectives in contemporary education.* Boston: Allyn & Bacon, 1971. Pp. 234–42.

Lovitt, T. C., Kunzelmann, H. P., Nolen, P. A., & Hulten, W. J. Dimensions of classroom data. *Journal of Learning Disabilities,* 1968, **1**, 710–21.

Lovitt, T. C., Lovitt, A. O., Eaton, M., & Kirkwood, M. The deceleration of inappropriate comments by a natural consequence. *Journal of School Psychology,* 1973, **11**, 149–54.

Lovitt, T. C., Schaaf, M. E., & Sayre, E. The use of direct and continuous measurement to evaluate reading materials and procedures. *Focus on Exceptional Children,* 1970, **2**, 1–11.

Lovitt, T. C., & Smith, D. D. Using withdrawal of positive reinforcement to alter subtraction performance. *Exceptional Children,* in press.

Lovitt, T. C., & Smith, J. O. Effects of instructions on an individual's verbal behavior. *Exceptional Children,* 1972, **38**, 685–93.

Smith, D. D., & Lovitt, T. C. The educational diagnosis and remediation of *b* and *d* written reversal problems: A case study. *Journal of Learning Disabilities,* 1973, **6**, 356–63.

Smith, D. D., & Lovitt, T. C. The use of modeling techniques to influence the acquisition of computational arithmetic skills in learning disabled children. In G. Semb (Ed.), *Behavior analysis in education—1973.* Lawrence: University of Kansas Press, in press.

Smith, D. D., Lovitt, T. C., & Kidder, J. D. Using reinforcement contingencies and teaching aids to alter subtraction performance of children with learning disabilities. In G. Semb (Ed.), *Behavior analysis and education—1972.* Lawrence: University of Kansas Press, 1972. Pp. 342–60.

Smith, J. O., & Lovitt, T. C. Speech, language and communication disorders. In G. O. Johnson (Ed.), *Behavioral research on exceptional children.* Washington, D. C.: Council for Exceptional Children, 1968. Pp. 226–61.

Smith, J. O., & Lovitt, T. C. Pinpointing a learning problem leads to remediation. *Teaching Exceptional Children,* 1973, **5**, 181–82.

10
Jeanne McRae McCarthy

Jeanne McRae McCarthy was born in Lakewood, Ohio, in 1923. She received her B.A. degree in psychology from Barat College, her M.A. in clinical psychology from Loyola University, and her Ph.D. in special education from the University of Illinois. She is presently professor of special education at the University of Arizona.

Dr. McCarthy has held a number of positions of leadership in special education. She was director of the Leadership Training Institute in Learning Disabilities at the University of Arizona from 1972 to 1975. From 1968 through 1969 she was professor of education at the University of Illinois at Chicago Circle. She served as adjunct professor of education at Barat College, Lake Forest, Illinois, from 1970 to 1972. From 1963 to 1972 she was director of special services for Shaumburg School District 54, Shaumburg Township, Illinois. During the years 1957 to 1960, she was director of special education and school psychologist, Niles Township Department of Special Education, Lincolnwood, Illinois. She began her work with learning disabled children as a clinical psychologist at the Loyola Center for Guidance and Psychological Service in 1944.

Dr. McCarthy has served in a variety of capacities within professional organizations. She was a member of the Board of Governors of the Council for Exceptional Children and president of the Division for Children with Learning Disabilities of the Council for Exceptional Children. She is a fellow of the American Psychological Association, a charter member of the School Psychology Division of the American Psychological Association, and chairman of the Professional Advisory Board of the Association for Children with Learning Disabilities. She also received the ACLD Award for Professional Contributions in 1970.

Since 1965, Dr. McCarthy has been a consultant for the United States Office of Education. She has been a visiting lecturer at many colleges and universities.

Dr. McCarthy is a frequent contributor to professional journals and is an associate editor of Exceptional Children. *A selected bibliography of her works is included on page 342.*

EVOLUTION OF MY INVOLVEMENT WITH LEARNING DISABLED CHILDREN

An enduring problem in psychology has been defined by Paul Bakan as "one that demands to be considered despite the best efforts of theorists to ignore it" (1966). Learning disabilities appears to meet this definition quite well. Because of the urgency of the demand to do something, with pressures from parents, administrators, physicians, and legislators, practitioners in the field began in the early years to function with the limited theoretical and research base available to them. Educational practices have multiplied as programs have proliferated in all fifty states, without a strong theoretical base to undergird many of them. And despite the best efforts of theorists to ignore it, the field of Learning Disabilities continues to flourish.

Perhaps it was this vitality and vigor that attracted me in the early years. Perhaps it was the relief we all felt with the advent of the work of Strauss and Lehtinen which seemed to offer more substance than the era we had lived through in the 1940s and early '50s when "tender, loving care" constituted the bulk of our recommendations to parents. As a young clinical psychologist, I was convinced that there had to be better ways of helping children than those culled so carefully but so naively from their Rorschachs, their T.A.T.s, and their Blacky Picture interpretations. In my daily contacts with children referred because of learning problems, and especially with those I was seeing for intensive individual tutoring, I knew that something was wrong that had little to do with the affective domain. I knew intuitively that poor motivation, an inadequate sense of self-worth, feelings of inadequacy, and so on could affect learning; but I also knew there had to be something more.

Recently the Professional Advisory Board of ACLD engaged in a learned discussion of a definition for the field. The old feelings of frustration which I felt so many days and for so many years began to engulf me. All of the Learning Disabilities children seen in the '40s and '50s in Child Guidance Centers and by well-meaning school psychologists seemed to rise up and mock us. For me the definition has always been crystal clear:

the learning disabled child is the child who seems so normal in so many ways, who is *obviously* not learning like his peers, and who is not eligible for services under any other category of the handicapped. It was this same frustration that led many of us, in the mid 1950s, to determine that such a child was educationally handicapped, emotionally disturbed, and, with the help of a selected pediatrician, "possibly brain damaged"—or in special educators' jargon, multiply handicapped. *Then* we could serve him in the public schools.

The Formative Years

My interest in children who could not learn was an offshoot of an early interest in and concern for people—all kinds of people. When I was 16, my maiden aunt, of which everyone had one in those days, took me to Winnepeg on the Minneapolis *Zephyr*. Her most significant report back to my parents suggested ominously that they "would have to watch Jeanne . . . *she talks to strangers!*" In this case it was the chair-car porter who pointed out in fascinating detail the head of the Mississippi River.

At about the same time, as a senior in high school, a psychiatric social worker visited Mercy High School and talked to us about careers in social work. Apparently my natural interest in people and my desire to have a dramatic response to the age-old question "what are you going to be when you grow up" found a match in my new awareness of social work as a way of responding to the unique needs of people. I am certain that I was unaware of the differences between a psychologist and a social worker and totally unaware of medical school as another avenue of helping people.

These embryonic ambitions were fostered and guided by some extremely perceptive teachers in elementary and high school: Sister Paula and Sister Evelyn, R.S.M., who demanded more of me than my other teachers, and who refused to let me slide by with less than my best work. Mother Margaret Reilly R.S.C.J. at Barat College joined in an unholy trinity with Mother Fox and Mother Burke to defeat my best efforts to slide by without putting out much energy. They provided my first introduction to psychology as a field of professional endeavor and guided me into an interdepartmental major in psychology and sociology with a minor in education. With a senior class of twenty-four, and a total enrollment in the college of 125, personal involvement by the faculty in shaping the character and lives of the students was as important an ingredient as the liberal arts program itself. Thus, I was not surprised when Mother Reilly, then president of Barat College, called shortly after graduation to ask if I would like a job as a psychologist at Loyola University in Chicago. Although I thought I was applying for a job, I found myself enrolled in the master's program in clinical psychology, with an internship of forty hours a week at the Loyola Center for Psychological Service under the direction of Charles I. Doyle, S.J. At that time, 1944, the answer to any child's problem in the parochial school system of Chicago was to "send them down to Father Doyle." It was in this program that I became formally involved in the problems of children with learning disabilities, although we didn't call them that. At that time, teachers described these children as "perfectly normal, but he has a mental block." The fields of psychology and education were still under the influence of Freudian concepts and viewed nonlearning in children as psychogenic manifestations of inner conflict or as the result of poor motivation. The child who *could not* learn was seen as the child who *would not* learn, because nonlearning served a conscious or unconscious role in his struggle with forces impeding the development of his ego. During this era of an essentially psychodynamic conception of learning problems, psychologists and educators encouraged parents to involve their child in extensive periods of psychotherapy in an effort to resolve the inner conflicts which were causing or contributing to the inability to learn. Most of the early psychological reports that I wrote emphasized the need of the child for success experiences, praise, and a relaxed, pleasant approach to school learning tasks.

In this early phase of my professional development several seeds were planted that were unusual in that era—one was a strong emphasis on parental involvement and on the parents' right-to-know. This emphasis resulted in a written report to parents containing complete diagnostic data translated from test scores to interpretations understandable by the parent unfamiliar with psychometric jargon. The second unusual part of my training as a clinical psychologist in the early 1940s was a strong educational emphasis, particularly on reading, with little but lip service paid to more traditional psychoanalytic concepts. Several years later I was mortified to have to admit to a group of my fellow psychologists at the Wichita Guidance Center that on my transcript was a course called "Psychology of the Reading Skills." The research of Marion Monroe (1932), Helen Robinson (1946), Samuel Orton (1928), and others active in the fields of reading and perception were considered a necessary part of a psychologist's training. Our daily tutoring cases provided the questions which we sought to answer.

The years that I spent at the Loyola Center for Guidance and Psychological Service formed an interesting contrast to my experience at the Wichita Guidance Center as a clinical psychologist. The center was one of the first intern training centers approved by the American Psychological Association for clinical psychology internships. Each year brought a new crop of bright young Ph.D. candidates from City College of New York, Brooklyn College, Indiana University, State University of Iowa, and other colleges and universities. Each of these schools had its own unique philosophy which had been ingrained into its students. It was fascinating to listen to a dyed-in-the-wool psychoanalytically trained psychologist trying to explain his rationale to a tried-and-true interbehaviorist from Indiana University. The result was a fascinating blend of eclecticism, with much emphasis on psychotherapy, play therapy (à la Virginia Axline), infant testing (à la Sybille Escalona, Raymond Cattell and Arnold Gesell), much Rorschach testing, scoring, and debating over interpretations.

In the midst of all of this psychiatric approach to children, minimal emphasis was placed on the work of two remedial reading specialists on the staff. It was fascinating to realize that the psychiatrically oriented staff apparently thought that reading would descend on these children like manna from heaven if, through psychotherapy, they could come to grips with their tensions and anxieties. The fact that someone would have to *teach* them to read was not a popular idea in those days. The daily experience of testing infants who were to be placed in adoptive homes in Sedgwick County, Kansas, helped to put standardized testing into proper perspective and to impress on me the importance of clinical intuition and careful observation. It was an experience I would not trade, as I work now with infant stimulation programs and preschool programs in my work with TADS, the Technical Assistance Delivery System of the Handicapped Children's Early Education Program.

This experience also provided me with a background for the next stage of my professional development: motherhood. With the impending arrival of my first daughter, Candy, I took a sabbatical leave from my profession. I learned possibly the most important lesson of all—how to combine professionalism with feminism, with being a wife and mother. It was not until after my second daughter, Sean, had been successfully launched into childhood that I felt I could return to fulltime professional work.

The position of school psychologist in Niles Township, Illinois, had just been created when I received a call asking if I was a "Q.P.E." I had never heard of it. The question was changed to "Are you a Qualified Psychological Examiner?" Although I was not, I soon became one, and so started my love affair with the public schools. I would probably still be a school psychologist if our director of special education had not suddenly become ill, creating a vacancy into which I was catapulted. I did such a fine job as the second director of special education in Niles Township that the state director of special education, Ray Graham, offered me the first fellowship funded under Public Law 85-926 to enter the doctoral program in special education at the University of Illinois. Or perhaps he just wanted to create a vacancy into which someone more competent could be catapulted.

It was at the University of Illinois, as a student of Samuel A. Kirk, that I began to formulate a sense of direction and a personal philosophy of special education. With a major in special education and a very heavy minor in psychology, I began to learn the reasons behind many of the decisions I had been making intuitively about children. My exposure to such giants as J. McV. Hunt, O. Hobart Mowrer, James J. Gallagher, and Samuel A. Kirk, both in class, on my doctoral committee, and in countless personal contacts, helped to shape my personal formulation and thinking. The other students who were involved in the struggle to integrate this new knowledge into their existing knowledge base included James Chalfant, Douglas Wiseman, Barbara Bateman, and Corrine Kass. From these and others with whom I came into contact—Bernard Farber (see Farber, 1968) and Herbert Goldstein (see Goldstein, Moss, & Jordan, 1965), who taught me much about the retarded; Celia Stendler Lavatelli (see Lavatelli, 1965), who taught me elementary classroom methods—I was able to fit much into my personal mosaic that was to form the theoretical structure from which I now operate. The structure is made up of concepts borrowed from Hebb (1949), Piaget (1966), Osgood (1965), Skinner (1938), Mowrer (1951), Gallagher (1964), Hunt (1961), Kirk (1972), Guilford (1957), Bruner (1966), and untold others. I would characterize my philosophy as developmental, epigenetic, cognitive, dynamic, and always optimistic and pragmatic. More recently the work of such neuropsychologists as Norman and Lindsay (1972), Broadbent (1958), and Miller, Galanter, and Pribram (1960) has added new dimensions to my thinking.

After receiving such massive amounts of new input in my doctoral program, it was a new challenge to go back to the public schools and see if it would work in the real world. I really felt that everything that happened so far had been preliminary to the main event. Could a program incorporating all of these exciting ideas be launched in the public schools?

Schaumburg (Illinois) Community Consolidated School District Number 54 may seem like an unlikely place for such a program to begin. But that would not take into account the drive of the superintendent, Kenneth Underwood, and the dedication of the Board of Education to provide the best possible program of special services and special classes for every handicapped child.

Our first major thrust, in 1964, was to develop a comprehensive program for children with learning disabilities. The proposal describing the program was submitted to the Bureau of Education for the Handicapped and was funded as a Research and Demonstration project. In the absence of trained learning disability teachers, it was necessary to expand the skills of remedial reading teachers to cover the broad spectrum of psychological processes involved in learning disabilities. Each member of the staff learned from and gave to each other member. Those in learning disabilities learned from those in mental retardation, speech and language, and from the school psychologists. Together we learned to maximize all of our skills into a smooth working team. Much of this inservice training took place during the child study team meeting in each building, attended by all special service personnel servicing the building plus the teacher, the principal, and the director of special services.

The developmental first grade emerged as an obvious effort to reduce the numbers of learning disabled children in the schools. The diagnostic class emerged as our final protest against categorical labels on classes for young children.

My final effort at innovative programming in Schaumburg involved a year of intensive planning for the program for three- and four-year-old handicapped children. This program now has over 250 children receiving direct service and is known as the Schaumburg Early Education Center program. Based on Piaget's developmental concepts, handicapped children and their parents are being served irrespective of handicapping conditions. The support that has been continuing since Wayne Schaible became superintendent in 1967 has resulted in the development of a sound program to meet the needs and respect the rights of all handicapped children in the district.

As more and more school districts became interested in initiating services for learning disabilities children, more visitors asked to come to visit our classrooms. I was being asked to share our experiences with groups at conferences or in other districts. Finally, I was asked by B.E.H. to become the director of the Leadership Training Institute in Learning Disabilities. The position seemed ideal, since my primary responsibility would be to help other districts develop programs for children in their own states. For the past few years I have been working with Children's Service Demonstration Centers funded under the Learning Disabilities Act in forty-three states in the development of their ideas for a model center for learning disabled children in their states.

The next transition will be from doing it directly to sharing my experiences with others in the classroom. My pleasures may be less direct and more vicarious, but will widen the impact I can have in improving programs and services for learning disabled children—which, by the way, is what it is all about.

PRESENT ASSESSMENT OF AND APPROACH TO THE FIELD

Issues and Problems

My present assessment of the field includes an almost naive amazement at the rapid growth we have all witnessed in the past fifteen years, as well as serious concerns over four issues:

1. Definition, characteristics, and prevalence;
2. Delivery of services at all levels, including legislation and funding;
3. Research methodology;
4. Apparently nonconstructive efforts to divide the field rather than to develop a sound base for progress.

Definition, characteristics, prevalence: The field of learning disabilities is at a crucial point at the present moment—probably more crucial even than the precarious moments in the late 1950s and early 1960s when the field was aborning. The most critical issue continues to be one of definition of the population. Because of the problems involved in defining a clear-cut set of characteristics unique to this group of handicapped children, prevalence figures continue to be elusive, eligibility criteria difficult to operationalize, and research findings contradictory and inconclusive.

Learning disabilities appears at this time to be a catch-all category with diagnosis largely by a process of elimination. As some professionals view the field, a child who is not mentally retarded, emotionally disturbed, blind, deaf, etc., but still is not learning *must* be learning disabled. The result appears to be a large group of slow learners, disabled readers, poorly taught, or behavior disordered children, with only a small percentage of learning disabled children in the group. In the Title VI-G Child Service Demonstration programs the percentage of the total population served ranged from 1 percent to 28 percent. The major area of remedial emphasis was in reading and spelling, followed by language and mathematics. In spite of a general acceptance of the National Advisory Committee on the Handicapped (1968) definition, there appeared to be little emphasis on deficits in "the psychological processes which underlie spoken or written language."

The problems in definition are not new. In 1972, after an intensive review of the field as a part of the work of the Leadership Training Institute in Learning Disabilities, Bryant (1972) concluded that "the most critical and primary need is to overcome the obstacles encountered in operationally defining the population to be served."

Dr. Bryant proposed three research steps which need to be reviewed and implemented:

(1) A series of criterion measures of learning ability needs to be developed,
(2) an encompassing model of learning disabilities needs to be generated with measures developed to validly reflect the model, and
(3) there need to be research studies on specific disability–treatment interaction.

The first recommendation is being met in part by those efforts of curriculum specialists and teachers to delineate skills in reading, language, mathematics, and other fields and to set up the scope and sequence of instruction. Many publishers are providing the sequence of crucial skill elements as a part of their basal reading or mathematics programs.

Such programs as the Systematic Approach to Reading Improvement, or Project SARI, from the Durham Unified School District in Durham, California, Fountain Valley, or Systems Fore from the Los Angeles City Schools are examples of such criterion measures currently available. Systems Fore includes the scope and sequence of skills, informal assessment tasks, and directories of instructional materials keyed to the strand, the level, and the task in reading, language, and mathematics from preschool to grade twelve.

The second recommendation involves "developing a model of disabilities in terms of the underlying processes involved in learning. Alternative models should be considered and tested against hard data" (Bryant, 1972).

I would concur with this thinking. It appears to me that the National Advisory Committee definition and the many state definitions which derive from it would be adequate, if more specificity could be given to the term "psychological processes." The lack of specificity in the definition is, however, a direct reflection of the state of knowledge of how human beings learn. Although progress is being made along many dimensions, no one yet knows precisely how human beings acquire information, how they process it, how or where they store it—in other words how they learn. There are wide gaps in knowledge in the basic fields of biochemistry, neuropsychology, neurology, endocrinology, neurophysiology, and others, gaps which continue to create problems for practitioners in the fields of pediatrics, ophthalmology, otology, psychology, neurology, speech, education, and psychiatry.

The efforts of cognitive and linguistic theorists to develop a model of human learning or of the communication process have resulted in such hypothetical constructs as Guilford's structure of intellect model, Hebb's cell assemblies and phase sequences, Piaget's sequential stages of the development of intelligence, and Osgood's model of the communication process. It appears to me that these, and most of the more than seventy-five other models of human information processing, have resulted in paradigms which exist largely in the heads of their authors, but which relate only tangentially to what is going on in a child's head as he is actively involved in the learning process.

If we are to move forward in our efforts to define the population to be identified as learning disabled, it appears to me that we need to sharpen our concepts of the processes involved in learning. Some of the neurophysiological models of human information processing which are based on experimental data on human subjects and which relate specifically to the function of the central nervous system appear to offer a different emphasis than is presently found in our field. Such models as those of Pribram (1969), Norman and Lindsay (1972), Mackworth (1972), Broadbent (1958, 1965), and Senf (1972) suggest a need to reemphasize the processes long considered the backbone of experimental psychologists, i.e., discrimination, attention, memory, inhibition, facilitation, mentation, motivation, filtering, habituation, arousal, etc.

The massive amounts of experimental data collected in each of these areas since the early days of Wundt and Titchener has been woven into a theory of human learning and presented in many of these recent models. The current need to sharpen and operationalize the term "psychological processes which underlie spoken or written language" is reminiscent of a statement made by William James (1890):

The immediate effects of attention are to make us:
(a) perceive—
(b) conceive—
(c) distinguish—
(d) remember—

better than otherwise we could—both more successive things and each thing more clearly. It also shortens 'reaction-time'!

From this extensive body of research and the research currently being generated by neuropsychologists and others interested in the neural substrate of attention and learning, we may be able to generate a theory of learning that will enable us to operationalize the definition and to describe and measure learning and nonlearning, and the processes involved with more specificity than we can at the moment. Such a theory would provide a set of check points to be observed in children's learning and would focus on psychological processes in a different way than is now the practice in psychology. Hopefully, we are on the verge of a new approach to psychometry.

Thus rather than denying the importance of psychological processes, I would hope that the field of learning disabilities would go back to our basic experimental psychology textbooks and to the laboratories of those concerned with the neural substrata of learning, and define and refine our concepts of psychological processes.

We need to be very certain of the fact that learning, or nonlearning, is a personal idiosyncratic process which takes place somewhere within the child's central nervous system. We need to be very certain that such constructs as perception, attention, memory, inhibition, scanning, discrimination, and set are the basic functions involved in learning, whether the learning consists of a discrimination task in an experiment or of reading or arithmetic in school. Thus, just as curriculum can be defined as "the content of instruction," these psychological processes are the mechanisms for learning.

Two directions for those seriously involved in the field of learning disabilities seem obvious: human information processing and the acquisition of symbolic language. The more competent those in the field can become in the analysis of the learning process, especially in how human beings acquire symbolic language, the better will we be able to facilitate or compensate for deficits in "the psychological processes which underlie spoken or written language."

In the meanwhile, the definition as we now have it can be operationalized in such a way as to effectively include those children who are learning disabled to the point where they need special educational intervention. The intent is to define a group of handicapped children who are unique from other handicapped children and from nonhandicapped children who may be experiencing some problems in learning extrinsic to themselves.

As I see it, any definition of learning disabilities needs to include three concepts:

1. A concept of *intactness;*
2. A concept of *discrepancy;*
3. A concept of *deviation.*

The learning disabled child is *intact* psychologically, emotionally, socially, and physically to the extent that he is not eligible for services under any other category of the handicapped. He is not blind, deaf, or orthopedically impaired. His learning disability is not caused by emotional disturbance, mental retardation, environmental disadvantage, or poor instruction. His learning disability exists *within* him in spite of adequate intelligence, adequate sensory processes, and adequate emotional stability.

The learning disabled child is characterized by *discrepancies* of two kinds:

1. Intraindividual discrepancies within the psychological processes involved in learning;
2. Discrepancies in academic learning, i.e., between mental-age grade expectancy and academic achievement in the skill subjects of reading, writing, spelling, or the quantitative skills of arithmetic and mathematics. The basic reading discrepancy will of course manifest itself in further problems in the content subjects of science, history, geography, English, shop, etc.

For a discrepancy to be indicative of a learning disability, the child's performance should fall more than two standard deviations below the mean of the normative population on whatever standardized measures are used to quantify the psychological processes or the achievement discrepancies.

The learning disabled child's learning style *deviates* so markedly from the norm of his peers as to require special educational intervention. If a six-year old Papago Indian boy learns like most other little six-year old Papago boys, he is *not* learning disabled, even though his scores may be discrepant from the norms of tests standardized on non-Papago boys.

The deviation concept helps to clarify the relationship between learning disabilities and cultural diversity. It also reflects the philosophy that curriculum and instruction in the regular class need to be responsive to the needs and learning styles of the majority of the children in the community, whether or not the majority is representative of standardization populations. Awareness of the deviation concept will prevent the learning disabilities label from being applied to large percentages of such minority groups as Mexican-American children, Black children, Indian children, Eskimo children, rural or isolated children, or Puerto Rican children on the mainland. This is not to say that a Black child cannot have a learning disability, i.e., be basically intact, have discrepancies in the psychological processes and between capacity and achievement, and have a learning style which deviates so markedly from the norm of his group as to require special education intervention. It *is* to say that not all children who are two years below grade level in reading have a learning disability.

Using such an interpretation of the definition, the prevalence rate would fall at 1 to 3 percent of the normal population who are in need of special educational intervention. A much larger percentage of children (15 to 17 percent) are in need of remedial help in academics or behavior, with most being served by the classroom teacher with or without specialized service to the child.

It would seem obvious that children with other primary handicapping conditions may also have learning disabilities. In order to emphasize this possibility, the professional advisory board of the Association for Children with Learning Disabilities in 1972 voted to add the following statement to the National Advisory Committee definition:

> Children with specific learning disabilities who also have sensory, motor, intellectual, or emotional problems, or are environmentally disadvantaged, should be included in this definition, and may require multiple services.

The major purpose of the National Advisory Committee definition was to differentiate those children with mild to moderate problems in learning who should be the responsibility of the classroom teacher from those children whose learning style deviates so markedly from the norm of their group as to make it impossible for them to learn with ordinary classroom methods, and who should be the responsibility of special education. If we consider all children whose scores fall within one standard deviation of the mean to be the responsibility of the regular program of curriculum and instruction, we are talking about 68 percent of the population. If we then add those children whose scores fall within two standard deviations of the mean as those who need individualized remedial or enrichment programs within the classroom, we are talking about another 27 percent of the population, or 95 percent of all children who should be reached by a teacher who has been trained to respond to a broad range of individual differences in children. It is not until we look at those children whose performance falls more than two standard deviations below the mean that we zero in on the severe learning disabled child who is in need of special educational intervention, the lowest 1 to 3 percent of children on measures other than intelligence. Thus, the learning disabled child falls within one standard deviation of the mean or higher on standardized intelligence tests, but is more than two deviations below the mean in achievement and in one or more of the psychological processes involved in learning.

At the present time it is imperative that special education delimit the learning disabilities population and prevalence rates in order to reduce the confusion and chaos which characterizes our field. If we are not able to clean our own house, legislatures and fiscal realities will clean it for us. The result could easily be a loss of the ability to serve those children who cannot learn by ordinary classroom methods, but who are not eligible for service under any other category of the handicapped—the severe learning disabled children.

Delivery of services, administrative rules and regulations, legislation, and funding: A second area of concern involves the delivery of diagnostic and remedial services to children with learning disabilities, rules and regulations written by state departments of education to implement the legislation for these children, and the present and future funding for service delivery systems.

It is impossible to discuss one of these topics without the other. In some states the rules and regulations state that the delivery system will be limited to resource room programs; in others, the rules and regulations of the state education agency require and reimburse only for self-contained classes. In some states, a school district may be reimbursed for no more than 1 percent of their total average daily attendance. In other states, a district may increase its programs by only 2 percent per year. In at least one state, a bill has been introduced to limit learning disabilities programs to children above the fourth grade. In another state, an effort is being made to reduce costs by eliminating from the learning disabilities population all children who can be mainstreamed. In some states, all self-contained classes have been eliminated, and all learning disabled children are handled in the mainstream. In most states, the learning disabled programs appear to be filled with mildly involved children with reading problems, not with severe learning disabled children. Even those districts serving just 1 percent of their population seem to be having difficulty identifying the most severely involved 1 percent. In other states, the rules and regulations require that the learning disabled specialist have twenty-five children in the class, thus limiting the kinds of service. Another state mandates 200 hours of instruction per week per teacher, which can only be met by serving at least eight children five hours a day for five days.

As I study these varied attempts to clarify the delivery of services, it seems important to say once again that the severity of the disability needs to be matched by the intensity of the service. Not all learning disabled children can be served in the mainstream. Not all need a self-contained class. Not all can have their needs met in a resource room. Not all will have their disabilities remediated in the elementary grades. I know of no panacea–program that will meet the varied needs of learning disabled students.

Usually the legislation is broad enough to permit the development of programs with a variety of service models. State rules and regulations need to reflect both the intent of the legislation and the varied needs of the children. Ideally, each state would make provisions for the following components of a total delivery system:

1. Early identification and preschool programs;
2. Self-contained classes;

3. Itinerant resource room programs;
4. Resource room programs;
5. Consultant help to the regular classroom teacher;
6. Inservice training for classroom teachers.

The various professions involved in the delivery of service to learning disabled children continue to have difficulty defining their roles and establishing territorial prerogatives. Questions about serving the learning disabled child with language problems continue to be raised by speech clinicians and learning disability specialists. Remedial reading teachers and Title I teachers frequently find themselves involved in conflict over the populations to be served. Federal and state regulations frequently contribute to the problem rather than clarifying it. Physical education teachers often find themselves questioning the role of the learning disabilities teacher in motor development programs. The list of problems in the multidisciplinary delivery of service is extensive.

The answer seems to be a simple one. The learning disabled student is entitled to his fair share of any of the special education services available within the school or the district. The speech clinician should be deeply involved with learning disabled children with language problems. Together with the learning disabilities specialist a program can be worked out through which the special knowledge and skills of both can be combined in a better program for the child. The same is true of the physical education teacher, the music teacher, the art teacher, the counselor, the social worker, and any other service available. The role of the reading specialist is a little more sticky, since a large percentage of learning disabled children have problems in reading. What is the difference between remedial reading and learning disabilities? Without going into a lengthy discussion, the learning disabled child is probably the flunk-out of a good remedial reading program. Where both services are available in a school, the delineation of population may well be on the basis of the severity of the disability and the presence of discrepancies in psychological processes. Where the learning disabilities teacher is the only service available, it may be necessary for him to include children in his program who need the same type of remediation, but in whom the diagnosis is not so clear.

As funding for schools continues to present problems for state and local administrators and legislators, the financial problems of programs for the learning disabled seemed destined to continue. This situation appears to argue for a careful delineation of this category of the handicapped rather than an expansion to include all children who are not learning for whatever reason.

Research methodology: The current furor over research methodology in the field of learning disabilities has both positive and negative connotations. My concern involves the apparent willingness of the field to blindly accept data from poorly designed and executed studies, using inappropriate statistical procedures. Before we can develop a research base from which we can draw reasonable inferences we need a method for selecting comparable groups. The heterogeneity which characterizes large groups of learning disabled children is creating serious problems in research design. Until we can delineate reasonably homogeneous clusters of children, it is impossible to do research of sufficient rigor that it should guide decision-making. At the present time, our field continues to be bombarded by studies using parametric statistics on children who do not meet the basic requirements of homogeneity of variance, normal distribution of errors, and comparability of groups. Although we know that aptitute-treatment interaction research using carefully defined sub-groups of children is necessary, few such studies are available. In an effort to explore more suitable statistical procedures, I have recently completed a study of the psychometric characteristics of learning disabled children enrolled in the Child Service Demonstration Centers funded under Title VI-G of the Education of the Handicapped Act. The statistical procedure used was Veldman's Adaptation of Ward's Hierarchical Grouping Procedure (Veldman, 1967). This is one of the cluster grouping procedures which matches profiles along such variables as *WISC* subscores or *ITPA* subscores. Using such a method it is possible to delineate statistically comparable sub-groups which can then be subjected to specific remedial procedures. Only with this type of approach can we begin to answer such questions as "Does psycholinguistic training work? For whom? What subgroups will respond to visual perceptual training?" At the present time, the most that can be said is that nothing works for any one, because differences in performance among heterogeneous children wash out when parametric statistics are used. As I see our research base, it is conflicting, confusing, or absent. The positive implications of this state of affairs suggest that we will sharpen our research skills, explore more appropriate procedures, strengthen our research designs, and develop a scientific pedagogy of which we can be justifiably proud.

Divisive influences in the field: A fourth concern which should bother all of us involves the apparently nonconstructive efforts within the field of learning disabilities to divide the field into factions. Although I will address this point further in the next section, my concern is great enough that I decided to list it in these introductory remarks. There seem to be divisive factions along several continua:

1. Those who speak for the mildly involved child with prevalence rates of 20 to 30 percent versus those who speak for the severely disabled child;

2. Those who argue for process training versus those who argue for academic remedial training;

3. Those who argue for a diagnostic–prescriptive approach versus those who argue for a task analytic-behavior modification approach;

4. Those who argue for a "brain-damaged" etiology and orientation versus those who argue for a psychoeducational orientation;

5. Those who tout panaceas versus those who see long, hard work ahead.

In a developing field, it is to be expected that a variety of approaches will be tried. In a field as heterogeneous as ours, diversity should be encouraged, not discouraged. My concern is that we do not seem to be using diversity to build a sound base for progress. Those with differing points of view need to turn their differences into a constructive approach to building the field of learning disabilities.

IMPACT AND VALUE OF DIVERGENT APPROACHES TO TEACHING LEARNING DISABLED CHILDREN

As the field of learning disabilities has emerged from a variegated heritage, we have witnessed a changing emphasis on first one area of learning disabilities and then another. The areas of emphasis stemming from the early work of Orton, Gillingham, Monroe, and others are still apparent in many clinical reading programs used in the field today. The emphasis on language stemming from the early studies of aphasia in adults by Head and John Hughlings Jackson is apparent in the recent stress on language development. It is understandable that each "expert" developed his or her unique view of learning disabilities in accord with the early training and the unique characteristics of the children seen in the programs with which each was working. Thus, it is understandable that Helmer Myklebust, with his early training and experience with hearing impaired children, began to look at those children referred with possible hearing losses through his unique "microscope" and to generalize from this striated group of referrals to a population of language impaired children. Children with a narrow range of symptoms typical of hearing impaired children constituted the bulk of the children seen in his daily practice. Many of these turned out not to be hearing impaired but rather language or learning disabled, thus delineating a symptom pattern or syndrome found in some learning disabled children. On the other hand, the kinds of children referred to Newell Kephart reflected his early background and work with brain-injured children at the Wayne County Training School. These children around whom he developed his theories and practices were quite different from those seen at the Institute for Language Disorders at Northwestern. For this reason, the theories of Myklebust and Kephart differ a great deal. The same is true of the theories and practices of Samuel Kirk, which developed out of his experiences with a different population of children and out of his early work with the mentally retarded. As I look at the divergent approaches in our field today, it becomes quite clear that these have evolved from varying subgroups of the population and varying delivery systems in which their proponents have functioned.

Thus, I see the role of the "specialists" as a critical one in the development of our field. I don't see any of these approaches as mutually exclusive. I see it as very dangerous to allow ourselves to feel that Dr. X is right and that therefore Dr. Y is wrong. Rather, I feel that it is incumbent upon all of us in a delivery system which serves all kinds of learning disabled children to learn as much about each specific point of view as possible, so that we can apply those methods and procedures to the child who seems to be most like the population of concern to each "expert." If a child is referred with a possible hearing loss, with symptoms characteristic of hearing impaired children, but is found to have adequate hearing, I would not hesitate to utilize the best of the work of such authors as Myklebust, Johnson, Flowers, Hardy, Costello, Wepman, etc., etc., etc. If a child were referred with obvious motor problems, clumsiness, midline problems, and feedback problems, I would turn to the work of the specialists in motor processes who have a reasonable data base underlying their practices.

Each divergent approach seems to have developed out of an emphasis by its early proponents on a specific subgroup of learning disabled children. The divergencies in points of view appear to be most significant at the theoretical level. The differences seem to disappear at the practical level. In most cases, it is very difficult to determine from watching a teacher teaching a child the specific theoretical orientations under which he or she was trained or is currently functioning.

A recent example of vast discrepancies apparent at the theoretical level and minimal discrepancies at the practical level involves the controversy over the diagnostic–remedial approach and the task analytic–behavior modification approach. Attempts have been made to divide the field over this issue, by creating what appears to me to be a straw man. The two approaches are not mutually exclusive and do not demand a dichotomous decision. Several years ago it became apparent to me that the essence of clinical teaching requires a precise match between the cognitive style of the learner and the cognitive demands of the task (see McCarthy 1975a, 1975b). The teacher needs to know at least as much about the task as he or she does about the learner.

The theoretical differences between cognitive psychology, which underlies the diagnostic–prescriptive approach, and behaviorism, which underlies the task-analytic approach, are great. Cognitive psychologists and behaviorists have been at odds since the days of Wertheimer and Watson. However, at the practical teaching level, the differences seem to disappear. If a child cannot talk, the diagnostic–prescriptive approach would emphasize the specific phonological skills which are deficient and attempt to elicit sounds and speech. The task-analytic approach would do the same. Positive reinforcement would play a significant role in any good teaching program. If a child cannot read, teachers from both orientations would try to teach him to read. In the diagnostic-prescriptive approach, an attempt would be made to identify the variables underlying the disability, and methods of reading would be selected which utilize the child's intact learning processes. If visual memory seems involved, with difficulties in the acquisition of sight words, a kinesthetic approach might be used, or a phonetic approach, or a linguistic approach. Through a careful analysis of the task, the same decision could be made. However, it appears to me that a careful analysis of the child is fruitless without a careful analysis of the task. It also seems fruitless to analyze the task without reference to the child. The combination of the two approaches seems most reasonable. Once as much as necessary has been learned about both the child and the task, and a reasonable match between the two effected, any good teacher would use sound principles of reinforcement and behavior modification in working with him. Thus the apparent divergencies between the two approaches disappear when implemented in a common sense way in a real-life situation.

The diversity in the *kinds* of disabilities found in children demand a wide range of diverse skills and approaches in the teacher. The varying *degrees* of disabilities in the children require varying degrees of intensity of service in the delivery system. I see the divergent approaches to teaching as necessary responses to the diversity in the children. The responsibility for appropriate selection and matching represents and will continue to represent the most critical challenge in our field until we discover the panacea that will "cure" all children.

SPECIFIC KINDS OF SCHOOL ENVIRONMENTS MOST CONDUCIVE TO THE EDUCATION OF LEARNING DISABLED CHILDREN

The most critical element in any learning disabled child's school environment is his teacher. The teacher's ability to transmit to the child a feeling of self-worth, of responsibility, of belonging, of competence is the most critical element in the many skills required of a good teacher. Second in importance would be the teacher's ability to modify the curriculum and instruction of the regular class in such a way as to minimize the impact of the disability in the child. Beyond the teacher—this most critical element in the school environment—a discussion of an effective milieu in the school becomes much less clear.

The design of an effective milieu would need to include a full range of services so that the degree of severity of the disability could be matched by the intensity of the service. Some learning disabled children can be served in a mainstream program with consultation service to the classroom teacher; some cannot. Some need a self-contained program; most do not. Many learning disabled children can be served in a parttime resource room program; some need more; some need less. The ideal program would be flexible enough to modify the service as the child's needs change.

Some of the educational innovations so prevalent in our schools today seem to enhance the educational milieu for the learning disabled child. Others seem to make his learning and adjustment more difficult. Some learning disabled children respond well to the open classroom plan and handle the increased noise level and lack of structure with no difficulty. For others, the structure and reduced stimuli of the self-contained class is imperative. The ungraded primary or the IGE school seem to fit some learning disabled children perfectly. For others, the confusion of any changes in procedure can be devastating. A flexible delivery system that can be responsive to the needs of the children would be most effective, especially if the hub of the delivery system is the effective teacher.

It is critical that the learning disabled child be kept in as normal a school environment as possible. Only an infinitesimally small percentage of the learning disabled population cannot profit from spending part of the school day with normal children in the regular classroom.

The design of an effective milieu would have *flexibility* as the cornerstone. With flexibility, the teacher can then be responsive to the extremely varied needs of each child. The child who needs a highly structured program, with distractions kept to a minimum, would be provided with a carrel and a tightly planned daily schedule. The child who can profit from the activities of the regular class on some days but not on others would be able to move to the learning disabilities class on those days when he needs more help and support. Such a milieu can be created by the skillful teacher who has built a strong support system within the school among teachers and administrators. Individualized programming of the academic parts of the day and of the child's social and affective program is a prerequisite of the effective milieu.

Such a design would require a full-size classroom close to other classes of students of similar age. It would require a high level of communication among the teachers involved so that continuity and reinforcement could be built into the child's program, whether he was being taught in the regular class or in the special class. Innovative instructional methods devised in the special class could be translated to the regular class. Most importantly, success would be built into all aspects of our effective milieu.

Essential Considerations in Educational Methodology for Learning Disabled Children

If a teacher is to be able to teach learning disabled children successfully, he or she must first be able to teach nonlearning disabled children successfully. The more I work in the field, the more convinced I have become that regular class teaching experience is essential to success as a learning disabilities teacher. Awareness of how normal children learn is a prerequisite to unlocking the mysteries of how learning disabled children can be taught to learn.

A second essential consideration is the ability to individualize instruction. A third essential consideration is the ability to do good diagnostic teaching, to probe the learning patterns of a child in order to form a basis for further instruction.

If the teacher is to be able to meet the needs of the varieties of learning disabled children whom she or he may be called upon to teach, it is imperative that the teacher have knowledge, skills, experience, and materials in at least eight areas of competence:

1. Sensory-motor processing;
2. Visual processing;
3. Auditory processing;
4. Language development;
5. Academics
   a. Reading
   b. Writing
   c. Spelling
   d. Arithmetic–mathematics
   e. Curriculum equivalents in each content area;
6. Social adjustment;
7. Emotional development;
8. Cognitive processing, including intersensory integration.

Within each of these areas of competence are included the many specific subskills which may need training or which may require the development of other compensatory skills in a particular child.

A teacher competent in sensory-motor processing would be skilled in training such subskills as body orientation, body awareness, directionality, laterality, movement, spatial orientation, time concepts, haptic processing, stereognosis, and the other skills subsumed under this area of competence (see Figure 1). Because of the teacher's competence as a diagnostic teacher, he would be aware of and recognize the symptoms of problems in these areas. Essential to such an approach are the materials necessary to teach each of these skills, whether teacher-made or commercially produced.

The second area in which a child may need help is visual processing, both perceptual and conceptual (see Figure 2). The learning disabilities teacher will need to develop or acquire materials to teach such perceptual processes as attention, discrimination, figure-ground, spatial relationships, closure, perceptual speed, constancy, and object recognition. The teacher competent in the area of visual processing should also be able to identify and remediate problems in abstracting a concept from a visual stimulus, analyzing, integrating, synthesizing, or remembering what is seen. Problems in visual-motor integration such as eye-hand coordina-

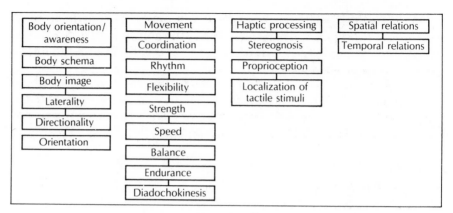

Figure 1: *Sensory-motor processes/functions*

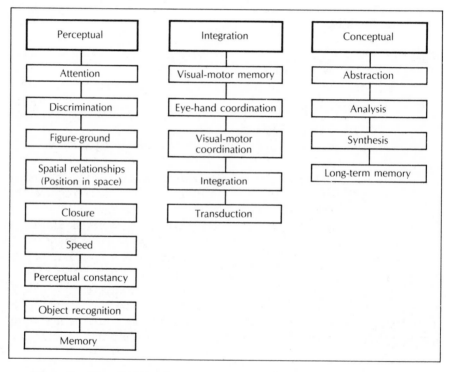

Figure 2: *Visual processing*

tion, eye-foot coordination, or visual-motor memory may also appear among the learning disabled population.

The ability to zero in on a specific deficit such as visual closure and then to know what to do to train it requires a high level of skill in the teacher, but is essential to his or her performance.

Some of the subskills subsumed under auditory processing would include attention, awareness, focus, screening, recognition, discrimina-

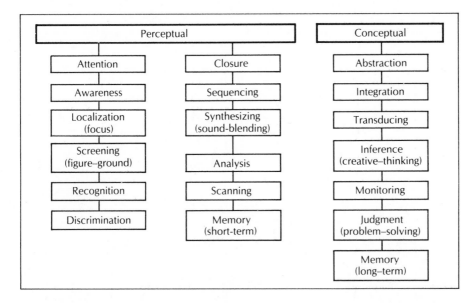

Figure 3: *Auditory processing*

tion, closure, sequencing, sound blending, analysis, scanning, and memory. Some of the problems the teacher may encounter in auditory processing at the conceptual level might include problems in abstraction, integration, inference, problem solving, or judgment. Any of these skills or any of them in combination may be critical to the child's progress.

In the same way, language development would be broken into at least four strands, i.e., phonology, morphology, syntax, and semantics (see Figure 4). The teacher needs to know whether the child's language problem stems from the inability to make the sound; to use such forms as plurals, possessives, tenses, prefixes, suffixes; to use such syntactical structures as phrases and sentences; or to understand, form associations, and express meaning. Materials to teach each of the microskills of language need to be available to the teacher competent to identify and remediate these skill deficits.

Remedial procedures would then need to be devised to teach each of these specific skills.

In the broad area of academics, the teacher will need to develop a variety of remedial approaches to each of the subskills, as well as a wide assortment of curricular equivalents, or "survival techniques" for use in the regular class.

Competence in reading is built upon the understanding that reading is a written symbol system superimposed upon a previously established oral language system (see Figure 5). Thus the teacher will need to be prepared to identify and remediate problems in phonetic analysis, structural analysis or comprehension, together with all of the micro-skills underlying each of these components of reading.

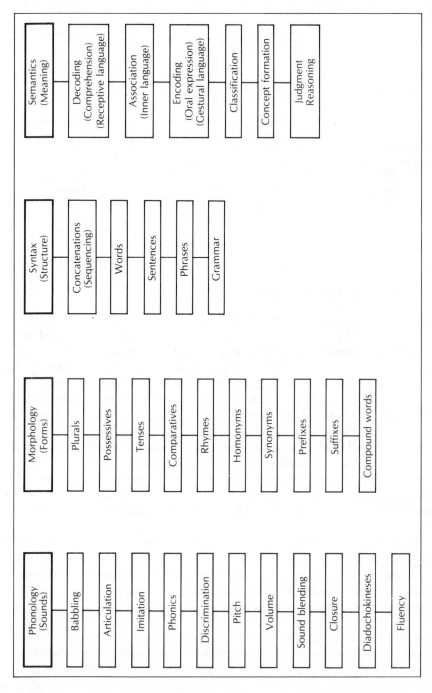

Figure 4: *Language development*

330

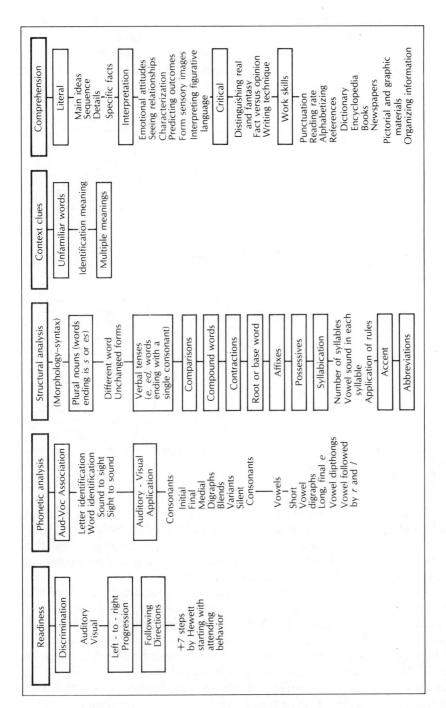

Figure 5: *Reading process*

331

Competence in the remediation of problems in arithmetic and mathematics includes the ability to identify and remediate problems in the four basic processes, as well as problems in the learning of fractions, geometry, numeration, symbols, money measurement, time, decimals, and so on (see Figure 6).

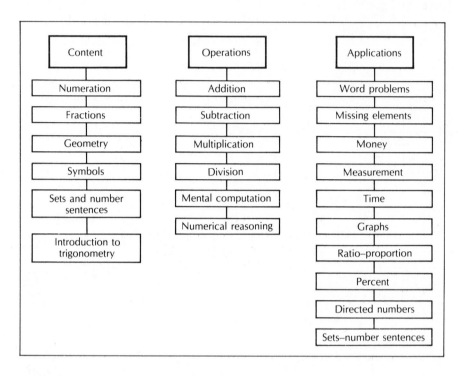

Figure 6: *Arithmetic and mathematics*

Awareness of the psychological processes involved in arithmetic and mathematics is essential in the remediation of learning disabled children. The teacher will be aware of the role played by at least four factors: spatial ability, verbal ability, problem-solving ability, and neurophysiological correlates (Chalfant & Scheffelin, 1969).

Since many learning disabled children demonstrate many of the same problems as children in public school classes for the emotionally disturbed (Kirk & Elkins, 1975; McCarthy & Paraskevopoulos, 1969), an essential part of the armamentarium of the teacher will be knowledges, skills, experiences, methods, and materials to handle the full range of social behaviors presented by learning disabled students (see Figure 7). This area would include skills in behavior modification and such other techniques of effecting behavioral change as transactional analysis (Berne, 1964), life space interviewing (Morse, 1963), group interaction techniques, role playing, and "boundary breaking." Each behavior manifested by the child may have a variety of causes which may or may not be subject to change by the teacher. However, the response of the child to conditions beyond his control can be the focus of the teacher's efforts. Emotional development may be much more difficult to affect than behavior, but needs to be a concern of the teachers and other mental health personnel in the schools.

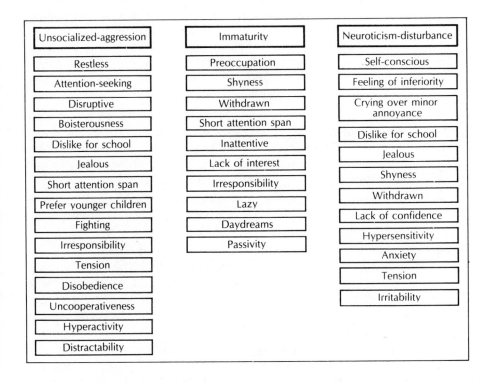

Figure 7: *Social adjustment and emotional development*

The eighth area of competence is that of cognitive processing, including intersensory integration. The teacher needs to know enough about intelligence, how it develops, how it is measured, how it can be enhanced, how to utilize the results of psychological diagnosis affecting the teaching program. In addition, the teacher needs to carry in her or his head a model of human information processing into which can be fit the confusing learning patterns of children. Such a model may range from the simplistic model of Kephart (1971) to a complex model of Mackworth (1972) or Senf (1972).

This array of competencies may seem overwhelming at first glance. Rather than being overwhelmed by it, I would hope that it could be used as a road map for the next article to read, the next speaker to listen to, or the next course to take.

CURRENT INVOLVEMENT

As I write this, I seem to be involved in a tremendous number of projects. By dint of great effort these can be collated into a manageable number:

1. My primary responsibility as director of the Leadership Training Institute in Learning Disabilities funded to the Department of Special Education, College of Education, University of Arizona, Tucson. Major activity in 1975: writing, editing, and disseminating the results of research done by the staff of the LTI-LD. Minor activity: the delivery of technical assistance to Child Service Demonstration Centers in forty-six states.

2. As a professor of special education at the University of Arizona, I have responsibilities to the Department of Special Education and the College of Education. As chairman of the Dean's Task Force on Research, I have been involved in designing new directions and new emphases for the research efforts of the college.

3. I have been developing a competency-based program for the preparation of learning disability teachers and plan to redesign the courses I will be teaching next year.

4. As a part of my interest in early childhood programs for the handicapped, I have been a major advisor to TADS, the technical assistance delivery system in early childhood, funded to the University of North Carolina. I am also involved in developing a training program in early childhood for the handicapped at the University of Arizona.

5. My interest and activity with the Association for Children with Learning Disabilities continues with my involvement on the program committee, as a member and this year, the newly elected chairman of the professional advisory board of ACLD. Locally, I am working closely with the Tuscon ACLD and the Kiwanis Clubs to launch a mobile van that will do vision, hearing, and developmental screening of three- and four-year olds.

6. I am also preparing to teach a graduate course next year in human information processing and have been researching this topic in depth.

Of all of the myriad of activities I find myself involved in, the "people" kinds of things excite me most. I can't sort out the activity that excites me most, because they all do. Perhaps early childhood programs would have highest priority. Human information processing is also high priority. Research into subgroups of learning disabled children or "*n* of 1" research is exciting to me. Teaching both inservice and graduate courses is highly stimulating. I feel that I have managed to reach one of my most cherished goals: *Getting paid to do what I really like to do the best.*

THE FUTURE OF THE FIELD

> *As Society goes*
> *So goes Education;*
> *As Education goes*
> *So goes Special Education;*
> *As Special Education goes*
> *So goes Learning Disabilities.*

This rather simplistic statement summarizes the few statements I can make with certainty about the future of the field.

Futures planning, or more precisely, prognosticating, is fraught with hazards. It can be approached from a variety of points of view, with the conclusions dependent on the abduction point of the predictor. If we define the future as "that strange kind of value imperative whose progeny is today" (Saunders, 1974), we see that the seeds of tomorrow are with us today.

If we approach the Future of the Field by looking at the past, as a series of events and data, we can predict the future by extrapolation. We then can say that the future will be today—only more so.

We can modify this extrapolation model by adding the undetermined influences which may change this flow of history and interrupt the direction of the past. We would then need to look at legislative changes, societal pressures, fiscal crises, and so on, that may require the development of new concepts, new designs, new methodologies, new data packaging.

Another way of approaching futures deals with the formulation of a set of values and plans for operationalizing these values by a group of concerned people. Such a planned adoption of values would need to reflect values agreed on by all affected. Think tanks and brain storming are examples of this type of futures research.

The recent Delphi Forecast, 1975–2000 (1974) completed by the National Association of State Directors of Special Education is one example of futures research in which expert opinion is polled and consensus reached on the basis of predominant thinking and value judgments by special education leaders. The participants were asked to predict when they thought sixty possible technological and sociological events would occur and to record the value they attached to each event. Among the highly valued events predicted in this study which have particular relevance to the field of learning disabilities are the following:

1. Due process procedures are guaranteed to all exceptional children in the public schools;

2. 70 percent of all teacher-training programs require six credits of course work with the exceptional child;

3. A special education information retrieval system incorporating instructional materials, model programs, and change process teaching strategies is operational nationwide;

4. 60 percent of all public school teachers practice prescriptive, individualized instruction.

Based on the many efforts to predict the future, culminated by the activity of my crystal ball, I see the following events as critical to the future of our field:

1. Mandatory legislation for all handicapped children resulting in the introduction of new populations of unserved children, at the severe end of the continuum.

2. Litigation reaffirming the rights of all children to an appropriate free public education, even children who are severely multihandicapped.

3. The absence of significant increases in funds to serve these new populations as children whom we are mandated to serve suggests the need to redeploy our troops—assigning those teachers with special training and skills to teach those children with the most special needs—those who deviate most markedly from the mean of their groups. This trend could result in a change of emphasis in special education from the mildly handicapped child across all categories to the severely handicapped child—to those children who cannot be mainstreamed effectively or served in a resource room program (from the educable to the trainable, subtrainable, or multihandicapped). This trend is gaining support from unexpected sources.

    a. The new AAMD definition of the educable mentally retarded child (see Kauffman & Payne, 1975) is one whose IQ falls more than two standard deviations below the mean—IQs of *70 or below.*

    b. State department revisions of eligibility requirements are lowering Educable limits to 70 or below on an individually administered IQ test administered in the language spoken in the home.

    c. New legislation in some states is aimed at tightening the emotionally disturbed category to include only the severely disturbed, the psychotic autistic, schizophrenic, etc., and eliminating the child with intermittent behavior problems.

    d. There has been lack of apparent success in many efforts to decategorize which has been received with open arms—

        (1) The noncategorical resource room, which appears to work only for children with minimal problems;

(2) The mainstreaming concept which appears at this time to be an administrative cop-out in too many cases, resulting only in lip-service for the truly handicapped child and in denial of service;

(3) The current trend to label all children who do not learn for whatever reason as learning disabled with resultant prevalence rates of 15 to 20 percent or higher;

(4) The upgraded—continuous progress—open school concepts which somehow do not extend to include the handicapped.

e. Another event which may have a significant effect on the direction of our field involves money. I am referring to the persistent struggle for funding for educational programs for handicapped children at state and federal levels, which seem to depend on emotional pleas for categorically labelled handicapped children.

Experience would suggest that legislators are responsive to pressure groups and that pressure groups are most effective when fighting a personal battle for their "own" group of handicapped youngsters. Thus experienced politicians and legislative experts see little hope of breaking the categories under current funding procedures.

f. The current effort in many states to devise a more equitable method of financing public education may result in more creative approaches to the financing of special education as well.

g. The militant note in negotiations between local school boards and representatives of teachers associations would suggest a cross current—a current running contra to the prevailing winds—which permits a teacher in some districts or in some states to exclude a child from school without recourse. Thus, in Hawaii, a child can be excluded from school by his teacher. This trend may well defeat our efforts to maintain handicapped children in the mainstream of education.

Revision of current methods of financing schools, coupled with continual emphasis on parents' rights to be involved in the educational decisions affecting their children, added to such experimental efforts as the voucher system, may well change the face of special education completely.

Given this state of affairs, if there is any value in this analysis, what should special education's thrust into the future involve? Where do we see our field, and our children, ten or twenty years from now? Which of these currents and cross currents do we want to lend our support to?

If our major goal is to prepare learning disabled children for a world which we may not even be able to imagine—the world of the twenty-first century—when handicapped children who are being born today will have reached adulthood and be assuming their places as contributing members of a competitive society, we must give careful thought to our direction *now*.

1. Unless the field of learning disabilities cleans its own house and is able to define a population of children who are truly handicapped, the field will cease to be seen as a part of special education. Responsibilities for the 15 to 20 percent of the population with problems in learning will be assigned to general education. An operational definition which will stand up in court whereby we can state definitively that a particular child *does* or *does not* have a learning disability because he does or does not meet these specific eligibility criteria is urgently needed if the field is to survive and grow.

2. Strenuous efforts will be made to build a sound research base, utilizing appropriate research methodology, to undergird our educational practices.

3. The current struggle to protect territorial rights between learning disabilities and speech, remedial reading, social work, physical education, etc., will subside as roles and responsibilities become realigned along competency-based lines.

4. As more knowledge is gained about how human beings learn, about the neural substrata of learning, about models of human information processing, more emphasis will be placed on the role of cognitive processing in academic learning. We will see a resurgence of interest in learning theory and a return to such basic elements of experimental psychology as attention, memory, symbolic learning, etc.

5. Since the future for mildly involved children includes assimilation into the normal, nonhandicapped society, our major efforts need to continue in the direction of serving these children within the mainstream—with the full range of services delivered with appropriate intensity and frequency.

6. Since experience has shown that the absence of earmarked programs and earmarked funds for the handicapped results too often in the diminution of service, we need to continue to provide such programs and such funds, resisting efforts to absorb special education funds into the general education budget. However, possibilities of using funds from the regular budget to employ specialists to serve minimally involved children is a viable one. In this way the more limited special education funds can be utilized for the most severely impaired children.

7. Although legislation and fund raising may need to continue to be categorical, it is feasible that teacher training programs and school programs for children can move toward an emphasis on the competencies required to move toward responsible adulthood. The

current move toward competency-based training programs with the emphasis on areas of overlap in categorical training programs seems to be pointing the way toward certification in more than one area of the handicapped, with a resultant reduction in emphasis on the categories, particularly learning disabilities, emotionally disturbed, behavior disordered, and educationally handicapped.

8. As mandatory legislation becomes more and more effective, it is imperative that all systems delivering services to handicapped children within a state be brought into proper alignment. If the public schools are mandated to provide an appropriate education program for all children, what should the role of the mental health delivery system be for such service? Perhaps all state programs involved in providing educational services to handicapped children need to be realigned in terms of funding and administrative structure.

9. If the field of learning disabilities is to survive as a distinct kind of handicapping condition and not be subsumed into the mainstream of general education, strenuous efforts need to be made to serve severely involved learning disabled children who require intensive modification of their educational programs. The mildly involved child would then become the responsibility of general education.

10. In the field of learning disabilities, as in all of special education, all we are talking about is the optimum in the individualization of instruction. Although this is mandatory for our children, let us not forget that it is our goal for all children.

REFERENCES

Bakan, P. *Attention.* New York: Van Nostrand, 1966.

Berne, E. *Games people play.* New York: Grove Press, 1964.

Broadbent, D. E. *Perception and communications.* London: Pergamon, 1958.

Broadbent, D. E. Information processing in the nervous system. *Science,* 1965, **150,** 457–62.

Bruner, J. *Toward a theory of instruction.* Cambridge, Mass.: Harvard University Press, 1966.

Bryant, D. *Final report of the Leadership Training Institute in Learning Disabilities.* (Vol. 1). Tuscon, Ariz.: University of Arizona, Leadership Training Institute in Learning Disabilities, 1972.

Chalfant, J. C., & Scheffelin, M. Central processing dysfunctions in children: A review of research. *NINDS Monograph,* 1969, No. 9. Bethesda, Md.: U.S. Department of Health, Education and Welfare.

Delphi Forecast, 1975–2000. Washington, D.C.: National Association of State Directors of Special Education, 1974.

Farber, B. *Mental retardation.* Boston: Houghton-Mifflin, 1968.

Gallagher, J. *Teaching the gifted child.* Boston: Allyn & Bacon, 1964.

Goldstein, H., Moss, J., & Jordan, L. J. *The efficacy of special class training on the development of mentally retarded children.* Cooperative Research Project No. 619. Washington, D.C.: U.S. Office of Education, 1965.

Guilford, J. P. *A revised structure of the intellect.* Reprints from the Psychological Laboratory, No. 19. Los Angeles: University of Southern California, 1957.

Hebb, D. O. *The organization of behavior.* New York: Wiley, 1949.

Hunt, J. M. *Intelligence and experience.* New York: Ronald Press, 1961.

James, W. *Principles of psychology.* (Vol. 1). New York: Holt, 1890.

Kauffman, J. M., & Payne, J. S. (Eds.) *Mental retardation: Introduction and personal perspectives.* Columbus, Ohio: Charles E. Merrill, 1975.

Kephart, N. C. *The slow learner in the classroom.* (2nd ed.) Columbus, Ohio: Charles E. Merrill, 1971.

Kirk, S. A. *Educating exceptional children.* (2nd ed.) Boston: Houghton-Mifflin, 1972.

Kirk, S. A., & Elkins, J. *Characteristics of children enrolled in the child service demonstration centers.* Preview Series. Tucson, Ariz.: Leadership Training Institute in Learning Disabilities, University of Arizona, 1975.

Lavetelli, C. B. Aspects of Piaget's theory that have implications for teacher education. *The Journal of Teacher Education,* 1965, **3,** 329–35.

Mackworth, J. F. Some models of the reading process: Learners and skilled readers. *Reading Research Quarterly.* Summer, 1972, **7,** 4.

McCarthy, J. M. Toward dispelling the mystique of learning disabilities. In S. A. Kirk & J. M. McCarthy (Eds.) *Learning disabilities: Selected ACLD papers.* Boston: Houghton-Mifflin, 1975. (a)

McCarthy, J. M. *Psychometric characteristics of children enrolled in the child service demonstration centers: The search for homogeneous clusters.* Preview Series. Tucson, Ariz.: Leadership Training Institute in Learning Disabilities, University of Arizona, 1975. (b)

McCarthy, J. M., & Paraskevopoulos, J. Behavior patterns of learning disabled, emotionally disturbed, and average children. *Exceptional Children,* 1969, **36,** 69–74.

Miller, G. A., Galanter, E., & Pribram, K. H. *Plans and the structure of behavior.* New York: Holt, Rinehart & Winston, 1960.

Monroe, M. *Children who cannot read.* Chicago: University of Chicago Press, 1932.

Morse, W. Life-space interviewing working paper: Training teachers in life-space interviewing. *American Journal of Orthopsychiatry,* 1963, **33,** 727–30.

Mowrer, O. H. Two-factor learning theory: Summary and comment. *Psychological Review,* 1951, **58,** 350–54.

National Advisory Committee on Handicapped Children first annual report. Subcommittee on Education of the Committee on Labor and Public Welfare, U.S. Senate, Washington, D.C.: 1968.

Norman, D., & Lindsay, P. *Human information processing.* Englewood Cliffs, N.J.: Prentice-Hall, 1972.

Orton, S. T. Specific reading disability—Strephosymbolia. *The Journal of the American Medical Association,* April, 1928, **90.**

Osgood, C., & Sebeak, T. A. (Eds.) *Psycholinguistics.* Bloomington: Indiana University Press, 1965.

Piaget, J. *Origins of intelligence in children.* Margaret Cooper (Tr.) New York: International Universities Press, 1966.

Pribram, K. H. The neurophysiology of remembering. *Scientific American,* 1969, **200,** 73–80.

Robinson, H. *Why pupils fail in reading.* Chicago: University of Chicago Press, 1946.

Saunders, T. F. Futures: Today and yesterday revisited. *Far West Philosophy of Education Journal,* September, 1974.

Senf, G. M. *An information-integration theory and its application to normal reading acquisition and reading disability.* Preview Series. Tucson, Ariz.: Leadership Training Institute in Learning Disabilities, University of Arizona, 1972.

Skinner, B. F. *The behavior of organisms.* New York: Appleton-Century-Crofts, 1938.

Veldman, D. J. *FORTRAN programming for the behavioral sciences.* New York: Holt, Rinehart & Winston, 1967.

A SELECTED BIBLIOGRAPHY OF WORKS BY JEANNE McRAE McCARTHY

Kirk, S. A., & McCarthy, J. M. (Eds.) *Learning disabilities—Selected ACLD papers.* Boston: Houghton-Mifflin, 1975.

McCarthy, J. M. How to teach the hard to reach. *Grade Teacher,* 1967, **84,** 97–101.

McCarthy, J. M. You can help these children. *Grade Teacher,* 1970, **87,** 48–49, 65–66, 68–70.

McCarthy, J. M. Providing services in the public schools for children with learning disabilities. In D. D. Hammill & N. R. Bartel (Eds.), *Educational perspectives in learning disabilities.* New York: Wiley, 1971.

McCarthy, J. M. Learning disabilities: Where have we been? Where are we going? In D. D. Hammill & N. R. Bartel (Eds.), *Educational perspectives in learning disabilities.* New York: Wiley, 1971.

McCarthy, J. M. Education: The base of the triangle. *Annals of the New York Academy of Science,* 1972, **205,** 362–67.

McCarthy, J. M. Exceptional child education: A dumping ground for all educational failures. Tallahassee, Fla.: Florida Department of Education, 1972.

McCarthy, J. M. *Psychoeducational characteristics of children in developmental first grade classes.* Preview Series. Tucson, Ariz.: Leadership Training Institute, University of Arizona, 1974.

McCarthy, J. M. *Remediation.* Preview Series. Tucson, Ariz.: Leadership Training Institute, University of Arizona, 1974.

McCarthy, J. M. Learning disabilities. In J. J. Gallagher (Ed.), *Review of research on exceptional children.* Washington, D.C.: Council for Exceptional Children, 1975.

McCarthy, J. M. Toward a clarification of programs for learning disabled and compensatory programs under Title I. Washington, D.C.: U.S. Office of Education, in press.

McCarthy, J. M., & Paraskevopoulos, J. Behavior patterns of learning disabled, emotionally disturbed, and average children. *Exceptional Children,* 1969, **36,** 69–74.

Paraskevopoulos, J., & McCarthy, J. M. Behavior patterns of children with special learning disabilities. *Psychology in the Schools,* 1969, **7,** 42–46.

11
Sheldon R. Rappaport

Sheldon R. Rappaport was born in 1926 in Jacksonville, Florida. He received his A.B. degree from Temple University in 1946 and his M.A. degree from the same university in 1947. His Ph.D. degree was earned at Washington University in 1950. From 1958 to 1961 he was a student of the Philadelphia Association for Psychoanalysis. At present he is president of Effective Educational Systems in Onancock, Virginia.

Dr. Rappaport was the founder of the Pathway School, a residential school for learning disabled children in Norristown, Pennsylvania, and served as its president from 1961 to 1970. During the years 1964 to 1966 he was research associate in psychiatry at the Jefferson Medical College, Philadelphia, Pennsylvania. From 1960 through 1966, he was medical research scientist III in the children's unit of the Eastern Pennsylvania Psychiatric Institute, Philadelphia, Pennsylvania. He was research associate in psychiatry, Hahnemann Medical College and Hospital, Philadelphia, Pennsylvania, from 1955 to 1960. From 1951 to 1964 he was in private practice and from 1951 to 1956 he was a consultant psychologist to Sklar School in Philadelphia, Pennsylvania. He also served as a psychologist at various times from 1948 through 1952 at Alton State Hospital, Alton, Illinois, and Embreeville State Hospital, Embreeville, Pennsylvania.

Dr. Rappaport is a member of numerous professional organizations. He is a diplomate in Clinical Psychology and a fellow of the American Psychological Association, American Association for the Advancement of Science, American Orthopsychiatric Association, the Virginia Psychological Association, and the Society for Personality Assessment. A well-known lecturer, he has given over 200 lectures, seminars, workshops, and keynote addresses.

Dr. Rappaport served as a task force participant for the Joint Commission on Mental Health of Children and as a consultant to the President's

National Advisory Council. In 1968 he received a Special Service Award from the Texas Association for Children with Learning Disabilities.

Dr. Rappaport has published several books and written many articles. A selected bibliography of his works appears on page 371.

ONCE A FAILURE

That school day had been like all others—bright with the joy of being with children and blurred in a kaleidoscope of activity. But in late afternoon, there was something different in the way Miss Joseph asked us to take our seats. Her customary calm and warmth were missing. On top of that, she announced that the principal had come to talk to us. My stomach squinched "danger."

The principal, small, grayed, and austere, spoke in her usual clipped fashion about the importance of working hard in school. As her train of thought thundered by, I was aware only of its ominous roar. The meaning of her words did not come into focus until she made the pronouncement: "Those boys and girls who have frittered away their time, and as a consequence will not be promoted to second grade, will stand when I call their names." Then she called *my* name.

The shock and mortification staggered me, making it difficult to struggle out of my seat to stand beside my desk. Who stood when she called the other names, the faces of those who remained seated, and what further remarks she intoned all blurred into a macabre dance that encircled my shame. Breathing was painful and had, I was sure, a ridiculously loud rasp which was heard by everyone. My legs rebelled at supporting my weight, so my fingers, aching tripods of ice, shared the burden. In contrast to the cold of my numbed face were the hot tears that welled in my eyes and threatened to spill down my cheeks to complete my degradation.

The principal left. Class was over. Amid joyous shouts, children milled through the door that for them was the entrance to summer fun and freedom. Some may have spoken to me, to tease or to console, but I could not hear them. The warm and pretty Miss Joseph was there, speaking to me, but I could neither hear nor respond. The borders of my mind had constricted like a hand clutching my pain.

Although that incident occurred in 1932, it has not lost its clarity, only its sting. The purpose of recounting it is to provide a view of our educational system seen only by those of us who have lived a learning disorder.

It is highly unlikely that Miss Joseph had either the administrative option or the training to find out why I could not learn. Otherwise, both of us might have found more fulfillment that year. I might have had a genuinely pleasant and gratifying first experience with education, rather than one that resulted in a fifteen-year fear of school and of tests. She, in turn, could have had the gratification of successfully helping a child in trouble, rather than the frustration and shame inherent in a teacher's failing a pupil.

In an age when the atom's energy has been harnessed to lift men through space and deposit them safely on the moon, it is inconceivable that we cannot guide small children successfully through the first grades of school. Yet surveys made in school district after school district across our nation indicate that an unconscionable number of our children find learning by conventional educational methods inordinately frustrating and painful.

Perhaps today there are more children who have, for a variety of reasons, malfunctions in their learning system. However, it is more likely that we now identify a higher percentage of the children who have trouble learning. Today's children are expected to absorb a greater quantity of information and to comprehend more abstract concepts earlier and quicker than ever before. The likelihood is that such educational expectations spotlight those who have trouble learning. Either way, I can assure you that failing at a child's life occupation, learning, is no less painful today than it was forty-two years ago. I am certain of that not only from my own experience, but also from the feelings children have shared with me during the past twenty-eight years.

A ten-year-old boy, who already had had five years of practice at failing school, said: "I feel like a basket case. I can't do anything right."

An elfin eight-year-old girl of winsome beauty, ridiculed both at school and at home for her awkwardness of movements, plaintively asked: "Will anyone ever want to marry me—will *I* ever be a mommy?"

A blonde youngster of eleven, Apollo-handsome except for the black and blue discolorations on his forehead where he daily beat his head with his fists, felt less adequate than every other person on earth. I felt his pain particularly, because between the ages of six and eleven *I* had beaten my head with my fists.

Daily I sat staring at a book that would not surrender to me its meaning. In my war with the book, now and again I was victorious over an isolated word, but the endless legion of pages ultimately defeated me. Repeatedly, I looked back over the unfriendly, unyielding rows of print to find a word that I could recognize. In doing so, my failures amassed by the minute, like a swelling mob jeering at me. Finally, the fury rising within me burst from my fists, while from between clenched teeth I silently cursed the head I was pounding. To me, the immutable reality was that my head was bad. It caused my frustration. It sponsored my shame. I knew no alternative but to beat it into becoming a smarter head. That failed, too, adding daily to my feelings of frustration and worthlessness.

Those feelings were particularly strong on my ninth birthday. I received a book from a cousin I adored. He lived with us while attending chiropody college. Tall, handsome, bright, athletic, and fun to be with, he was in reality all the things I could only dream of being. I *so* wanted to read the book he gave me. I still remember its title, *The Gladiator's Revolt.* I laboriously learned to read it the following year. Its opening words were: "With the clash of swords on swords and swords on shields . . ."

During those painful years, I had no way of knowing that at least part of the reason I could not read was because I could not see clearly enough to understand the world around me. As a result, I did not do what other children did. Consequently, I did not have the experiences necessary to enable me to bring meaning to the words in a book. Nor did I know that to others, letters and words had a constant shape; whereas to me, their form never seemed the same twice in a row.

Not only could I not see the world around me clearly, but I also could not move through it easily or accurately. I felt clumsy, awkward, and a nuisance. In their exasperation with me, others repeatedly confirmed those feelings. And outdoor games like baseball were not only incomprehensible, but constantly to be feared lest they highlight my ineptitude and underscore my shame.

Daily terrors were walking the eight blocks to and from school and going into the school yard for recess. Being all flab and clumsiness *and* wearing thick glasses made me a ready target for any kid who needed to prove his prowess by beating me up. And the number who needed that were legion. Consequently, a rainy day became a reprieve. To awaken to a rainy morning was like an eleventh-hour stay of execution. It meant no recess outdoors. And nobody who wanted to fight. But even better than a rainy morning was being ill. Only then, in *my* bed, in *my* room, did I feel really secure. In the fall of third grade I missed twenty-two days of school. I was confined to bed with rheumatic fever, as I learned from the family doctor when I didn't have the desired wind for distance running while in college. Despite pains which I can still vividly recall, that confinement is the most peaceful of all my childhood memories.

The only outdoor activities I enjoyed were pretend ones. (The woman who lived in the next row house must have been sainted.) To get me out of the house, my mother put on the open porch the piano stool I played with. It became the steering wheel of a huge, powerful truck (you know how loud *they* are), which I guided flawlessly along endless highways, gaining the admiration of all whom I passed. At other times, I ventured across the street where the vacant lot became a battlefield on which I, clothed in my father's army tunic and overseas cap, performed feats of heroism and distinction for which I received countless medals and accolades. Those fantasized moments of glory apparently nourished my thin strand of self-respect enough to enable it to withstand the daily siege on my pride.

At night, when the cannonade of derision was still and my imperiled pride temporarily safe, I implored God and the Christ, Jesus, to see to it that tomorrow would not hold for me the tortures of today. I offered all possible concessions and deals, but relentlessly the tomorrows of Monday to Friday were no better.

I do not believe that my learning disorder was due solely to poor vision. By fourth grade, learning had become at least possible. That was the year I reached puberty. If the force with which the sexual drive then hit me is any indication, the biological upheaval going on within me must have been of hurricane proportion. Quite suddenly, words and numbers no longer were alien symbols. Working with them required a great deal of time and effort, but I *could* manage them. By fifth grade, reading was easy, and arithmetic began to make some sense. Then I no longer regarded my head as my enemy. Instead, I funneled the accumulated shame and self-derogation into the thick, eighteen-diopter lenses that I had worn since age five. For me, those glasses were a blatant badge of inadequacy. Consequently, I stayed to myself and paradoxically took refuge in my former arch enemy, reading.

For the next five years, encyclopedias, magazines, atlases, and dictionaries all showed me a world full of places, people, and ideas with a clarity unavailable to me when I looked at anything farther away than the length of my arm. Hundreds of hours also were spent trying to translate with the aid of a dictionary my cousin's anatomy and physiology books from medical jargonese into English. My original motivation was to understand the tremendous sexual force within me, but, after a while, the mechanics and dynamics of the body held their own fascination.

While I was learning about the human body, I had a counselor at a camp one summer who helped make the words and diagrams of those books real for me. We called him Blacky—probably because his surname was Black. I never saw him after that summer and never could tell him how he changed my life. Because he was on the wrestling team at college, he worked out daily. Recognizing my flabby incoordination, he offered to teach me how to build myself up. His tutelage opened a whole new world to me. The anatomical and physiological words I had learned became real as I became friends with my muscles and gained some first-hand understanding of how they functioned and what they were capable of doing. By fifteen, I could move easily with grace and effectiveness. My body, which had been 5 feet 11 inches tall since I was twelve years old, no longer was a thing of derision. Broad shouldered, slim hipped, and well-muscled, it brought kind words and admiring glances.

With my newly developed body and newfound ability to move effectively, a sense of well-being, self-esteem, and confidence emerged. I began to analyze the sequential steps involved in swimming, hitting a baseball, throwing a football, riding a horse, rowing a boat, shooting a rifle, and other activities that previously had been only incomprehensible globs of failure for me. Analyzing those skills was accomplished by observing how others did what I could not do. Once I knew the sequence involved in an activity, I learned to rely on kinesthetic information as compensation for inadequate vision. With practice, I was able to make a fair showing on the high-school track team, and I even became quite successful as a boxer, using a fast left jab as a substitute for seeing. To achieve in sports (especially boxing) was, for obvious reasons, essential to my self-concept. What I did not know at the time was that boxing and, later, diving would cost me irrevocable retinal damage. Regardless of that, feeling fit became so highly valued that I still do seventy pushups and other exercises each morning before breakfast.

Music added still another dimension to my life. When my parents started me on piano lessons at age seven or eight, I had no rhythm, no motivation, and I could neither see nor read the notes. After puberty, music became an important daily component of my life. With the help of Ben Greenblatt, a well-known jazz pianist, the piano became an enjoyable, socially rewarding means of emotional release. The Philadelphia Academy of Music, and especially its Dr. Rollo F. Maitland, provided an understanding of theory and harmony that allowed me the gratification of writing pop songs and a tone poem by age fourteen. In junior high, that brought me recognition and praise both from the faculty and from other students. And my malnourished self-pride gobbled it up. Although for many years I have had no desire to compose music, listening to music and playing my favorite of favorites, the Thomas Celebrity Electronic Organ, are daily gratifications whose threads reach back to that era of my life.

Another boost to my self-esteem was being awarded the competitive American Legion Scholarship to Temple University. I took the examination with no hope of winning it. That summer, while I was working as a lifeguard at the Germantown Boys Club, the notice came. I read it and reread it, feeling about six inches taller each time.

Going as a scholarship recipient made the whole prospect of college brighter, but it did not eradicate the gnawing self-doubt. As a child, I had vomited each morning before going to school. The carryover continued in my not being able to stomach breakfast and in my coughing and gagging before leaving for class. Later, I understood the childhood vomiting and the residual coughing as a way of trying to expel the fear and noxious thoughts associated with school. While in college and for many years thereafter, I also had nightmares of walking into an examination unprepared.

During my third year in college, I worked as an assistant in the psychology clinic. Early in that year, the director, Harold C. Reppert, was certain my visual problem could be cured, and so he sent me to what he regarded as the best help available: the head of the department of ophthalmology at Johns Hopkins. After briefly examining my eyes through a slit lamp, the doctor pronounced sentence on my ambition: "You might as well drop out of college because your eyes aren't good enough to complete undergraduate work, let alone go on to graduate school." On the return train ride, all the fury accumulated during all the years of frustration focused like a laser beam of determination to prove him wrong. As I read even more voraciously, my stomach writhed and churned. Frequently the feeling of tension became almost unbearable, but I completed a B.A. degree that year, by the end of the summer.

Then I met an optometrist, Dr. Luther Garnes, of Philadelphia, who found that I needed two sets of glasses—one for distance and one for reading. The proper lenses made reading a luxuriant comfort that I had never before experienced. I could explore the vast panorama of knowledge available through books *comfortably*—without tension, without headache, without blurred vision, and, best of all, without my stomach feeling as though it were being drawn up through my chest by a magnet attached to my retinas. With that enhanced freedom, I completed an M. A. in eleven months and then a Ph.D. in two years, while concurrently working fulltime as the head of the department of psychology at Alton (Illinois) State Hospital.

What did my learning disorder cost me? It cost years of feeling so inadequate and tense that I lived with chronic pain in my stomach and muscles. It cost years of feeling absolutely convinced that I could not do anything worthwhile or admirable. It produced a residual anxiety always present when I embark on something new. On the other hand, it helped me to realize that being able to read, to think, and to learn are wondrous miracles of daily delight. If learning had not been so inordinately difficult for me as a child, perhaps it could not have become, by contrast, such a sustained source of pleasure as an adult. I think that struggling so hard to achieve played a role in my developing a deep, abiding regard for human potential. And that has provided me with the bounteous pleasure I get from interacting with those who choose the always arduous route of self-potentiation.

I remember getting into Grand Central Station after midnight and having to wait among its hollow echoes for a connecting train. I sat on one of the wooden benches, feeling very alone and very tired. Nearby, a man was mopping the floor. He did that menial chore with such rhythm, precision, and artistic grace that I became enthralled by the beauty of his performance. My loneliness and fatigue vanished. The joy of watching such beauty had refreshed me. That was but one of the rich dividends I might have missed if I never had learned to prize human potential.

And such dividends occur daily—in listening to an orchestra, seeing a painting, watching a gymnast or a skier, reading poetry, coming across a particularly poignant phrase, hearing a child laugh, or watching him skip off, content with his accomplishment. For these alone, the investment of childhood suffering was worthwhile. Although I do not regret what I lived through, I would like to spare children the necessity of going through similar experiences. I know that is possible because there are other, far better routes now available to children to find joy in potentiation. Those routes involve learning the process of clarifying their own goals and values, of understanding how their behavior affects others and what options are open to them as to how they handle any given situation. Those will be discussed a bit more later in this chapter.

PERSONS TO GROW WITH

Many persons in diverse fields have contributed to my professional development. As a graduate assistant in the reading clinic at Temple University, I had the opportunity to learn from Emmett A. Betts and Russel G. Stauffer. Russ was working on his doctorate and I on my master's degree.

That was my first opportunity to understand the many causative factors involved in a reading problem. Emmett Betts had masterfully opened the door to communication among the disciplines involved, directly or indirectly, with children who had reading problems. With his leadership at a case conference, specialists shared their information and views while respecting the findings and opinions of the others. The process by which he arranged for and led this type of interaction was to me more fascinating even than the content of the discussion. To a lowly graduate student, Betts' skill in getting nationally known specialists to work together on behalf of a child was miraculous. That was in 1946. Now, thirty years later, openness and respectful sharing among different disciplines still is not a widely accepted way of life.

Another intriguing concept I learned from Stauffer and Betts was that learning could be fun. Their formula was to present complex issues with clarity and tie them to specific children with whom we all had first-hand experience, and then to mix that with abundant laughter and gentle humor. Such experiences established roots in me that later would be nurtured by the open-education movement.

Although interning at the Institute for Living in Hartford did not give me the personal supervision and experience I had enjoyed at Temple's reading clinic, it did point out the importance of the environment and of structuring the life space of mental patients (who were *always* to be referred to as guests). The role of the environment and of structuring relationships were also to germinate into major areas of my endeavor.

In hope of finding personal supervision and experience with mental patients, I switched my internship to Elgin State Hospital in Illinois. There I was first introduced to psychodynamic concepts by Seymour Fisher and his wife, Rhoda, by Phyllis Witman, and by the psychiatrists and social workers. Phyllis, who then was head of psychology for the state of Illinois, was brave enough to send me to Alton State Hospital to revitalize its psychology department.

At Alton, I had the good fortune of a close association with two psychiatrists, Doctors Siegfried and Frances Gruenwald. Not only did they share fully the richness of their friendships, but they also shared me —very patiently—their vast knowledge of psychiatry and neurology. The holistic approach to human development was practiced by them daily, and I was privileged to be part of it. I also had the opportunity to work closely with physicians who were taking their residencies at Alton. That provided in-depth probes which nurtured the holistic concept.

While at Alton, I worked on my doctorate at Washington University in St. Louis. Washington U., with Arthur H. Compton as chancellor, was far ahead of its time in personalizing education. For instance, the several other universities at which I had applied insisted on fulltime residency. Because I had to work to pay for my education, such a requirement was an insurmountable hurdle. At Washington U., where John Paul Nafe was head of the psychology department, the response was different. Certainly his work in perception was as prestigous as could be found at any university. Yet when I asked him whether I could work fulltime and also be a doctoral student, his answer typified his humanistic and earthy approach: "Keep a 3.5 average and I don't give a damn what else you do—but you better get the Dean's permission first."

Moreover, in courses both at the graduate school and at the medical school, there was concern for the student as a person. Real—not lipservice—attempts were made to meet my needs, to tailor the curriculum to be most stimulating to my professional development. Getting my doctorate at Washington U. was not a trip through Disneyland. There was a notable absence of Mickey Mouse courses that had no relevance to professional growth. That, which I experienced during 1948 to 1950, has been a prized example of the responsibility that all universities should take with students to prepare them to function ably in their chosen profession from day one on the job.

Another phase of my development was as a student with the Philadelphia Association for Psychoanalysis. There I discovered that to be psychoanalyzed was not a destination, but a journey. Its termination was not a graduation, but a beginning. It provided an opportunity to start clarifying what I really valued, what I wanted my life to count for. And that led me into studying the how-to of value clarification.

As a student in the association, I was privileged to interact with such eminent thinkers as Gerald H. J. Pearson and Robert Waelder. Delving into patient-therapist interactions with Gerald Pearson, John Eichloltz, Phyllis Blanchard, Eli Markowitz, Paul Sloane, Mitch Dratman, Herm Belmont, Morrie Gelinsky, and others highlighted two functions that I have valued ever since: observational skills and awareness of the process of interpersonal interaction.

During that period, I also had the pleasure of associating with the gifted pediatric neurosurgeon, Eugene B. Spitz, which enabled me to pursue my study of the interaction between affective and cognitive functions, a study which I had begun at Alton and on which I had done my doctoral dissertation. This appeared in two publications (Rappaport, 1951, 1953).

I also had the extreme good fortune to get to know David Rapaport (no relation) during that time. For five years I had tried to synthesize my ideas on the ego development of children who suffered obvious brain damage. On several occasions I used David as a sounding board for those ideas. His response was that the organic child was an altered organism and, therefore, could not be viewed from the standpoint of expected ego development. The ideas in my mind would not be dismissed, however. Finally, they gelled sufficiently for me to present them so that they made sense. Then David quickly seized the ideas, helped me to elaborate on them, and encouraged me to publish them. Unfortunately, David's brilliance was snuffed out at the age of forty-nine. His death, which was a loss to the whole professional world, I felt keenly because he had been both friend and mentor. The paper David Rapaport had been helping me with (Rappaport, 1961) reached final draft with the aid of Jerry Pearson.

After a while, working with brain-dysfunctioned children and their families in private practice and in hospital settings was not sufficiently satisfying. The key role that education played in habilitating these children was missing. I wanted to explore that. Consequently, I founded The Pathway School in 1960.

The previous year, while trying to assess what the public schools were doing or wanted to do for these youngsters, I had asked the superintendent of schools in Philadelphia what was the incidence of brain-damaged and aphasic children in his school system. He replied "None." I suggested that we file immediately for a grant from NIMH to study the water in the Schuylkill River, because it might harbor the secret of why Philadelphia was the only city in the nation so blessed. My recommendation went over like a pregnant pole-vaulter.

It seemed logical to me to start a private school for handicapped children in a church's Sunday School facilities, because these went unused from one Sunday to the next. But that did not seem logical to the ministers. There were countless refusals. Undoubtedly, they were afraid of the children. Because I could not show them what youngsters with brain damage were really like, the fear of the unknown again prevailed.

Finally, I approached a young minister, newly appointed to the congregation at the Narberth (Pa.) Presbyterian Church. I ended my marathon of words describing the children and their needs with "and please don't tell me there's no room at the inn." We enjoyed our stay there for several years, with no serious mishaps.

There was one close call, though. A youngster had pulled the fire alarm just as the assistant minister happened by. He dove for the box and kept his finger in it to prevent it from going off. I came along minutes later to hear him intoning, "Oh, Grand Coulee, oh, Grand Coulee . . ." Later, when I asked why he was saying that, he replied, "It's the biggest dam I could think of!"

My purpose in founding Pathway was to learn what children with brain dysfunctions really require to return to public education and succeed where they had previously failed dismally. Many persons were financially helpful in supporting that endeavor, but it was mainly supported by the generosity of John and Chara Haas. Their foundation grants made the exploration possible. It permitted experimentation with various interdisciplinary melds to find which worked best for those children. Once those factors were identified, for me the task became one of finding how to adapt that program economically enough for it to be implemented in public schools. In 1970, I left Pathway to work fulltime at helping public school systems to develop such programs.

Pathway provided many opportunities for growth. In its early years, I was teacher, psychologist, parent counselor, and wiper of noses and bottoms. The kids taught me a tremendous amount about how they learn and how they feel—facts that were not in any textbooks. Their parents were equally fine teachers. From them I learned how extensive were their feelings of guilt and despair, how deeply they had been wounded by the scorn of relatives and neighbors and by the ridicule of their physicians. The valuable support parents gave each other in groups proved superior to the orthodox approach of working with parents individually. And the worth of working with families as a unit became clear.

Soon after founding the school, I asked Bill Cruickshank if he would serve on my advisory council. He agreed, with the stipulation that I use his services and not only his name. Bill may have regreted that stipulation, because over the years I sought his counsel many times on many matters. Thus, I became one of the recipients of his caring. In the process, I developed an abiding affection for Bill Cruickshank both as a person and as a teacher. He does not give lip service to humanism; he *lives* it. His reservoir of caring is boundless. His availability when he is needed has a constancy second to none. And he shows his caring as though he had nothing else to do, as though he were not a prolific writer and an organizer *par excellence.* Although he has pioneered on many fronts in behalf of the exceptional child, to me Bill Cruickshank's zenith is his ability to combine efficiency with love. I have met no one who teaches that better.

During my years at Pathway, I also was fortunate enough to have Jerry Getman join me. He introduced me to the concepts of developmental optometry, which I had only glimpsed while working for Emmett Betts. Many of his concepts of how learning takes place helped to clarify and then became integrated into my own ideas on the learning system. His emphasis on observing the performance of the child as *the* criterion for the child's educational program was also syntonic with my background and became a major dimension of my thinking. And observing Jerry work so magnificently with children added still another dimension and additional depth to my understanding of the child's process of learning. Although we came from very different professional backgrounds, Jerry contributed much to my understanding of learning. Working with Jerry Getman added to my development in a number of ways, one of which was his introducing me to Darell Boyd Harmon.

Darell was, in some ways, the most unique of all persons I have been privileged to learn from. He had an extraordinary talent for delving in depth into seemingly diverse disciplines and synthesizing from them information directly applicable to the development and education of children. (See Rappaport, 1975.)

Before I knew Darell, I was not very pleased with the professional role I had played—that of a synthesizer. I think the reason I could not value it is because I never saw it done with the brilliance with which Darell had done it. Watching him synthesize was like being enthralled by a splendid mystery novel. The pertinent factors were first identified and categorized singly. Then they were fit nearly together so that the bewildering complexity that once appeared to be insoluble became transformed by decisive logic into a self-evident solution. To synthesize with a skill even approaching his excellence is now a highly valued aspiration of mine.

Darell also demonstrated that the other side of the coin of being a synthesizer is to be a catalyst. When a synthesis is presented with clarity, it becomes a highly effectual motivator, giving those who have been stalled and discouraged the desire to proceed. And when that synthesis has been long awaited, they tackle the problem joyfully and with renewed vigor. Certainly the field of education, particularly the area of learning disorders, needs that quality of synthesis and catalyst.

As you can see, my debt is to many teachers. They are of different ages and of variegated backgrounds. What they have taught me most clearly, by being living demonstrations, is the value of caring about others as persons, of being open, and of inviting others to enjoy what they have enjoyed. They have enabled me to realize what Kahlil Gibran (1923) meant when he said: "The teacher ... gives not of his wisdom but rather of his faith and his lovingness. If he is indeed wise he does not bid you enter the house of his wisdom, but rather leads you to the threshold of your own mind" (p. 56).

LEARNING DISORDERS: MY PERSPECTIVE

Since 1946, when I first started to work with children who had learning problems, knowledge of those problems and of possible solutions to them has burgeoned in a manner unprecedented in the history of education. Concomitantly, there have been some major shifts in my beliefs and concerns. In the 1950s, my main objective for children with learning disorders was a special education classroom that would save them from torment and would have some basic understanding of how to meet their needs. I was opting for special education classes not to be garbage dumps designed to cleanse mainstream education of all its undesirables. Therefore, I was also searching for a standardized battery of tests that would quickly and accurately identify the LD child, so that he could be extricated from the garbage dump and placed instead with others who shared his needs.

Those are not my prime concerns today. I believe that there is sufficient knowledge about how learning takes place to be able to mainstream the majority of LD students. I also believe that no standardized tests provide us with information that is as *reliable* and as *useful* as the information obtained from practiced, daily observations. Those two beliefs have been substantiated by public school projects which I have helped to parent and nurture during the past five years.

The model for such public school projects is the Bay-Arenac Developmental Learning Program. It is coordinated through the Bay-Arenac Intermediate School District, located in Bay City, Michigan, with Jack C. McConkey as superintendent and Mary E. DuBois as director of special education. Seven independent school districts actively participate in the developmental learning program within their elementary schools and now are moving the program into their secondary schools. One district, Essexville-Hampton, has an ESEA Title III project, FAST, which has been nationally validated and was selected as a demonstration center. Information on FAST's objectives and research findings are available from Herb Escott, Project Director, 303 Pine St., Essexville, MI 48732. Both project FAST and the developmental learning program are built on principles which demonstrably have enabled public education to accomplish the fundamental goal of personalized and effective educational service to most students. This goal is achieved (1) through systematically training the mainstream teacher to become aware of and then program for the overall needs of each student, and (2) by providing mainstream teachers the support service they need to help students overcome their problems and learn optimally. Briefly, those principles are:

1. The ultimate goal of education is development—preparing students to cope with whatever their adult environment demands of them. To accomplish that goal, teachers must understand *how* learning takes place. Otherwise, teachers are likely to continue in the historical tradition of emphasizing only *what* is learned. Because of the existing knowledge explosion, it is highly improbable that the facts taught in school today will prepare students to meet the demands of their world tomorrow.

2. To insure each student's right to development requires that each teacher gains an understanding of (1) the learning process, (2) how to identify developmental needs, and (3) how to devise educational programming to meet those needs. To achieve that, teachers re-

quire a systematic opportunity to accomplish their own learning. Similarly, parents require ongoing opportunities to learn how they can team with teachers to help their chidren to grow. Consequently, no student can develop optimally unless provision is made for the educational system also to change and develop as it provides the opportunities for the development of both students and teachers and as it facilitates parental participation in their child's growth process (see Figure 1).

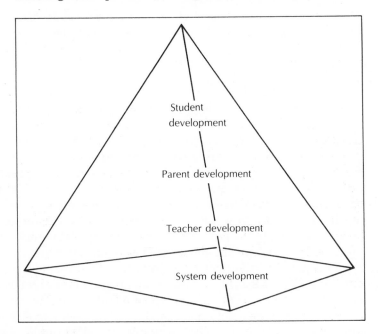

Figure 1: *Educational development*

3. In view of our burgeoning knowledge and technology, a delivery system of education which is fact-centered is neither effective nor efficient. The delivery system instead must become centered on the process by which students learn. For that to become a reality, the system must enable teachers to have the tools they need to understand the learning process. That requires, first of all, training in the understanding and application of nine basic teaching tools (see Figure 2). These nine teaching tools are not startlingly new. Their concepts have been around for a long time, but have not been implemented systematically in education. Nor have teachers had the opportunity to practice, organize, and refine the skillful use of these tools so that they in fact can employ them comfortably on a day-to-day basis.

1. Observing how students go about learning.
2. Analyzing what each task really demands of a student.
3. Deciphering the developmental level of the various skills a student needs to build for successful learning.
4. Prescribing the educational program a student needs next for his development.
5. Organizing the classroom to promote active participation in learning.
6. Helping students to direct their own behaviors appropriately.
7. Applying support help meaningfully.
8. Sharing teaching concepts and strategies so more students are helped.
9. Teaming with parents to provide their children consistent opportunities for development.

Figure 2: *The teacher's tool kit*

The first tool is observing the child in the process of learning. The second tool is knowing what is being presented to him. The third tool is knowing how each task fits with his developmental level. When those tools are used together, an educational prescription emerges that meets the *student's* needs—not some prejudged, arbitrarily chosen needs. The educational prescription highlights the student's developmental needs at that time, and it provides the teachers a way to get feedback about what the youngster needs to be able to climb to the next rung on his own developmental ladder.

The fifth tool means devising classroom activities that help students get actively involved in learning. That includes working out the mechanics of how students go about their daily activities so that the teacher is not in the role of a traffic cop. The sixth tool recognizes that the emotional climate of the classroom either will hinder or help learning. The success of the educational prescription will depend greatly on the emotional climate. A vital part of the curriculum then is helping students to become aware of how we are influenced by the behavior of others and to see the options each of us has in how we behave in a particular situation.

The seventh tool enables teachers to relinquish the traditional oracle role. Oracles are expected to have all the answers, so they never need help. But teachers readily admit that they need all the help they can get, to understand better what experiences their students need to grow on. The eighth tool enables colleagues to share teaching strategies, materials, and also problems and possible solutions. As that is done routinely, students are provided a much broader opportunity for learning than is available only in any one classroom. It also is comforting for teachers to know that they are not expected to be the perfect oracle, completely self-sufficient behind the closed door of the classroom.

The ninth tool enables teachers to team with parents. Traditionally, parents have been invited out of school. The only time parents have been called in is when there were complaints. Consequently, many parents feel uncomfortable in school. But if educators first share with them their child's strengths and positive aspects, most parents are willing to team with teachers to foster their child's development.

The nine teaching tools all work together (see Figure 3). The first tool, observing the child, tells *how* he learns. Task analysis tells *what* he can learn. Understanding how his skills emerge tells *when* he is ready to learn a task successfully. Classroom organization enables active participation in learning. Appropriately structuring the emotional climate promotes understanding of how to find satisfaction in relating to others. Using help from others makes finding solutions easier. Sharing teaching strategies enables many more students to get appropriate learning opportunities. Teamwork with parents provides more consistent opportunities for learning. All eight of those tools are necessary for an educational prescription to be effective.

4. To assist in the implementation of the teaching tools, the learning system needs to be explored so it can serve as a roadmap to devel-

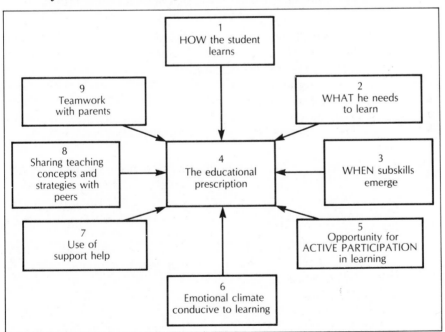

Figure 3: *Components of a successful educational prescription*

opment. The basic purpose of the learning system (see Figure 4) —which is the same in child and adult, slow learner and fast learner—is to enable the individual to cope with whatever demands the environment makes on him. Toward that end, he has information-processing modes that inform him of the environment. Information concerning the environment becomes increasingly integrated and codified into more economical, usable bodies of knowledge, so that the student's performance is an index to the effectiveness and efficiency that is possible for him at that point in his development. As teachers learn how to understand the functions of the learning system, and as they become comfortable in applying the nine teaching tools, they can devise learning opportunities that best promote the student's total development.

Then, rather than cram the pupil's cranium with facts, they give him an opportunity to explore the world around him, as well as the process by which he, himself, learns. Instead of rote drill, the teacher provides the student with the opportunity to practice whatever he is learning—reading, spelling, math—in activity and game form. Because we all like to play games, learning then does not become boring. Boredom is a formidable deterrent to learning. Instead, enjoyable activities and games which provide the opportunity for practice enhance both the student's learning and his total development.

5. Because the delivery system enables the teacher to be process-oriented rather than fact-oriented, pupils do not need to sit in rows, at military-erect attention. Instead, they can explore a variety of sources of knowledge and technology, as well as how they themselves learn, using learning centers and various other classroom organizations. The more a student actively participates in his own learning, the more use he makes of educational opportunities.

6. In this delivery system, teachers are not expected to be all things to all students. Through ongoing training, they are expected to develop a facility in understanding the process of learning, so that they can observe a malfunction in the learning system and, when needed, refer the student to the appropriate specialist in the community for help. Similarly, teachers are not expected to know everything about all accrued knowledge and technology. Instead, they are expected to help students find out what they need to know. They also are expected to make school a place in which students enjoy the experience of living and of developing their learning systems, so that later in life the whole world can be a classroom in which they learn whatever additional facts and skills they then need.

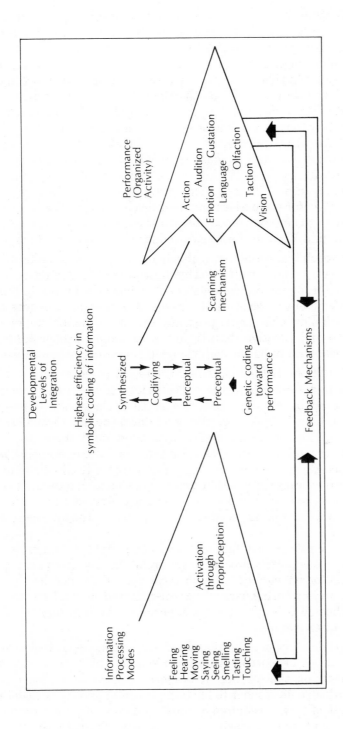

Figure 4: *Functional learning system*

7. Teachers also are expected to develop their understanding of how students grow emotionally—how they interact and how they learn to manage their own behavior so that they do not need adults to police them constantly. Instead of policing pupils and keeping them in a rigid lockstep order, teachers help them become aware of who they are, of who they can become, of how they influence each other through their behavior, and of what options they have in how they behave toward others in any given situation. Teachers share with students the process of making goals and evaluating progress, as well as what they can hope to accomplish by doing certain activities. The key to the teacher's role is *with* the student, not *to* him. Through such means, teachers help pupils develop respect for themselves and, thereby, for others. Teachers also help them to become responsible for themselves and their own behavior, and, thereby, for others and for the society in which they live.

8. As each teacher becomes able to implement those skills, his or her effectiveness is multiplied by the number of students in that class, that is, by the number of students who benefit from that teacher's effectiveness. Meeting the needs of almost all students through such a developmental program, therefore, is much more economical and effective than trying to remediate school failures on a one-to-one basis through the traditional use of specialists.

9. Traditionally the mainstream classroom teacher has been unable to find solutions to the wide variety of learning problems presented by pupils within the regular classroom. Consequently, "problem" pupils have been sent down the hall to various specialists. The specialists worked with them on a one-to-one basis for short periods of time. Despite attempts at conferencing between specialists and teacher, many mainstream teachers did not leave those conferences with a comprehensive understanding of the total student or with a comprehensive picture of the specific educational strategies needed to help that student overcome his problem.

    Similarly, the fast learner in the conventional class has not been adequately programmed for, either. Too often his opportunities for educational growth have been restricted by the narrow scope and boring pace of the fact-centered curriculum. As a result, school has been a failure experience for him and for the slow learner equally.

10. The delivery of educational services is conceptualized in terms of modules of existing school personnel. The first service module pivots on the teacher. It is more effective and efficient for the mainstream teacher to have the training necessary to deliver the bulk of service required by most students within a classroom than to send many students to specialists. Through retraining, the

building principal then becomes the first line of support to the mainstream teacher in delivering comprehensive service to most pupils in that classroom. Educational programs help the parents also to become an integral part of the first service module.

In the second service module are school personnel who provide additional support to the teacher, the building principal, and the parents. Module II is formed by providing additional training to such school personnel as psychologists, speech pathologists, and reading specialists. The purpose of that additional training is to enable them to provide two-fold service: (1) generalized support to mainstream teachers in classroom organization and management, identifying learning needs, aiding in the implementation of educational prescriptions, and assisting with emotional development, and (2) consultation to other support persons, sharing with others their background of disciplinary training and experience. By training specialists to provide a broader range of services to a larger number of teachers, help is provided to a much larger number of students, making the service of those specialists more effective and more economical.

In the third service module, consultants and also specialists from the community are used to help find solutions to those problems presented by the relatively few pupils for whom persons in Modules I and II cannot find answers. By exhausting the resources of Module I before Module II is called upon, *existing* school personnel are used more effectively and efficiently to meet a broader spectrum of needs for more students than would be possible under the traditional educational system.

I shall not go into the specifics of the training program that encompasses the principles just summarized, because that would require volumes in itself. Neither shall I cite the results, because the interested reader can obtain those from Herb Escott and Mary DuBois. Suffice it to say that applying those principles developmentally and humanistically *has* worked, as measured by a variety of criteria ranging from parent satisfaction to achievement testing. But those principles have been successful *only* when applied in a developmental and humanistic fashion. Such a program's effectiveness can be sabotaged by a superintendent's, or any other administrator's, disregard for the human dignity of the school district's personnel. For example, not listening to what teachers *really* need and *really* are asking for is a dehumanization that must ultimately have impact on student development. On the other hand, when superintendents and all other administrators do participate actively and caringly in implementing the program, the results can be rewarding to the whole community.

And it is the whole community that needs to understand and become involved in learning—all kinds of learning, including the disorders of learning. I do not believe that today the community should be sold on the need for separate, segregated programs and buildings for those who do not progress at a preordained rate in remembering facts arbitrarily prescribed as relevant to their growth and development. In every community, everyone develops at his own pace in whatever he learns. The fact that this is how learning occurs *in everyone* is important to convey to all members of the community. Equally, it is important for the community to realize that it is okay for us to learn at our own pace and then to learn only what we select, because learning *that* has real value to us at that time in our lives. Then, perhaps, there is a better opportunity to view not only education, but all community systems from a developmental standpoint.

There *are* many ways that the educational system can deliver service to students. The goal is to find the way that best meets the needs of those specific students. To accomplish that the educational system needs the opportunity to be self-examining: what types of education are needed by whom, and for what purposes, and how they can best get it. That concept is alien to many educational and community leaders. To them, there is but one kind of education—the kind they know from their own school attendance—and everybody needs it! Moreover, to them, the whole community exists only as they presently perceive it. Buildings, businesses, natural resources all are related only to the current needs of the perceivers. There is no room in their perceptions to regard those or other aspects of the community as a passing scene which *must* change in one way or another. Consequently, those educational and community leaders who have such constricted perceptual fields also have no concept that the educational system should serve to enable all persons in the community to accommodate to those changes.

How change occurs does not have to be left to chance. Today, persons and, therefore, communities can be taught how to optimize change. But before that can be learned, many must discover that change and inconstancy are not synonomous. For some, to learn that is not easy, because they are well-steeped in our cultural heritage which says that to hold a belief less than forever is fickle.

For the aforementioned educational and community leaders with the constricted perceptual fields and hardening of the concepts, the only game in town is to enhance their own prestige and preserve their own power. When playing that game, they have neither the need nor the desire to perceive what the individuals in their community really want or need from the educational system. Neither do such leaders care about personal development or human potentiation. Much more important to them, for example, is the number of buildings erected during their regime, because buildings are impressive, lasting monuments to their builders. Consequently, the need for providing students with alternatives to education, or with flexible space, or, more important, with the opportunity to learn how to live in that space harmoniously is not permitted to interfere with those leaders' edifice complex.

My concern about community education is not irrelevant to my abiding concern for children who have learning problems. The link is my conviction that those who have a learning disability or those who have any other type of disability cannot reach their optimal potentiation except in a community that has learned how to clarify its attitudes and values. And *that* learning rightfully begins in the elementary grades. Many times have I contrasted the jeers and taunts and degradations I received as a learning disabled child with the manner in which similar children are treated today by peers and by adults who have had the opportunity to clarify which feelings and behavior toward others they truly value. At a comparable state of development, the progress those children are making far exceeds mine.

Whether the concern is about community education or finding the educational prescription that will most efficiently provide a student the opportunity to overcome a specific learning disability, I believe that today we have the capacity to specify the process needed to accomplish the goal. And that, to me, is thrilling. Equally exciting to me is the fact that we also can examine a variety of ways in which the process can be learned. Once a training procedure has been decided upon and the reasons for its selection specified, we have the capacity to initiate ongoing assessment of how well that procedure serves those who want to learn a particular process. Consequently, two goals are accomplished simultaneously: (1) no one has to be stigmatized on the inherent assumption that the training procedure is infallible and, therefore, that anyone who does not immediately master the process-to-be-learned must be inferior, and (2) utilizing feedback from the participants—not from desk-bound administrators—the training procedure can be improved so that it continuously evolves better ways of serving those who want that service. Thus, today, education does not have to be anachronistic, irrelevant, or denigrating. From where I have been in education, that capacity is a beautiful dawning which must not be wasted.

TOMORROW'S HISTORY OF EDUCATION

The loud ones
and overly-proud ones,
Teachers had sent
To the specialist gent
Down the hall.

The ones who couldn't read
And those no one would need
Also were sent
To the specialist gent
Down the hall.

The kids diagnosed as unteachable
and those who were labelled unreachable
Urgently were sent
To the specialist gent
Down the hall.

Then school boards demanded more dollars
To transform instantly into scholars
All the failures being sent
To the specialist gent
Down the hall.

Universities answered the need
For more specialists to be degreed,
So more kids could be sent
To the specialist gent
Down the hall.

Fresh from college they came to the schools,
Applying pathology and taxonomy rules
To all the children sent
To the specialist gent
Down the hall.

There were doctors and misters and Ms.
All practicing away at the specialist biz,
So, of course, larger numbers were sent
To each specialist gent
Down the hall.

September through June you then found
Classrooms with few kids around.
Most had been sent
To the specialist gent
Down the hall.

The remaining few did no balking
At teacher's oracular talking and chalking,
Because only troublemakers *went*
To the specialist gent
Down the hall.

While that occurred in suburbia,
Inner-city kids really worried ya.
They just couldn't be sent,
Having no *specialist gent*
Down the hall.

Instead, they turned off or tuned out,
Taking the suspension or delinquency route.
Courts and judges made no dent,
Impotent as any specialist gent
Down the hall.

Costs rose from San Diego to Montpelier,
So increased were the number of failures,

Even among kids who went
To the specialist gent
Down the hall.

Finally the feds said, "The system is failing,"
Despite teachers demanding and wailing
For more kids to be sent
To the specialist gent
Down the hall.

Amidst cries of "Alas" and "Oh, woe,"
The feds said, "No more dough
From Uncle Sam will be spent
For a specialist gent
Down the hall."

Teachers then couldn't stay oracular
While they expected the miracular
For all the kids they sent
To the specialist gent
Down the hall.

Instead, teachers had to be retrained,
If federal money was to be retained,
So they too were sent
To a specialist gent
Down the hall.

They discovered that a child is whole,
That with, *not* to *is the teacher's role.*
Into that, and more, they went
With the specialist gent
Down the hall.

How-to's for reading, math, and behavior,
And how to synthesize, since no one method is the
   savior,
All were explored by the teachers sent
To the specialist gent
Down the hall.

Then they began to approach their classes
With less concern about failures and passes,
Because they lived their own *development*
With the specialist gent
Down the hall.

They found how to make learning be fun,
How not to put pupils under the gun.
As teachers practiced that bent,
Fewer kids had need of the specialist gent
Down the hall.

Higher education recognized later,
That for superintendents to alma their *mater,*
College courses must be relevant

Or their *grads would need that specialist gent*
Down the hall.

When colleges finally became real,
Instead of a let's-build-my-empire deal,
Very few teachers, or kids, then were sent
To any specialist gent
At all.

REFERENCES

Gibran, K. *The prophet.* New York: Knopf, 1923.

Rappaport, S. R. The role of behavioral accessibility in intellectual function of psychotics. *Journal of Clinical Psychology,* 1951, **7,** 335–40.

Rappaport, S. R. Intellectual deficit in organics and schizophrenics. *Journal of Consulting Psychology,* 1953, **17,** 389–95.

Rappaport, S. R. Behavior disorder and ego development in a brain-injured child. *The Psychoanalytic Study of the Child,* 1961, **16,** 423–50.

Rappaport, S. R. A pioneer in vision and educational environments: Salute to Darell Boyd Harmon. *Journal of Learning Disabilities,* 1975, **8,** 332–35.

A SELECTED BIBLIOGRAPHY OF WORKS BY
SHELDON R. RAPPAPORT

Rappaport, S. R. The role of behavioral accessibility in intellectual function of psychotics. *Journal of Clinical Psychology,* 1951, **7,** 335–40.

Rappaport, S. R. Intellectual deficit in organics and schizophrenics. *Journal of Consulting Psychology,* 1953, **17,** 389–95.

Rappaport, S. R. Behavior disorder and ego development in a brain-injured child. *The Psychoanalytic Study of the Child,* 1961, **16,** 423–50.

Rappaport, S. R. (Ed.) *Childhood aphasia and brain damage: Vol. I, A definition.* Narberth, Pa.: Livingston, 1964.

Rappaport, S. R. (Ed.) *Childhood aphasia and brain damage: Vol. II, Differential diagnosis.* Narberth, Pa.: Livingston, 1965.

Rappaport, S. R. Personality factors teachers need for relationship structure. In W. M. Cruickshank (Ed.), *The teacher of brain-injured children: A discussion of the bases for competency.* Syracuse: Syracuse University Press, 1966.

Rappaport, S. R. (Ed.) *Childhood aphasia and brain damage: Vol. III, Habilitation.* Narberth, Pa.: Livingston, 1967.

Rappaport, S. R. *Public education for children with brain dysfunction.* Syracuse: Syracuse University Press, 1969.

Rappaport, S. R. Education or imprisonment. In M. Robb (Ed.), *Foundations and practices in perceptual motor learning—A quest for understanding.* Washington, D.C.: AAHPER, 1971.

Rappaport, S. R. A pioneer in vision and educational environments: Salute to Darell Boyd Harmon. *Journal of Learning Disabilities,* 1975, **8,** 332–35.

Rappaport, S. R. Ego development in learning disabled children. In W. M. Cruickshank & D. P. Hallahan (Eds.), *Children with perceptual and learning disabilities: Vol. I: Psychoeducational practices.* Syracuse: Syracuse University Press, 1975.

Rappaport, S. R., & McNary, S. R. Teacher effectiveness for children with learning disorders. *Journal of Learning Disabilities,* 1970, **3,** 75–83.

12
Unsettled Issues in Learning Disabilities

From reading the previous chapters in this volume, you should be under the impression that the field of learning disabilities is in a state of flux. There are really very few concepts which are shared by the vast majority of professionals in learning disabilities, and there are many controversies which permeate all phases of this new discipline.

The newcomer to the field of learning disabilities is faced immediately with a number of seemingly crucial polarities. Not finding many of his or her new colleagues to be undecided on any of these issues, the novitiate soon learns that it is the "proper" thing to pick sides on issues and to do it quickly. This cavalier attitude is displayed not only among the rank-and-file classroom teachers, but also among university professors, who often serve as models of this kind of behavior.

The situation is most unfortunate. Today, when an issue arises, there is little room for careful scrutiny of both sides. For some reason, individuals feel compelled to take a side immediately. Once having decided on which of the two sides is the "right" one, the individual must soon defend his position. Since all of the evidence on the matter is not yet in, he is forced to use irrational arguments. The scientific debate soon evolves into an emotionally charged argument. There is rarely any middle ground. A person maintaining a position in the middle or reserving final judgment until more evidence is accrued rarely gains an audience. The popular press, which frequently becomes embroiled in the volatile debates, tends to give coverage to extreme viewpoints. Unfortunately, sensationalistic reporting can do much to hinder rational consideration of emotionally charged issues (see *Journal of Learning Disabilities*, 1975).

While we lament the fact that more professionals do not refrain from completely accepting one side of many debatable dichotomies, we recognize that in order that each side be heard there must be individuals who make it their responsibility to champion a given position. Likewise, it is appropriate and scientifically productive for people to be identified as advocates. It should be kept in mind, however, that there is a distinct difference between an advocate and a zealot.

SOME FUTURISTIC ISSUES

There are obviously a number of topics which, when brought up in conversation with a group of learning disabilities professionals, can stir up debate. It is the purpose of this chapter to identify a few of the issues which we see as worthy of further consideration. The topics discussed should *not* be considered an exhaustive survey of all of the pertinent issues, nor should it be considered an intensive treatment of each of the issues. The intention here is to familarize the introductory student with some of the controversial topics which we believe will continue to be pursued for some time.

Definition

On the surface, it would appear impossible to have controversy or heated debate concerning such a mundane and lackluster topic as definition. While all areas of special education have had and continue to have some debate concerning definition, none of the fields has undergone any more controversy than learning disabilities. One reason for this may be the particular mood of the special education community at the time during which the first "official" definition of learning disabilities was being set forth. In the 1960s there was growing concern over labelling and the potential dangers of misclassification. The special education profession was becoming aware of the impact a definition can have in how potentially large numbers of children would be treated attitudinally and educationally.

The popularly accepted definitions of learning disabilities usually include the following elements:

1. The child evidences a significant degree of academic retardation.
2. The child has an uneven pattern of development.
3. The child may or may not have central nervous system (CNS) dysfunction.
4. The child does not have a learning problem which is primarily due to mental retardation, emotional disturbance, or environmental disadvantage.

It is with items (3) and (4) that the most controversy has risen. A look at the development of the field shows that many of its forefathers believed the learning problems of these children to be neurologically based (Hallahan & Cruickshank, 1973). In recent years, however, disenchantment with the neurological position has grown. Educators (the profession for which the definition will have most relevance), in particular, have questioned the utility of attempting to diagnose brain injury. The attack has been primarily on two questions. First, a goodly amount of research data supports the idea that it is extremely difficult to diagnose accurately the presence or nonpresence of a brain lesion. Second, given that the presence of a brain lesion has been shown, of what practical use is this information *to the teacher* in terms of development of an educational strategy for that particular child? This negative reaction to consideration of the neurological status of the child has undoubtedly influenced the definitions of learning disabilities, so that most definitions state that the learning problem "may or may not be due to CNS dysfunction." To some people, this phrase is meaningless, since the learning disabled child "may or may not" have anything you want to name. The reason the phrase appears at all is probably that it is extremely difficult to deny that the act of learning is in some way associated with events within the brain.

The other aspect of the definition frequently debated is the "exclusion clauses," the statements that the learning problem of the LD child is not the result of mental retardation, emotional disturbance, or environmental disadvantage. This last etiological consideration was the first to raise questions in the minds of some people. Some of the arguments against using this exclusion clause have been: (a) There is ample evidence that environmental factors (e.g., inadequate nutrition, medical care, and socialization practices) can lead to learning problems [see Cravioto & DeLicardie (1975) and Hallahan & Cruickshank (1973) for reviews of this literature]. (b) A child with a learning disability who happens to be from a disadvantaged environment would not be treated any differently in terms of educational programming than a child who is from a middle-class home. (c) This exclusion clause may result in denial of needed services to many children.

The rationale for disagreement with the exclusion of mental retardation and emotional disturbance has been elaborated elsewhere (Hallahan & Cruickshank, 1973; Hallahan & Kauffman, 1975, 1976). Questioning these clauses goes along with the trend toward noncategorical special education, as evidenced by such introductory texts to special education as Dunn (1973) and Hewett and Forness (1974). The position espoused by Hallahan and Kauffman is that mildly handicapped children—learning disabled, mildly emotionally disturbed, and educable mentally retarded—have more characteristics in common than not in common. They maintain that teaching methods for the three areas do not differ significantly; and, in fact, many of the educational strategies that have come to be associated with learning disabilities were actually originally used with the retarded and disturbed, particularly the former. Hallahan and Kauffman (1975) suggest, *if the term "learning disabilities" is to continue to be used, "that it be used to refer to learning problems found in children who have traditionally been classified as mildly handicapped, whether it be emotionally disturbed, mildly retarded, or learning disabled."* Under this broad, umbrella-like term they suggest that a child could be further grouped according to *specific* behavioral characteristics, regardless of the etiology or traditional category into which the child falls.

A recent definition from the national project on the classification of exceptional children directed by Nicholas Hobbs is destined to create some controversy. A committee dealing with learning disabilities recommended the following definition:

> *Specific learning disability,* as defined here, refers to those children of any age who demonstrate a substantial deficiency in a particular aspect of academic achievement because of perceptual or perceptual-motor handicaps, regardless of etiology or other contributing factors. The term *perceptual* as used here relates to those mental (neurological) processes through which the child acquires his basic alphabets of sounds and forms [Wepman, et al., 1975].

This definition, like the one presented by Hallahan and Kauffman, also merges across previously separate categories. However, the crucial criterion in the Wepman committee's definition is whether or not the learning problem exists because of a perceptual handicap.

Motivational Variables

Closely related to the issue of definition is a topic which is likely to be of increasing concern—the effects of motivational variables on the performance of learning disabled children. Amazingly little research has been done on this question. This lack of concern is surprising, since it would seem crucial to look into a factor which, on the surface, appears to have a close association with classroom learning. For example, the results of two interesting studies (Stevenson, Iscoe, & McConnell, 1955; Weir & Stevenson, 1959) reported by Stevenson (1972) can be interpreted to highlight the importance of the individual's conception of the difficulty of the tasks he is asked to perform. They found that tenth grade and college students did just as poorly as preschoolers on discrimination tasks, because they had expected something harder or assumed that the right answer was random. These assumptions lead one to respect the power of motivational variables. The many past failures of the LD child may influence him to expect that many of the tasks with which he is presented are more difficult than they actually are or that answers are randomly determined. The work on external locus of control (Crandall, Katkovsky, & Preston, 1962; McGhee & Crandall, 1968) is relevant here in that it indicates that poor achievers are more apt than normal achievers to believe that their own behavior has little to do with how they ultimately perform (see Lawrence & Winschel, 1975, for a review of research).

If research in learning disabilities follows the general trend of the field of mental retardation, personality and motivational variables are due more consideration in the future. In mental retardation, the work of such researchers as Zigler [see Zigler (1973) for a summary of this work] has shown the importance of these noncognitive variables on cognitive performance. Systematic study of this area with the learning disabled, however, remains to be done.

Underlying Psychological Processes Versus Observable Behavior

Already becoming a debate of major proportions is the growing concern that the field of learning disabilities assumes that learning problems are due to deficits in psychological processes. For example, the model of the *ITPA*, which has been of considerable influence, is composed of a number of psychological processes. It has recently been attacked. Hammill and Larsen's (1974) article and Newcomer and Hammill's book (1976) are examples of the disenchantment with the *ITPA*. Hammill and Larsen have stated:

> Psycholinguistic training is based upon the assumption that discrete elements of language behavior are identifiable and measureable, that they provide the underpinning for learning, and that if defective they can be remediated. When using this approach, an additional assumption is made that the cause of the child's learning failure is within himself and that strengthening weak areas will result in improved classroom learning [1974, pp. 5–6].

They then review a number of studies looking at the efficacy of psycholinguistic training and conclude that it has not proven effective. Three possible explanations are offered:

> (*a*) The *ITPA* is an invalid measure of psycholinguistic functioning; (*b*) the intervention programs and/or techniques are inadequate; and (*c*) most psycholinguistic dimensions are either untrainable or highly resistant to simulation [p. 11].

The last explanation has a note of finality about it. The other two explanations leave some hope for a solution to the problem, but if underlying processes cannot be trained, then it would be useless to be concerned about them.

Advocates of behavior modification, in particular, are often critical of those who look for underlying psychological processes. In this volume, for example, Lovitt emphasizes that only observable behavior should be considered worthy of concern. Getman, on the other hand, stresses the importance of underlying processes. One actually has to wonder if these positions are as far apart as some would think. The crux of the problem is whether or not one can *observe and quantify* the behavior in question. After all, when "behavior modifiers" engage in task analysis, they, too, are looking for underlying behaviors. The major difference is that they are only concerned with those behaviors that they can measure.

Early Identification

For the last decade or so one watchword in special education circles has been "early identification," which has been viewed as extremely critical in learning disabilities, since this area deals with *subtle* deviations. The widespread acceptance of the importance of early identification has probably led to the philosophy that anything short of total adherence to this concept would be practically heretical. A thought-provoking article by Keogh and Becker (1973), however, should cause professionals to do some rethinking regarding the benefits of early identification.

Keogh and Becker note that, in general, identification measures have proven to be a failure in terms of predicting later achievement. In addition, the possible dangers associated with misplacing children lead them to the following conclusions:

> Programs of early identification will be effective relative to the educational programs which are available to accommodate the child. Identification of a given child as high risk for school learning is in essence a *prediction* [italics added] that he will fail or have problems in the existing school program; to place him in the program which has been predefined as failure producing for him without modifying that program puts the child in double jeopardy and maximizes the possibility of a self-fulfilling prophecy.
>
> It should be emphasized that program modification and special class placement are not necessarily the same. Support for segregation of children who may develop learning problems into special classes is indeed tenuous. Bloom (1968) proposed that most children are able to perform school tasks at a mastery level given adjustments in time, materials, and teaching strategies, for example. Too often, however, the major portion of time and funds are spent on extensive diagnosis and evaluation so that neither time nor money is left to modify educational programs in light of the identification data. It may well be that focus on effective educational programming per se is a more productive route than is the search for precise measures for early identification of individual children [p. 10].

These cautions against early identification are pointed toward the placement of children based upon that identification. From a research and theory point of view, quests for new methods of early identification may eventually lead to some of the most exciting discoveries in special education. As an example, the work of Lewis (1975) using attentional measures in infancy appears to hold promise for prediction of later learning problems.

Medical Issues

There are also a number of growing controversies regarding medical aspects of learning disabilities. The issue of drug therapy, of course, is probably the best known controversial area and has been written about extensively (see Kornetsky, 1975, for a review of the research). In the rest of this chapter, we will briefly discuss those medical issues which are gaining momentum as topics of concern (hypoglycemia, vitamins, food additives, genetics). One reason for the spread of these controversies is also a partial reason for the delay of scientific progress in these areas. The lay press has frequently reported on some new methods without concern for their scientific merit. As you will note, much more controlled research is needed on each of these questions before any of them can be answered.

Hypoglycemia: The symptoms of hypoglycemia are caused by a deprivation of glucose to the brain, reflecting inadequate intrauterine nutrition or inadequate glucose homeostasis. Hypoglycemia is sometimes present in the brain-damaged child, manifesting itself as lethargy, mental confusion, or convulsions in the more severe cases. Neonatal hypoglycemia most frequently occurs in infants of low weight at birth, infants born of toxemic and diabetic mothers, and twins. Often hypoglycemia has been associated with other neonatal disorders, such as asphyxia or cerebral damage. It has also been reported among "normal" newborns not included in the high-risk groups (Koivisto, Blanco-Sequeiros, & Krause, 1972).

A relationship between symptomatic neonatal hypoglycemia and subsequent central nervous system damage has been a common clinical condition reported in the literature. Whether the central nervous system abnormality is primary and precedes the hypoglycemia, or whether the hypoglycemia causes the central nervous system damage, has been the source of much controversy. Autopsies in cases of fatal hypoglycemia have revealed degeneration of the nerve cells with degeneration of the entire central nervous system in the most severe cases (Koivisto, Blanco-Sequeiros, & Krause, 1972).

Little has been done to define brain biochemical alterations resulting from hypoglycemia, though a great deal has been learned from animal experiments about pathogenic mechanisms leading to brain damage. Since a controlled study in the newborn infant is impossible, lower order animals have had to serve as the models. Chase, Marlow, Dabiere, and Welch (1973) induced hypoglycemia in newborn rats once daily for the first eighteen days of life. Diffuse biochemical alterations in the fore- and hindbrain were found; reductions in brain weight, cellularity, and protein were present throughout the brain, as were markedly lower brain glucose concentrations. Thus the contention that neonatal hypoglycemia may be harmful to the development of the central nervous system was supported.

Conversely, Griffiths and Laurence (1974) studied brain sections from thirty-four infants who died following an episode of clinical hypoxia in the perinatal period. These subjects were divided into two groups ($n = 17$), depending on the presence or absence of a recorded episode of hypoglycemia. The brain sections were then studied for neural alterations. It was found that infants who suffered hypoxia in the newborn period and were exposed to a limited degree of hypoglycemia showed no histological evidence of central nervous system damage over and above that produced by hypoxia.

A study investigating symptomatic and asymptomatic hypoglycemia in the newborn child and a control group between a period of one to four years after birth was conducted by Koivisto and his colleagues (1972). One hundred fifty-one children diagnosed as having hypoglycemia during the first few days of life were followed one to four years after birth. Of the 151, 8 had had hypoglycemia with convulsions, 77 had had only hypoglycemia without convulsions but with other symptoms, and 66 had been asymptomatic. Hypoglycemia had been diagnosed at mean ages of thirty-nine hours in the group with convulsions, ten hours in those without convulsions, and nine hours in the asymptomatic group; therapy was begun at mean ages of forty-three, twenty-one, and fourteen hours respectively. A control group of fifty-six normal children was also included. The findings suggested that *time* is the crucial factor affecting the onset of symptoms in the newborn period and that symptomatic hypoglycemia with convulsions can lead to permanent central nervous system damage. On the other hand, asymptomatic hypoglycemia, if diagnosed and treated before convulsions occur, appeared to have no permanent, detrimental influence. It is also interesting to note that at the time these data were collected (1967 to 1969), breast-feeding was not started until the age of twenty-four hours. The infants were given only 5 percent saccharose for the first day. Since then, Koivisto found that early feeding has resulted in neonatal hypoglycemia occuring less frequently than it did previously.

Several recent studies have focussed on the relationship of hypoglycemia to certain personality characteristics. Anthony, Dippe, Hofeldt, Davis, and Forsham (1973) administred the *Minnesota Multiphasic Personality Inventory* (*MMPI*) to thirty-seven hypoglycemic patients and to twenty-one patients with various endocrine disorders without hypoglycemic symptoms. The hypoglycemic patients differed significantly from the mixed endocrine group on the hypochondriasis and hysteria scales, falling two standard deviations above normal. Further, hypoglycemic patients of varying etiology showed the same *MMPI* pattern. The authors concluded that a relationship between hypoglycemia of whatever origin and this specific personality pattern is suggested, since the pattern differed from that shown in previous *MMPI* studies of diabetic patients and patients with gastric surgery without hypoglycemia. Research into the effects of hypoglycemia on learning is just beginning. From even the few studies reviewed here, it is obvious that the issue is complex. Before the etiological status of hypoglycemia can be established, more research is needed. (See News, *Journal of Learning Disabilities*, 1974a, 1974b).

Vitamins: Drugs have been widely used in the treatment of children with psychological and learning problems and have controlled hyperactivity, destructiveness, and other similar behaviors. However, many medical, psychological, and educational personnel are demanding a closer investigation into the neurological and biochemical processes of the disturbed and the learning disabled child in order to treat these areas more efficiently. Moreover, due to such possible adverse side effects as loss of appetite, insomnia, and abdominal pain, alternative methods of treatment are being sought. Among the most controversial has been the administration of massive doses of vitamins, the orthomolecular approach or megavitamin therapy, which directs attention to the treatment of the central processes.

During the past fifteen years, nine vitamin-dependent diseases have been identified, associated with six vitamins, mainly of the B-complex. As early as 1954, A. D. Hunt at the Stanford Medical Center reported on two infant siblings who responded only to massive doses of vitamin B_6 in treating violent convulsive seizures (Cott, 1972). Later investigations at the University of Texas have led researchers to conclude that many cases of infantile seizures were due to a dysfunction in the metabolism of vitamin B_6 and not to a simple dietary deficiency. More recent research has suggested the close monitoring and administration of vitamin D in order to offset possible serious adverse reactions to long-term anticonvulsant therapy (Villareale, et al., 1974).

One of the strongest advocates of megavitamins is Allan Cott, who originally applied the megavitamin therapy in the treatment of psychoses. In investigating the treatment of such childhood psychoses as autism and childhood schizophrenia, he states that he has found a significant decrease in hyperactivity, an improved concentration, and an increased attention span, leading to improved capacities for learning. Trials were next begun using megavitamin therapy on those children exhibiting learning disabilities. Until these investigations were begun, the biochemical basis of disturbed behavior was ignored; instead specialists stressed "the more peripheral aspects of a handicapped child's performance" [Cott, 1972, p. 246]. A research project now underway at the New York Institute for Child Development is studying the effectiveness of remediation using megavitamin therapy along with perceptual-motor training. Remedial efforts are being directed toward brain function and body chemistry through the application of perceptual-motor techniques and the employment of orthomolecular therapy to improve the child's biochemical balance. It has been reported that rarely are the treatment results quick and dramatic, since two to six months normally elapse before significant changes are observed. It is also stated that the therapy can last for years, with children who begin early in life and are treated the longest generally making the greatest progress (Cott, 1972).

Disturbed or learning disabled children are being given niacin (B_3), ascorbic acid (C), pyridoxine (B_6), and calcium pantothenate, a member of the B complex. Frequently riboflavin, thiamine, vitamin E, folic acid, and glutamic acid are used. Cott reports that all these vitamins are water soluble and readily excreted. He also believes that most physicians feel the behavioral and physical harm caused by vitamins is much less than that caused by synthesized drugs. It is stated that side effects such as nausea, diarrhea, or skin reactions may occur, but usually disappear after the fifth or sixth dose.

Butcher, Brunner, Roth, and Kimmel (1972) administered massive doses of vitamin A to rats on the eighth, ninth, and tenth day of gestation. The offspring were tested on maze learning performance at fifty days of age; the performance of the offspring receiving vitamin A was significantly lower than that of the controls. A low frequency of minor malformations was also observed in an examination of fetuses aborted from treated rats sacrificed on the twentieth day of gestation. The authors concluded that when substances capable of producing malformations of the central nervous system are given in dosages too low to yield anatomic effects, enduring behavioral deficits are observed. (However, Cott states that vitamins A and D are fat soluble rather than water soluble and are not commonly used in megavitamin therapy.)

Many critics of vitamin therapy attribute the improvement seen when using vitamins to the placebo effect. However, Cott notes that adherents state that, following the interruption of the medication, the child again displays the disturbed behavior. However, the former level of improvement is attained within two to five days after medication is resumed. The necessity for more controlled research studies to investigate these clinical observations is keenly felt in this area.

A recently reported study from the Yale University School of Medicine offered a caution on the use of vitamins (Pediatric News, 1974). If vitamin utilization is governed by specific genes and affected by mutational events, many different kinds of vitamin-responsive disorders are possible. Therefore, differential diagnosis of patients with a wide variety of neurologic deficits is necessitated. Although response has generally been favorable among patients suffering from seizures, schizophrenia, mental retardation, or learning and emotional disturbances, it does not follow that *all* patients will respond accordingly. It was also found that patients with neurologic or psychiatric problems of an unknown nature responded well to a short course of vitamins in large amounts. However, the researchers cautioned against long-term, uncritical use of pharmacologic doses of vitamins. Although megavitamin therapy has been called harmless since the water soluble vitamins have no known overdose and few adverse side effects, doctors in the field do not condone the use of massive dosages without a physician's direction. As of January 1, 1974, it was reported that the Food and Drug Administration will set limits on the sale of nonprescription vitamins to extremely low dosages, which will force people to go to their physician to obtain prescriptions. Not all orthomolecular practitioners agree with this decision. Some feel that vitamins are foods rather than drugs and constitute a much less grave danger than such over-the-counter drugs as aspirins or cold remedies (Issues in *Journal of Learning Disabilities*, 1973).

With an estimated patient population of twenty million children (Cott, 1972), the implication for much needed controlled research in this area is clear. In order to make more universal application of these findings, carefully planned studies must be instigated. Clearly, some researchers believe that this treatment *could* benefit many children with learning and emotional problems.

Food additives: Much research is now being done to assess the effect of food additives on the physical and behavioral conditions of children. One such questionable ingredient is monosodium glutamate, a substance often found in canned and boxed foods, especially baby foods. Olney and colleagues have found lesions in the hypothalamus of rhesus monkeys after multiple monosodium glutamate treatments in infancy (Lowe, 1970). Citing various methodological problems with this study, Lowe finds the most critical fault to be the treatment and evaluation of only one animal. Further, the researchers provided neither data on the concentrations of glutamatic acid in the blood nor control data for the experiment. In an experiment similar to Olney's, Adamo and Ratner (1970) injected infant rats with a dose of monosodium glutamate four times greater than that administered by Olney. The results showed no adverse monosodium glutamate effects on the neural morphology or reproductive system other than significantly smaller ovaries. However, a later investigation conducted by Olney (1971) found the average weight of the ovaries and adenohypophyses in a treated group to be about half that of the controls. Neural lesions and depressed pituitary concentrations were also reported. Olney is critical of the few animals Adamo and Ratner studied. Further, these animals were only exposed to one injection of monosodium glutamate, with no attempt made to measure the weights or hormonal concentrations of adenohypophyses or to compare the reproductive capacities of the experimental and control rats. Thus, Olney concludes that Adamo and Ratner's failure to find a deleterious effect on the reproductive function is a faulty interpretation based on insufficient data.

Other experiments have also contradicted Adamo and Ratner's results. Varied methods and concentrations of monosodium glutamate produced brain lesions similar in location and extent of damage in the hypothalamus of treated mice (Arees & Mayer, 1970). Rats later injected with a much lower concentration than that used by Adamo and Ratner also developed lesions. In addition, Lemkey-Johnston and Reynolds (1974) found neural damage in the hypothalamus of neonatal rats treated with monosodium glutamate. However, they warn that the comparison of any neuropathological findings must consider the critical aspects of species variation, developmental age, route of administration, time of examination of brain material after dosage, and thoroughness of the sampling methods. A number of amino acids besides monosodium glutamate are now believed to produce neuronal damage in the hypothalamus of infant mice following an injection. Johnston (1973) injected mice with excitant amino acids which all produced convulsions. The onset of the seizures was dependent on the dosage and was used to compare the relative potencies of these excitant amino acids. Johnston concludes:

> Olney and his colleagues have pointed out that "the close correspondence in molecular specificity associated with neurotoxic and neuroexcitatory properties of simple amino acids suggest the two phenomena may be governed by similar mechanisms of action." The present study indicates that the neuroexcitatory properties are also directly related to the ability of these amino acids to produce convulsions in ten-day-old rats. It is suggested that any excitant amino acid should be suspect as a food additive [p. 139].

Some have said that as yet there has been no quantitative relation to the dosage of monosodium glutamate that could be expected to be given to an infant or adult. In addition, it is reported that all the studies have used dosages far exceeding those consumed by humans. From the research conducted thus far, it is obvious that issues surrounding monosodium glutamate are complex. Whether to continue including it in foods is yet to be determined by research.

A medical specialist in allergies has gained widespread attention for claiming that a diet free of artificial food flavoring and coloring can eliminate hyperactive behaviors affecting approximately five million children in this country. Ben F. Feingold, chief emeritus of the Department of Allergy of the Kaiser Foundation Hospitals and Permanente Medical Center in San Francisco, has designed a nutritionally balanced diet prohibiting these substances as well as various fruits and vegetables containing salicylates, natural chemicals which are believed to produce similar adverse effects to the artificial additives. However, Brown (1974) has criticized Feingold's research and the appropriateness of his methodology.

In an article in the *Washington Post* (Mintz, 1973) it was stated that as yet the Food and Drug Administration had not reacted to the Feingold diet. With the authority to control the use of food additives, the FDA usually requires strictly controlled studies to establish the effectiveness of medical claims. Such experimentation would be very lengthy as well as expensive, because of the vast amount and numbers of additives. However, the National Institute of Education of the Department of Health, Education and Welfare has been considering funding these studies. Feingold realizes his findings need to be supported by these more extensive clinical studies. He admits he has not yet established a cause-effect relationship between food additives and hyperactivity. However, he feels that the gains he and other physicans have observed when using the diet are too great to be ignored when they could greatly benefit the hyperactive child. Meanwhile he has called for clear labeling specifying artificial flavors and colors. Wilson (1972) also advocates new labeling laws for the food industry in light of his recent finding of the potentially dangerous interaction of aspirin and benzoic acid, a commonly used food preservative. When simultaneously used, teratogenic effects may be produced. Until further research is completed, Wilson cautions women of childbearing age to be aware of the possible danger involved with these two agents interacting, and to avoid these substances if possible.

Genetics: Few studies dealing with the genetic aspects of learning problems are found in the literature, although many diverse fields of investigation are capable of providing information in this area. Recent biomedical advances have been of particular interest and value to family and genetic studies. Studies in the United States have indicated a high incidence of diabetes in the family backgrounds of students with learning problems. Family studies relating to learning disabilities have focused on metabolic problems. A list of vitamin-responsive inherited dysfunctions may be able to afford valuable information in identifying and working with these children. Most of the research deals with the problems in reading, while other fields are left relatively unexplored.

Hallgren (1950), an earlier investigator into the familial aspects of reading disorders, studied 276 cases of "dyslexia," 116 affected children and 160 secondary cases (siblings and parents of these children). From his data, he concluded that he had demonstrated genetic transmission of dyslexia. Results obtained from studies comparing the frequencies of disorders in monozygotic and dizygotic twins (Hallgren, 1950; Norrie, 1959) suggest that heredity is a critical etiological factor in certain types of learning problems. Walker and Cole (1965) reported more recent research into the familial patterns of specific reading disability. Spelling test performance was used as an index to identify children with reading problems. They found a highly significant concentration of specific reading disability within families.

Several cases of inherited reading disability have been reported more recently in the literature. In most of these, a dominant mode of inheritance has been observed. Hof and Guldenpfennig (1972) have described a South African family in which the inheritance of specific reading disability was traced through four generations. All individuals were given psychological, neurological, and scholastic evaluations approximating those currently used in western Europe and the United States. Specific reading disability was attributed to specific neurological dysfunction, resulting in the inability to learn to read when having normal intelligence, intact motor and sensory function, proper motivation, and no gross neurological dysfunction or cultural deprivation. The disability appeared to follow a dominant mode of inheritance through four generations. There was no significant common EEG deviation. In addition, writing was generally unclear, and unconventional methods of arithmetical calculation were employed. All subjects also experienced considerable difficulty in the form board and pattern completion subtests. Thus, the disability appeared to be associated with a visuo-spatial integration problem.

A more comprehensive research project was undertaken by Owen, Adams, Forrest, Stolz, and Fisher (1971). Children with normal intelligence who performed poorly in school were studied in an attempt to discover whether the characteristics of these children could be more precisely identified and described as well as to clarify further the causes and familial patterns of learning disorders. The sample was composed of seventy-six quartets of children and their parents. Seventy-six academically handicapped children and their same-sex siblings were compared to seventy-six academically successful children and their same-sex siblings. The children were evaluated and compared on educational, psychological, and medical criteria. The parents of both groups were contrasted on adult reading ability, high school transcripts, and perceptions and attitudes toward children. Neurological, emotional, and familial factors were not as clearly defined, and a great deal of overlapping among these three areas was seen. Familial learning disorders were seen most clearly in those children with markedly high performance discrepancies on the Wechsler test. Further, siblings of these subjects displayed many similarities of impairment such as the concordance of neurological differences, speech problems, and Wechsler subscale patterns. The poor adult reading skill of the mothers also emphasized the familial aspect of the language-learning handicap in this group.

Whether this familial aggregation is genetically determined cannot be answered definitively. The inherent problem in genetic research is that children with similar hereditary backgrounds also have similar environmental backgrounds. It is, thus, difficult to isolate the genetic component in order to determine its status as a *causal* agent.

The role of the physician in identifying and managing learning problems has been nominal. In many cases, the information furnished is fragmentary, with the interpretation of medical terms lacking clarity and specificity. Thus, global diagnoses have often served to confound educational programming. However, with persistent and consistent evidence suggesting that a significant number of children with learning problems have some associated medical conditions, this profession is making strides to overcome these obstacles. Recent medical research into such areas as hypoglycemia, allergies, vitamins, and food additives has shown a comprehensive and insightful involvement having relevant implications for today's educator. Yet these studies are only the beginning; they should serve to guide further imperative medical contributions.

REFERENCES

Adamo, N. J., & Ratner, A. Monosodium glutamate: Lack of effects on brain and reproductive function in rats. *Science,* 1970, **169,** 673–74.

Anthony, D., Dippe, S., Hofeldt, F. D., Davis, J. W., & Forsham, P. H. Personality disorder and reactive hypoglycemia. *Diabetes,* 1973, **22,** 664–75.

Arees, E. A., & Mayer, J. Monosodium glutamate-induced brain lesions: Electron microscopic examination. *Science,* 1970, **170,** 549–50.

Bloom, B. S. Learning for mastery. *U.C.L.A. Evaluation Comment,* 1968, **1** (2), 1–12.

Brown, G. W. Food additives and hyperactivity. *Journal of Learning Disabilities,* 1974, **7,** 652–53.

Butcher, R. E., Brunner, R. L., Roth, T., & Kimmel, C. A. A learning impairment associated with maternal hypervitaminosis-A in rats. *Life Science,* 1972, **11,** 141–45.

Chase, H. P., Marlow, R. A., Debiere, C. S., & Welch, N. N. Hypoglycemia and brain development. *Pediatrics,* 1973, **52,** 513–20.

Cott, A. Megavitamins: The orthomolecular approach to behavioral disorders and learning disabilities. *Academic Therapy, 1972, 1, 245–58.*

Crandall, V. J., Katkovsky, W., & Preston, A. Motivational and ability determinants of young children's intellectual achievement behaviors. *Child Development,* 1962, **33,** 643–61.

Cravioto, J., & DeLicardie, E. Environmental and nutritional deprivation in learning disabilities. In W. M. Cruickshank & D. P. Hallahan (Eds.), *Perceptual and learning disabilities in children. Vol. 2: Research and theory.* Syracuse: Syracuse University Press, 1975.

Dunn, L. M. (Ed.) *Exceptional children in the schools.* (2nd ed.) New York: Holt, Rinehart & Winston, 1973.

Griffiths, A. D., & Laurence, K. M. The effect of hypoxia and hypoglycemia on the brain of the newborn human infant. *Developmental Medicine and Child Neurology,* 1974, **16,** 308–19.

Hallahan, D. P., & Cruickshank, W. M. *Psychoeducational foundations of learning disabilities.* Englewood Cliffs, N.J.: Prentice-Hall, 1973.

Hallahan, D. P., & Kauffman, J. M. Learning disabilities: A behavioral definition. Paper presented at the Second International Scientific Conference on Learning Disabilities. Brussels, Belguim, January 3–7, 1975.

Hallahan, D. P., & Kauffman, J. M. *Introduction to learning disabilities.* Englewood Cliffs, N.J.: Prentice-Hall, 1976.

Hallgren, B. Specific dyslexia (Congenital word blindness: A clinical and genetic study). ACTA Psychiatrica et Neurologica, 1950, Suppl. **65.** (Cited in F. W. Owen, et al., *Monographs of the Society for Research in Child Development,* 1971, **36**(4), Serial No. 144).

Hammill, D. D., & Larsen, S. C. The effectiveness of psycholinguistic training. *Exceptional Children,* 1974, **41,** 5–14.

Hewett, F. M., & Forness, S. R. *Education of exceptional learners.* Boston: Allyn & Bacon, 1974.

Hof, J. O., & Guldenpfennig, W. M. Dominant inheritance of specific reading disability. *South African Medical Journal,* 1972, **46,** 737. (Cited in *Journal of Learning Disabilities,* 1973, **6,** 160–61).

Issues, *Journal of Learning Disabilities,* 1973, **6,** 466.

Johnston, G. A. R. Convulsions induced in 10-day-old rats by intraperitoneal injection of MSG and related excitant amino acids. *Biochemical Pharmacology,* 1973, **22,** 137–40.

Journal of Learning Disabilities, 1975, **8,** 316–25.

Keogh, B. K., & Becker, L. D. Early detection of learning problems: Questions, cautions, and guidelines. *Exceptional Children,* 1973, **40,** 5–11.

Koivisto, M., Blanco-Sequeiros, M., & Krause, V. Neonatal symptomatic and asymptomatic hypoglycemia. *Developmental Medicine and Child Neurology,* 1972, **14,** 603–14.

Kornetsky, C. Learning disabilities, behavior, and medication. In W. M. Cruickshank & D. P. Hallahan (Eds.), *Perceptual and learning problems in children. Vol. 2: Research and theory.* Syracuse: Syracuse University Press, 1975.

Lawrence, E. A., & Winschel, J. F. Locus of control: Implications for special education. *Exceptional Children,* 1975, **41,** 483–90.

Lemkey-Johnston, N., & Reynolds, W. A. Nature and extent of brain lesions in mice related to ingestion of monosodium glutamate. *Journal of Neuropathology and Experimental Neurology,* 1974, **33,** 74–97.

Lewis, M. The development of attention and perception in the infant and young child. In W. M. Cruickshank & D. P. Hallahan (Eds.), *Perceptual and learning disabilities in children. Vol. 2: Research and theory.* Syracuse: Syracuse University Press, 1975.

Lowe, C. V. Monosodium glutamate specific brain lesion questioned. *Science,* 1970, **167,** 1016–17.

McGhee, P. E., & Crandall, V. C. Beliefs in internal-external control of reinforcements and academic performance. *Child Development,* 1968, **39,** 91–102.

Mintz, M. Hyperactivity linked to additives. *Washington Post,* Oct. 29, 1973, A9.

Newcomer, P., & Hammill, D. D. (Eds.) *Psycholinguistics in the classroom.* Columbus, Ohio: Charles E. Merrill, 1976.

News. *Journal of Learning Disabilities,* 1973, **6,** 12.

News. *Journal of Learning Disabilities,* 1974, **7,** 47. (a)

News. *Journal of Learning Disabilities,* 1974, **7,** 324. (b)

Norrie, E. Ordblindhedens. In L. J. Thompson, *Reading disability.* Springfield, Ill.: Charles C Thomas, 1959. (Cited in F. W. Owen, et. al., *Monographs of the Society for Research in Child Development,* 1976, **36,** No. 4, Serial no. 144).

Olney, J. W. Monosodium glutamate effects. *Science,* 1971, **172,** 294.

Owen, F. W., Adams, P. H., Forrest, T., Stolz, L. M., & Fisher, S. Learning disorders in children: Sibling studies. *Monographs of the Society for Research in Child Development,* 1971, **36** No. 4 (Serial No. 144).

Pediatric News. *World News Reports,* March, 1974, **8,** 4. (Cited in *Journal of Learning Disabilities,* 1974, **7,** 361–62).

Stevenson, H. W. *Children's learning.* New York: Appleton-Century-Crofts (Prentice-Hall), 1972.

Stevenson, H. W., Iscoe, S., & McConnell, C. A developmental study of transposition. *Journal of Experimental Psychology,* 1955, **49,** 278–80.

Villareale, M., Gould, L. V., Chiroff, R. T., & Bergstrom, W. H. Diphenylhydatoin: Effects on calcium metabolism in the chick. *Science,* 1974, **183,** 671–73.

Walker, L., & Cole, E. M. Familial patterns of expression of specific reading disability in a population sample. *Bulletin of the Orton Society,* 1965, **15.** (Cited in F. W. Owen, et. al., *Monographs of the Society for Research in Child Development,* 1971, **36,** No. 4, Serial No. 144).

Weir, M. W., & Stevenson, H. W. The effect of verbalization in children's learning as a function of chronological age. *Child Development,* 1959, **30,** 143–49.

Wepman, J. M., Cruickshank, W. M., Deutsch, C. P., Morency, A., & Strother, C. R. Learning disabilities. In N. Hobbs (Ed.), *Issues in the classification of children. Vol. I.* San Francisco: Jossey-Bass, 1975.

Wilson, J. Birth defects—Fetal defects, drugs, and environmental agents. *Pediatric News,* 1972. (Cited in *Journal of Learning Disabilities,* 1973, **6,** 617–18).

Zigler, E. C. The retarded child as a whole person. In D. K. Routh (Ed.), *The experimental psychology of mental retardation.* Chicago: Aldine, 1973.

INDEX

James M. Kauffman, Ed.D., is associate professor of education, Department of Special Education, at the University of Virginia. He is a member of the Council for Exceptional Children, the Association for the Advancement of Behavior Therapy, and the Society for Research in Child Development. Dr. Kauffman's experience with children includes teaching emotionally disturbed children at the Menninger Clinic, Topeka, Kansas, and instructing disturbed and normal children in public schools. He is the co-author of many books and journal articles in special education.

Daniel P. Hallahan, Ph.D., is assistant professor of special education at the University of Virginia. Dr. Hallahan completed his doctorate in the Combined Program in Education and Psychology at the University of Michigan, where he served as a research associate at the Institute for the Study of Mental Retardation and Related Disabilities. He is the author of numerous books and articles in the field of learning disabilities and mental retardation.

Sara G. Tarver received her Ph.D. in special education with a major in learning disabilities at the University of Virginia. Before obtaining her doctorate she was a classroom teacher for ten years, nine of which involved the instruction of learning disabled children. She is now an assistant professor of special education at the University of Virginia.

Elizabeth Heins received her B.A. degree in psychology from Florida Technological University, Orlando, Florida, in 1972. In 1974 she received her M.Ed. degree in special education from the University of Virginia. After a year of teaching mentally retarded children, she began advanced graduate work at the University of Virginia, where she is now a doctoral student.